ISLAMIC ACTIV

Islamic Activism

*A Social Movement
Theory Approach*

Edited by Quintan Wiktorowicz

INDIANA
University Press
Bloomington & Indianapolis

This book is a publication of
Indiana University Press
601 North Morton Street
Bloomington, Indiana 47404-3797 USA

http://iupress.indiana.edu

Telephone orders   800-842-6796
Fax orders   812-855-7931
Orders by e-mail   iuporder@indiana.edu

The paper used in this publication meets the minimum requirements of American National Standard for Information Sciences—Permanence of Paper for Printed Library Materials, ANSI Z39.48-1984.

Manufactured in the United States of America

Library of Congress Cataloging-in-Publication Data
Islamic activism : a social movement theory approach / edited by Quintan Wiktorowicz.
p. cm. — (Indiana series in Middle East studies)
Includes bibliographical references and index.
ISBN 0-253-34281-3 — ISBN 0-253-21621-4 (pbk.)
1. Social movements—Arab countries. 2. Social movements—Middle East. 3. Islam and politics—Arab countries. 4. Islam and politics—Middle East. I. Wiktorowicz, Quintan, date II. Series.
HN766.A8I85 2004
303.48'4'09174927—dc21
2003008458

2 3 4 5   09 08 07 06 05

For Aidan

Contents

Contents

PART III

Culture and Framing

Foreword

Charles Tilly

Suppose you wanted to appropriate insights from some visibly vigorous body of theory for description and explanation of some phenomenon to which that body of theory had not yet been systematically applied. You might, for example, think that chaos theory had something valuable to say about corporate corruption or that evolutionary theory could contribute usefully to explanations of changes in family structure. You would have a choice among several forms of appropriation:

1. Subsuming the phenomenon of interest directly under the theory, for example, by claiming that corporate corruption is indeed a kind of chaos—a pushing of normal corporate dynamics beyond the limits within which they operate normally.

2. Borrowing an informative metaphor without insisting on strict correspondence: for example, by saying that family structures evolve through some variety of competitive selection but probably not through genetically transmitted mutations.

3. Using the well-developed theory to pose telling questions about your phenomenon, but not supposing that the answers would remain the same: for example, by asking whether conventional corporate brakes on corruption stop working beyond some identifiable limit of size, wealth, or heterogeneity.

4. Extracting certain mechanisms and processes from the existing theory, rather than adopting the theory as a whole, in the hope that those same mechanisms and processes work in the same way within the new domain: for example, by singling out sexual selection as a mechanism by which family structures change.

In reaching for something called "social movement theory," the outstanding authors whom Quintan Wiktorowicz has brought together in this volume cannot be following strategy 1, for no sufficiently coherent body of theory concerning social movements exists. Instead, the ideas about mobilizing structures, political opportunities, framing, and repertoires on which they draw repeatedly offer them and other students of contentious politics two main services. First, the ideas incorporate a standard set of concepts for the description and comparison of contentious episodes: to the extent, for example, that political opportunities have common properties over a wide variety of circumstances, the concept calls attention to those common properties. Second, they constitute a questionnaire to discipline the explanation of contentious episodes. For example, which mobilizing structures are important? How do participants respond to threats and opportunities? And what kinds of frames are employed to mobilize contention? But the explanations themselves involve specifications of how and why those elements—mobilizing structures, political opportunities, and so on—behave and interact as they do. At least for the moment, no available theory provides general specifications of the how and why.

For the most part, this volume's authors pursue strategies 2 and 3. They treat Islamic activism as something like a social movement and/or they adopt the standard social movement questionnaire to ask telling questions about Islamic activism. The two strategies have merits both in what they prevent and in what they facilitate. On the side of prevention, they make it easier to avoid the reduction of Islamic activism to a straightforward product of distinctive Islamic mentalities or of a peculiar social milieu. They lead away from explaining activism as a solo performance in which the doctrine or biography of one actor at a time causes that actor's behavior. On the side of facilitation, they make it easier to grasp interactions between groups of activists (as well as between activists and governments) that shape and reshape the locus, intensity, and form of Islamic activism. As I read the book, its contributions gain most from theories about social movements by thinking of Islamic activisms (plural) as a changing family of interactive political episodes. On the whole, the book's authors generally avoid the greatest risk of strategies 2 and 3: to imagine that Islamic politics should resemble Western social movements down to such details as what sorts of programs they espouse and how they broadcast their claims, with the implication that if such resemblances fail, either the theory is defective or the movements themselves lack essential features.

We who study Western social movements can only applaud the effort. So long as it helps students of Islamic activism to exploit their special knowledge of Muslim countries more effectively rather than suppressing their knowledge in the service of false analogies, informed comparison of Islamic and non-

Islamic activism can only enrich our knowledge of contentious politics at large. Moreover, close analysis and comparison will contribute to the solution of problems that Western specialists have not resolved: under what conditions, how, and why governmental repression diminishes or accelerates popular mobilization, how extreme polarization actually works, why apparently similar negotiations sometimes end in agreements and sometimes in massacres, what determines the effectiveness of peaceful but risky forms of protest such as hunger strikes, and so on through a long list of conundrums familiar to students of social movements everywhere.

Students of Islamic mobilization and conflict may even promote adoption of the fourth choice I laid out above: concentrating on specific mechanisms and processes instead of broad analogies. Contributors to *Islamic Activism*, for example, repeatedly encounter the powerful process of boundary activation: making one of several previously existing divisions among social locations so salient that it suppresses other divisions and organizes most political interaction around (and across) that division alone. Of course, boundary activation occurs widely in social movements around the world. Divisions by gender, by race, by language, by national origin, between adjacent communities, or between capital and labor that have long existed and organized some aspects of routine social life suddenly (if temporarily) come to dominate public politics in some locale. Us/them divisions of this sort recurrently form the fulcrum of lethal combat, even of genocide. Islamic activists have no monopoly on boundary activation. Yet the division between "true" and "false" Islamists and the division between Muslims and non-Muslims do figure so regularly in this book's stories that all students of contentious politics can learn from clearer descriptions and explanations of their activation—not to mention their deactivation.

Let me come clean: I doubt that any interesting regularities and explanatory principles exist at the scale of *whole* social movements. As I see it, the apparatus of mobilizing structures, political opportunities, repertoires, frames, and contentious action can never serve as more than an orienting device for the sorting of observations that investigators will then have to explain by other means. As a horde of critics have complained without much effect, no one has identified powerful empirical regularities or compelling causal models that account for all sorts of political opportunity structures, framing processes, or sequences of political mobilization. Regularities and explanatory principles operate at the level of mechanisms and processes, not at the level of these descriptive categories.

Nevertheless, the challenge of Islamic activism, as analyzed so acutely in this book, should drive students of social movements away from their tendency to treat social movement mobilization across the world as a series of approximations—more or less similar and successful—to the sorts of social movements that have prevailed in Western democracies over the last century or so. It would be delightful if students of Islamic activism, having adopted the frameworks of social movement researchers to shake up their own field, ended up jolting students of Western social movements into recognizing where effective explanations lie. This volume's authors have opened up a crucial collaboration.

Introduction

Islamic Activism and
Social Movement Theory

Quintan Wiktorowicz

In October 2001, the U.S. decision to launch a military campaign in Afghanistan in response to the September 11 attacks by al-Qaeda unleashed a maelstrom of protest throughout the Muslim world. Despite the variegated contexts of activism and the multivocality of the demonstrations, several common patterns emerged during the early stages of the war in Afghanistan. First, many of the strongest demonstrations erupted after prayers and the Friday *khutba* (sermon) at mosques. In Kenya, for example, 3,000 protesters ran through the streets of Nairobi waving placards and chanting slogans after attending prayers at a mosque controlled by Shaykh Ahmed Mussallam, the chairman of the Council of Imams and Scholars (*Africa News*, October 13, 2001). In an episode in Jakarta after Friday prayers, 10,000 Muslims marched from the National Monument to the U.S. embassy and then filled the southbound lanes of Jalan Thamrin with protesters, buses, motorcycles, and trucks (*Agence France Presse*, October 19, 2001). In Kuala Lumpur, 2,000 members of the Pan-Malaysian Islamic Party (PAS) demonstrated outside the U.S. embassy after gathering for Friday prayers at a nearby mosque. Representatives of the PAS were eventually allowed into the embassy to present a note protesting the bombings in Afghanistan (*Deutsche Presse-Agentur*, October 12, 2001). Certainly, demonstrations took place on other days as well, but as social sites of collective action, the Friday gatherings in mosques provided opportunities for organizing contention.

Second, although nonaffiliated Muslims frequently participated in demonstrations, Islamic movement groups organized many of the protest events. Well-known Islamic organizations, such as the Muslim Brotherhood (Egypt and Jordan), the Justice Party (Indonesia), and the Jamiat Ulama-I-Islam (Pakistan), coordinated massive protests and rallies opposed to the war in Af-

1

ghanistan and Muslim government support for the United States. Smaller, more radical groups, such as Lashkar Mujahidin (Indonesia), also actively organized demonstrations against the U.S. bombings.

Third, the demonstrations were frequently used as opportunities to articulate an indictment of U.S. foreign policy that reversed attributions of fault and reassigned definitions to the terminology used by the American administration to justify its actions. In particular, America was framed as the embodiment of evil, terrorism, and injustice because of its support for Israel against the Palestinians, policy toward Iraq, and attacks that killed civilians in Afghanistan. Banners denounced the U.S. war in Afghanistan as "a crusade against Islam" (*Jordan Times*, October 12, 2001) and charged that "Bush is the greatest terrorist" (*Deutsche Presse-Agentur*, October 12, 2001). Others pledged to "save the world from global terrorism [i.e., the United States]" and to "drag Bush to an international tribunal" (*Agence France Presse*, October 11, 2001). These slogans were accompanied by the ubiquitous "Death to America" and placards proclaiming support for Osama bin Laden. At a rally in northern Nigeria, attended by more than 3,000 Muslims, the president of the Kano State Council Ulama aptly summarized the general sentiment on the Muslim street: "America's definition of terrorism differs from the rest of the world. America is the biggest terrorist nation, given its record of unprovoked attacks on countries like Libya, Iraq, and Sudan" (*Agence France Presse*, October 7, 2001).

Fourth, many of the protests exhibited a consistent repertoire of contention (Tilly 1978; Traugott 1995). In addition to marches and rallies intended to demonstrate opposition to the United States, protesters utilized other tools of dissent. Petitions were directed to U.S. representatives as well as to Muslim governments. Protesters unveiled banners in indigenous languages as well as English, the latter indicating a strategy to target broad audiences in the era of globalization. Symbolic props and actions were also common, especially religious idioms and burning American flags and effigies of President George W. Bush. Violence did occur, but usually in response to protest policing techniques, which tended to be repressive.

All of these forms of contention are part of what we term "Islamic activism"—*the mobilization of contention to support Muslim causes.* Our definition of "Islamic activism" is purposefully broad and attempts to be as inclusive as possible. In doing so, it accommodates the variety of contention that frequently emerges under the banner of "Islam," including propagation movements, terrorist groups, collective action rooted in Islamic symbols and identities, explicitly political movements that seek to establish an Islamic state, and inward-looking groups that promote Islamic spirituality through collective efforts. We believe that given the plethora of differences within the Muslim world as to what is truly "Islamic," it would be folly to artificially construct a narrow delineation that includes some self-declared definitions of what is "Islamic" while excluding others.

The patterns of contention in anti-U.S. protests identified above are not unique to Islamic activism. Petitions, banners, marches, and other tactics of dissent, for example, enjoy illustrious careers in modern protest. While the precise timing and choice of tactics may vary according to local contexts, there are common instruments in repertoires that exhibit consistency across time and space. As Sidney Tarrow (1994) argues, such tactics are so common that they reflect modular forms of protest that can be used by different actors at different moments and places. In addition, other collective actors also respond to grievances, use institutional and organizational resources to muster support, and produce mobilization frames rooted in symbols, discourse, and practice, often designed to evoke a sense of injustice to encourage activism.

This indicates that the *dynamics, process, and organization* of Islamic activism can be understood as important elements of contention that transcend the specificity of "Islam" as a system of meaning, identity, and basis of collective action. Though the ideational components and inspiration of Islam as an ideological worldview differentiate Islamic activism from other examples of contention, the collective action itself and concomitant mechanisms demonstrate consistency across movement-types. In other words, Islamic activism is not *sui generis*.

Despite these similarities, the study of Islamic activism has, for the most part, remained isolated from the plethora of theoretical and conceptual developments that have emerged from research on social movements and contentious politics. Instead, most publications on Islamic activism are either descriptive analyses of the ideology, structure, and goals of various Islamic actors or histories of particular movements. Other sociological dynamics typically remain unexamined or are downplayed as contingent upon the unique ideological orientation of Islam, thus implicitly essentializing Islamic activism as unintelligible in comparative terms and perpetuating beliefs in Islamic exceptionalism. Where comparative analysis is used (beyond examining multiple examples of Islamic activism), it is typically limited to comparisons with other "religious fundamentalisms" that share similar ideological foundations and religious orientations, thus emphasizing the comparability of ideas rather than the mechanisms of activism (Antoun and Hegland 1987; Lawrence 1989; Sivan and Friedman 1990; Kepel 1994; Marty and Appleby 1995). The consequence is that scholarship has tended to ignore developments in social movement research that could provide theoretical leverage over many issues relevant to Islamic activism.

An additional obstacle to theory building in the study of Islamic activism is that multidisciplinary research is not unified by a shared research agenda. Scattered among a variety of disciplines, publications on Islamic activism tend to follow narrow sets of research questions, theoretical frameworks, and methodologies, each determined by a particular disciplinary focus. Political scientists, for example, are mostly concerned with how Islam impacts the state and politics; sociologists are interested in exploring the demographic roots of Islamist recruits; religious studies scholars predominantly focus on the ideas that motivate Islamic activism; and historians detail the histories of particular Islamist groups. The result is that disciplinary fragmentation has produced greater understanding about each particular element of Islamic activism without developing models or frameworks that explain how all of these elements fit together, interact, and influence patterns of Islamic contention. A cooperative research agenda, in contrast, would produce a set of shared working questions, concepts, and lines of theory that help provide a comprehensive, interconnected understanding of Islamic activism.

The purpose of this book is to propose social movement theory as a unifying framework and agenda that can provide effective modes of inquiry to further the boundaries of research on Islamic activism. Whereas the majority of studies on Islamic activism tend to assume that a particular set of grievances, translated into religious idioms and symbols, engenders mobilization, various generations of social movement theory and concomitant debates have demonstrated that other factors are inextricably linked to mobilization processes, including resource availability, framing resonance, and shifts in opportunity structures. By engaging social movement theory, this book demonstrates the efficacy of a shared language for comparative analysis and theory building.

At the same time, our hope is not only to demonstrate the ways in which social movement theory offers theoretical leverage over many of the issues germane to the study of Islamic activism but also to show how the study of Islamic activism provides new testing grounds for social movement theory. Dominated by empirical research on the United States and Western Europe, social movement theory building has been heavily contextualized by liberal democratic polities and Western societies, thus narrowing the generalizability of findings and conclusions. As several social movement scholars lament, "The new comparative riches available to movement scholars are based, almost exclusively, on research rooted in core liberal democratic polities. . . . If our understanding of collective action dynamics has benefited as much as we contend by comparing cases across this relatively homogeneous set of polities, imagine what we are likely to learn from broadening our perspective to include those set in very different times and places" (McAdam et al. 1996, xii).

To be certain, the universe of cases has expanded to include less open polities and non-Western societies. But the Muslim world has yet to be fully integrated into social movement theory. The ubiquity of Islamic activism and its global ramifications (in both the Muslim and non-Muslim world, especially since September 11) means that this oversight is significant. Given the variety of collective actors that operate in the name of "Islam" (prayer groups, terrorists, propagation movements, study circles, political parties, nongovernmental organizations, cultural societies, etc.), one might even make a strong claim that Islamic activism is one of the most common examples of activism in the world. It is thus an important topic and may challenge social movement theory to reflect and modify its assumptions and conclusions about contention.

In demonstrating the fecundity of a social movement theory approach to the study of Islamic activism, this book provides form to an interest that has been emerging in strength over the past few decades. David Snow and Susan Marshall (1984) initiated the first published call to incorporate research on Islamic activism into social movement theory. Their analysis of the relationship between cultural imperialism and Islamic movements effectively utilizes the theoretical tools that were current in social movement research at the time, including structural strains as catalysts, mobilizing ideologies, and resource mobilization. Religion is depicted as the source of a mobilizing ideology and organizational resources that are used to combat perceived cultural imperialism. They conclude by calling for "the integration of research on both religious and political movements" and note that "[t]oo frequently students of both kinds of movements have ignored each others' work, the result of which is a fragmented understanding of social movements" (1984, 146). Others have argued for the more general elimination of an artificial bifurcation between the studies of religious and nonreligious movements (e.g., Hannigan 1991; Williams 1994), and a handful of scholars have encouraged the study of Islamic activism in particular (either directly or indirectly by way of example) (Foran 1994; Vergés 1997; Tehami 1998; Wolff 1998; Munson 2001; Wiktorowicz 2001; Schatz 2002; Wickham 2002; Clark 2003; Hafez 2003). Sidney Tarrow's decision to include a brief discussion of Islamic fundamentalism in the second edition of *Power in Movement* (1998) reflects the broader recognition among social movement theorists that Islamic activism represents an important topic of inquiry, especially as scholars broaden to study new regions and movements.

At the same time, specialists on Islamic activism have been actively searching for a new framework for understanding Islamic contention. Driven by an overall shift in area studies to become more broadly comparative and theoretical (Tessler 1999), those interested in Islamic activism have sought to engage more comprehensive theoretical debates. As the following sections explain, this search has led Islamic activism scholars through theoretical developments that parallel trends in social movement theory. Although these two areas of research historically enjoyed little interaction, similar developments intimate commonalities and the possibility of cross-fertilization. The remainder of this introduction details areas of convergence that have emerged over the past several decades before concluding with an outline of the structure of the book.

Structural Strains as Proximate Causes?

Early approaches to the study of social movements derived from functionalist social psychology accounts of mass behavior. The starting point for such analyses was an assumption that system equilibrium is a natural societal condition. From this perspective, societies organically generate institutional infrastructure that regulates the balance between inputs and outputs in the political system. Societal demands are accommodated by responsive institutions that channel and address myriad interests to produce optimal policies. These policies, in turn, assuage demands and function to maintain the equilibrium of the system. For functionalists, system *disequilibrium* derives from exogenous structural strains that produce new grievances and erode the efficacy of institutions, producing pathological dysfunctions that can cause political instability. If institutional capacity cannot accommodate newly mobilized societal demands, the result is social frustration and political disorder (Huntington 1968).

The first generation of social movement theory was rooted in functionalism and focused on the structural and psychological causes of mass mobilization (see McAdam 1982, chapter 1). The classic models posited a linear causal relationship in which structural strains produce psychological discomfort, which, in turn, produces collective action. Various strains, such as industrialization, modernization, or an economic crisis, disrupt social life and accepted routines, thereby creating a degree of social and normative ambiguity about how to respond to changing conditions. Theories of mass society, in particular, argued that the erosion of intermediary groups that integrate individuals into society and politics creates a growing sense of social anomie, despair, and anxiety. A psychological sense of isolation and impotence in the face of broad societal changes was believed to prompt individuals to join social movements. Movements were thus seen as escapist coping mechanisms through which individuals regain a sense of belonging and empowerment (for various renditions, see Turner and Killian 1957; Kornhauser 1959; Smelser 1962). While there are different variants of the early social movement theories, they all shared a common understanding of social movements as mechanisms for alleviating psychological discomfort derived from structural strains.

The logic of the sociopsychological approach dominates much of the scholarship on Islamic activism. For many scholars, the underlying impetus for activism derives from the structural crises produced by the failure of secular modernization projects (Waltz 1986; Dekmejian 1995; Hoffman 1995; Faksh 1997). During the pinnacle of developmentalism, leaders in Muslim countries, especially in the Middle East, adopted Western modernization models to promote economic development. Steeped in Western education systems, elites frequently viewed modernization and Westernization as part of the same process, thus advocating not only policies of industrialization, but also the incorporation of Western practices, including clothing styles, secularization, and Western languages. Even in states borne from brutal confrontations with Western powers, elites frequently adopted Western cultural attributes, despite anti-Western rhetoric. This was particularly the case in North Africa, where the ruling elite preferred to speak French. While this small minority drifted apart from the cultural mainstream of its own societies, regimes attempted to placate their populations by promising economic growth, national wealth, and social protection.

Rapid socioeconomic transformations tended to concentrate wealth among the Westernized elite, state bourgeoisie, and corrupt state officials, while concurrently generating negative side effects that impacted large segments of the population. Municipal infrastructure, for example, was insufficient to accommodate the influx of rural-urban migrants seeking employment, leading to housing shortages, the expansion of shantytowns, and the growth of unwieldy mega-cities such as Cairo, Tehran, and Algiers. At the same time, prices on basic commodities rose while real wages and employment declined. By the late 1960s and early 1970s, the standard of living for many in society had suffered under failed state-controlled economic policies. The sense of general economic malaise was compounded by exclusion from political power, which was monopolized by a small elite coterie that seemed to espouse an alien value system. These failures and the growing impoverishment of larger portions of the population were magnified by the devastating and bitter Arab defeat in the 1967 war with Israel, which served as a catalyst for societal introspection (Haddad 1992).

Although proponents of this sociopsychological understanding agree that Islamic activism is a response to the psychological distress produced by these conditions, scholars have debated the relative importance of different precipitants. Some argue that socioeconomic factors are the principal cause and tend to emphasize the common socioeconomic background of Islamic activists (Ibrahim 1980; Ansari 1984; Munson 1986; Waltz 1986). The underlying assumption of such an approach is that socioeconomic background tells us something about grievances and therefore why individuals join an Islamic movement or group. Early research indicated that most militants had high levels of education and recently migrated to urban centers, often in search of employment opportunities. Scholars argued that because these recruits were cut off from their rural roots and family, lived in a new urban environment with different values, and faced blocked social mobility, they suffered a sense of social alienation and anomie that rendered them vulnerable to the Islamist message of tradition. Later studies showed that the base of support shifted toward the less educated strata of society, but recruits were still seen as motivated by psychosocial pressures created by socioeconomic crisis (Ibrahim 1996).

Others view Islamic activism as a response to cultural imperialism. From this perspective, the most important societal strain is the growing influence of Western culture, as supported by an assortment of foreign and international political, economic, and military instruments (Burgat and Dowell 1993; Keddie 1994; Esposito 1998).

Islamists themselves tend to emphasize this dimension of the crisis. Whether such claims mask other interests, Islamists frequently couch their grievances and goals in language akin to Huntington's (1996) "clash of civilizations," whereby mobilization is viewed as a response to insidious Western desires to undermine the culture of Muslim societies. A direct corollary of this cultural infiltration argument is that the erosion of Islamic values and practices will inexorably lead to deeper problems in various spheres of social life, including economics, politics, and military defense. The Western "attack on Islam" (whether by foreign enemies or Western proxies in the Muslim world) is thus conceptualized as the first stage in a conspiracy to undermine, weaken, and eventually dominate Muslim countries (see Burgat and Dowell 1993; Wiktorowicz and Taji-Farouki 2000).

Still others favor political strain explanations for the rise of Islamic activism. Under authoritarian rule, the masses lack formal political access to mitigate the adverse effects of modernization projects and the deterioration of quality of life. With few open channels for political recourse, the result is societal frustration and a sense of alienation. The feeling of political impotence is exacerbated in the face of security service repression and administrative processes that attempt to depoliticize civil society and prevent oppositional activities. Since political movements are banned under most authoritarian regimes, Islamic activism becomes a natural vehicle for political discontent. Rooted in established social sites of religious practice and widely accepted values, contention through Islam represents one of the few remaining effective options for confronting a sense of political exclusion.

Some scholars take the strain argument even further and assert that the precise shape of Islamic activism is directly correlated with the intensity of the crisis. Dekmejian represents this perspective when he argues that "The scope and intensity of the fundamentalist reaction, ranging from spiritual awakening to revolutionary violence, depends on the depth and pervasiveness of the crisis environment" (1995, 6). Increased strain is assumed to elicit increased responses whereby individuals seek to re-anchor themselves or redress grievances through religion (Esposito 1992, 12–17).

The early sociopsychological approach to the study of social movements met with stark criticism for its overly simplistic formulation of an inexorable linkage between structural strain and movement contention (e.g., McAdam 1982), a criticism that is equally applicable to similar approaches in the study of Islamic activism. Systems are not inherently balanced or static, but rather consistently dynamic as they experience the pressures and strains of societal changes, events, and interactions. More importantly, structural strain and the discontent it produces (the alleged catalyst for contentious action) are ubiquitous in all societies (though the precise content varies according to local conditions), yet do not always elicit a movement. In reality, social movements do not correspond to the strain-movement paired logic. In fact, poor countries with limited resources or political freedom often produce few social movements, despite the ubiquity of strain and discontent. Western democracies, on the other hand, which enjoy much higher standards of living, political freedom, and stability, are ripe with robust movements.

Not only did early strain models of social movements ignore the innumerous instances where strains did not actually engender movement mobilization, but they also tended to disregard the purposive, political, and organized dimensions of movement contestation. Movements are not merely psychological coping mechanisms; they are often explicitly focused and directed toward the political arena (McAdam 1982; Buechler 1993). In addition, participants are not "dysfunctional" individuals seeking psychological comfort, but instead frequently represent educated and well-adjusted members of society.

While social movement theory moved to redress this theoretical deficiency, the study of Islamic activism has, to a large extent, remained circumscribed by the inherent limitations of the sociopsychological model. Building on the underlying suppositions of the model, recycled renditions have mostly sought to create more complex lists of strains and grievances. Explanations for the emergence of Islamic activism no longer narrowly focus on a single category of strains or concomitant discontent (political, socioeconomic, or cultural), but rather combine these factors into single explanatory frameworks that include extensive lists of precipitating causes. The massive accumulation of different societal problems makes mobilization seem virtually inevitable.

But by unreflectively replicating the weaknesses of strain-based explanations, scholars cannot effectively answer central questions about the emergence and dynamics of Islamic activism. Under conditions of repression, how do movements collectivize individual grievances and mobilize participants? Given similar structural conditions, strains, and grievances, what explains cross-national and diachronic variance in patterns of Islamic mobilization? In shared political contexts, what explains intra-movement tactical differences? Why do some groups use violence while others adamantly eschew violent contention? And why did aggrieved individuals turn to Islam rather than liberal democracy, nationalism, socialism, or other "isms"? Questions such as these raise comparative issues about the dynamics of contention that prioritize the *mechanisms* of collective action. Structural strain and discontent may be necessary, but they are not a sufficient causal explanation for Islamic activism.

Resources and Mobilizing Structures

Resource mobilization theory (RMT) emerged in response to the shortcomings of the early sociopsychological approaches to social movements. Rather than viewing movements as constituted by irrational or psychologically deprived individuals who join in response to structural strains, RMT views movements as rational, organized manifestations of collective action. As an approach, its central contention is that while grievances are ubiquitous, movements are not. As a result, there must be intermediary variables that translate individualized discontent into organized contention. For RMT, resources and mobilizing structures, such as formal social movement organizations (SMOs), are needed to collectivize what would otherwise remain individual grievances. Movements are not seen as irrational outbursts intended to alleviate psychological distress, but rather as organized contention structured through mechanisms of mobilization that provide strategic resources for sustained collective action.

Steeped in Western societies, RMT emphasizes the rational and strategic dimensions of social movements in liberal democratic polities (Oberschall 1973; Gamson 1975; Tilly 1978; Jenkins 1983; McCarthy and Zald 1987a, 1987b). Movements create crucibles of mobilization, communication mechanisms, and professional staffs through a process of bureaucratization and institutional differentiation designed to coordinate and organize contention. With a sturdy and enduring infrastructure, formal institutions, resources, organic community organizations, and a division of labor, movements can strategically direct activism to maximize impact and efficaciousness. In cases where resource availability for disempowered collectivities is limited, third party intervention may be necessary to create mobilizing structures (Jenkins and Perrow 1977). At the same time, movement entrepreneurs offer selective incentives (Olson 1965) (material, solidary, as well as purposive) to entice actors to join an SMO, sharply contrasting the rational recruit of RMT with the psychologically distressed joiner of early sociopsychological models. For both entrepreneurs and professional SMO staffs, employment depends upon the ability of the organization to attract and maintain membership, thus creating a movement-business model designed to promote organizational continuity. The consequence of such a formulation is that mature social movements use resources to evolve into organizational models akin to other bureaucratic entities and forms of institutionalized politics.

Although most research on Islamic activism does not directly address RMT debates, scholarship highlights the importance of organizational resources. The mosque, for example, is a central institution for religious practice in Muslim societies and is frequently utilized as a religiospatial mobilizing structure by various Islamist groups (e.g., see Parsa 1989). Within the physical structure of the mosque, Islamists offer sermons, lessons, and study groups to propagate the movement message, organize collective action, and recruit new joiners. Mosques also provide an organic, national network that connects communities of activists across space. In this manner, mobilization through the mosque is analogous to the use of churches by the civil rights movement in the United States (McAdam 1982; Morris 1984), though the role of the mosque as a "free space" has declined in recent years as regimes have extended state control over public religious institutions.

Islamic nongovernmental organizations (NGOs) constitute another set of widely used meso-level organizations (Sullivan 1994; Clark 1995, 2003; Shadid 2001; Wiktorowicz 2001). Islamic NGOs, such as medical clinics, hospitals, charity societies, cultural centers, and schools, provide basic goods and services to demonstrate that "Islam is the solution" to everyday problems in Muslim societies. Within these organizational contexts, Islamic activists not only provide needed social services (often in areas where state programs are absent or ineffective), but use social interactions with local communities to propagate and recruit followers as well. In at least a few instances, employment opportunities at Islamic NGOs provide patronage rewards (selective incentives) for loyal constituents, thus reinforcing solidarity ties to the movement. Rooted in socioeconomic development activities, these organizations represent a friendly public face that promotes the Islamic message without directly confronting the regime, even though the activities themselves may highlight the inability of the state to effectively address socioeconomic problems (Sullivan 1994). They also offer concrete, visible examples of what Islam can provide, in contradistinction to the state's secular modernization failures. Islamic NGOs are commonly used by peaceful, reform minded movements, but they also constitute organizational resources for radical groups such as Hizbullah and Hamas (Shadid 2001; Robinson in this volume). Where the regime constrains formal political space, outreach programs through Islamic grassroots activities can provide tangible resources for mobilization (Wickham 2002).

Within civil society, Islamic activists also mobilize through the structure of professional and student associations (Wickham 1997; Fahmy 1998). Frequently in Muslim countries, these associations function as surrogate political arenas where various social tendencies compete for control of institutional po sitions and resources. With the decline of leftist ideologies and movements, especially after the end of the Cold War, Islamic movements have successfully gained control over various associations and utilize them to promote a religious message, even while providing services to the professional or student body. Islamic activists do not create these organizational resources; rather, they capture and usurp "potential resources" for movement purposes (Kurzman 1994).

In addition to these organizational fora, a number of Islamic groups have responded to limited political liberalization measures by mobilizing through political parties (Esposito and Voll 1996; Robinson 1997; Akinci 1999; Langhor 2001; Lust-Okar 2001). While many Islamists reject democracy as unIslamic, reform-oriented movements have taken advantage of new political openings. In Jordan, for example, the Islamic Action Front (IAF) has demonstrated remarkable electoral strength and organizational capacity since its legalization in 1993. It is the most widely recognized party in the kingdom and has seriously contested municipal and parliamentary elections (despite a national electoral boycott in 1997). In Turkey, Indonesia, Malaysia, Yemen, and elsewhere, moderate Islamists have demonstrated remarkable skill in mobilizing support through political parties as well (Langhor 2001). Even radicals-cum-reformists from the Islamic Group and Islamic Jihad in Egypt have attempted to create political party vehicles (the Shariʿa Party and the Islah Party), though state opposition and repression have proved daunting hurdles.

While RMT has tended to emphasize these types of formal organizations, it also accommodates the role of informal institutions and social networks. A multitude of studies, for example, highlight the importance of social networks for movement recruitment, particularly in high-risk activism where social ties provide bonds of trust and solidarity and encourage activism (McAdam 1986). Still others point to the decentralized, polycephalous, and reticulated structure of movements such as the Pentecostal and black power movements (Gerlach and Hine 1970). And a number of scholars have embraced less formal understandings of social movements by conceptualizing informally structured movements as "social movement communities," understood as "informal networks of politicized participants who are active in promoting the goals of a social movement outside the boundaries of formal organization" (Buechler 1990, 61). As opposed to the bureaucratic model of SMOs, social movement communities exhibit "fluid boundaries, flexible leadership structures, and malleable divisions of labor" (ibid., 42). Examples include elements of the women's movement (Buechler 1990), lesbian feminists (Taylor and Whittier 1992), some neighborhood movements (Stoecker 1995), the alternative health movement (Schneirov and Geczik 1996), and Earth First! (Ingalsbee 1996). At least a few scholars have argued that informality, as opposed to formal organizations, is more effective for protest since the organizational survival imperatives of SMOs can undermine the purpose of a movement (Piven and Cloward 1979).

The use of social networks and informal resources for mobilization is especially common in less open polities where visibility is dangerous. In such contexts, formal resources are inviting targets for regime repression and may actually make it easier for security services to undermine the institutional capacity of the movement. As a result, movements may instead use informal institutions and social networks for activism, since they are embedded in everyday relationships and thus more impervious to state control (Scott 1990; Opp and Gern 1993; Schneider 1995; Zuo and Benford 1995; Pfaff 1996; Loveman 1998; Zhao 1998). In his analysis of the 1989 "revolution" in Eastern Europe, for example, Pfaff (1996, 99) finds that in "societies in which the state virtually eliminates an open public sphere and organization independent of regime control, informal ties are of critical importance. Tightly knit networks nurture collective identities and solidarity, provide informal organization and contacts, and supply information otherwise unavailable to individuals." Addressing the same question of mobilization under repressive conditions in the Chinese context, Zuo and Benford (1995) find that the Chinese student movement overcame similar impediments to mobilization by utilizing social networks, campus study groups, student unions, dormitory networks, and informal communications, such as protest notices, all of which facilitated the social construction of grievances and protest.

Given the decentralized nature of Islamic authority, the importance of social connections and personalism, and political repression in Muslim societies, scholarship on Islamic activism has much to offer the study of informality in social movement theory. In Jordan, for example, a number of Islamic activists have utilized informal social networks as viable mobilization structures and resources for contention (Wiktorowicz 2001). Despite political liberalization in 1989, the Jordanian regime has maintained social and political control through the "management of collective action"—the manipulation of bureaucratic processes to set limits and channel movement activism in particular, less oppositional, directions. Legal codes and administrative procedures are manipulated to favor the creation of moderate Islamic SMOs while disempowering more radical activists. Radical activists have, in turn, responded to these limitations by mobilizing through informal social networks and institutions. Through a loose web of personal relationships, study circles, and informal meetings, these activists mobilize outside the boundaries of formal institutions. While personalism and informality may ultimately limit the reach of a social movement, social networks provide viable resources for movement survival and activism, especially in contexts where authoritarianism limits formal resource availability.[1] In Muslim contexts, informal networks are an indelible component of the social matrix and are frequently used as resources for political, social, and economic purposes (Denoeux 1993; Ismail 2000).

Opportunities and Constraints

Social movements do not operate in a vacuum; they belong to a broader social milieu and context characterized by shifting and fluid configurations of enablements and constraints that structure movement dynamics. Regardless of level of grievances, resource availability, or the prevalence of mobilizing structures, collective actors are both limited and empowered by exogenous factors, which often delimit movement viability and the menu of tactics, actions, and choices. Such understandings contextualize collective action by incorporating the influence of external factors and concomitant structures of opportunity and constraint. While many scholars describe these structures as "*political* opportunity structures" and incorporate them into a political process model of social movement mobilization, in practice they encompass cultural, social, and economic factors as well.

Social movement theorists do not necessarily share a common delineation of the most important exogenous factors, but most scholarship in this area focuses on "the opening and closing of political space and its institutional and substantive location" (Gamson and Meyer 1996, 277). Some of the most cited variables in determining access to political space include the level of formal and informal access to political institutions and decision-making, the degree of political system receptivity to challenger groups, the prevalence of allies and opponents, the stability of the ruling elite coalition, the nature of state repression, and state institutional capacity (Tilly 1978; Kitschelt 1986; Tarrow 1994; McAdam et al. 1996a). While these dimensions may impact social movements by either opening or closing possibilities for activism, movement responses are contingent upon recognition and interpretation of opportunities and threats (Kurzman 1996; McAdam et al. 2001).

Although this approach focuses its attention on structural factors, it shares similar assumptions with RMT. In particular, despite the micro-macro differences between the two approaches, they both share an underlying assumption that social movement contention derives from rational actors. For RMT, movement entrepreneurs construct SMOs and institutional infrastructure and strategically mobilize resources and personnel to produce efficacious choices and actions, whether for individual preferences or movement goals. Movement participants are not irrational, but rather join because of a variety of incentives and goals. Similarly, while a structuralist analysis of social movements is primarily concerned with the ways in which structural conditions shape social movement dynamics, there is an assumption that actors, once they perceive opportunities and threats, will respond rationally to maximize openings or limit adversity (Berejikian 1992). A focus on structural factors is thus an additive piece of an overall understanding of social movements and reflects a difference in emphasis, rather than a fundamental ontological disagreement.

Since the late 1990s, a number of scholars have shifted to reconceptualize Islamic activists as strategic thinkers embedded in a political context which influences choices and decisions (Anderson 1997; Alexander 2000; Ismail 2001). Recent research, for example, has demonstrated that despite widely accepted understandings of Hamas as an uncompromising movement trapped by rigid adherence to doctrine, the movement has strategically responded to changes in the surrounding political context. Prior to the Palestinian *intifada* (uprising) that began in 2000, there was growing popular support for the peace process, which posed a dilemma for the movement. Strict adherence and an intransigent position vis-à-vis peace was likely to erode the support of bystander publics that sought an end to the economic and social hardships of occupation, thus threatening the organizational survival of Hamas as an alternative to Arafat and his supporters. As a result, Hamas tactically adjusted its doctrine to accommodate the possibility of peace with Israel by framing peace as a temporary pause in the jihad that would strengthen Muslim forces before a final assault. Islamic concepts such as *sabr* (patience) and *hudna* (truce) were used to legitimize doctrinal flexibility within the overall objectives of the movement (Mishal and Sela 2000; see also Hroub 2000). The uprising and escalation of violence that started in September 2000 increased public support for Hamas and provided an opportunity for the movement to reinstate earlier militant positions and actions. Additional studies of the Armed Islamic Group in Algeria (Kavylas 1999) and various chapters in this volume (Hafez, Hafez and Wiktorowicz, Lawson, and Robinson) concur that radicals respond rationally and strategically to structures of opportunity. At least a few studies of moderate Islamist groups also depict activists as strategic thinkers who are affected by opportunities and constraints (Mufti 1999; Alexander 2000).

Culture and Framing Processes

Since the 1980s, social movement theorists have been interested in the role of ideational factors, including social interaction, meaning, and culture (Morris and Mueller 1992; Laraña et al. 1994; Johnston and Klandermans 1995). In addition to the strategic and structuralist dimensions of mobilization outlined in RMT and the political process model, social movement theory has increasingly addressed how individual participants conceptualize themselves as a collectivity; how potential participants are actually convinced to participate; and the ways in which meaning is produced, articulated, and disseminated by movement actors through interactive processes. In the development of a theoretical approach to social movements, this interest has predominantly manifested itself through the study of framing.

Frames represent interpretive schemata that offer a language and cognitive tools for making sense of experiences and events in the "world out there." For social movements, these schemata are important in the production and dissemination of movement interpretations and are designed to mobilize participants and support. As signifying agents engaged in the social construction of meaning, movements must articulate and disseminate frameworks of understanding that resonate with potential participants and broader publics to elicit collective action. Although extant ideas or ideologies may underlie contentious action, they are arranged and socially processed through grammatical constructs and interpretive lenses that create intersubjective meaning and facilitate movement goals. The term "framing" is used to describe this process of meaning construction (see Snow et al. 1986; Snow and Benford 1988; Snow and Benford 1992; Benford and Snow 2000; Williams and Benford 2000).

David Snow and Robert Benford (1988) identify three core framing tasks for social movements. First, movements construct frames that diagnose a condition as a problem in need of redress. This includes attributions of responsibility and targets of blame. Second, movements offer solutions to the problem, including specific tactics and strategies intended to serve as remedies to ameliorate injustice. And third, movements provide a rationale to motivate support and collective action. While potential participants may share common understandings about causation and solutions to a particular problem, motivational frames are needed to convince potential participants to actually engage in activism, thereby transforming bystander publics into movement participants.

One of the most critical dimensions of the framing process for movement mobilization is frame resonance. The ability of a movement to transform a mobilization potential into actual mobilization is contingent upon the capacity of a frame to resonate with potential participants. Where a movement frame draws upon indigenous cultural symbols, language, and identities, it is more likely to reverberate with constituents, thus enhancing mobilization. Such reverberation, however, depends upon not only its consistency with cultural narratives, but also the reputation of the individual or group responsible for articulating the frame, the personal salience of the frame for potential participants, the consistency of the frame, and the frame's empirical credibility in real life (Benford and Snow 2000, 619–22).

Islamic movements are heavily involved in the production of meaning and concomitant framing processes. Like many "new social movements" driven by issues of identity, culture, and post-materialism (as opposed to class, economic, or narrow political interests) (Laraña et al. 1994), Islamic movements are embroiled in struggles over meaning and values. While a great deal of research has focused upon politicized movements that seek to create an Islamic state, the core imperative of Islamic movements is a desire to create a society governed and guided by the *shariᶜa* (Islamic law). Control and reconstruction of state institutions may be an effective instrument for accomplishing this transformation, but it is only one of many routes for change. In other words, the state is a means for the production of meaning, not an end. In fact, most Islamic struggles are waged through society and cultural discourse rather than state institutions or government decision-making bodies. Such efforts challenge dominant cultural codes and create networks of shared meaning about the proper functions of society, groups, and the individual (Melucci 1996).

An important component of most Islamic movement diagnostic frames is to blame the spread of Western values and practices for a wide variety of social ills, including rising unemployment, stagnant economic development, soaring debt, housing shortages, dwindling public social and welfare expenditures, and so forth. The argument is that the true path to development and success is outlined in the sources of Islam. So long as Muslims follow this straight path, they will be rewarded for their faithfulness. The onslaught of Western cultural codes, however, erodes the sanctity of Islamic mores and devalues the very Muslim institutions and social relationships necessary for a healthy society. Following or mimicking Western practices (styles of dress, culture, public behavior, etc.) is thus viewed as an egregious departure from Islam and the cause of crisis (Wiktorowicz and Taji-Farouki 2000).

Most frames go a step further and argue that this process of cultural imperialism is a conscious Western strategy to weaken Muslim societies for economic, political, and military purposes. International institutions, media outlets, the marketplace, and secular modernization projects are all framed as vehicles for the strategic infusion of alien value systems calculated to undermine the strength of Islam. For some Islamic activists, the ultimate manifestation of this imperialist design is Western support for pliant "non-Islamic" regimes, which are framed as Western puppets controlled through International Monetary Fund structural adjustment programs, Western foreign aid, and U.S. military forces. From this perspective, regimes are merely extensions of Western interests determined to weaken and control Muslim societies (Burgat and Dowell 1993).

Social movements, however, are embedded in a field of multiple actors that often vie for framing hegemony. Frequent disagreements and framing contests over meaning encourage competitive pressures as various groups produce and disseminate interpretive schemata (Benford 1993). Such competition takes place not only between a movement and its adversaries, but within the movement itself as well. Intramovement divisions (such as hardliner-softliner, conservative-liberal, young-old, ideologue-pragmatist) can create internal framing disputes as each faction attempts to assert its own frame for movement-wide adoption. Prognostic framing, in particular, tends to produce numerous intramovement-framing disputes. While social movements often share a common understanding about responsibility for a problem, there is far less cohesion over strategies and tactics (Benford 1993; Benford and Snow 2000, 625–27).

These prognostic framing differences are common among Islamic activists. Many concur that some break with the West is necessary and that "Islam is the solution," but there are important divergences over specific tactics and strategies. Some groups, for example, believe that the transformation of individual beliefs will eventually affect broader circles over time. Thus missionary movements, such as Jamaᶜat Tabligh, focus on *daᶜwa* (propagation) to affect shifts in individual attitudes toward the role of religion in regulating society and personal behavior. The hope is that these individuals will then promote proper Islamic practices among friends, families, neighbors, communities, and other collectivities. Eventually, this process expands to incorporate the entire society, after which point state institutions naturally evolve to accommodate shariᶜa principles. Other groups advocate formal political participation to restructure state policy and institutions. Advocates of this approach typically have formed political parties and successfully contested elections (where possible). Many such groups also rely upon grassroots activities as tangible manifestations of Islam in action and frame participation in terms of a "new ethic of civic obligation" (Wickham 2002; also in chapter 9 in this volume). Still others advance violent prognostic frames that support the use of military coups or revolutions. Particular Islamic groups may support multiple tactics or shift prognostications, but the existence of multiple prognostic frames is the cause of a great deal of internal conflict and competition.

In addition to intramovement framing contests, social movement groups often compete with "official frames" as well (Noakes 2000). Because regimes throughout the Muslim world depend on Islam in a variety of ways for legitimation, they are actively engaged in what Dale Eickelman and James Piscatori term "Muslim politics"—"the competition and contest over both the interpretation of symbols and the control of the institutions, both formal and informal, that produce and sustain them" (Eickelman and Piscatori 1996, 5). In an effort to maintain this source of legitimacy, regimes articulate innocuous frames that support regime interests and power. These frames do not call for broad societal or state transformations, but rather emphasize individual piety and concern for personal salvation, thus supporting a politically quiescent variant of Islam. At the same time, regimes also attempt to limit the institutional resources and public space available for the dissemination of alternative frames that could challenge regime legitimacy. State control of mosques, sermons, and other public religious institutions and practices is designed to amplify regime frames while muting other perspectives.

As with other social movements, the success of Islamic groups vis-à-vis the state to a large extent derives from the reputation of frame articulators and the use of publicly recognized symbols and language that tap into cultural experiences and collective memories. Failed modernization experiments and political repression have eroded popular support for regimes in the Muslim world; and although many Muslims still follow publicly employed *ulama* (religious scholars), *muftis* (Islamic legal experts), and *imams* (prayer leaders), "official Islam" has lost credibility among disaffected and marginalized communities. These collectivities instead frequently turn to "popular" Islam and reputable community leaders, including Islamic activists. To maximize access to these discontented populations, Islamists have in many cases melded religious themes with nonreligious elements to garner broad support among those who are merely seeking a change from the status quo rather than an Islamic transformation. Meriem Vergès (1997), for example, shows how the Islamic Salvation Front (FIS) in Algeria strategically framed itself as the heir to the revolutionary mantle of the war of independence. Using the language and symbols of the revolution, the FIS attempted to portray itself as a natural extension of the struggle while denouncing the regime as a usurper of Algeria's historic memory. In less auspicious political conditions, Islamists may avoid publicly denouncing a regime and instead produce "clandestine frames" via safe social sites that can escape state surveillance (Tehami 1998).

The use of framing by Islamic groups reflects the cultural and ideational components of contentious politics; and while frames alone do not explain every dimension of collective action, they are important interpretive devices that translate grievances and perceived opportunities into the mobilization of resources and movement activism. To be sure, there are still boisterous debates about whether frames alone have an explanatory value, whether they are post-hoc justifications to take advantage of opportunities, the differences between "frames" and "framing," and the degree of analytic precision, but this area of research has provided a useful tool for examining the interaction of ideas and mobilization.

Structure of *Islamic Activism*

This book should not be understood as a response to the September 11 terrorist attacks by al-Qaeda. The contributors to this book are all specialists in Islamic activism who have maintained an interest in social movement theory for a number of years. Many of the authors have already published work that synthesizes research on Islam and social movement theory and joined this project to further a shared research agenda with broader implications. Their comparative advantage lies in a synthesis between broader theoretical orientations and extensive fieldwork with Islamic activists. All of the authors have engaged in rigorous field research and thus bring to bear empirical prowess situated within comparative theoretical frameworks. Certainly, we hope this book will influence perceptions of Islamic activism in the post–September 11 period, but our driving purpose is to integrate two disparate areas of research in an effort to augment theory building. This book thus echoes earlier calls among area specialists for greater social science and comparative breadth (Tessler 1999).

The book is organized according to areas of research that we believe specialists on Islamic activism are well situated to address—violence and contention, networks and alliances, and culture and framing. Though there are many other possibilities, these three general areas are offered as a starting point for engaging social movement theory, an entrance into a theoretical foray where specialists may have something new to add to the debates. In addressing these areas, each of the chapters builds upon the various theoretical developments outlined above, in many cases addressing multiple theoretical concerns and issues.

In the process, the chapters cover diverse empirical ground that reflects the breadth of the contributors' research strengths. Topics range from the Iranian revolution to women's groups to Islamism and the marketplace. The authors' specialties also allow the volume to address a variety of country contexts in North Africa, the Levant, and the Gulf. A total of eight countries are addressed, including two non-Arab countries (Turkey and Iran). Egypt is given emphasis (two chapters) because of its centrality in the development of research on Islamic activism, and Yemen receives treatment in two chapters because of its growing importance and the paucity of information on Islamic activism there. Two chapters deal specifically with Shiʿite activism. The wide coverage is intended to demonstrate the fecundity of a social movement theory approach for a variety of topics and contexts. In all cases, the chapters address one of the three research areas of focus—violence and contention, networks and alliances, and culture and framing; and each contributor attempts to contribute to ongoing social movement theory debates.

Violence and Contention

Perhaps no other topic has received more attention recently than the use of violence by Islamic groups. In the aftermath of 9/11, scholars, policy makers, and the general American public struggled to fathom the rationale and motivation for the use of mass violence. Concern about Islamic violence was further heightened by the proliferation of suicide bomb attacks by Hamas beginning in the spring of 2002. For many, especially those with little knowledge about Islamic activism, such events and episodes tend to confirm the worst stereotypes about Islamic contention and Islam in general. Self-proclaimed "experts" on "Islamic terrorism" frequently are of little help, since few have actually met their subjects and therefore rely on open public sources such as newspapers and Internet resources, which are often superficial, uninformed, and biased.

In contradistinction to popular perceptions of radical Islamic groups as irrational, "crazy," or deviant, these groups frequently follow a particular dynamic that mirrors the rational calculus of other non-Islamic social movement actors who have used violence as part of their repertoire of contention. In the first section of this book, all of the chapters demonstrate the strategic and tactical dimensions to the use of violence by groups as varied as the Armed Islamic Group (GIA) in Algeria, the Gamaʿa Islamiyya (Islamic Group) in Egypt, Hamas, and Shiʿites who revolted during the 1990s in Bahrain. In each of these different country settings, the use of violence was, to a large extent, a tactical response to shifting opportunity structures and emerged under particular conditions and circumstances.

Mohammed Hafez's opening chapter on the GIA in Algeria effectively represents this argument with an extreme case (chapter 1). During the 1990s, the GIA was responsible for an outbreak of civilian massacres that were notorious for their brutality. Members of the GIA descended on villages in the dead of night and massacred women, children, the elderly, and others, using machetes and burning many of the victims alive. The sheer viciousness was reminiscent of ethnic genocide and raises important questions about the use of violence in contention, especially the indiscriminate killing of noncombatants. Hafez argues that such massacres are most likely to occur where the political opportunity structure is characterized by repression and three related conditions converge: (1) state repression creates a political environment of bifurcation and brutality; (2) insurgents create exclusive organizations to shield themselves from repression; and (3) rebels promote anti-system frames to motivate collective action to overthrow agents of repression. Repression creates a sense of injustice, legitimates a call to arms, and forces insurgents into clandestine organizations that become increasingly isolated from the rest of society and countervailing pressures. Where the regime is framed as fundamentally corrupt through anti-system frames, these radical, encapsulated organizations become further radicalized through a growing belief in total war.

Although the low intensity insurgency led by the Gamaᶜa Islamiyya in Egypt during the 1990s was not colored by massacres (aside from the attack in Luxor in 1997), the dynamics of violence were quite similar. As in Algeria, regime repression seems to have had a causal effect. However, Mohammed Hafez and Quintan Wiktorowicz (chapter 2) argue for a more specific understanding of repression that breaks it down into relevant dimensions. In particular, they argue that repression is most likely to engender violent movement responses where the movement is excluded from institutional politics and suffers *indiscriminate, reactive* state repression (as opposed to *selective, preemptive* repression). Political exclusion is likely to provide credibility for those in the movement who argue for violence because it limits the number of reasonable tactical options, especially those related to system reform. The Egyptian regime accelerated its exclusion of even moderate Islamic groups, such as the Muslim Brotherhood, thus inadvertently weakening calls for reform. At the same time, the regime's repression against the Gamaᶜa Islamiyya was reactive and took place after the movement had already developed organizational resources and mobilization capacity. In part as a counter to leftist forces, the regime had previously allowed the Gamaᶜa organizational space, and the movement took advantage by organizing social services, "taking over" mosques, and developing relationships with local communities. As a result, by the early 1990s, the Gamaᶜa not only had something to lose, but the movement also had developed resources and a capacity to protect its interests. The fact that the regime's repression was indiscriminate and targeted non-activists, including Gamaᶜa families and supportive bystanders, lent credence to arguments that the system could only be changed through violence.

Fred Lawson (chapter 3) addresses the use of violence within the overall context of a protest cycle in Bahrain during the 1990s that included violent *and* nonviolent dissent. Rather than isolating violence as a tactic, Lawson seeks to explain *changes* in repertoires, particularly transitions toward and away from violence. In tracing the different phases of the Shiʿite uprising against the Sunni-dominated al-Khalifa regime, he finds that contrary to the expectation of most social movement theorists, violence was not necessarily pervasive during the last stages of protest when mass mobilization declined. Instead, the pattern of violence in the different stages seems best explained in terms of regime responses to challenger initiatives. Harsh regime response measures that limited moderate tactics tended to radicalize the rebellion and push tactics toward violence. This understanding shifts attention away from macro-level opportunity structures to the micro-level of tactics and regime-challenger interactions.

Glenn Robinson's chapter on Hamas is the final selection in this part of the book (chapter 4). Robinson follows the general theme of this section that Islamic activists who use violence are rational tacticians who respond to exogenous contingencies. Although frequently labeled a terrorist group, Hamas is a social movement that, like the Gamaʿa in Egypt, provides an assortment of social services for the Palestinian community. Its leadership is well educated, modern, and rational—hardly the vision of the radical fanatic. A narrow focus on the violence misses the larger dynamics of the movement, which are better understood in terms of social movement mobilization. From this perspective, Robinson shows how a social movement framework, which focuses on political opportunities, mobilizing structures, and cultural framings, is an effective tool for providing a comprehensive understanding of Hamas. This helps "deorientalize" groups like Hamas by pointing to commonalities shared with other social movements, violent and nonviolent alike. The chapter also highlights the need to sharply distinguish terrorist groups with strict political agendas from "terrorist groups," such as Hamas and Hizbullah, that are more effectively understood as complex social movements. Labels such as "terrorism" may serve to obfuscate more than they clarify.

Networks and Alliances

Islamic activists are embedded in complex network-oriented societies that tend to favor informality over formalized institutionalization. Whereas Western social movements typically mobilize through SMOs, movements in Muslim societies are more likely to utilize the dense associational networks of personal relationships that characterize much of politics, economic activity, and culture. Even formal Islamic organizations, such as the Muslim Brotherhood, are constituted by dynamic networks that extend beyond the parameters of formal organizational space to connect activists to other Islamists, friends, families, and associates.

The reliance on network-based activism among many Islamic activists makes the topic relatively opaque for research. Press reports, organizational charts, and secondary material are often insufficient for delineating and studying these networks and their relationship to contention since networks are by their nature embedded in personal interactions and social relationships. To complicate matters further, repressive conditions in Muslim societies mean that networks are often as much a tactical evasion of public surveillance as they are an organic manifestation of the structure of society. Even those well acquainted with Islamic activism encounter difficulties accessing these networks for study, since access is contingent upon a degree of trust and familiarity that takes time to build.

Many of the authors in this volume have conducted extensive fieldwork explicitly designed to gain access to these networks and assess their impact on the dynamics of contention, fieldwork that is measured in terms of months and years, not days or weeks. Understanding only comes about through repeated interactions, the cultivation of friendships and trust, and through patience and endurance. This puts specialists engaged in political or social anthropology with experience in the field in a unique position to augment and expand social movement debates on the role of networks. Although social movement theory has elucidated the role of networks at the level of recruitment, far less is known about how networks influence social movements beyond the initial recruitment process.

Diane Singerman, whose work on popular networks in Cairo has inspired a great deal of research on network-based activism in the Middle East (see Singerman 1995), explores the cultural resonance of networks and the ways in which they signify authenticity, legitimacy, and efficacy for Muslim communities (chapter 5). Because they are culturally legitimate, networks serve as resources for movement building, even if they remain hidden or submerged as the movement grows and expands. The use of less formal institutions for Islamic activists is increasingly important as regimes throughout the Middle East "criminalize politics" and choose strategies of control, co-optation, and repression rather than inclusionary politics. Through these informal institutions, Islamic activists mobilize and construct collective identities that inspire solidarity within a context of repression and authoritarian politics.

Janine Clark's study (chapter 6) of Islamist women in Yemen explores how individual members of dominant Islamic SMOs, such as Hizb al-Islah and the Islah Charitable Society, use social networks and informal institutions as vehicles for Islamic activism. In particular, SMO activists use *nadwas* (Qurʾanic study groups) to reproduce the movement message, support SMO agendas and activities, and engage women through personal relationships. Because *nadwas* are embedded in social networks, they provide informal institutional resources and comfortable micromobilization contexts where women can participate in forms of activism that are not directly tied to formal movement organizations. In many cases, SMO activists break down existing social network ties and reconstruct new relationships through *nadwa* activities to foster supportive communities and networks of shared meaning. Networks are thus more than recruiting devices; they are informal resources that can be utilized by SMOs to support movement goals. From this perspective, networks are not just umbilical cords that provide sustenance to movements through recruitment; they can be actively manipulated, and thus impacted and reshaped, by formal organizations.

Both Benjamin Smith (chapter 7) and Jillian Schwedler (chapter 8) explore a different kind of network: alliance relationships. Their chapters highlight the fact that networks are not always shared by like-minded individuals and that connections and linkages may result out of tactical considerations or because two actors share a common goal or enemy. Smith cautions against an assumption that all of the actors involved in the "Islamic movement" during the Iranian revolution were equally motivated by religion. While certain members of the *bazaari* (merchant) community did share the ideology of Khomeini and his supporters, evidence indicates that groups in the bazaar joined the revolution through different organizations and for different reasons. Even though political entrepreneurs may have "borrowed" the resources of the bazaar, as a collectivity the bazaar still retained those resources for its own purposes and later used them to protect the merchant class from incursions and economic threats by the Islamic state. The alliance between the ulama and the bazaar was therefore a temporary relationship, one that was subject to change depending upon the strategic interests of the partners.

This kind of alliance and network of convenience among Islamic and non-Islamic activists was also found in Yemen. Jillian Schwedler's chapter shows how the regime sought to use the Islah Party (an Islamic political party) as a strategic ally in party politics to offset the Yemini Socialist Party (YSP) after unification and political liberalization. Embedded in a continuing North-South political struggle, the Northern-dominated ruling party sought to stymie the political aspirations of the YSP, which represented the former political ruling class of Southern Yemen. This initial alliance helped propel the Islah Party to national prominence and provided the Islamic movement with powerful political access and positions. However, as both Schwedler and Smith demonstrate, alliances of this nature are prone to defections if one of the partners no longer deems the relationship as in its best interest. In Iran, the bazaaris defected when their economic interests were threatened by the state. In Yemen, the regime withdrew from the alliance with Islah once it was clear that it no longer needed the movement to offset the socialists from the South. After the civil war in 1994, the political power of the YSP weakened, and the regime determined that it could dominate politics without resorting to alliances or partners. The result was a decline in Islah influence and power.

Culture and Framing

Islamic activism is rooted in the symbolism, language, and cultural history of Muslim society and as a result has successfully resonated with increasingly disillusioned populations suffering from political exclusion, economic deprivation, and a sense of growing impotence at the expense of outside powers and a faceless process of globalization. Much of the work of Islamic activism is devoted to creating frames that motivate, inspire, and demand loyalty. But because Islamic activism operates in contexts of repression, the dynamics of framing may differ from similar processes in Western, liberal democracies. Since work on this area of research in the Muslim world is only now beginning, this possible difference is really an empirical question. Specialists on Islamic activism, historically well versed in the arguments and frames of activism, can use their expertise to answer such questions and further theory.

Carrie Wickham (chapter 9) examines framing within the context of recruitment and Islamic outreach. Whereas most social movement theorists argue that successful recruitment results from selective incentives and the gravity of social networks and relationships, Wickham's study of Islamic outreach to lower-middle-class graduates in Egypt indicates that ideas also matter. In particular, while individual (or rational) interests often attracted graduates to the movement initially, it was the ability of the movement to frame activism as a "moral obligation" that led to its success, especially with respect to recruitment into high-risk activism. "Moral obligation" frames encouraged graduates to embrace an ideology that mandates participation as a moral duty, demands self-sacrifice, and encourages unflinching commitment. The appeal of the frame derived from dynamics familiar to social movement scholars: (1) its resonance with the life experiences of graduates; (2) the credibility and effectiveness of the Islamic agents responsible for articulating and transmitting the frame; and (3) the reinforcement of the frame through intensive, small group interactions that built solidarity, trust, and loyalty. The success of the frame led to what Wickham calls the "transvaluation of values"—a reordering of the priorities that guide individual action. Belonging to the movement was no longer about selective incentives and personal relationships; it was about the morality of religious activism.

Gwenn Okruhlik (chapter 10) draws on social movement concepts such as cognitive liberation, framing, cultural tool kits, and cultural repertoires to explain how Islamists in Saudi Arabia shifted cultural understandings about permissible forms of activism. Within the conservative society of the kingdom, only Islam could provide the language and medium for contention and oppositional activities because of its cultural authenticity and resonance. The use of the *nasihi*, or "memorandum of advice," by an assortment of Islamic activists fundamentally reshaped societal discourse and debate by opening space for criticism through a mode of contention routed in religious legitimacy and sanctioned by Islamic sources and scholars. Okruhlik argues that the *nasihi* provided cognitive liberation for ordinary Saudis because permission for conversation about formally taboo topics came in an Islamic vocabulary. While the Islamic opposition in Saudi Arabia did not topple the regime, it did successfully restructure discourse and meaning.

The last chapter in this section is Hakan Yavuz's study of the impact of economic liberalization on Islamic activism in Turkey (chapter 11). The program of economic liberalization created a variety of new "opportunity spaces"—"social sites and vehicles for activism and the dissemination of meaning, identity, and cultural codes." New vehicles for meaning production included television, newspapers, magazines, financial institutions, and businesses. Yet despite these new opportunities for affecting culture in Turkey, which has been tightly regulated by the Kemalist secularization project, not all Islamic groups responded the same way to market openings. Society-oriented movements, which seek to challenge dominant culture codes and shift networks of shared meaning in society, took advantage of the changes, to a large extent because they were supported by economic groups capable of mobilizing into capitalist venues. State-centered Islamic groups, which seek transformation from above through the state, did not fare as well. Because support for state-centered movements derives from less privileged socioeconomic groups, these movements have always emphasized socioeconomic justice. This goal, however, was undermined by economic liberalization, which disrupted welfare policies. The result was that state-oriented movements generally opposed the reform measures. Yavuz's chapter combines political economy, a political opportunity structure approach, and an emphasis on cultural contention to highlight the differential impact of large-scale change on various movement groups, even if these groups share a common cultural reference point.

Conclusion

In addressing these three general areas, our hope is to contribute to theory building in both social movement theory and the study of Islamic activism. This introduction has argued that the divisions between these two traditions are not all that wide and that parallel developments intimate possibilities for cross-fertilization. Charles Kurzman seconds this view in the conclusion and points to similar paradigmatic developments, especially concerning the relationship between the researcher and the subject. In both the study of collective action and Islam, scholars moved from a view of the subject as irrational to a perspective that emphasized rationality. In social movement research this was precipitated by the entry of movement activists into the academy. In research on Islamic activism, the shift derived from a transition away from Orientalism to an approach that emphasized the authenticity and rationality of indigenous subject voices. This was accompanied by the entry of Muslim scholars into academic debates and discourse. As these two areas of research move in similar directions, the "chasm" (as Kurzman calls it) between them is narrowing.

This book, however, should be viewed only as a first step, an opening for debate and dialogue and an effort to be more consciously theoretical. We fully recognize that theory is dynamic and that there are a variety of ongoing developments and even contention about the social movement theory project itself (see, e.g., McAdam et al. 2001), but social movement theory still flourishes and is exploring new directions. New work on "passionate politics" (Goodwin et al. 2001), for example, may join with broader trends in comparative politics to incorporate emotions into social science (even rational choice) approaches (see, e.g., Monroe 2001). And other possibilities still abound. The study of Islamic activism has much to learn from all of these developments. We hope it can offer much to teach as well.

Notes

Parts of this chapter are adapted from "Islamic Activism and Social Movement Theory: Toward a New Direction for Research," *Mediterranean Politics* (2003).

1. This survival is not limited to informal social networks. Munson (2001), for example, shows how the Muslim Brotherhood in Egypt utilized a decentralized (formal) organizational structure that facilitated movement survival during periods of regime repression.

Works Cited

Akinci, Ugur. 1999. "The Welfare Party's Municipal Track Record: Evaluating Islamist Municipal Activism in Turkey." *Middle East Journal* 53, 1 (Winter): 75–94.

Alexander, Christopher. 2000. "Opportunities, Organizations, and Ideas: Islamists and Workers in Tunisia and Algeria." *International Journal of Middle East Studies* 32, 4 (November): 465–90.

Anderson, Lisa. 1997. "Fulfilling Prophecies: State Policy and Islamist Radicalism." Pp. 17–31 in *Political Islam: Revolution, Radicalism, or Reform?* ed. John Esposito. Boulder: Lynne Rienner.

Ansari, Hamied N. 1984. "The Islamic Militants in Egyptian Politics." *International Journal of Middle East Studies* 16, 1 (March): 123–44.

Antoun, Richard T., and Mary E. Hegland, eds. 1987. *Religious Resurgence: Contemporary Cases in Islam, Christianity, and Judaism.* Syracuse: Syracuse University Press.

Ayubi, Nazih N. 1980. "The Political Revival of Islam: The Case of Egypt." *International Journal of Middle East Studies* 12, 4 (December): 481–99.

Benford, Robert D. 1993. "Frame Disputes within the Nuclear Disarmament Movement." *Social Forces* 71, 3 (March): 677–701.

Benford, Robert D., and David A. Snow. 2000. "Framing Processes and Social Movements: An Overview and Assessment." *Annual Review of Sociology* 26: 611–39.

Berejikian, Jeffrey. 1992. "Revolutionary Collective Action and the Agent-Structure Problem." *American Political Science Review* 86, 3 (September): 647–57.

Buechler, Steven M. 1990. *Women's Movements in the United States.* New Brunswick, N.J.: Rutgers University Press.

———. 1993. "Beyond Resource Mobilization? Emerging Trends in Social Movement Theory." *Sociological Quarterly* 34, 2: 217–35.

Burgat, François, and William Dowell. 1993. *The Islamic Movement in North Africa.* Austin: Center for Middle Eastern Studies, University of Texas.

Clark, Janine Astrid. 1995. "Democratization and Social Islam: A Case Study of Islamic Clinics in Cairo." Pp. 167–84 in *Political Liberalization and Democratization in the Arab World: Theoretical Perspectives,* ed. Rex Brynen, Bahgat Korany, and Paul Noble. Boulder: Lynne Rienner.

———. 2003. *Faith, Networks, and Charity: Islamic Social Welfare Activism and the Middle Class in Egypt, Yemen, and Jordan.* Bloomington: Indiana University Press.

Dekmejian, R. Hrair. 1995. *Islam in Revolution: Fundamentalism in the Arab World.* 2d ed. Syracuse, N.Y.: Syracuse University Press.

Denoeux, Guilain. 1993. *Urban Unrest in the Middle East: A Comparative Study of Informal Networks in Egypt, Iran, and Lebanon.* Albany: SUNY Press.

Eickelman, Dale F., and James Piscatori. 1996. *Muslim Politics.* Princeton, N.J.: Princeton University Press.

Esposito, John L. 1992. *The Islamic Threat: Myth or Reality?* New York: Oxford University Press.

———. 1998. *Islam and Politics.* 4th ed. Syracuse, N.Y.: Syracuse University Press.

Esposito, John L., and John O. Voll. 1996. *Islam and Democracy.* New York: Oxford University Press.

Fahmy, Ninette S. 1998. "The Performance of the Muslim Brotherhood in the Egyptian Syndicates: An Alternative Formula for Reform?" *Middle East Journal* 52, 4 (Autumn): 551–62.

Faksh, Mahmud A. 1997. *The Future of Islam in the Middle East.* Westport, Conn.: Praeger.

Foran, John, ed. 1994. *A Century of Revolution: Social Movements in Iran.* Minneapolis: University of Minnesota Press.

Gamson, William A. 1975. *The Strategy of Social Protest.* Homewood, Ill.: Dorsey.

Gamson, William A., and David S. Meyer. 1996. "Framing Political Opportunity." Pp. 275–90 in *Comparative Perspectives on Social Movements: Political Opportunities, Mobilizing Structures, and Cultural Framings,* ed. Doug McAdam, John D. McCarthy, and Mayer N. Zald. Cambridge: Cambridge University Press.

Gerlach, Luther P., and Virginia H. Hine. 1970. *People, Power, Change: Movements of Social Transformation.* Indianapolis: Bobbs-Merrill.

Goodwin, Jeff, James M. Jasper, and Francesca Polleta, eds. 2001. *Passionate Politics: Emotions and Social Movements.* Chicago: University of Chicago Press.

Haddad, Yvonne Y. 1992. "Islamists and the 'Problem of Israel': The 1967 Awakening." *Middle East Journal* 46, 2 (Spring): 266–85.

Hafez, Mohammed M. 2003. *Why Muslims Rebel: Repression and Resistance in the Islamic World.* Boulder: Lynne Rienner.

Hoffman, Valerie J. 1995. "Muslim Fundamentalists: Psychosocial Profiles." Pp. 199–230 in *Fundamentalisms Comprehended*, ed. Martin E. Marty and R. Scott Appleby. Chicago: University of Chicago Press.

Hroub, Khaled. 2000. *Hamas: Political Thought and Practice.* Jerusalem: Institute for Palestine Studies.

Huntington, Samuel P. 1968. *Political Order in Changing Societies.* New Haven, Conn.: Yale University Press.

———. 1996. *The Clash of Civilizations and the Remaking of World Order.* New York: Simon and Schuster.

Ibrahim, Saad Eddin. 1980. "Anatomy of Egypt's Militant Islamic Groups: Methodological Notes and Preliminary Findings." *International Journal of Middle East Studies* 12, 4 (December): 423–53.

———. 1996. "The Changing Face of Egypt's Islamic Activism." In *Egypt, Islam, and Democracy*, S. E. Ibrahim. Cairo: American University in Cairo Press.

Ingalsbee, Timothy. 1996. "Earth First! Activism: Ecological Postmodern Praxis in Radical Environmentalist Identities." *Sociological Perspectives* 39, 2: 263–76.

Ismail, Salwa. 2000. "The Popular Movement Dimensions of Contemporary Militant Islamism: Socio-Spatial Determinants in the Cairo Urban Setting." *Comparative Studies in History and Society* 42, 2 (April): 363–93.

———. 2001. "The Paradox of Islamist Politics." *Middle East Report* 221 (Winter): 34–39.

Jenkins, J. Craig. 1983. "Resource Mobilization Theory and the Study of Social Movements." *Annual Review of Sociology* 9: 527–53.

Jenkins, J. Craig, and Charles Perrow. 1977. "Insurgency of the Powerless: Farm Worker Movements (1946–1972)." *American Sociological Review* 42 (April): 249–68.

Johnston, Hank, and Bert Klandermans, eds. 1995. *Social Movements and Culture.* Minneapolis: University of Minnesota Press.

Kalyvas, Stathis N. 1999. "Wanton and Senseless? The Logic of Massacres in Algeria." *Rationality and Society* 11, 3: 243–85.

Keddie, Nikki R. 1994. "The Revolt of Islam, 1700 to 1993: Comparative Considerations and Relations to Imperialism." *Comparative Studies in Society and History* 36, 3 (July): 463–87.

Kepel, Gilles. 1994. *The Revenge of God: The Resurgence of Islam, Christianity, and Judaism in the Modern World.* University Park: Pennsylvania State University Press.

Kitschelt, Herbert P. 1986. "Political Opportunity Structures and Political Protest: Anti-Nuclear Movements in Four Democracies." *British Journal of Political Science* 16: 57–85.

Kornhauser, William. 1959. *The Politics of Mass Society.* Glencoe, Ill.: Free Press.

Kurzman, Charles. 1994. "A Dynamic View of Resources: Evidence from the Iranian Revolution." *Research in Social Movements, Conflict, and Change* 17: 53–84.

———. 1996. "Structural Opportunity and Perceived Opportunity in Social-Movement Theory: The Iranian Revolution in 1979." *American Sociological Review* 61 (February): 153–70.

Langhor, Vicky. 2001. "Of Islamists and Ballot Boxes: Rethinking the Relationship between Islamisms and Electoral Politics." *International Journal of Middle East Studies* 33, 4 (November): 591–610.

Laraña, Enrique, Hank Johnston, and Joseph R. Gusfield, eds. 1994. *New Social Movements: From Ideology to Identity.* Philadelphia: Temple University Press.

Lawrence, Bruce. 1989. *Defenders of God: The Fundamentalist Revolt against the Modern Age.* Columbia: University of South Carolina.

Loveman, Mara. 1998. "High-Risk Collective Action: Defending Human Rights in Chile, Uruguay, and Argentina." *American Journal of Sociology* 104, 2 (September): 477–525.

Lust-Okar, Ellen M. 2001. "The Decline of Jordanian Political Parties: Myth or Reality?" *International Journal of Middle East Studies* 33, 4 (November): 545–69.

Marty, Martin, and R. Scott Appleby, eds. 1995. *Fundamentalisms Comprehended.* Chicago: University of Chicago Press.

McAdam, Doug. 1982. *Political Process and the Development of Black Insurgency, 1930–1970.* Chicago: University of Chicago Press.

———. 1986. "Recruitment to High-Risk Activism: The Case of Freedom Summer." *American Journal of Sociology* 92: 64–90.

McAdam, Doug, John D. McCarthy, and Mayer N. Zald, eds. 1996. *Comparative Perspectives on Social Movements: Political Opportunities, Mobilizing Structures, and Cultural Framings.* Cambridge: Cambridge University Press.

McAdam, Doug, Sidney Tarrow, and Charles Tilly. 2001. *Dynamics of Contention.* Cambridge: Cambridge University Press.

McCarthy, John D., and Mayer N. Zald. 1987a. "Resource Mobilization and Social Movements: A Partial Theory." In *Social Movements in an Organizational Society*, ed. Mayer N. Zald and John D. McCarthy. New Brunswick, N.J.: Transaction Books.

———. 1987b. "The Trend of Social Movements in America: Professionalization and Resource Mobilization." In *Social Movements in an Organizational Society*, ed. Mayer N. Zald and John D. McCarthy. New Brunswick, N.J.: Transaction Books.

Melucci, Alberto. 1996. *Challenging Codes: Collective Action in the Information Age.* Cambridge: Cambridge University Press.

Mishal, Shaul, and Avraham Sela. 2000. *The Palestinian Hamas: Vision, Violence, and Coexistence.* New York: Columbia University Press.

Monroe, Kristen Renwick. 2001. "Paradigm Shift: From Rational Choice to Perspective." *International Political Science Review* 22, 2 (April): 151–72.

Morris, Aldon D. 1984. *The Origins of the Civil Rights Movement: Black Communities Organizing for Change.* New York: Free Press.

Morris, Aldon D., and Carol McClurg Mueller, eds. 1992. *Frontiers in Social Movement Theory.* New Haven, Conn.: Yale University Press.

Mufti, Malik. 1999. "Elite Bargains and the Onset of Political Liberalization in Jordan." *Comparative Political Studies* 32, 1 (February): 100–29.

Munson, Henry, Jr. 1986. "The Social Base of Islamic Militancy in Morocco." *Middle East Journal* 40, 2 (Spring): 267–84.

Munson, Ziad. 2001. "Islamic Mobilization: Social Movement Theory and the Egyptian Muslim Brotherhood." *Sociological Quarterly* 42, 4 (Fall): 487–510.

Noakes, John A. 2000. "Official Frames in Social Movement Theory: The FBI, HUAC, and the Communist Threat in Hollywood." *Sociological Quarterly* 41, 4 (Fall): 657–80.

Oberschall, Anthony. 1973. *Social Conflict and Social Movements.* Englewood Cliffs, N.J.: Prentice-Hall.

Olson, Mancur. 1965. *The Logic of Collective Action.* Cambridge, Mass.: Harvard University Press.

Opp, Karl-Dieter, and Christiane Gern. 1993. "Dissident Groups, Personal Networks, and Spontaneous Cooperation: The East German Revolution of 1989." *American Sociological Review* 58: 659–80.

Parsa, Misagh. 1989. *Social Origins of the Iranian Revolution.* New Brunswick, N.J.: Rutgers University Press.

Pfaff, Steven. 1996. "Collective Identity and Informal Groups in Revolutionary Mobilization: East Germany in 1989." *Social Forces* 75, 1 (September): 91–118.

Piven, Frances Fox, and Richard A. Cloward. 1979. *Poor People's Movements: Why They Succeed, How They Fail.* New York: Vintage Books.

Robinson, Glenn. 1997. "Can Islamists Be Democrats? The Case of Jordan." *Middle East Journal* 51, 3 (Summer): 373–88.

Schatz, Edward. 2002. "Framing Islam: The Role of Anti-Americanism in Central Asia." Paper presented at the annual meeting of the American Political Science Association, Boston, August.

Schneider, Cathy Lisa. 1995. *Shantytown Protest in Pinochet's Chile.* Philadelphia: Temple University Press.

Schneirov, Matthew, and Jonathan David Geczik. 1996. "Alternative Health's Submerged Networks and the Transformation of Identity." *Sociological Quarterly* 37, 4: 627–44.

Scott, James. 1990. *Domination and the Arts of Resistance: Hidden Transcripts.* New Haven, Conn.: Yale University Press.

Shadid, Anthony. 2001. *Legacy of the Prophet: Despots, Democrats, and the New Politics of Islam.* Boulder: Westview.

Singerman, Diane. *Avenues of Participation: Family, Politics, and Networks in Urban Quarters of Cairo.* Princeton, N.J.: Princeton University Press.

Sivan, Emmanuel, and Menachem Friedman, eds. 1990. *Religious Radicalism and Politics in the Middle East.* Albany: SUNY Press.

Smelser, Neil J. 1962. *Theory of Collective Behavior.* New York: Free Press.

Snow, David A., and Robert D. Benford. 1988. "Ideology, Frame Resonance, and Participant Mobilization." Pp. 197–218 in *From Structure to Action: Comparing Movement Participation across Cultures, International Social Movement Research,* vol. 1, ed. Bert Klandermans, Hanspeter Kriesi, and Sidney Tarrow. Greenwich, Conn.: JAI Press.

———. 1992. "Master Frames and Cycles of Protest." Pp. 456–72 in *Frontiers in Social Movement Theory*, ed. Aldon Morris and Carol McClurg Mueller. New Haven, Conn.: Yale University Press.

Snow, David A., and Susan Marshall. 1984. "Cultural Imperialism, Social Movements, and the Islamic Revival." Pp. 131–52 in *Research in Social Movements, Conflict, and Change*, vol. 7, ed. Louis Kriesberg. Greenwich, Conn.: JAI Press.

Snow, David A., E. Burke Rochford Jr., Steven K. Wordon, and Robert D. Benford. 1986. "Frame Alignment Processes, Micromobilization, and Movement Participation." *American Sociological Review* 51: 464–81.

Stoecker, Randy. 1995. "Community, Movement, Organization: The Problem of Identity Convergence in Collective Action." *Sociological Quarterly* 36, 1: 111–30.

Sullivan, Denis J. 1994. *Private Voluntary Organizations in Egypt: Islamic Development, Private Initiative, and State Control*. Gainesville: University of Florida Press.

Tarrow, Sidney. 1994. *Power in Movement: Social Movements, Collective Action, and Politics*. Cambridge: Cambridge University Press.

———. 1998. *Power in Movement: Social Movements and Contentious Politics*. 2d ed. Cambridge: Cambridge University Press.

Taylor, Verta, and Nancy E. Whittier. 1992. "Collective Identity in Social Movement Communities: Lesbian Feminist Mobilization." Pp. 104–29 in *Frontiers in Social Movement Theory*, ed. Aldon D. Morris and Carol McClurg Mueller. New Haven, Conn.: Yale University Press.

Tehami, Amine. 1998. "The Social Construction of Political Islam, in Najd (1739–86), Iran (1963–79), and Algeria (1954–95)." Paper presented at the annual meeting of the American Political Science Association, Boston, September 3–6.

Tessler, Mark, ed. 1999. *Area Studies and Social Science: Strategies for Understanding Middle East Politics*. Bloomington: Indiana University Press.

Tilly, Charles. 1978. *From Mobilization to Revolution*. Reading, Mass.: Addison-Wesley.

Traugott, Mark, ed. 1995. *Repertoires and Cycles of Collective Action*. Durham, N.C.: Duke University Press.

Turner, Ralph H., and Lewis Killian. 1957. *Collective Behavior*. Englewood Cliffs, N.J.: Prentice-Hall.

Vergès, Meriem. 1997. "Genesis of a Mobilization; The Young Activists of Algeria's Islamic Salvation Front." Pp. 292–305 in *Political Islam*, ed. Joel Beinin and Joe Stork. Berkeley: University of California Press.

Waltz, Susan. 1986. "Islamist Appeal in Tunisia." *Middle East Journal* 40, 4 (Autumn): 651–70.

Wickham, Carrie Rosefsky. 1997. "Islamic Mobilization and Political Change: The Islamist Trend in Egypt's Professional Associations." Pp. 120–35 in *Political Islam*, ed. Joel Beinin and Joe Stork. Berkeley: University of California Press.

———. 2002. *Mobilizing Islam: Religion, Activism, and Political Change in Egypt*. New York: Columbia University Press.

Wiktorowicz, Quintan. 2001. *The Management of Islamic Activism: Salafis, the Muslim Brotherhood, and State Power in Jordan*. Albany: SUNY Press.

Wiktorowicz, Quintan, and Suha Taji-Farouki. 2000. "Islamic Non-Governmental

Organizations and Muslim Politics: A Case from Jordan." *Third World Quarterly* 21, 4 (Summer): 685–99.

Williams, Rhys H. 1994. "Movement Dynamics and Social Change: Transforming Fundamentalist Ideology and Organizations." Pp. 785–833 in *Accounting for Fundamentalisms: The Dynamic Character of Movements,* ed. Martin E. Marty and R. Scott Appleby. Chicago: University of Chicago Press.

Williams, Rhys H., and Robert D. Benford. 2000. "Two Faces of Collective Action Frames: A Theoretical Consideration." *Current Perspectives in Social Theory* 20: 127–51.

Wolff, Kristin. 1998. "*New* New Orientalism: Political Islam and Social Movement Theory." Pp. 41–73 in *Islamic Fundamentalism: Myths and Realities,* ed. Ahmad S. Moussalli. Reading: Garnet.

Zhao, Dingxin. 1998. "Ecologies of Social Movements: Student Mobilization during the 1989 Pro-Democracy Movement in Beijing." *American Journal of Sociology* 103, 6 (May): 1493–1529.

Zuo, Jiping, and Robert D. Benford. 1995. "Mobilization Processes and the 1989 Chinese Democracy Movement." *Sociological Quarterly* 36, 1: 131–56.

PART I
VIOLENCE AND CONTENTION

One

From Marginalization to Massacres
A Political Process Explanation of GIA Violence in Algeria

Mohammed M. Hafez

In 1997, the Armed Islamic Group (Groupe Islamique Armé, GIA) perpetrated a wave of massacres against civilians in villages and hamlets south of Algiers. These massacres featured the most barbaric forms of brutality and execution, including throat slitting, decapitation, mutilation, rape, kidnapping, and the slaughter of children, women, and the elderly. The massacres, which claimed thousands of lives, continued well into the new millennium.[1]

The massacres in Algeria took place in a context of mass Islamist insurgency, which included attacks on security forces, government officials, journalists, intellectuals, foreigners, and public workers. What is mystifying about the massacres of 1997 is that they overwhelmingly targeted civilians in Islamist strongholds.[2] Why would Muslim rebels turn against the people who at one point supported them and provided aid and shelter? Indeed, massacres were concentrated in Algiers and towns to the southwest, including Medea, Blida, and Ain Defla, all of which constituted the geographic backbone of support for Islamism. Many of the victims backed the Islamic Salvation Front (Front Islamique du Salut, FIS) during the 1991 elections and subsequently gave help to the armed groups fighting the Algerian regime.

Anticivilian violence and massacres are not unique to the Islamist movement in Algeria. The recent history of Islamist violence in Afghanistan, Chechnya, Kashmir, Egypt, Indonesia, Israel, and southern Philippines serves as a reminder that anticivilian bloodshed is a recurrent phenomenon in the Muslim world. Nor are radical Islamists unique in engaging in mass butchery. The histories of ethnic nationalism, fascism, socialism, and non-Islamic fundamentalism are replete with examples of anticivilian carnage. One need only recall contemporary events in Bosnia, India, Rwanda, Sierra Leone, and Sri Lanka.

The pervasiveness of anticivilian violence during the course of mass insurgency raises important questions: How can we explain massacres of helpless civilians? Which variables help us make sense of the near genocidal violence against ordinary people? And what conditions seem to engender the indiscriminate killing of noncombatants?

This chapter presents a political process explanation of anticivilian violence and contends that massacres and other forms of anticivilian violence are part and parcel of a radicalization process. Perpetrators of mass violence are not simply driven by motivational imperatives, such as relative deprivation, ideological orientation, or rational calculation. They must undergo a progression of radicalization that is intimately connected to the broader political process of violent contention. Specifically, massacres are more likely to appear when three conditions related to repression converge: (1) state repression creates a political environment of bifurcation and brutality; (2) insurgents create exclusive organizations to shield themselves from repression; and (3) rebels promote antisystem frames to motivate violent collective action to overthrow agents of repression.

State repression, particularly indiscriminate repression against movement supporters, creates a generalized environment of brutality and injustice that gives insurgents a shared sense of victimization and legitimacy, which in turn can be used to justify unspeakable acts of terror. This repression also creates a need for exclusive mobilization structures to shield insurgents from external repression and discourage internal defections. These exclusive organizations tend to create "spirals of encapsulation" (Della Porta 1995a, 12) that gradually pull insurgents away from the broader society, isolating them in the underground where they lose touch with reality and increasingly begin to view the goals and strategies of their movement in emotive, rather than strategic, terms.

In addition, state repression often facilitates the diffusion of antisystem collective action frames within the insurgent movement. These frames— condensed symbols of meaning that fashion shared understandings of the insurgent's world to legitimate and motivate collective action (McAdam, McCarthy, and Zald 1996; Moss 1997)—portray the institutionalized political system as fundamentally corrupt, thereby denying the possibility of reform. Moreover, antisystem frames depict the struggle as a fight to the death between two irreconcilable forces, limiting the possibility of neutrality. According to such frames, opponents and those who directly and indirectly support them must be displaced.

The confluence of a repressive political environment, exclusive insurgent organizations, and antisystem collective action frames in Algeria occurred during the 1990s and best explains GIA violence against civilians. The de facto military coup that ended the Islamic movement's drive to parliament in 1992 and subsequent indiscriminate repression created a political context of "injustice" that intensified Islamists' sense of rage and righteousness. The realities of repression forced Islamists to abandon the inclusive organization of the FIS, and they instead chose to rely on hundreds of exclusive armed groups to protect themselves against informants and infiltration. These groups promoted antisystem frames to motivate "total war" against the ruling regime, frames that readily resonated within the movement given the brutal repression of Islamists. Once exclusive organizations and antisystem ideologies proliferated in the movement, the spiral of violence began to expand against civilians, many of whom were neutral observers in the conflict. Eventually, the killing reached its apex in the form of massacres after five years of radicalization.

In addition to answering an important empirical inquiry, this chapter, similar to Robinson's contribution to this volume (chapter 4), aims to contribute theoretically to the emerging synthesis in social movement research by charting how the interplay of political environments, mobilization structures, and collective action frames shapes the development and behavioral repertoires of social movements (McAdam, McCarthy, and Zald 1996; McAdam, Tarrow, and Tilly 1997; Tarrow 1998; Hafez 2003). The explanation presented here is not unique to Islamist movements, nor is it limited to the case of Algeria. The dynamic of radicalization and its concomitant categories of indiscriminate repression, exclusive organizations, and antisystem frames can be leveraged to study ethnonationalist, leftist, and other fundamentalist violence.

Theorizing Anticivilian Violence: A Political Process Framework

The political process approach to mass insurgency developed largely in response to socioeconomic and psychosocial theories of social movements that mechanistically link grievances generated by economic deprivation or alienation to collective action (e.g., Gurr 1970). It contends that movement behavior is shaped by the broader political context (or political opportunity structure), which can facilitate or hinder collective action. The availability of allies, the absence of effective repression, and the emergence of elite schisms create opportunities for collective action, while the opposite conditions tend to discourage mobilization (Jenkins and Perrow 1977; McAdam 1982; Tarrow 1994). From this perspective, an analysis of insurgency and mass violence must investigate the political environment in which violence develops.

The political process approach further maintains that collective action, including mass violence, involves organizational structuring and normative framing to facilitate the mobilization of resources and motivate individuals to sacrifice their time, money, energy, and lives. In other words, organizational dynamics and cognitive processes mediate between the political environment and collective action (McAdam 1988; Voss 1996; McAdam, Tarrow, and Tilly

1997). A movement's inability to effectively allocate movement resources due to inappropriate organizational structures will result in missed opportunities. Similarly, an inability on the part of movement organizers to articulate grievances in a manner that resonates with potential supporters will result in failed collective action, even if grievances and opportunities abound. How movements structure and restructure their organizations to respond to the opportunities and constraints in their political environment and the ways in which they frame grievances are important processes that impact movement behavior and success. The following explains how political contexts characterized by severe repression encourage exclusive mobilization structures and antisystem collective action frames, and how the convergence of three variables—repression, exclusive organizations, and antisystem frames—influences the trajectory of mass violence.

Linking Environments, Organizations, and Frames

A movement in a repressive environment encounters several constraints that it must overcome to effect change. First, there is the problem of government infiltrators, informers, and *agents provocateurs*, who threaten to undermine the plans of movement groups and destroy the movement from within. To overcome this problem, movement organizers must find ways to recruit only trustworthy activists. Second, there is the threat that a decisive blow from the security forces could decimate a movement. Movements under a repressive environment accumulate material and organizational resources slowly and must be careful not to lose them to state repression. To overcome this problem, movement organizations must find ways to absorb the inevitable blows of state repression without suffering disintegration (O'Neill 1990). Finally, clandestine activities under repressive systems demand a high degree of group solidarity and cohesion; disunity and discord could bring about the loss of lives and destroy the movement. The need to maintain secrecy when conducting movement activities increases the dependency of individual activists on one another. If one activist decides to defect, the whole organization is vulnerable to the defector's subsequent actions. As Crenshaw (1992, 32) explains, "The pressures toward cohesion and uniformity that exist in all primary groups are likely to be intensified under the circumstances of underground life." To overcome this constraint, movement organizations must find ways to forge group cohesion and reduce the possibility of defections.

The tasks necessary to overcome constraints generated by a repressive environment strongly encourage movements to develop *exclusive organizations*. In their seminal article on movement organizations, Zald and Ash (1987, 125–26) define an exclusive organization as one that establishes strict criteria for membership. Only those who share a set of beliefs and meet a demanding standard of conduct are accepted as members.[3] An exclusive organization usually "requires the recruit to subject himself to organization discipline and orders, and [draws] from those having the heaviest initial commitments." It not only "requires that a greater amount of energy and time be spent in movement affairs, but it more extensively permeates all sections of the member's life, including activities with non-members." Such organizations also "attempt to reduce the claims of competing roles and status positions on those they wish to encompass within their boundaries" (Della Porta 1995b, 107). In contrast, an inclusive organization is one with relatively unrestricted criteria for membership. It usually "requires minimum levels of initial commitment —a pledge of general support without specific duties, a short indoctrination period, or none at all." An inclusive organization "typically requires little activity from its members—they can belong to other organizations and groups unselfconsciously, and their behavior is not as permeated by organization goals, policies, and tactics" (Zald and Ash 1987, 125–26).

Frequently, exclusive organizations only include like-minded individuals and regulate the behavior of activists by limiting external ties and demanding adherence to a strict mode of conduct, all of which aids in the development of committed activists and group cohesion. By limiting the interaction field of activists, often through acts of "bridge burning" (Gerlach and Hine 1970), the group succeeds in neutralizing countervailing influences that could entice activists to defect. Wasmund (1986, 214), drawing on the example of West German terrorism, argues that in clandestine groups the militants' "total dependence on the group, its pressure of adjustment, as well as the internal assignment of roles and division of labor lead to the loss of their own needs, interests and desires, and finally of their own identity." In these circumstances, each activist begins to identify his needs and interests with those of the group. This pattern has been observed in Italian left-wing movements (Moss 1997) and the Shining Path in Peru (McClintock 1998). In both cases, frequent regulation of behavior created what Della Porta (1995a, 12) terms "spirals of encapsulation" whereby activist links to the external world are all but completely cut off as intragroup ties mature. Defection from the group, therefore, comes at a double cost: lost friendships and a loss of the identity forged through extensive indoctrination and interaction within the group (Crenshaw 1981, 1992; Laqueur 1987; Post 1987).

In addition to encouraging exclusive organizations, repressive political environments facilitate the diffusion of antisystem collective action frames in the movement. Antisystem frames portray the institutional political system and the state elite as fundamentally corrupt and deny "legitimacy to the routinized functioning of the political process" (Diani 1996, 1057). Moreover, antisystem frames depict social ills and individual grievances as manifestations of deeply rooted problems in the system, rather than as products of misguided policies or ineffective leadership. The solution is to displace the incumbent regime and begin anew. Unlike revitalization frames, which portray adversaries as competitors with whom one can negotiate in order to reconcile differences and reach an agreement that will lead to non–zero–sum outcomes, antisystem frames preclude reform and insist on the displacement of opponents to achieve movement goals.

Clandestine high-risk activities, especially violence, require a great deal of justification and motivation. As Apter (1997, 2) argues, "People do not commit political violence without discourse. They need to talk themselves into it." In chapter 9 of this volume, Wickham illustrates how Egyptian Islamists "facilitate a progression toward high–risk activism" by framing participation "as a moral 'obligation' that demands self-sacrifice and unflinching commitment to the cause of religious transformation." Antisystem frames accentuate the need for violence because the struggle is not against a few individuals or parties but against an entrenched social order that is incapable of reform. Wasmund's (1986, 215) analysis of the antisystem Red Army Faction in Germany is illuminating:

> In the process of defining symbolic figures of the political system as the personification of everything evil and bad, terrorists repress their guilt feelings and provide themselves with a "good conscience," justifying their deeds. The liquidation of the political enemy thus does not become a necessity but also a legitimate act.

A repressive system that does not allow for the possibility of reforms through institutional opposition can be more readily portrayed as a monolithic entity incapable of change.

Moreover, antisystem frames facilitate anti–institutional strategies by solidifying cohesion within movement organizations and groups. Antisystem frames, characterized by ideological intransigence, emphasize the purity of the movement's cause and imbue movement activists with a sense of historical righteousness. The fight is not against a particular individual or party; it is a fight for a new and better social order. Antisystem frames, therefore, lead to a moral demarcation between the insurgents' world and the system against which they are fighting. The former is the realm of the wretched who sacrifice and fight against an iniquitous order, while the latter is the realm of exploitation, corruption, and denial. This division is essential for the solidification of exclusive organizations because it makes defection to the other side more than just a strategic decision for survival; defection is "selling out" or reconciling oneself to an illegitimate order. As Jabri (1996, 7) explains in relation to international and civil conflicts:

> The discourse of inclusion and exclusion cannot allow uncertainty or doubt, so if such are expressed, they must be represented as irrational or even treacherous. Any representation which blurs the inclusion/exclusion boundary breaks down certainties constructed in the name of war and

forms a counterdiscourse which deconstructs and delegitimates war and thereby fragments myths of unity, duty, and conformity.

Repressive political environments that do not allow for the legitimate participation of opposing voices often reinforce the boundary of inclusion/exclusion by giving such discourses fertile soil.

Exclusive Organizations, Antisystem Frames, and Expansive Violence

Exclusive organizations often lose touch with political reality. This is, in part, because alternative sources of information are less available and there is an absence of effective debate within the organization. But it is also because there are few countervailing influences, thereby denying the organization evaluative mechanisms by which to assess its performance and goals.[4] To put it differently, since spirals of encapsulation replace external affiliations with in-group associations, the "entrapped" activists increasingly cease to give outsiders, who might have a more objective viewpoint concerning the movement's activities, any say over their behavior. Instead, activists rely solely on their "comrades" or "brothers" for evaluation. At the same time, an exclusive group often "cannot afford an honest, self-critical appraisal of its theoretical premises and positions; questioning its theoretical assumptions would endanger the group's *raison d'être* and could activate a destabilizing effect on the group consciousness" (Wasmund 1986, 220). Under such circumstances, objective assessments of the political environment necessary for strategic calculations disappear; groups become increasingly driven by emotive and abstract appeals to justice and retribution (Crenshaw 1992, 1995; Apter 1997; Wieviorka 1997; Post 1998).

Exclusive organizations with antisystem frames do not readily accept the idea of "neutrality," thus leading to a broad categorization of legitimate targets. Anyone perceived as either supporting an "unjust" social order or opposing the legitimacy of total war is part of the problem and hence fair game. History is replete with examples of guerrilla movements and militant groups initiating greater violence against noncombatants than against government soldiers and officials. Wickham-Crowley (1991, 74, 79–80) points out that the Vietnamese Viet Cong and the Venezuelan Armed Forces of National Liberation (FALN), among others, unleashed terror campaigns against ordinary civilians to impose territorial control and deter defections. In the case of Vietnam, approximately 80 percent of the Viet Cong's victims were nonofficial types of civilians. Crenshaw (1995, 477, 483–84) notes a similar pattern in the Algerian National Liberation Front (FLN), which carried out a violent campaign against rival groups and civilians who refused to abide by FLN edicts during its war of liberation against France. Expansive violence, however, is best exemplified in Peru's Shining Path movement: only 17 percent of its victims over the course of 12 years were security forces. Instead, most of its victims were ordinary civilians, including preachers, nuns, foreign development workers, journalists, human rights activists, teachers, students, and, above all, peasants (McClintock 1998, 67–68).

What is interesting about all these examples is that in each instance the movement was an antisystem movement that sought to oust foreign forces and/or overthrow incumbent regimes. None adopted reconciliatory or revitalization frames, but instead portrayed insurgency as an uncompromising struggle for social and political transformation. Recruits had to be effectively indoctrinated and scrutinized to be included within clandestine movement organizations. Finally, each group justified the expansion of violence by claiming that it was necessary for the good of the nation, society, or the struggle.

The case of Algeria offers empirical support for the propositions offered above and calls our attention to the importance of political environment, mobilization structures, and ideological frames for understanding anticivilian violence. As explained below, in the early 1990s the Islamist movement in Algeria was well on its way toward building an inclusive movement organization behind the FIS. However, the shift toward a repressive political environment forced the movement to increasingly rely upon exclusive organizations that could shield it from repression. The radicals, which hitherto were politically marginal, became a predominant force because their antisystem ideology resonated with an increasingly repressed movement. The combination of repression, exclusive organizations, and antisystem frames resulted in expansive violence, which culminated in civilian massacres.

From the Margins to the Massacres:
The Rise of the GIA in Algeria

The contemporary Islamist movement in Algeria was forged during the late 1970s and early 1980s. From 1979 to 1988 Islamists engaged in very little overt political opposition or extra-institutional protest. Instead, Islamic activism in this period was fragmented and largely limited to preaching and proselytizing on university campuses and in mosques. A radical trend did emerge in the Mouvement Algérien Islamique Armée, better known as the Bouyali group (named after its founder and leader, Mustapha Bouyali), but it received little support and was largely shunned by the broader movement (Roudjia 1993; Burgat and Dowell 1997).

It was not until the state announced a shift to a more pluralistic political system in 1989 that the Islamist movement began to exert itself politically. A series of constitutional reforms guaranteed freedom of expression, association, and assembly; afforded the right to unionize and strike; and restricted the role of the military to the protection of stability and national sovereignty (Rashid 1997). Reforms were not limited to constitutional matters alone. Algerians witnessed palpable changes in their political life in the aftermath of the 1988 October riots that began the reform process. The press was given tremendous freedom to publish, and "During the spring of 1990, marches, demonstrations, and rallies became virtual daily occurrences" (Mortimer 1991, 583).

The Islamists took advantage of almost every aspect of reform. Numerous religious parties emerged, including the FIS, Harakat al-Mujtama al-Islami (HAMAS), and Mouvement de la Nahda Islamique (MNI). Along with these registered Islamist organizations and parties, a number of small groups with a radical Islamist orientation emerged as well. These groups carried titles such as Amr bil Ma'rouf wal Nahi 'an al-Munkar, Takfir wal-Hijra, Jama'at al-Sunna wa al-Shari'a, and Ansar al-Tawhid (Ayyashi 1993; al-Tawil 1998; Martinez 2000).

The permissive political context after 1989 led the Islamist movement to move in the direction of inclusive organizations. From 1989 to 1991, Islamist mobilization was more or less organized behind the FIS. Although there were 14 other Islamist parties, the FIS was by far the most dominant.[5] It participated in local elections in June 1990 and was able to control many of the communes and departments of Algeria (Mus'ad 1995, 235). More significantly, the FIS expressed serious ambitions to participate in the national elections of 1991 and mobilized myriad social forces for support (Willis 1996).

The FIS succeeded in leading the Islamist movement for two reasons. First, it took the lead in organizing an Islamic political party in 1989 and thus positioned itself as the movement vanguard. Once the FIS was able to draw thousands of supporters through rallies, demonstrations, and local government elections in 1990, it proved it was the most effective mechanism for mobilization and consequently attracted more activists (al-Tawil 1998, 23–24). In contrast, other new Islamist parties garnered little support, mostly because they appeared reactive and divisive. They were seen as splitting the voters by competing with the well-established FIS.

Second, the inclusive nature of the FIS facilitated its rapid expansion in the movement because the membership criteria made room for less committed activists. It divided its members into sympathizers, supporters, and activists. Only the active members had to abandon any association with other religious or political groups. Furthermore, only activists had to devote their time and energy to the activities of the organization and contribute 5 percent of their monthly income to the organization. Finally, only activists had to obey the commands of the leadership (Labat 1995, 187).

In addition, the FIS did not impose obstacles to the inclusion of other tendencies and leaderships in the Islamist movement. Its only rule for alliances was that whoever joined the FIS had to do so as an individual promoting the broad aims of the organization, not as a representative of other groups. The FIS did reject a broader Islamic alliance with HAMAS and MNI, which were viewed as competitors. But despite this rejection, the FIS remained an inclusive organization as evinced by the composition of its consultative council, which incorporated various tendencies—*Salafiyya*,[6] Jazaira,[7] "Afghans,"[8] Takfir wal-Hijra,[9] and former Bouyali activists[10] (Labat 1995; al-Tawil 1998). As Roudjia (1995, 74–75) notes, "The FIS must be considered, in light of experience, as a melting-pot for very diverse factions which have little more in common than Islam and the desire to put an end to a political situation in Algeria."

State Repression

The rising power of the FIS and its imminent victory in the national elections of 1991 led the military to carry out a bloodless coup, nullify the electoral process, and initiate anti-FIS measures that included its ban in March 1992. In February of that year, the authorities opened five detention centers in the Sahara desert to hold thousands—estimates range from 6,000 to 30,000[11]—of FIS activists, including 500 mayors and councilors. Special courts, which had been banned under the 1989 constitution, were reestablished to prosecute "terrorists," and in July one of these courts sentenced Abassi Madani and Ali Belhaj (the top FIS leaders) to twelve years in prison. As time went on, the state closed down all the cultural and charitable organizations of the FIS and ordered the destruction of all unofficial mosques, which were popular with Islamists. In 1992 and 1993, a total of 166 Islamists were sentenced to death, mostly in absentia.[12] By 1996, according to an Algerian human rights organization, there were 116 prisons with 43,737 prisoners, half of whom were accused of terrorism.[13] The gravest development since 1993, however, was the almost daily killing of Islamists, either through manhunts or clashes during searches. Many human rights organizations condemned the military regime's use of torture, "disappearances," and the extrajudicial killing of suspected Islamists.[14]

The political exclusion and indiscriminate repression of the FIS resulted in the migration of many FIS activists toward radical organizations that rejected democracy, the electoral process, and the Algerian ruling regime altogether (al-Tawil 1998; Martinez 2000). Hitherto small and marginal groups began to win over hundreds of FIS supporters in the months following the military coup.[15] By the end of 1992, many of the FIS's activists united around one of three militant organizations: the Islamic State Movement (le Mouvement pour l'Etat Islamique, MEI), Mouvement Algérien Islamique Armée, and a conglomeration of armed groups in Takfir wal-Hijra and Amr bil-Maᶜrouf and from the informal network of Algerian "Afghans."

In September 1992, a meeting took place in Tamesguida to unite the ranks of some of the armed groups, and it appeared the movement was about to unite behind the leadership of "The General," Abdelkader Chebouti, a former Bouyali activist who received a death sentence in 1987 (amnestied in 1990). However, security forces launched a surprise attack on the leaders of the armed groups during the conference, killing several people, including the leader of one of the armed groups. The attack led to suspicions that state agents had infiltrated the armed groups, putting an end to unity talks. Instead, some of the disparate radical groups decided to form a new organization —the Jama'a al-Islamiyya al-Musalaha or GIA (Willis 1996; al-Tawil 1998), which became the most prominent armed group in 1993 because of its daring attacks against security forces. The GIA attracted a number of former FIS activists and leaders (Labat 1995, 308–309), including Muhammad Said, Abderrazak Rejjam, Yousuf Boubras, and Said Mekhloufi (head of MEI), who all joined in May 1994.

Exclusive Organization

Despite the rapid growth of the GIA, it became an exclusive organization bent on a total war against the ruling regime. Initially, the GIA operated as a conglomeration of armed militias dispersed over at least nine zones, each of which was under an appointed *amir* (or commander). The size of each of these groups ranged from 20 to 300 militants.[16] Some initially organized into small cells in urban areas, but subsequently took refuge in the mountains where they set up camps in caves and constructed underground tunnels for shelter, safe havens, and supply caches.

All groups and individuals who wanted to join the GIA had to declare their allegiance to the *Salafiyya* tradition and abandon any previously held "innovations." In contrast to the FIS, which accommodated various tendencies including Jazairas, Salafis, and "Afghans," the GIA forced Jazairas and Takfir groups to renounce their views in order to be part of the group. The GIA refused any unity with the FIS and made it clear that it was not its armed wing. Despite symbolically appointing Abassi Madani and Ali Belhaj to its consultative council, the GIA unequivocally opposed the electoral strategy of the FIS and insisted that any unity with the latter had to be based on a renunciation of elections, parliaments, and democracy.[17]

In May 1994, after several senior FIS leaders joined the GIA, the latter issued a communiqué declaring that the GIA was the only legitimate organizational framework for conducting jihad in Algeria (al-Tawil 1998, 152–54). In 1995, Jamal Zitouni, the leader of the GIA at that time, issued *Hidayat Rab al-ʿAlamin fi Tabyeen Usul al-Salafiyeen wama Yajib min al-ʿAhd ʿala al-Mujahedeen* (The Guidance of the Lord of the Universe in Clarifying the Traditions of the Salafis and the Requirements of Allegiance among the Holy Fighters). In this pamphlet he rejected any alliance with groups such as Hizb al-Tahrir (Islamic Liberation Party) and Takfir wal-Hijra, both considered radical groups by many standards. Zitouni went on to specify GIA membership rules: (1) A member had to adopt the *Salafiyya* tradition; (2) obey the *amir* (commander) on order; and (3) repent if he at one point or another belonged to the FIS, Islamic Salvation Army (AIS, which developed as the armed wing of the FIS in 1994), HAMAS, MNI, Takfir wal-Hijra, Muslim Brotherhood, Jazaira, or secular parties. Former FIS members who wanted to join the GIA had to "proclaim the banner of the [FIS] a polytheist, democratic banner; repent from political, electoral, and democratic activities; and declare their innocence from all calls for dialogue with the apostate tyrants [i.e., the regime]." Individuals who at one point belonged to Takfir or non-Islamist groups had to sever all ties with non–GIA groups and their members and provide information on their activities. Any *imam* (prayer leader or cleric) who sought entry into the GIA had to "issue a *fatwa* [Islamic legal ruling] to motivate jihad." Finally, those who wanted to leave the GIA were considered apostates, defectors, opportunists, or potential informers and corrupters. Whatever the case, their punishment was death.

The exclusive orientation of the GIA manifested itself in behavior toward other groups in the Islamist movement. When it became clear that the FIS was not going to abandon its demand for a return to the electoral process, the GIA completely broke relations with it. On May 4, 1995, the GIA issued communiqué #30, declaring that FIS/AIS leaders had a month to get in touch with the GIA, to repent, and to join the ranks of the GIA. On June 13, 1995, the GIA issued communiqué #36 ("An Open Letter to Abassi Madani and Ali Belhaj") in which it "proclaims its innocence from the FIS by announcing that the GIA is not the armed wing of the FIS." The GIA communiqué concluded by ousting Abbasi and Belhaj from its consultative council and encouraging "the shedding of the blood of those 'blood merchants' [FIS members] inside and outside (Algeria) unless they repent." This series of warnings and threats culminated with an explicit declaration of war against the AIS on January 4, 1996.[18]

Antisystem Frames

The GIA's exclusive orientation went hand-in-hand with its antisystem frames. Although the military coup of 1992 was the impetus for armed struggle, the leaders of the GIA portrayed jihad as a struggle against apostasy (*ridha*), infidelism (*kufr*), and tyrannical rule (*tughma al-hakima*). Moreover, the GIA did not make distinctions among non–GIA Algerians. Anyone who sustained the regime in one way or another (even through tacit approval) was considered an apostate (*murted*), infidel (*kafer*), or tyrant (*taghout*), and consequently deserved death.

In contrast to the FIS/AIS, the pronouncements of the GIA rarely made reference to the military coup of 1992. To the extent it did so, it was only to deny that its struggle was a response to the coup.[19] On the contrary, it viewed its "jihad" as a broader struggle to rid the Muslim world of un-Islamic rulers and establish the "rule of God." As Abdelhaq Layada, the first leader of the GIA, declared:

> The great tragedy the Muslim community is living in this era is the collapse of the Caliphate, because it is now living an abnormal and disharmonious life due to the separation between its high values, ideals and principles in which it believes and the pagan (*jahili*) reality imposed upon it. (Quoted in al-Tawil 1998, 79)

For the GIA, the struggle in Algeria was part and parcel of the larger struggle against apostasy and infidelism. The Algerian regime was seen as a willing partner in this scheme, and none of its polity members or constituency was considered innocent. In a fatwa issued on December 2, 1992, Layada declared:

> [Algerian] leaders in this age are, without exception, infidels. Their ministers, soldiers, and supporters and anyone who works under them and helps them and all who accept them or remain silent to their deeds are also infidels outside of the creed.[20]

In an ominous communiqué issued on September 13, 1994, the day after Abassi Madani was released from prison in preparation for negotiations with the regime, the GIA declared that they fought the state "on the basis of apostasy and nothing else."[21] Zitouni maintained in *Hidayat Rab al-ʿAlamin* (1995, 27) that "the [GIA] considers the institutions of the [Algerian] state, from its agencies and ministers, to its courts and legislative and parliamentary assemblies, to its army, gendarme and police, to be apostate institutions."

Describing the Algerian ruling regime as apostate and infidel is not merely charged hyperbole; these terms are condensed symbols rooted in Islamic traditions and full of implied meaning. They suggest mutual negation, irreconcilability, and total war. In Islam, infidelism—nonbelief in the creator—is one of the greatest sins one can commit, especially when ruling over Muslim societies. The Qurʾan implores Muslims to struggle against infidels and promises great suffering toward the unbelievers. Apostasy (turning away from Islam after upholding the creed) implies that reconciliation with the ruling regime is virtually impossible. In Islam, the punishment of an apostate is death; there can be no compromise with apostates unless they repent. Entire wars were fought against apostates after the death of the prophet Muhammad in what came to be known as *huroub al-ridha* or apostasy wars. One cannot reconcile with apostates and maintain the sanctity of Islam and the Muslim community. The GIA's oft repeated mantra of "no dialogue, no cease-fire, no reconciliation, and no security and guarantee with the apostate regime" was justified with reference to the Qurʾanic verse "So, fight them [the unbelievers] till all opposition ends, and obedience is wholly God's."[22]

To consolidate the antisystem framing of the conflict, the GIA insisted that "jihad is an Islamic obligation [*faridha*] until judgment day."[23] In contrast to the AIS, which portrayed jihad as a means (*wasila*) to an end, the GIA saw the war as a religious one imposed by God on Muslims. As the insurgency developed, the GIA portrayed its struggle as one against historic "enemies" of Islam—the West, Crusaders, and Jews. In a communiqué issued in August 1993, the GIA declared: "Our struggle is with infidelism and its supporters beginning with France and ending with the leader of international terrorism, 'The United States of Terrorism,' its ally Israel, and among them the apostate ruling regime in our land."[24] The problem, in other words, was framed as a systemic problem whereby Muslims were being governed by un-Islamic states and besieged by un-Islamic forces inside and outside of Algeria. The crisis was not the fault of a few putchists or even a ruling elite that monopolizes power, as the AIS portrayed the conflict, but a crisis rooted in the national and international system.

Exclusive Organizations, Antisystem Frames,
and Expansive Violence in Algeria

Political violence in Algeria initially took the form of clashes with security forces and assassinations of policemen and military personnel. In 1993, violence expanded to include government officials. Violence eventually expanded to include representatives of opposition groups, foreigners, journalists, intellectuals, and ordinary civilians killed randomly through bombings or deliberately through executions and massacres.

The antisystem framing of the struggle resulted in the GIA's refusal to distinguish between the Algerian state and those that work for it in one way or another. It did not differentiate between soldiers and tax collectors, nor did it distinguish between government officials and state gas workers. As Zitouni states in *Hidayat Rab al-ᶜAlamin* (1995, 27), "The [GIA] does not distinguish between those who fight us with arms or money or tongue." Few people were viewed as neutral in the conflict. As a result, the GIA politicized individuals and groups that were not political or interested in taking sides.

Antisystem frames were repeatedly utilized by the GIA in their communiqués to justify expansive violence against "enemies." In 1993, the GIA expanded its violence to include journalists and intellectuals. GIA communiqué #2 issued on January 12, 1993, justified this expansion of violence by reference to the "obfuscation and distortion" of the "mercenary press" that "maligns" the *mujahidin* and refuses to report the truth. Another communiqué in August 1993 simply declared, "He who fights us with the pen, we fight him with the sword" (quoted in al-Tawil 1998, 74–76).

In 1993, the GIA expanded its violence to foreigners. This was justified in the following terms:

The jihadist operations commenced with prior planning and scheming, targeting all the symbols of the infidel regime from the head of state through the military, and ending with the last hypocrite working for the regime. Into this equation enters *all who support the unjust, infidel system whether inside or outside [Algeria]*. . . . As we previously stated in our communiqués, the nationals of the resentful crusading countries are a target for the *mujahidin because they represent part of the wicked colonialist plan,* which is led by the leader of international terrorism [United States], succored by its crusading friend [France].[25]

In 1994 the GIA expanded its threats to state employees. It justified this expansion in a communiqué issued in July 1994, which declared: "The Armed Islamic Group issues its order to all customs and tax employees to leave their positions through which they support the tyrants [*tawaghit*]. . . . Whoever refuses to obey this order his judgment will be the judgment of the tyrants."[26] The GIA also made public schools a target of violence and justified the attacks in an August 1994 communiqué, which claimed that "continuing with schooling is aiding the tyrants to achieve stability. . . . It is known in [Islamic] law that it is not permissible to work in the institutions of apostate rulers."[27]

The logic of the GIA's antisystem discourse, which was solidified and sheltered from countervailing frames by an exclusive mobilization structure, led to barbaric violence and the massacres of entire towns and villages around Algiers. The shift from targeting select categories of civilians to the mass butchery of villages and hamlets was part and parcel of the gradual radicalization of the struggle. In a series of communiqués beginning in 1994, the GIA sought to impose its control by regulating the behavior of citizens in its strongholds and Algeria in general. In February, March, and April 1995, the GIA ordered the wives of men employed by the state to leave their husbands because it deemed the latter to be apostates.[28] In January 1996, it threatened to kill young men of draft age if they traveled outside their area of residence for an extended period (presumably to prevent them from being trained in government military camps).[29] In September 1996, it issued a communiqué forbidding contractual agreements with the state.[30] In October 1996, it threatened to kill those who do not pray and Muslims who fail to pay the *zakat* (Islamic alms) to the GIA. It threatened to kill women who left their homes without donning the *hijab* (head covering). It also forbade people from going to state courts, demanding that they instead turn to the GIA for arbitration.[31] Even government mosques were considered off limits, and those who prayed in them were labeled collaborators.[32] In its "liberated zones," the GIA demanded food, supplies, contributions, and shelter from local inhabitants (Martinez 2000). In *Hidayat Rab al-ʿAlamin,* Zitouni (1995, 9) demanded that Muslims direct financial resources to the *mujahidin* until the condition of sufficiency (*kifaya*) was achieved.

During this period, GIA leaders reinforced their exclusive hold on the group by executing many of their commanders for disagreeing with the increasingly radical orientation. In 1995 and 1996, some of the militias in the GIA began to break away from the group, claiming the GIA had "deviated from the correct path of jihad" and committed crimes against innocent people. Abderrazak Rejjam and Yousuf Boubras, two former FIS leaders who joined the GIA in 1994, withdrew their group, accusing the GIA of killing women.[33] Others defected after the GIA executed Muhammed Said (a former FIS leader and a member of the GIA's consultative council), Abderrazak Rejjam, Yousuf Boubras, Mahfouz Tajeen (the former leader of the GIA), and Abdelwahab Lamara (a leader within the GIA).[34]

Having come this far down the path of excommunication and anticivilian killings, one can readily see how the GIA could extend its violence to innocent people, even those who had at one time provided the movement with a helping hand. As the conflict persisted, people who were initially sympathetic to the GIA's cause could no longer endure the material costs of the insurgency. Many stopped giving support; others turned against the movement. As a resident of Bentalha (site of a gruesome massacre on September 22, 1997) recalls:

> We were forbidden to smoke a cigarette, read a newspaper, watch television, listen to radio, or have a satellite. . . . They tried to impose their viewpoint on the people, and the straw that broke the camel's back (for the militants) was the mass participation in the 1995 elections despite the many communiqués the GIA posted on the walls, in which it threatened to cut off the heads of those who vote.[35]

After a few years of sheltering the movement, either willingly or because of coercion, some residents in and around Islamist strongholds agreed to form government-sponsored militias. Many others accepted the AIS's 1997 cease-fire call. As Kalyvas (1999) shows, a number of massacres targeted individuals and families who participated in the government-sponsored militias, which were formed to protect secluded regions from radical Islamists.[36] Other massacres targeted the families of AIS and GIA militants who had abandoned the armed struggle in 1997.[37] In September 1997, the GIA issued a communiqué in its *al-Ansar* pamphlet (published in London), in which it declared: "The infidelism and apostasy of this hypocrite nation that turned away from backing and supporting the mujahidin will not bend our determination and will not hurt us at all, God willing. . . . All the killing and slaughter, the massacres, the displacement [of people], the burnings, and the kidnappings . . . are an offering to God."[38]

In February 2002, Algeria's security forces succeeded in killing Antar Zouabri, the sixth commander of the GIA and the purveyor of mass slaughter in Algeria. His death, however, did not bring about an end to violence. On the contrary, his successor, al-Rashid Abu Turab, issued a communiqué promising more "blood and blood, destruction and destruction."[39] To prove that the GIA would not succumb to repression, the new commander escalated the violence by carrying out a number of massacres and random bombings in public places, such as the one that took place on the fortieth anniversary of Algeria's independence, killing 38 civilians and injuring more than 80.[40]

Conclusion

This chapter set out to answer an important question: Why do insurgents in mass movements resort to anticivilian violence? To that effort, it presented a testable model of radicalization rooted in a synthetic approach to social movement theory. It charted the interplay of three dimensions of contentious politics—political environment, mobilization structures, and collective action frames—to explain how anticivilian violence is an outcome of an ill-fated convergence of three variables—indiscriminate repression, exclusive organizations, and antisystem ideologies.

GIA violence in Algeria illustrates this dynamic of radicalization. Before 1992, the permissive political context in Algeria encouraged the formation of inclusive Islamist movement organizations that marginalized radicals and accommodated the state regime through institutional participation. The closure of the political system in 1992, combined with indiscriminate state repression of Islamists, made possible the expansion of the radical wing. The radicals organized in exclusive movement organizations largely to shield themselves from counterinsurgency measures, solidify the cohesion of their members, and minimize defections. The nature of these organizations led to "spirals of encapsulation" whereby counterframes were marginalized and actively repressed. The antisystem frames promoted by these groups gained empirical credibility in the context of state repression and provided a rationale for the expansion of violence that included anyone supporting the regime and its legitimacy.

The convergence of state repression, exclusive organizations, and antisystem frames facilitated the expansion of violence to those who were either unable or unwilling to support the Islamist cause. This was especially the case with state employees and civilians caught up in Islamist strongholds. They did not wish to take sides in the conflict and simply wanted to carry on with their lives. However, such neutrality was viewed as treachery by the GIA, and it began punishing civilians with impunity. The expanding violence against civilians led to greater defections to the regime, principally in the form of anti-insurgent militias. This response further enraged GIA militants and led them to take revenge, even against those who at one point had offered moral, financial, and physical support. Hence, the massacres.

Anticivilian violence by Islamist insurgents will continue to warrant our attention. Protracted Islamist rebellions in Algeria, Chechnya, Indonesia, Kashmir, and the Philippines, to name a few, suggest that the potential for anticivilian carnage is ever present in the Muslim world. More recently, the wave of suicide bombings against civilian targets in Israel has brought to the forefront the bewildering question of what motivates ordinary people to volunteer their lives for the sake of killing men, women, and children? Yet, despite the descriptive attention this violence has received, the current research on Islamist movements lacks a sustained theoretical treatment of the phenomenon. The political process approach to Islamist violence begins to fill this theoretical gap and offers us replicable categories and a model with which to analyze and predict anticivilian violence in the future.

The dynamic of radicalization presented in this chapter also has implications for the broader study of contentious politics. The targeting of civilians is likely to persist as a "legitimate" repertoire in the eyes of many insurgents across the world. Thus far, socioeconomic, psychological, and rational actor approaches have dominated the theoretical field when it comes to explaining this violence. The preceding analysis, however, suggests that an alternative political process approach based on the synthesis of environment, mobilization structures, and ideological frames can offer a more robust and convincing explanation of anticivilian violence in social movement contention.

Notes

1. I define a massacre as the deliberate execution of 15 or more civilians in one episode of violence. At least 76 massacres took place between November 1996 and July 2001, but most of the massacres took place in 1997 (42 massacres). For the dates and places of the massacres, refer to the quarterly chronology sections of *Middle East Journal*. For a description of some of the massacres, see *Amnesty International* (MDE 28/23/97, November 1997).

2. This led some observers to accuse Algerian security forces of involvement in several massacres. See, for instance, the interview of former Algerian prime minister Abdelhamid al-Ibrahimi with *al-Wasat* (March 15, 1999), in which he claims that government-sponsored militias are behind the massacres. Yous (2000) implicates the authorities in the Bentalha massacre of September 22, 1997, and Souaïdia's (2001) book *The Dirty War* is often cited as evidence of state complicity in the massacres.

3. To overcome the fear of infiltration and the obstacles of a repressive environment, exclusive organizations typically begin by dipping into the pool of relatives, friends, and neighbors where trust is already established (Lofland 1966; Snow et al. 1980; Della Porta 1988, 1992).

4. When faced with countervailing ideologies that do manage to penetrate the movement, exclusive organizations are likely to up the ante to maintain internal cohesion and subvert attempts at reconciliation.

5. HAMAS and MNI, the two major competitors of the FIS, did not win any

seats in the first round of the 1991 national elections. Their combined total of votes was 518,790, compared with 3,260,359 votes for the FIS.

6. The *Salafiyya* tendency in contemporary Algeria shares a common belief that Muslims should be ruled by an Islamic state organized according to the precepts of the Qurᵓan, the Sunna (the traditions of the prophet Muhammad), and the righteous forefathers (*al-Salaf al-Salih*). The latter include the companions of the Prophet and the Rightly Guided *Caliphs*—Abu Bakr, Umar Ibn al-Khattab, Uthman Ibn Afan, and Ali Ibn Abi Talib—and numerous Islamic *ulama* (religious scholars), including Ibn Hanbal, Ibn Taymiyya, and Muhammad Ibn Abd al-Wahhab. Contemporary *salafiyya* thought tends to be literalist in its reading of the Islamic tradition and believes Islamic law is a set of religious, social, and economic rules that should be applied in every Muslim society; Islamic law is not subject to change from one place to another. The contemporary *Salafiyya* movement generally rejects democracy as an "innovation" (*bidᶜa*) and hence un-Islamic. For more on Salafis, see Wiktorowicz (2001a, 2001b).

7. The *Jazaira* (literally "Algerianist") is a derisive title given to a strand of Algerian Islamists in the early 1980s by the *Salafiyya*. The *Jazaira* rejects the rigidity of the contemporary *Salafiyya* movement, especially its belief that Islamic law could be applied in the same manner across the Muslim world—hence the title Algerianists. They are closer to the "modernists" who believe Islam must be reinterpreted in light of historical transformations and adapted to different times and places. Also, they tend to be more accommodating of democracy.

8. This title was given to Algerians who returned from Afghanistan after volunteering to fight the Soviets in the 1980s. For an excellent account of their history, see the series of seven articles by Muhammed Muqadem entitled "Rihlet al-Afghan al-Jazaireen: Min al-Jamaᶜa ila Tanzim al-Qaᵓida" (The Journey of the Algerian Afghans: From the [Armed Islamic] Group to the Qaeda Organization), *al-Hayat*, December 23–29, 2001.

9. Hachemi Sahnouni, a prominent member and fiery preacher within the FIS, was a former member of the Takfir wal-Hijra group.

10. Ali Belhaj, who was the second in command within the FIS, was a Bouyali activist in the 1980s.

11. President Boudiaf put the number at 6,000, but Abderrazak Rejjam of the FIS put the figure at 30,000 (see the *Middle East Journal* chronology sections for February 16 and 23, 1992).

12. *Middle East Journal* chronologies for 1992 and 1993.

13. *Al-Hayat*, July 6, 1999.

14. Amnesty International, "Algeria: 'Disappearances'—The Wall of Silence Begins to Crumble" (MDE 28/01/99, March 3, 1999); Amnesty International, "Algeria: Who Are the 'Disappeared'?—Case Studies" (MDE 28/02/99, March 3, 1999); Middle East Watch/Human Rights Watch, "Human Rights Abuses in Algeria: No One Is Spared" (1994); Human Rights Watch, "'Neither among the Living nor the Dead': State-Sponsored 'Disappearances' in Algeria" (February 1998); Human Rights Watch, "Algeria's Human Rights Crisis" (August 1998); *Independent*, October 30 and 31 and November 1, 1997; and *Observer*, May 25, 1997.

15. Ben Hajjar, the commander of the Rabita al-Islamiyya lil-Dawa wal Jihad (The Islamic League for Preaching and Holy Struggle, LIDD), which joined the

GIA in 1994, maintained that few opposed the electoral option before 1992. But when the FIS was "hit twice" (June 1991 and January 1992), these extremists were the only leaders left to guide the movement (interview in *al-Hayat*, February 5, 2000). Qameredin Kharban, a former FIS leader, maintained in a published interview that "the hesitation of the [FIS] in declaring jihad was a mistake that led to other grave mistakes, one of which is the [GIA]" (al-Tawil 1998, 103). Many FIS activists were angered at the hesitation of the leadership in the immediate aftermath of the coup. Some went so far as to argue that FIS leaders should be tried for their mistake. Although the GIA's leadership initially consisted of non-FIS activists, by 1994 it managed to win over many activists who were with the FIS.

16. The size of these GIA groups could be gathered from a series of communiqués issued in 1996 declaring GIA splits and from reports of groups laying down their arms in 1999 (*al-Hayat*, January 1, 1996; March 3 and 23, 1996; June 8, 1999; and September 9 and 14, 1999). In January 2000, 22 GIA militias composed of approximately 800 militants—an average of about 36 militants per militia—were granted complete amnesty after abiding by the AIS cease-fire call (*al-Hayat*, January 12, 2000).

17. Madani Merzaq, the national commander of the Armée Islamique du Salut (Islamic Salvation Army, AIS), which is the armed wing of the FIS since 1994, maintains that several attempts were made in 1992 and 1993 to bring the GIA and other groups together to form a unified armed movement under the leadership of the FIS. However, the GIA did not respond to these initiatives. Instead, "we began to hear claims that it is not appropriate to fight under the banner of parties, and the FIS should change its name because it contains opportunists" (see *al-Hayat*, July 26, 1996).

18. For communiqué #30, see *al-Ansar*, no. 96, May 12, 1995; for the open letter to Abbasi Madani and Ali Belhaj, see *al-Ansar*, no. 101, June 15, 1995; and for the declaration of war of the AIS, see *al-Hayat*, February 7, 1996.

19. For example, in a GIA communiqué issued in August 1993, the third *amir* of the group, Jafar al-Afghani, declared, "The Armed Islamic Group was not born today; it was in secret preparation for years, but its entry into open *jihadist* military operations was precisely a year and 10 months ago, that is since the Guemmar operation [less than two months prior to the coup]." This claim is repeated by Zitouni, the sixth *amir* of the GIA, in *Hidayat Rab al-ᶜAlamin* (1995, 14). By dating the start of the insurgency to the Guemmar attack in November 1991, the GIA implicitly, but consciously, rejected the argument that the military coup was the source of the violence.

20. *Al-Wasat*, September 19, 1994.

21. *Al-Hayat*, September 15, 1994. See similar statements by GIA leaders in *al-Ansar*, no. 16, October 16 and 28, 1993, and no. 111, August 24, 1995, and in *al-Hayat*, August 6, 1994, July 25, 1995, and November 23, 1996.

22. Sura VIII, al-Anfal, verse 39: "wa qatiluhum hata la takuna fitnatun wayakuna al-din kulluhu li-llah."

23. These claims were made in the unification communiqué of May 1994 (text in al-Tawil 1998, 152–54).

24. *Al-Hayat*, August 27, 1993. Also see GIA's communiqué in *al-Ansar*, no. 16, October 28, 1993.

25. *Al-Ansar*, no. 16, October 28, 1993 (emphasis added).

26. *Al-Hayat*, July 25, 1994.

27. *Al-Hayat*, August 6, 1994.

28. See communiqué #26 in *al-Ansar*, no. 87, March 9, 1995; communiqué #28 in *al-Ansar*, no. 95, May 4, 1995; and communiqué in *al-Hayat*, March 10, 1995.

29. Communiqué #41 in *al-Hayat*, February 14, 1996.

30. Communiqué #48 in *al-Hayat*, September 13, 1996.

31. Communiqué #49 in *al-Hayat*, November 3, 1996.

32. *Middle East Contemporary Survey* 20 (1996): 235.

33. See their communiqué in *al-Hayat*, July 5, 1995.

34. For other splits, see communiqués in *al-Hayat*, February 3, 1996; March 3 and 23, 1996; July 23, 1996; September 17, 1998; and December 28, 1999; and *al-Sharq al-Awsat*, November 24, 1996.

35. See interview in *al-Hayat*, May 31, 2002.

36. Kalyvas attributes the massacres to strictly the rational calculation on the part of GIA to prevent mass defections to the regime. This analysis, while not without merit, cannot account for the numerous other massacres that continue to take place to this day. Moreover, Kalyvas cannot explain why the AIS, which had as much interest in preventing defections from 1994 until 1997, did not engage in mass anticivilian violence.

37. Mustapha Karatali, the commander of al-Rahman militia, which split from the GIA in December 1995, accused the GIA of massacring relatives of the Larbaa militias who split from the GIA at fake checkpoints (see interview with *al-Hayat*, February 8, 2000).

38. The communiqué was published in *al-Ansar* on September 27, 1997. Also see *Agence France-Presse International*, September 26, 1997.

39. *Al-Hayat*, April 1, 2002.

40. On March 18, 2002, a powerful bomb was detonated in central Algiers. A month later, 13 people were killed near southern Algiers by GIA gunmen who entered a bus and started shooting passengers (see *al-Hayat*, March 22 and May 16, 2002). On May 30, 2002, 25 Bedouins, including 15 children, were slaughtered in the village of Sanjas in the Chelf province after the GIA promised violence on election day in a communiqué a few days earlier (*al-Hayat*, May 31, 2002). The Larbaa market bombing took place on July 5, 2002. According to the French Press Agency, approximately 810 people were killed in Algeria between January and July 2002 (*al-Hayat*, July 11, 2002).

Works Cited

Apter, David E. 1997. "Political Violence in Analytical Perspective." In *The Legitimization of Violence*, ed. David E. Apter. New York: United Nations Research Institute for Social Development.

Ayyashi, Ahmeda. 1993. *Al-Haraka al-Islamiyya fi al-Jazair: al-Joudhour, al-Rumouz, al-Masar.* Casablanca: Uyun al-Magalat.

Burgat, François, and William Dowell. 1997. *The Islamic Movement in North Africa.* Austin: Center for Middle Eastern Studies, University of Texas.

Crenshaw, Martha. 1981. "The Causes of Terrorism." *Comparative Politics* 13, 4: 379–99.

——. 1992. "Decisions to Use Terrorism: Psychological Constraints on Instrumental Reasoning." In *Social Movements and Violence: Participation in Underground Organizations,* International Social Movement Research, vol. 4, ed. Bert Klandermans and Donatella Della Porta. Greenwich, Conn.: JAI Press.

——. 1995. "The Effectiveness of Terrorism in the Algerian War." In *Terrorism in Context,* ed. Martha Crenshaw. College Park: Pennsylvania State University Press.

Della Porta, Donatella. 1988. "Recruitment Processes in Clandestine Political Organizations: Italian Left-Wing Terrorism." *International Social Movement Research* 1: 155–69.

——. 1992. "Introduction: On Individual Motivations in Underground Political Organizations." In *Social Movements and Violence: Participation in Underground Organizations,* International Social Movement Research, vol. 4, ed. Bert Klandermans and Donatella Della Porta. Greenwich, Conn.: JAI Press.

——. 1995a. *Social Movements, Political Violence, and the State: A Comparative Analysis of Italy and Germany.* Cambridge: Cambridge University Press.

——. 1995b. "Left-Wing Terrorism in Italy." In *Terrorism in Context,* ed. Martha Crenshaw. University Park: Pennsylvania State University Press.

Diani, Mario. 1996. "Linking Mobilization Frames and Political Opportunities: Insights from Regional Populism in Italy." *American Sociological Review* 61 (December): 1053–69.

Entelis, John P. 1992. "Introduction: State and Society in Transition." In *State and Society in Algeria,* ed. John P. Entelis and Phillip C. Naylor. Boulder: Westview.

Gerlach, Luther P., and Virginia H. Hine. 1970. *People, Power, Change: Movements of Social Transformation.* Indianapolis: Bobbs-Merrill.

Gurr, Ted Robert. 1970. *Why Men Rebel.* Princeton, N.J.: Princeton University Press.

Hafez, Mohammed M. 2000. "Armed Islamist Movements and Political Violence in Algeria." *Middle East Journal* 4: 572–91.

——. 2003. *Why Muslims Rebel: Repression and Resistance in the Islamic World.* Boulder: Lynne Rienner.

Jabri, Vivienne. 1996. *Discourses of Violence: Conflict Analysis Reconsidered.* Manchester: Manchester University Press.

Jenkins, J. Craig, and Charles Perrow. 1977. "Insurgency of the Powerless: Farm Worker Movements (1946–1972)." *American Sociological Review* 42: 249–68.

Kalyvas, Stathis N. 1999. "Wanton and Senseless? The Logic of Massacres in Algeria." *Rationality and Society* 11, 3 (August): 243–85.

Labat, Séverine. 1995. *Les Islamistes algériens: entre les urnes et le maquis.* Paris: Seuil.

Laqueur, Walter. 1987. *The Age of Terrorism.* Boston: Little, Brown.

Lofland, John. 1966. *Doomsday Cult.* New York: Irvington.

Martinez, Luis. 2000. *The Algerian Civil War, 1990–1998.* New York: Columbia University Press.

McAdam, Doug. 1982. *Political Process and the Development of Black Insurgency, 1930–1970.* Chicago: University of Chicago Press.

——. 1988. "Micromobilization Contexts and Recruitment to Activism." In *From Structure to Action: Comparing Social Movement Research across Cultures,* ed.

Bert Klandermans, Hanspeter Kriesi, and Sidney Tarrow. Greenwich, Conn.: JAI Press.

McAdam, Doug, John D. McCarthy, and Mayer N. Zald, eds. 1996. *Comparative Perspectives on Social Movements: Political Opportunities, Mobilizing Structures, and Cultural Framings*. Cambridge: Cambridge University Press.

McAdam, Doug, Sidney Tarrow, and Charles Tilly. 1997. "Toward an Integrated Perspective on Social Movements and Revolution." In *Comparative Politics: Rationality, Culture, and Structure*, ed. Mark Irving Lichbach and Alan S. Zuckerman. Cambridge: Cambridge University Press.

McClintock, Cynthia. 1998. *Revolutionary Movements in Latin America: El Salvador's FMLN and Peru's Shining Path*. Washington, D.C.: U.S. Institute of Peace.

Mortimer, Robert. 1991. "Islam and Multiparty Politics in Algeria." *Middle East Journal* 45, 4 (Autumn): 575–93.

Moss, David. 1997. "Politics, Violence, Writing: The Rituals of 'Armed Struggle' in Italy." In *The Legitimization of Violence*, ed. David E. Apter. New York: United Nations Research Institute for Social Development.

Musᶜad, Nevien Abdelmunᶜim. 1995. "Al-ᶜAnf al-Siyyasi lil-Harakat al-Ijtimaᶜiyya al-Diniyya (Dirasa lil-Jabha al-Islamiyya lil-Inqadh bil-Jazair)." In *Dhahiret al-ᶜAnf al-Siyyasi fi Manzour Muqarin*, ed. Nevien Abdelmunᶜim Musᶜad. Cairo: Center for Political Research and Studies.

O'Neill, Bard E. 1990. *Insurgency and Terrorism: Inside Modern Revolutionary Warfare*. Washington, D.C.: Brassey's.

Post, J. M. 1987. "Group and Organizational Dynamics of Political Terrorism: Implications for Counterterrorist Policy." In *Contemporary Research on Terrorism*, ed. Paul Wilkinson and Alasdair M. Stewart. Aberdeen: Aberdeen University Press.

———. 1998. "Terrorist Psycho-logic: Terrorist Behavior as a Product of Psychological Forces." In *Origins of Terrorism: Psychologies, Ideologies, Theologies, States of Mind*, ed. Walter Reich. Washington, D.C.: Woodrow Wilson Center Press.

Rashid, Samih. 1997. "Al-Taᶜadidiyya al-Hizbiyya fi al Jazair." *Shuʾun al-Awsat* 65 (September): 57–77.

Roudjia, Ahmed. 1993. *Al-Ikhwan wal-Jamiᶜa: Istitlaᶜa lil-Haraka al-Islamiyya fi al-Jazair*. Translated by Khalil Ahmed Khalil. Beirut: Dar al-Muntakhab al-ᶜArabi.

———. 1995. "Discourse and Strategy of the Algerian Islamist Movement (1986–1992)." In *The Islamist Dilemma: The Political Role of Islamist Movements in the Contemporary Arab World*, ed. Laura Guazzone. Reading, U.K.: Ithaca.

Shabad, Goldie, and Francisco José Ramo. 1995. "Political Violence in a Democratic State: Basque Terrorism in Spain." In *Terrorism in Context*, ed. Martha Crenshaw. University Park: Pennsylvania State University Press.

Snow, D. A., L. A. Zurcher, and S. Ekland-Olson. 1980. "Social Networks and Social Movements." *American Sociological Review* 45: 787–801.

Souaïdia, Habib. 2001. *La sale guerre*. Paris: La Découverte.

Tarrow, Sidney. 1994. *Power in Movement: Social Movements, Collective Action, and Politics*. Cambridge: Cambridge University Press.

———. 1998. *Power in Movement: Social Movements and Contentious Politics*. 2d ed. Cambridge: Cambridge University Press.

al-Tawil, Camille. 1998. *Al-Haraka al-Islamiyya al-Musalaha fi al-Jazair: min al-Inqadh ila al-Jamaʿa*. Beirut: Dar al-Nahar.

Vergès, Meriem. 1997. "Genesis of a Mobilization: The Young Activists of Algeria's Islamic Salvation Front." In *Political Islam*, ed. Joel Beinin and Joe Stork. Berkeley: University of California Press.

Voss, Kim. 1996. "The Collapse of a Social Movement: The Interplay of Mobilizing Structures, Framing, and Political Opportunities in the Knights of Labor." In *Comparative Perspectives on Social Movements*, ed. Doug McAdam, John D. McCarthy, and Mayer N. Zald. Cambridge: Cambridge University Press.

Wasmund, Klaus. 1986. "The Political Socialization of West German Terrorists." In *Political Violence and Terror: Motifs and Motivations*, ed. Peter H. Merkl. Berkeley: University of California Press.

Wickham-Crowley, Timothy P. 1991. *Exploring Revolution: Essays on Latin American Insurgency and Revolutionary Theory*. New York: M. E. Sharpe.

Wieviorka, Michael. 1997. "ETA and Basque Political Violence." In *The Legitimization of Violence*, ed. David E. Apter. New York: United Nations Research Institute for Social Development.

Wiktorowicz, Quintan. 2001a. *The Management of Islamic Activism: Salafis, the Muslim Brotherhood, and State Power in Jordan*. Albany: SUNY Press.

———. 2001b. "The New Global Threat: Transnational Salafis and Jihad." *Middle East Policy* 8, 4 (December): 18–38.

Williams, Rhys H. 1994. "Movement Dynamics and Social Change: Transforming Fundamentalist Ideology and Organizations." In *Accounting for Fundamentalism*, ed. Martin E. Marty and R. Scott Appleby. Chicago: University of Chicago Press.

Willis, Michael. 1996. *The Islamist Challenge in Algeria: A Political History*. Reading, U.K.: Ithaca.

Yous, Nesroulah. 2000. *Qui a tué à Bentalha? Algérie, chronique d'un massacre annoncé*. Paris: La Découverte.

Zald, Mayer N., and Roberta Ash. 1987. "Social Movement Organization: Growth, Decay, and Change." In *Social Movements in an Organizational Society: Collected Essays*, ed. Mayer N. Zald and John D. McCarthy. New Brunswick, N.J.: Transaction Books.

Zitouni, Jamal. 1995. *Hidayat Rab al-ʿAlamin fi Tabyeen Usul al-Salafiyeen wama Yajib min al-ʿAhd ʿala al-Mujahedeen*. A 62-page pamphlet carrying the name Abu Abdel Rahman Amin and dated 27 Rabiʿa al-Thani 1416.

Two

Violence as Contention in the Egyptian Islamic Movement

Mohammed M. Hafez and
Quintan Wiktorowicz

In the 1990s, Islamic political violence escalated dramatically, frequently embroiling broader publics in conflict. In Algeria, the civil war between a nebulous Islamic insurgency and the military-backed regime led to more than 120,000 casualties, including substantial civilian deaths. The brutality of the conflict, which included widespread massacres of women, children, and the elderly, captured international attention and raised concerns about the nature of Islamic activism. This violence was reproduced at lower levels throughout the Middle East, including Jordan, Yemen, Kuwait, Bahrain, Libya, the Sudan, and Egypt. At the same time, a transnational network of radical Salafis loosely affiliated with Osama bin Laden attacked U.S. targets in Saudi Arabia, Tanzania, Kenya, and Yemen. Bin Laden's February 1998 *fatwa* (Islamic legal opinion) legitimizing attacks against U.S. military targets and civilians sparked nervous debates in Western circles about how to address rising levels of Islamic-sponsored terrorism, a debate given new urgency since the September 11 attacks. Outside the Middle East, Islamic groups engaged in violent forms of contention in China, South Africa, Eritrea, Kashmir, the Philippines, Chechnya, Tajikistan, Uzbekistan, and Dagestan, redefining the geography of violent Islamic struggles.

Although radical tactics are at the fringe of Islamic movements, the growing use of violence in the 1990s raises important questions about Islamic activism and social movement contention. In particular, given the broad repertoire of contention, which includes preaching, religious lessons, social and welfare services, publications, and general *da'wa* (religious proselytizing) activities, why did a number of Islamists turn to violence? More generically, why do social movements utilize violence as contention, given other tactics? What explains cross-national and diachronic variance in the level of violence?

61

In this chapter, we use the cycle of violence between Hosni Mubarak's regime and the Gamaʿa Islamiyya in Egypt as a case study to explore some of these questions. Although episodes of Islamic violence have a history in Egypt, the most recent confrontations differ in scope. Running gun battles, bombings, assassinations, and ambushes claimed hundreds of lives between 1990 and 1998. Deaths included not only Islamists and agents of the state but also foreign nationals, intellectuals, civilians, and Coptic Christians. The cycle of violence culminated in the massacre of 58 tourists and 4 Egyptians by members of the Gamaʿa Islamiyya (henceforth Gamaʿa) in November 1997, shocking the entire nation, including the jailed leaders of the Gamaʿa who tried to distance themselves from the perpetrators. The attack marked the turning point in the low-intensity conflict, and the number of deaths attributed to Islamic violence declined precipitously.[1] This pause (or end), in turn, provides an opportunity to look back at the previous decade to explain the explosion in violent Islamic contention and why social movements turn to radical tactics.

In contrast to popular views of Islamic radicals as fanatics engaged in irrational, deviant, unpredictable violence, we argue that violent contention is the result of tactical considerations informed by the realities of repressive contexts. Islamists engage in a rational calculus about tactical efficacy and choose modes of contention they believe will facilitate objectives or protect their organizational and political gains. Violence is only one of myriad possibilities in repertoires of contention and becomes most likely where regimes attempt to crush Islamic activism through broad repressive measures that leave few alternatives. In Egypt, the cycle of violence began largely in response to a broad crackdown on the Islamic movement that ensnared moderates, radicals, and a number of tangential bystanders. The crackdown included arrests, hostage taking, torture, executions, and other forms of state violence.

From this perspective, violent Islamic contention is produced not by ideational factors or unstable psychological mentalities but rather by exogenous contingencies created through state policy concerning Islamists. Particular Islamic groups may engage in violence irrespective of state actions, but the stability of tactics for these outlier groups cannot explain the overall level of violence nor its timing. Instead, we must examine the inputs into repertoire calculations that lead increasing numbers of activists toward the use of violence. This perspective does not entail an outright rejection of ideational explanations that focus on the ideology and beliefs of violent militants; rather, it serves as a corrective to long-standing traditions in research on Islamic activism that tend to highlight the role of ideational factors at the expense of structural imperatives and voluntarist dynamics. This study maintains that while it is tempting to blame Islamic activists for the outbreak of violence, exogenous factors, such as regime repression, hold some culpability.

Islamic Activism and Violent Contention

Despite the notoriety of violent episodes of Islamic contention, such as the Egyptian cycle of violence in the 1990s, there is surprisingly little empirical work on the subject. Most studies of Islamic activism instead examine the underlying causal factors that provide impetus for the emergence of an overall Islamic revival or resurgence. These include socioeconomic crises prompted by the failure of secular modernization projects (Dekmejian 1995; Faksh 1997); demographic pressures; the residual effects of colonialism, neo-imperialism, and concomitant foreign hegemony (Burgat and Dowell 1993; Keddie 1994); and the Arab defeat in the 1967 war with Israel (Haddad 1992). Islamism is seen as an indigenously constructed response to the realities of everyday life, conditioned by housing shortages, rising unemployment, declining social services, rising prices, and a general sense of cultural, political, military, and economic weakness. From this perspective, deprivation has created a legion of disaffected recruits who seek culturally acceptable explanations that address their marginalization and social anomie (Ayubi 1980; Ibrahim 1980). Rooted in the shared symbols and language of Muslim societies, Islamism offers an appropriate *weltanschauung* and diagnostic framing for understanding and ameliorating difficult living conditions.

Although such studies point to the general conditions that give rise to Islamic movements, they do not effectively explain the emergence and proliferation of violence in repertoires of contention. In most cases, Islamic movements are not "born" violent. Instead, proponents of violence develop coteries of militants from within established, predominantly nonviolent Islamic movements. Groups such as the Armed Islamic Group (GIA) of Algeria, the Gamaʿa of Egypt, and violent Salafi fringes in Jordan all emerged from broader mainstream Islamic movements. And while violent Islamic groups may represent constituent elements of a general reaction to intense crisis conditions, this does not in itself explain decisions to utilize violence rather than other mechanisms of collective action. What leads to shifts in repertoires of contention so that violence becomes an acceptable instrument of collective action within Islamic discourse? In a shared milieu, why do some Islamic groups turn to violence while others promote peaceful contention? And why do Islamic groups decide to use heightened violence at particular moments? To a large extent, the study of Islamic activism has been unable to effectively address these questions because of a tendency to favor the descriptive analysis of the textual sources, ideology, and social roots of Islamic groups that espouse violence at the expense of deeper sociological understandings about tactical choice.[2]

Since the Iranian Revolution, scholars have sought to explicate the underlying belief systems and demographic support of Islamic militancy, leading to two loosely clustered approaches on the subject of Islamic violence. The first is what we call "the ideational school." According to this approach, the immutable sources of the religion—the Qur'an and Sunna (traditions of the prophet Muhammad)—inform decisions about behavior. According to a well-trodden Islamic adage, unchanging religious principles and understandings must be used to address new challenges and circumstances. As a result, violence becomes something rooted in the traditions and sources of Islam itself, revived under particular circumstances that meet specific, religiously sanctioned criteria. There is thus a certain degree of ideational constancy (Voll 1983; Sivan 1985; Vatikiotis 1987). More recent manifestations of this perspective embrace the multiplicity of religious interpretations that derive from ambiguities in ideational sources, but still place ideology at the center of analysis (Jansen 1986; Hafez 2000).

Despite the role of ideology in structuring behavior, radical Islamic groups often demonstrate remarkable doctrinal flexibility in response to a changing political environment. For example, despite popular perceptions of Hamas as an uncompromising movement trapped by rigid adherence to dogma, the movement has displayed doctrinal flexibility designed to enhance the movement's standing in the Palestinian community and its long-term viability in the struggle against Israel. Before the *intifada* (uprising) that began in 2000, there was growing popular support for the peace process, which posed a problem for the movement. Strict adherence and an intransigent position regarding peace was likely to erode the support of bystander publics that sought an end to the economic and social hardships of occupation, thus threatening the organizational survival of Hamas as an alternative to Arafat and his supporters. As a result, Hamas adjusted its doctrine to accommodate the possibility of peace with Israel by framing peace as a temporary pause in the jihad that would strengthen Muslim forces before a final assault. Concepts such as *sabr* (patience) and *hudna* (truce) were used to legitimize doctrinal flexibility within the overall objectives of the movement (Mishal and Sela 2000). Thus, while ideology, beliefs, and text play a role, they may be subordinated to other considerations under certain circumstances.

The second dominant approach, what Salwa Ismail (2000, 366) terms the "psychosocial model," privileges the socioeconomic background of violent activists in analysis. Studies in this tradition seek to explain the emergence of violent groups by understanding their demographic roots. Early research indicated that most militants had high levels of education and had recently migrated to urban centers, often in search of employment opportunities. Scholars argued that because these recruits were cut off from their rural roots and family and were living in a new urban environment with different values, they suffered a sense of social alienation and anomie that rendered them vulnerable to the Islamic message of tradition (S. E. Ibrahim 1980; Ansari 1984). Later studies showed that the base of support shifted toward the less educated members of society, but recruits were still seen as motivated by psychosocial pressures (S. E. Ibrahim 1996). The underlying assumption of such an approach is that socioeconomic background tells us something about grievances and therefore why individuals join violent groups (Hoffman 1995).

The demographic profile of violent Islamists, however, tells us little about patterns of violence for a number of reasons. First, radicals and moderates seem to share many of the same characteristics, including levels of education. While violent militants tend to be younger, this alone does not explain why violence is used, since a number of young people also belong to peaceful movements. Second, demographic characteristics do not explain the variance of violence over time. Radical Islamic groups have not engaged in unending violent hostilities since their formation. Instead, there is an ebb and flow in the level of violence, and individuals choose to support and/or use violence at particular moments. Assuming that their socioeconomic background does not suddenly shift, and there is no evidence to indicate this, demographics alone cannot explain the choice.

Research on violent Islamists has thus failed to explain patterns of tactical choices or recognize the dynamic nature of repertoires of contention. Ideological orientation or background characteristics do not inexorably lead to violence; cross-national and internal group variance in the use of violence indicates otherwise. It is more effective to view violent activists as rational actors operating within a context of opportunities and constraints that inform decisions about appropriate tactics. We believe that only by accommodating the role of exogenous factors in structuring movement choices can social scientists fully explain the level and timing of Islamic violence. This is not to argue that beliefs or background characteristics are irrelevant, but rather that other theoretically relevant variables must be incorporated into our understanding of Islamic activism and violence as contention.

Political Opportunity Structure
and Violent Contention

Social movement theorists have long emphasized the importance of exogenous factors on social movement behavior through the concept of "political opportunity structure," which captures the myriad conditions propitious for the rise and growth of social movement contention. These conditions include the availability of allies (Gamson 1975; Jenkins and Perrow 1977), the nature of state repression (Tilly 1978; Brockett 1991; Smith 1991), the instability of elite alignments (Tarrow 1989, 1994, 1996), and the institutional strength of the state (Kriesi et al. 1992, 1995). An analysis of the political opportunity structure informs us of the broader context of opportunities and constraints under which movement actors seek to acquire and allocate resources for collective action. The opportunities and constraints present in the political environment enter into the rational calculus of movement actors and help shape intramovement debates over the efficacy and legitimacy of violence. Two aspects of the political opportunity structure, in particular, help shape decisions regarding whether or not to rely on violent contention: accessibility of the institutionalized political system and the nature of state repression.

Access to Institutionalized Politics

The institutionalized political system refers to the set of *formal* institutions of the state—parliaments, government ministries, policy-implementing agencies—and *informal* mechanisms, procedures, and "policy styles" (Kitschelt 1986, 63) by which the state elite governs. A political system is accessible to the movement when the state grants it procedural and substantive access through which it can exert formal or informal influence. It is inaccessible when the movement lacks substantive access to formal and informal policy-making channels, and thus lacks the possibility of influence over public policy through state institutions.

System accessibility is important for investigating levels of violent contention because it bears directly on the question of reform versus revolution. An accessible political system, as Jeff Goodwin (1997, 18) explains, "discourages the sense that the state is unreformable or an instrument of a narrow class or clique and (accordingly) needs to be overhauled." Many studies have substantiated the claim that the more accessible the state, even an authoritarian state, the less likely it is to unify opposition behind a violent strategy (Huntington 1968; Skocpol 1979; Dix 1984; Goldstone 1991; Wickham-Crowley 1991). In contrast, the more exclusionary and inaccessible the political system, the more likely opposition will coalesce around a violent strategy (Goodwin and Skocpol 1989). "Exclusionary regimes," argues Goodwin (1997, 18), "tend to 'incubate' radical collective-action: those who specialize in it tend to prosper, because they come to be viewed by many people as more realistic and potentially effective than political moderates, who themselves come to be viewed as hopelessly ineffective."

Recent history supports the contention that political access quells violent rebellion. The Iranian and Nicaraguan revolutions of 1979, for instance, were made by a broad-based movement against "personalist authoritarian" regimes characterized by "institutional detachment from the majority of the population" (Farhi 1990, 32). Similarly, the Cuban revolutionary movement of 1959 engendered cross-national opposition to the state largely because Fulgencio Batista's regime was a personalistic, rather than collective, form of dictatorship. Martha Crenshaw's (1978, 7–8) study of revolutionary nationalism in Algeria points out that many of the leaders of the National Liberation Front (FLN) at one point sought political office but were denied through fraud. In contrast, revolutionary movements in Colombia, Venezuela, Peru, and Bolivia in recent history were unable to forge unified movements partly because elected governments "contributed greatly to the weaknesses of the revolutionary opposition since the reformist option seemed to provide the opposition with an alternative path" (Wickham-Crowley 1992, 170).

System inaccessibility, however, may be a necessary but insufficient cause for widespread and sustained violent contention. Much like economic deprivation, dictatorial regimes abound. Yet the levels of violence across illiberal polities vary. This fact has led many social movement theorists to look to the nature of state repression for a more complete explanation of violent contention.

②The Nature of State Repression

Comparable to system accessibility, state repression is a palpable and often tragic way for a movement to gauge the tolerance limits of the political system. Indeed, despite ongoing disagreements over the dimensions of the political opportunity structure, very few scholars exclude the variable of repression from their analysis.

However, assessing the impact of repression on movement behavior is as difficult as it is important. Theoretically, there is little agreement regarding the logical consequences of state repression on movement behavior. Some contend that repression increases the cost of collective action so as to make it unlikely (Snyder and Tilly 1972; Hibbs 1973; Oberschall 1973; Oliver 1980; Hardin 1982). Others maintain that repression generates additional grievances that motivate further mobilization to punish an "unjust" opponent (Eckstein 1965; Gamson, Fireman, and Rytina 1982; Goldstein 1983; White 1989). We reject these two perspectives on empirical grounds; there are many instances where repression both quells and provokes insurgency (Zimmermann 1980; Khawaja 1993).

Attempts to solve the paradox of the repression-rebellion nexus led some to investigate how varying levels of repression—too much or too little repression—are likely to induce protest or hinder it (Gurr 1970; Lichbach and Gurr 1981; Muller 1985; Muller and Weed 1990). Others look to the timing of repression (Snyder 1976; Gurr 1986; Brockett 1995), its perceived illegitimacy (Opp and Roehl 1990), the institutional context under which repression is applied (Gupta, Singh, and Sprague 1993), the targeting of repression (Mason and Krane 1989), the consistency of repression in relation to accommodative strategies (Lichbach 1987), or a combination of these variables (Della Porta 1995a, 1996). These studies suggest that there are many dimensions to repression, each generating variables that could explain different outcomes. Therefore, rather than hypothesize the effect of repression per se, it is more useful to clarify some of the dimensions of repression and how they encourage or deter violent movement strategies.

There are at least two dimensions of repression that deserve careful attention: timing and targeting. The timing of repression refers to whether repression is applied preemptively or reactively. Repression is *preemptive* when it is applied before the opposition movement has had an opportunity to organize and mobilize disparate supporters and sympathizers around a common goal. Repression is *reactive* when it is applied in the ascendant phase of the protest cycle—that is, after activists gain organizational momentum (Brockett 1995). The targeting of repression refers to the range of targets encompassed under state repression (Mason and Krane 1989). State repression is *selective* when it only targets the leaders and core activists of the movement. It is *indiscriminate* when repression expands to include supporters, sympathizers, and ordinary citizens suspected of involvement in the movement.

The manner in which the state combines the timing and targeting of repression is a primary determinant of movement strategic calculations. We argue that preemptive and selective repression will deter violent contention on a mass scale, while reactive and indiscriminate repression is likely to encourage it. Preemptive repression predisposes the movement toward nonmilitant strategies for two reasons. First, preemptive repression denies activists the opportunity to rapidly expand material and organizational resources and thus disempowers supporters and sympathizers. They may wish to act but perceive few feasible means for effecting change. Uncertainty as to the power of the movement will force activists to become cautious and will deter supporters from backing radical groups who may appear overzealous or "ahead of their time." "In the absence of organizational mobilization and support," explains Khawaja (1993, 67), "potential activists are more likely to keep their anger and grievances to themselves, fearing retributions by authorities." Brockett (1995, 132) illustrates this argument with reference to peasant mobilization in Guatemala in the mid-1960s and Nicaragua in the mid-1970s. The peasants in both cases, despite encountering widespread and arbitrary murders, shied away from revolutionary groups because the latter were "small and isolated from other political forces." Peasant support for revolutionaries only came when political space for organized collective action opened during the 1970s, which facilitated more support groups and social networks.

Second, insurgency, especially in a highly repressive context, involves high-risk activities that require committed and trustworthy participants. "Recruitment is less risky when the recruiter can trust the recruit, and vice versa" (Della Porta 1988, 159). Commitment and trust beyond the core activists involved in initial organizing, however, usually develops through the actual process of mobilization. In other words, to induce rebellion on a mass scale, prior mobilization is necessary because it is in this phase that activists and supporters become acquainted with each other, gauge the level of commitment and numerical support in the movement, and develop bonds of friendship and camaraderie in organized settings. Many studies point out that the strongest incentive for recruitment into high-risk activities is through friendship ties with someone who is already in the movement (Gerlach and Hine 1970; Snow, Zurcher, and Ekland-Olson 1980; Della Porta 1992; McAdam and Paulsen 1993). This observation is confirmed by Wickham's study of Islamist mobilization in Egypt, discussed in chapter 9 of this volume. She notes that recruitment into Islamist networks was facilitated by the fact that "most residents had a brother, cousin, friend, or neighbor involved in Islamic prayer circles or study groups, and Islamist participants frequently maintained close social relationships with nonactivist peers." By depriving activists of the opportunity to repeatedly link with other activists and supporters through mobilization, preemptive repression isolates militants from their potential supporters and other political forces, raises doubt as to the size of their support, and precludes the cultivation of high levels of commitment and trust across the movement.

Reactive repression, on the other hand, predisposes the movement to rebellion for three reasons. First, activists will have acquired material resources, mainly through the expansion of membership contributions. This means that activists encountering repression after a series of mobilizations will not only become more aggrieved but will also command resources that can be used to fight back.

Second, in contrast to preemptive repression, reactive repression comes after sympathizers and supporters have had a chance to develop trust and bonds of friendship with the core activists of the movement as well as to realistically gauge the level of support and commitment in the movement. If commitment and support are deemed high, then supporters will feel empowered to join insurgent organizations, act on their grievances, and try to bring about change (Klandermans 1984; Opp 1988; Lichbach 1995; Kurzman 1996). As Brockett (1995, 133) argues with reference to Central American revolutionaries, repression of collective action in the ascendant phase of the protest cycle encourages further protest because "the active opposition of large numbers of people and of many organizations from many different sectors of society sustains the belief that the regime will be defeated."

Finally, reactive repression that seeks to eradicate an organized and mobilized movement is more likely to induce mass rebellion than preemptive repression because activists and supporters will seek to halt the loss of resources accumulated over time. As Bayat (1997, 163) points out, "Extrakinship mobilization and campaigning do not usually develop under repressive conditions, unless the actors feel a common threat to their gains." In other words, movements will act not only because they are empowered but also because they may believe that inaction will lead to the loss of hard-earned movement resources. As Berejikian (1992, 652) explains, the "decisional determinant [to revolt] is not the expected outcome, but how the choice is perceived relative to the status quo (reference point)." If inaction entails continued losses, then there will be a greater inclination toward risk to mitigate losses. Kriesi et al. (1995,

40) make a similar point: when repression threatens to considerably worsen the challengers' ability to exert influence in the future, "the costs of collective action decrease relative to the now costly path of inaction." In such circumstances, movement organizations may choose to fight back "even though it may be expected to accomplish little more than a continuation of the present situation or even a mere reduction of the expected deterioration."

The targeting of repression—whether it is selective or indiscriminate—is also important. Selective repression predisposes the movement toward nonmilitancy while indiscriminate repression pushes it toward militant strategies. Selective repression signals to supporters and sympathizers that only "troublemakers" will be punished, and therefore those who keep their distance will not become victims of repression. Moreover, selective repression is not likely to create "martyrs" out of uncommitted supporters. This does not mean that proponents of revolutionary violence will discontinue militancy, but it does mean that selective repression will deprive them of mass support, limiting the scale of their militancy. In chapter 3 of this volume, Lawson points out that support for violent contention in Bahrain during the 1990s was influenced by whether state repression was "selective" or "diffuse." He shows that while selective targeting did not necessarily diminish protest, it did decrease the level of public support for acts of violence.

In contrast, indiscriminate repression antagonizes hitherto inactive supporters and sympathizers and intensifies the moral outrage of activists. Although selective repression could result in moral outrage and thus expand the legitimacy of the movement, indiscriminate repression is likely to do so many times over. A state that throws the net of repression widely is more likely to be viewed as illegitimate. Moral outrages committed by the militants of the movement will be seen as the "natural" response to indiscriminate repression. In his study of liberation theology movements in Latin America, Smith (1991) points out that brutal repression which targeted not only political parties, labor unions, and students but also many Catholics engaged in pastoral activities facilitated the development of insurgent consciousness and made possible the diffusion of "injustice frames" that motivated insurgency. Similarly, Gurr and Goldstone (1991, 334) and Kiernan (1996, 20–25) offer evidence that American punitive bombings of Cambodian and Vietnamese villages suspected of aiding rebels drove many peasants into the ranks of revolutionary armies. And Horne (1987, 104) shows that the French policy of "collective responsibility" during Algeria's war of independence (1954–1962) expanded the membership of the rebellious National Liberation Front (FLN).

Furthermore, indiscriminate repression may push occasional activists and known supporters of the movement to seek the protection of violent groups. In a study of left-wing terrorism in Italy during the 1970s, Della Porta (1995b, 118) notes that "many of the new members of terrorist organizations were in fact members of radical groups who joined terrorist organizations in order to have logistical support while evading arrest." Similarly, Davis and Hodson (1982) and May (2001) show that many Guatemalan villagers joined guerrilla groups because the guerrillas came to be viewed as the only remaining source of defense against government-sponsored massacres that targeted innocent *campesinos*. And Mason and Krane (1989) correlate the expansion of peasant support for the El Salvadoran FMLN (Faribundo Marti National Liberation Front) during the late 1970s with the escalation of indiscriminate repression by government-sponsored death squads.

One of the paradoxes of state repression in response to social movement activism is that while governments often repress movements because of their potentially violent or destabilizing nature, the very act of repression creates a crisis and the conditions for violence (Melucci 1996, 303, 369). It is a collective action variant of the spiral of escalation in arms races where each side escalates its violent contention as a defensive measure while viewing opponent actions as offensive and provocative, thereby reinforcing perceptions about the need for continued violence.

In the following section, we show how the 1992 Islamic insurgency in Egypt was, at least in part, a response to a changing political opportunity structure. In the late 1980s and early 1990s, the state increasingly blocked peaceful avenues of opposition and legitimized violent contention in the Islamic movement. In contrast to prevailing studies of Islamic violence, which imply that violence is endogenously produced as a result of either ideology or the socioeconomic characteristics of activists, the case of Egypt highlights how the degree of system accessibility and the nature of state repression play a large role in the decision to adopt violent forms of contention.

Violent Contention in Egypt

Islamic violence in Egypt has been a recurring phenomenon since the resurgence of Islamism in the 1970s. The 1981 assassination of President Anwar al-Sadat was a milestone in the history of sporadic violence between radical Islamists and the state. During the 1990s, however, Islamic violence took a distinct turn toward a more sustained insurgency. Between 1992 and 1997, there were 741 incidents of violence, which is in stark contrast to the 143 incidents that took place between 1970 and 1991.[3] The years 1993 to 1995 were the bloodiest, witnessing almost daily incidents of violence. Whereas violence between 1970 and 1989 produced an estimated 120 deaths (Mubarak 1995, 374), violence between 1992 and 1997 resulted in 1,442 deaths and 1,779 injuries.[4]

Islamic violence in the 1990s featured a number of attributes that distinguished it from earlier periods. Whereas violence in the 1970s and 1980s largely struck at "soft" targets—leftist students, Copts, "places of sin"—

violence in the 1990s targeted the state and its institutions much more than in previous periods, as evinced by attacks on policemen, security forces, and prominent government officials.[5]

Moreover, violence was characterized by greater sophistication as Islamists increasingly relied on high-tech explosives, intelligence gathering, and military training to better enable their units to inflict damage (Fatah 1995; Bakr 1996). In addition, for the first time since its inception, the Gamaʿa formed a clandestine armed wing with its own leadership separate from the daʿwa wing.[6] The decision to form an armed wing marked a clear shift in strategy from earlier periods when the Gamaʿa rejected clandestine work as both an un-Islamic innovation and a politically unsound strategy for building a mass movement (Mubarak 1995, 188).

Furthermore, in an unprecedented escalation, Islamic violence targeted tourists,[7] the tourism industry,[8] and various financial centers—principally state and foreign banks.[9] Islamic violence was expansive, and Coptic Christians increasingly became targets. While estimates indicate that there were 20 violent incidents against Copts between 1982 and 1991, the years 1992 and 1993 alone witnessed 58 violent attacks against the Coptic community (Abulala 1998), and the attacks continued well into the late 1990s.[10] Islamists also struck at secular intellectuals and ordinary civilians suspected of collaborating with security forces.[11] Beginning in 1996, the Gamaʿa escalated its rhetoric against the United States, Israel, Jews, and "Crusaders."[12]

The Islamic insurgency, however, was a relatively limited one, despite the significant increase in violence. It was largely confined to Upper Egyptian towns—Asyut, Aswan, Souhaj, al-Minya, Qina, and Beni Swayf—even though the Gamaʿa tried to expand its recruitment and attacks to Cairo (Mubarak 1995, 370–71; al-Din 1998, 506).

The turn to violent contention coincided with three important changes in the Egyptian political opportunity structure. First, Egypt witnessed the deliberalization of institutional politics in the 1990s. Second, the authorities in Egypt began to dismantle the network of the Gamaʿa in Upper Egypt after years of "permissive repression" that enabled them to foster organizational and societal gains. Finally, repression against the Gamaʿa was indiscriminate; it did not distinguish between core militants, sympathizers, and neutral observers. Each of these developments legitimized violent Islamic frames in the broader movement and thus made violent contention possible and sustainable.

Political Deliberalization in Egypt

During the late 1970s and 1980s, the Egyptian ruling regime took some tangible steps toward greater liberalization of the polity. Some previously banned parties were permitted to come back and participate in parliamentary elections, and the unsanctioned Muslim Brotherhood, the largest Islamic organization in Egypt since the late 1920s, was allowed to join legal parties and hold positions in the People's Assembly (Ansari 1986; Hinnebusch 1985; Springborg 1989; Mustapha 1996; Korany 1998). To be sure, political liberalization in the late 1970s and 1980s did not give the Islamic movement substantive policymaking power in the political system. Nonetheless, many Islamists saw formal access to the system as a tangible gain because it provided a platform for Islamic agitation.

In the 1990s, the state reversed its liberalization stance and imposed greater restrictions on the opposition, especially the Muslim Brotherhood (MB). The reversal began when the regime issued electoral law 206, which redrew (or gerrymandered) voting districts in a blatantly unfair way that privileged the ruling National Democratic Party (NDP) candidates. The ruling party continued to receive financial subsidies from the state, and it maintained its monopoly over the radio and television during election campaigns (al-Shourbaji 1994; Auda and Ibrahim 1995). These policies led the opposition, including the MB, to boycott the 1990 parliamentary elections. As a result, only 7 seats went to the official opposition, which is less than 2 percent of the seats. If we include the estimated 8 seats that went to independent Islamic candidates and 23 seats that went to independent candidates from the New Wafd, secular Labor, Liberal, and Nasserist Parties (38 seats, or a little over 8 percent), we still have a parliament that is proportionally less representative of the opposition than the 1979 one, which had allotted the opposition almost 11 percent of the seats (Zaki 1995, 94–96).

The 1995 elections resulted in a comparable outcome, but for entirely different reasons. The opposition, including the Muslim Brotherhood, did not boycott the elections. However, before both rounds of the election, the state carried out a wave of arrests against hundreds of MB representatives and cadres to preclude them from running an effective campaign—indeed, to prevent their candidates from running altogether.[13] Days before the elections, the state sentenced 54 members to prison terms ranging from three to five years (al-Shawkabi 1995). As a result, only 1 of the 150 MB candidates made it to the People's Assembly, and he was removed in 1996 for membership in an illegal organization.

The lack of real opposition in the national assemblies of the 1990s meant that the legislature was in effect nothing more than a legal secretary to the executive, putting regime orders into proper legal form and doing so with due speed and no questions asked. One illustrative example of this subservience is Law 100 of 1993. This law regulated the elections of the professional associations purportedly to make them representative of their constituencies. In practice, however, it was widely perceived as a way of countering the hegemony of Islamists in the associations (al-Shourbaji 1994). The law stipulated, *inter alia*, that at least 50 percent of syndicate members must cast a vote for election results to be valid, a rule that hurt the Islamic movement, whose loyal and organized cadres had previously taken advantage of low voter turnout in syndicate elections, which rarely exceeded 10 percent (Fahmy 1998). After news of the proposed law reached the opposition, it demanded input into the formulation of the measures. The government simply denied that such a law was in the making. On February 15, however, the law was proposed in parliament and enacted two days later. The speed with which the controversial law passed the legislature is a striking example of collusion between the legislative and executive against the opposition (Qandil 1995).

Four factors help explain the reversal in liberalization. First, during the 1980s, the MB took advantage of its national platform to raise its demands for Islamic laws and vociferously challenge the ruling regime's policies with regards to internal security, economic planning, foreign relations, use of torture, and the lack of democracy and human rights in Egypt (Radhi 1990/1991; al-Tawil 1992). By refusing to play a quiescent role in parliament, the MB challenged the legitimacy of the state regime. During the early 1980s, Mubarak wanted to consolidate his legitimacy by giving the opposition parties, especially the Islamists, an opportunity to express themselves through institutional channels while simultaneously enhancing the democratic image of the presidency, which had been tarnished by Sadat's excesses in the two years before his assassination. By the early 1990s, Mubarak was firmly in control and no longer needed to maintain an accommodative stance toward his most open and effective critics.

Second, while the political inclusion of the MB was intended to contain its influence, by the late 1980s the MB became the leading opposition force in parliament with 36 seats. Other political parties began vying for an alliance with the MB by Islamizing their discourse and political programs. In the 1987 "Islamic Alliance" that united the MB with the Labor and Liberal Parties, the MB was able to set the terms of the alliance. For example, it was able to exclude Marxists and Nasserists from the alliance list. It also enticed the Labor Party to amend its political program to include "applying the *shari*ᶜ*a*" atop its list of objectives (Auda and Ibrahim 1995, 310).

Third, the legitimacy of the MB in parliament spilled over into civil society. The MB began to expand its influence in professional associations of engineers, lawyers, and doctors. These syndicates became a vehicle for the expression of political aims and criticism of the regime's "impotence" at home and in foreign policy. They also allowed the MB to mobilize financial resources to aid social and political causes locally and abroad (Qandil 1995, 1996). Such influence was deemed threatening to the ruling regime because it turned the MB into an "alternative" to the state.

Finally, the inclusion of the MB did not result in the complete containment of the Gamaᶜa. The state's strategy during the 1980s was to isolate the militants by rewarding the MB with political access. However, as we shall see below, mere formal inclusion of the MB in political institutions did not placate the ideological radicals. To be sure, the Gama‘a and Islamic Jihad shunned parliamentary participation on religious grounds. They believed democracy was heresy because it allowed people, not the "word of God," to rule. Yet despite this fundamental objection, they did not hesitate to criticize the MB for its failure to advance Islamic aims through institutional participation. Aboud Zumur, the leader of Islamic Jihad, chided the MB for failing to secure a political party during the 1980s by pointing out that "whereas France, Germany, and Italy permit the formation of a religious party, Egypt is proud of the fact it does not permit such a party" (quoted in Ahmed 1995, 109). More significantly, the ideological radicals accused the MB of legitimating the regime and dividing the Islamist movement. According to Aboud Zumur, "The government carefully responds to some of the limited demands of Islamists inside of the [People's] Assembly to fulfill its containment conspiracy to the point of convincing Muslims that there is a possibility of applying Islamic law through the assembly" (quoted in Ahmed 1995, 287).

In a document by Islamic Jihad entitled *Falsafit al-Muwajaha* (The Philosophy of Confrontation), Tariq Zumur wrote: "The goal of permitting Islamists to enter the People's Assembly is nothing more than an attempt to drag a wide section of the youth behind a course of action in which the path (of the movement) is lost and its goals concealed. The presence of Islamists inside the regime's legislative assembly bestows upon the regime legitimacy it never dreamed of. The mere direction of Islamists toward the ballot box guarantees the fulfillment of [the state's] goal" (quoted in Mubarak 1995, 355).

As the formal inclusion of the MB during the 1980s turned into outright political exclusion in the early 1990s, the Gama‘a and Islamic Jihad felt vindicated in their assessment of the political strategy of the state. In one communiqué, the Gama‘a rhetorically asked, "What has the Muslim Brotherhood, since its inception until now, achieved of the goals and objectives of Islam, the hopes and needs of the Muslims, and the duties and requirements of the age?" It added, "What is astonishing is that every time the Muslim Brotherhood rushes to issue their statements of moral condemnation, denunciation, and disavowal of all that is jihad—they call it terrorism—the more the government redoubles its constraints against them and strikes them nonstop."[14] In its publication *al-Mujahedin,* Islamic Jihad wrote, "All the peacefulness and gradualism upheld by the [Muslim Brotherhood] during their political struggles, and their work through the regime's legitimate, legal channels did not save them from being handcuffed, tried in front of military courts, and dragged to prisons. All the while their preachers declare that they will not be provoked and will not attempt confrontation."[15]

The inability of the legal and semilegal opposition to effect major political changes gave the radicals, as they saw it, added justification for violent contention. The demands of the opposition in the early 1990s reiterated the demands of the early 1980s: application of Islamic law, electoral reforms, repeal of the state of emergency imposed after Sadat's assassination, an end to mass arrests and torture, and respect for political freedom and human rights. The repetition of the demands highlighted the limited political progress of the opposition over the past several decades. As Ahmed (1995, 287) explains, "The inability of the Muslim Brotherhood to achieve substantial political gains during the two parliamentary experiences of 1984 and 1987 resulted, on the one hand, in a loss of support for the Muslim Brotherhood and, on the other, an intensification of the jihadist's criticism toward them. It also consolidated the jihadist's conviction in their rejectionist position toward parliamentary work and predisposition toward greater reliance on violence."

The deliberalization of the political system in the 1990s was a necessary but not sufficient cause for the cycle of violence that began in 1992. The nature of state repression, particularly the reactive and indiscriminate application of repression, contributed to the legitimization of violent contention in the Islamic movement as well.

Reactive State Repression

In the 1980s, as the Islamic movement gained social momentum, the state adopted what Hisham Mubarak (1995, 382) aptly terms a policy of "permissive repression" (*al-tasamuh al-qumᶜai*). This policy aimed to contain militant Islamists in their Upper Egypt strongholds by acquiescing to some of their organizational activities while repressing more outwardly confrontational behavior.

During the 1980s, the Gamaᶜa branches were allowed to hold regular conferences and meetings around their mosques, and the gatherings were often overtly political and critical of the state and "enemies" of Islam. During the meetings, the Gamaᶜa employed its own security guards and drew a large number of supporters. As Mubarak (1995, 257) points out: "The Gamaᶜa was the only political force in Egypt that conducted mass conferences without acquiring a security permit as the law declares, not to mention the repetition of slogans, declarations and words that represented a violation of and a challenge to the law. Meanwhile, security men—at that time—could not come near conference areas for fear of clashing with the Gamaᶜa's paramilitary groups, which were given the task of 'protecting' the conferences."

The Gamaᶜa was even able to establish "liberated zones" in some of the towns of Upper Egypt and Greater Cairo (Mubarak 1995; Bakr 1996). In the Asyut city of Dairut, the Gamaᶜa controlled approximately 150 mosques, and in some neighborhoods they imposed complete control. In the 1980s, the Gamaᶜa began expanding into the shantytowns and peripheral areas of Cairo —Ain Shems, al-Zawiyya al-Hamra, Imbaba, and Boulaq al-Dakrour. In a place like Imbaba, where the Islamists nearly established an "Islamic republic," the Islamists hardly encountered any repression. As one Gamaᶜa activist in Imbaba relates, "Our work was conducted and expanded without any security provocations or intervention from the security apparatuses, which gave us a better opportunity to grow. After a short while the Gamaᶜa al-Islamiyya became an influential force in Imbaba and everyone took it into account" (quoted in Mubarak 1995, 247).

The Gamaᶜa established roving bands that often engaged in "forbidding vice"—segregating the sexes, preventing girls from engaging in sporting activities at schools, and breaking up concerts (Ramadan 1995, 241). The movement also regularly enforced its own laws through threat and force at the universities of Upper Egypt, something it began doing in the 1970s (Springborg 1989, 228). Just as important, the activities of the Gamaᶜa against the Copts went largely unpunished so long as it did not rise to an "alarming" level—that is, to a level that attracted national and international press attention. This was especially the case in Dairut, where there were repeated incidents of sectarian violence (see Egyptian Organization for Human Rights 1992).

The acquiescence of the state to Islamic activism in Upper Egypt also extended to social services. The Gamaᶜa organized social welfare services that operated out of the movement's mosques to help impoverished communities. These activities included distributing meat and rice during religious holidays and passing out school supplies and clothing to poor families at the beginning of each school year. They also set up "reconciliation committees" to mediate conflicts in neighborhoods on the basis of Islamic laws (Mubarak 1995, 260–65). Because the Gamaᶜa made it a point to publicize these activities to enhance its legitimacy in the community, the authorities were well aware of what the Gamaᶜa was doing.

But this policy of permissive repression had limitations, and, eventually, escalating provocations prodded the state to intervene and limit the power of the Gamaᶜa. In 1990, the state responded to the growing strength of the Gamaᶜa by assassinating ᶜAla Muhyi al-Din, the movement's official spokesman. The Gamaᶜa retaliated by forming an armed wing of preexisting security groups and by assassinating Rifᶜat al-Mahjoub, former speaker of parliament (Mubarak 1995). Mahjoub's assassination led to massive sweeps in Asyut, Cairo, and Beni Swayf, among other places, which resulted in hundreds, if not thousands, of arrests. The only comparable sweep occurred in May 1987, when thousands were picked up immediately after the attempted assassination of former interior minister Hasan Abu Basha.

A shift from a policy of permissive repression to one that favored the elimination of the Gamaᶜa in Upper Egypt accelerated dramatically in 1992 following several critical events: clashes between Muslims and Christians in Manshiyat Nasir in Upper Egypt in March, where at least 13 people were killed; the assassination of the prominent intellectual Faraj Fuda in June 1992; and attacks on tourists (also in June).

In May 1992, the state deployed 2,000 soldiers in the Asyut district of

Dairut to impose a curfew after a series of demonstrations and clashes between Islamists and the police. A month later, a state of emergency was declared in some areas of Asyut. In November 1992, the authorities declared their intention to speed up the closure of private mosques, and in December 1992 the state sent 16,000 soldiers to "liberate" Imbaba in Greater Cairo. In January 1993, 8,000 soldiers sought Islamists in Masarah, Dairut, Sanaba, Manshiyat Nasir, and Dairut al-Sharif. In April 1993, an additional 5,000 soldiers were deployed in Asyut.[16]

The attempt to uproot the militants of the Gama'a was reactive and somewhat late. As one Egyptian analyst noted, "Since the emergence of the phenomenon [of violence] in Egyptian society in 1991, and even until 1993, it is possible to say that the security apparatus had no strategy. It dealt with events individually without linking them together and without forming a single political agenda to deal with [Islamic violence]" (Markaz al-Dirasat al-Istratijiyya fi al-Ahram 1995b, 425). Another observer comments that it was with the "liberation" of Imbaba in late 1992 and early 1993 that the state began developing a comprehensive strategy against Islamic violence (see *al-Wasat*, no. 60, March 22, 1993).

But after a decade of organizing social and political networks in Upper Egypt, the Islamists had the capacity to fight back. Just as important, the Gama'a had much to lose if it did not fight the state's attempt to roll back its organizational and societal gains. By 1992, the state was bent on depriving the Gama'a of its mosques, informal associations, and, as the insurgency developed, lives. In short, the Islamic insurgency of 1992 may well have been as much a defensive as an offensive strategy. And the indiscriminate nature of state repression gave Islamists further justification to rebel (Hafez 2003).

Indiscriminate State Repression

Islamic militancy in the 1990s did not produce a targeted state response. Instead, repression was brutal, swift, and indiscriminate. State repression encompassed not only the hard-core militants of the Gama'a and Islamic Jihad, but also supporters, sympathizers, families, and, for that matter, anyone wearing a beard with a trimmed moustache (see Human Rights Watch 1993; Amnesty International 1996). The arrest numbers in the 1990s indicate that the state threw its net too widely.[17] Between 1992 and 1997, more than 47,000 people were arrested, a number that is surely greater than the number of active militant Islamists. It was only in 1998 and 1999 that the state released more than 7,000 of these prisoners in response to the cessation of violence (see *al-Hayat*, April 27, 1999).[18]

In addition to mass arrests, the regime began using "hostage taking," whereby they detained the families and relatives, especially the wives, of suspected militants until the militants turned themselves over to the authorities (see Human Rights Watch 1995). Those arrested were regularly mistreated and tortured. As suggested previously, torture was not a new phenomenon in Egypt. What distinguished it in the 1990s was its indiscriminate application.

In addition to being indiscriminate, state repression was heavy-handed. For the first time since 1981, the state began referring Islamists, including those from the Muslim Brotherhood, to military courts, where "justice" was delivered hastily and without an appeal process. For example, in early June 1994, five defendants were brought to a military court to face capital charges. By mid-July 1994, they were found guilty and sentenced to death. They were executed in late August.

In the mid-1990s, the state increasingly adopted a shoot-to-kill policy, as evinced by the decline in the number of Islamists "injured" and the increase in the number of Islamists "killed."[19] The policy had a self-fulfilling dynamic because Islamists began to fight back.

Insurgents cited mass arrests, hostage taking, and torture by the authorities as the main reasons for the rebellion of 1992. In one of its documents, *Hawla al-Muqif al-Rahin bayna al-Gamaʿa al-Islamiyya wal-Nizam al-Misri* (Concerning the Current Situation between the Islamic Group and the Egyptian Regime), the Gamaʿa cites the following reasons for the increase in violence since 1992:

1. The storming of mosques controlled by the Gamaʿa.
2. The execution of some of the leaders of the Gamaʿa.
3. Torture of Gamaʿa members under arrest.

The document goes on to say that the Gamaʿa operated "peacefully" and limited its activities to holding conferences, distributing leaflets, and protest and strikes until the regime decided to eliminate it.[20] In another document, *Hata Mata* (How Long), issued in July 1991, the Gamaʿa argued that the main reason for the violence was the imprisonment of Islamists and their "torture and the torture of their wives and mothers that has become a daily habit in police branches and in the buildings of the central state security investigators."[21]

The fact that repression was indiscriminate gave added incentive to hitherto uncommitted activists to join the ranks of militants, either as a way to evade long prison sentences and torturous confinement or to take revenge against an "iniquitous" state that unfairly punished them and their families. H. T. Ibrahim (1996, 412–13) aptly sums up the effect of indiscriminate repression on Egyptian Islamists: "The logical consequence of the randomness in applying security measures in some areas was to create tensions between the public and the agencies of the police. In the midst of conducting a sharp confrontation with some of the Islamic groups, these agencies did not receive the sympathy of the public, which did not provide them a truly helping hand. . . . [Likewise,] the politics of arresting the wives and relatives of fugitives and taking them as hostages aided in inculcating the spirit of revenge between security agents and [the Islamic] groups."

Conclusion

Violent contention in the Egyptian Islamic movement became an increasingly acceptable protest repertoire in the 1990s due to three developments relating to the political opportunity structure. First, the deliberalization of the political system, after some tangible albeit limited progress in the 1980s, set the context for a delegitimized ruling government bent on limiting access to institutional contention. The inability of moderate Islamists to expand their political influence through state institutions during the 1990s gave the message of revolutionary Islamists empirical credibility. Second, the reactive nature of state repression against militant Islamists in Upper Egypt meant that Islamists had the organizational means to fight repression. It also meant that Islamists had organizational and societal gains worth protecting. Finally, indiscriminate repression gave Islamists added justification to rebel, as indicated by their communiqués and pamphlets. Indiscriminate repression meant that nonrebellion was no guarantee against state persecution. It also allowed the "injustice frames" promoted by insurgents to resonate with the broader Islamic field.

The case of Egypt highlights the necessity of focusing on exogenous political conditions that are propitious for violent contention. Contrary to prevailing ideational and socioeconomic perspectives on Islamic violence, the ideology and demographic backgrounds of militant Islamists are insufficient to explain the decision to rely on violence as a means to an end. As the case of Egypt illustrates, violent contention was a reaction to predatory state policies that threatened the organizational and societal gains of a movement, as well as a defensive reaction against an unpredictable future created by indiscriminate repression.

The case of Egypt also highlights the importance of investigating political violence, especially Islamic political violence, as a component of social movement theory. Violence in the Egyptian Islamic movement was not the domain of a marginal terrorist group. It was adopted by one of the major actors in the movement, one that organized social services, recruited members, and had adherents in several of Egypt's towns and cities. Moreover, the Gamaʿa was not born violent, but developed in that direction due to the political opportunity structures that prevailed in the 1980s and 1990s. The probability of future Islamic rebellions in the context of resurgent Islamism across the Muslim world points to the need for greater theoretical attention to Islamist violence by social movement theorists.

Notes

1. For an explanation of the end to the heightened violence, see Gerges (2000).

2. This tendency is represented in an array of descriptive publications that outline the structure and history of various radical groups and episodes of violence without comprehensively elucidating tactical choices (e.g., Rubin 1991; Kepel 1993; Martinez 2000).

3. The data for 1971–1993 were gathered from Abulala (1998, appendix). The data for 1995–1996 were collected from the 1995 and 1998 al-Hala al-Diniyya fi Misr reports (Cairo: Markaz al-Dirasat al-Siyasiyya wal-Istratijiyya). The data for 1997 were taken from the Taqrir Misr al-Mahrousa wal-ᶜAalam, 1997 (Cairo: Markaz al-Mahrousa lil-Nashr wal-Khidmat al-Sahafiyya wal-Mᵓaloumat, 1998). The data for 1994 and 1998 were collected from the Middle East Journal chronology.

4. The numbers were gathered from Ahmed 1995 (299–305); Ibn Khaldun files on Islamist activism; Abulala (1998) appendix; al-Hala al-Diniyya fi Misr (1998, 241); and Taqrir Misr al-Mahrousa wal-ᶜAalam, 1997 (1998, 679–80).

5. Some of the prominent government officials who were subject to assassinations and assassination attempts are Atif Sidqi (prime minister), Hasan al-Alfi (minister of interior), Safwat al-Sharif (minister of information), and President Mubarak in Adis Ababa, Ethiopia, in 1995.

6. The decision to form an armed wing was taken in late 1990, after a series of mosque raids by security forces and the assassination of ᶜAla Muhyi al-Din, the official spokesman of the Gamaᶜa, in September of that year (Mubarak 1995, 399–400). In the late 1980s and early 1990s, the Gamaᶜa, under the pretext of fighting Soviet forces in Afghanistan, sent some of its leaders and activists to set up training camps in Pakistan and Afghanistan to instruct militants in guerrilla and clandestine warfare (al-Hayat, September 25, 1999).

7. The Gamaᶜa also repeatedly claimed responsibility for attacking tourists. See its communiqués in al-Hayat (October 1, 1994, and April 21, 1996).

8. The Gamaᶜa repeatedly issued communiqués declaring responsibility for attacking tourist sites and trains. See al-Hayat (February 24, 1994; March 10, 1994; January 18, 1995; and November 10, 1995).

9. The Gamaᶜa repeatedly issued communiqués claiming responsibility for bombing banks and exchange bureaus. See al-Hayat (February 10, 1994; February 25, 1994; March 21, 1994).

10. The Gamaᶜa did not regularly claim responsibility for attacks on Copts, but it did not deny them or condemn them until two gruesome massacres took place in 1997. The first was in Abu Qurqas on February 12, when nine Coptic Christians were gunned down during prayer services. The second was on March 13 in Naj Dawud, where 13 Copts were killed (New York Times, March 15, 1997). See communiqués denying responsibility in al-Hayat (February 16, 1997, and March 16, 1997). The denials of the Gamaᶜa were not consistent. In one communiqué it denied all responsibility; in another it said misguided youth within the Gamaᶜa, lacking proper leadership due to the arrest of their leaders, were behind the attacks.

11. Among the notable intellectuals to come under attack were Faraj Fuda, an outspoken critic of Islamism killed in June 1992, and Najib Mahfouz, a Nobel Prize-winning novelist wounded in October 1994. Threats were also issued against intellectuals and entertainers: former Judge Said al-Ashmawi, feminist writer Nawal al-Sʾadawi, writer and professor Nasr Hamed Abu Zeid, and actor ʿAdel Imam. For the killing of "collaborators," see al-Hala al-Diniyya fi Misr (1995, 191, and 1998, 241).

12. See its communiqués in al-Hayat (January 21, 1996; May 1, 1996; February 13, 1997; June 26, 1997).

13. For a detailed account of the interference encountered by the Muslim Brotherhood candidates and cadres, see Egyptian Organization for Human Rights (1995).

14. Communiqué in al-Hayat, August 8, 1995.

15. The article was quoted at length in al-Hayat, January 28, 1996.

16. Information was gathered from the *Middle East Journal* chronology for 1992–1993.

17. The data for 1992–1994 were gathered from Ahmed (1995, 299–305); the 1995 figure was taken from Abulala (1998); the 1996 figure was taken from al-Hala al-Diniyya fi Misr (1998, 241); the 1997 figure was taken from *Taqrir Misr al-Mahrousa wal-ʿAalam, 1997* (1998).

18. The release of 7,000 prisoners within two years after the end of the insurgency indicates that the state had arrested many people on the mere suspicion of being militant.

19. Based on data collected from Abulala (1998); al-Hala al-Diniyya fi Misr (1998); and *Taqrir Misr al-Mahrousa wal-ʿAalam, 1997* (1998).

20. The document is extensively quoted in Mubarak (1995, 396–98).

21. The document is quoted in Markaz al-Dirasat al-Siyasiyya wal-Istratijiyya (1995a, 189).

Works Cited

Abulala, Muhammed Hussein. 1998. *Al-Anf al Dini fi Misr: Dirasat fi ʿalm al-Ijtimaʿa al-Siyyasi.* Cairo: al-Mahrousa.

Ahmed, Abdel Aati Muhammad. 1995. *Al-Harakat al-Islamiyya fi Misr wa Qadhiyet al-Tahawal al-Dimuqrati.* Cairo: Markaz al-Ahram lil-Tarjama wal-Nashr.

Amnesty International. 1996. "Egypt: Indefinite Detention and Systematic Torture— The Forgotten Victims." MDE 12/13/1996, July.

Ansari, Hamied N. 1984. "The Islamic Militants in Egyptian Politics." *International Journal of Middle East Studies* 16, 1 (March): 123–44.

———. 1986. *Egypt: The Stalled Society.* Albany: SUNY Press.

Auda, Huda Ragheb, and Hasanin Tawfiq Ibrahim. 1995. *Al-Ikhwan al-Muslimun wal-iyasa fi Misr: Dirasa fi al-Tahalufat al-Intikhabiya wal-Mumarasat al-Barlamaniya lil-Ikhwan al-Muslimin fi Dhal al-Taʿadudiya al-Siyasiyya al-Muqayada, 1984–1990.* Cairo: Markaz al-Mahrous lil-Bihouth wal-Tadrib wal-Nashr.

Ayubi, Nazih N. 1980. "The Political Revival of Islam: The Case of Egypt." *International Journal of Middle East Studies* 12, 4 (December): 481–99.

Bakr, Hasan. 1996. *Al-ʿAnf al-Siyyasi fi Misr, 1977–1993.* Cairo: Markez al-Mahrousa lil-Bihouth wal-Tadrib wal-Nashr.

Bayat, Asef. 1997. *Street Politics: Poor People's Movements in Iran*. New York: Columbia University Press.

Berejikian, Jeffrey. 1992. "Revolutionary Collective Action and the Agent-Structure Problem." *American Political Science Review* 86, 3 (September): 647–57.

Brockett, Charles D. 1991. "The Structure of Political Opportunities and Peasant Mobilization in Central America." *Comparative Politics* 23: 253–74.

———. 1995. "A Protest-Cycle Resolution of the Repression/Popular-Protest Paradox." Pp. 117–44 in *Repertoires and Cycles of Collective Action*, ed. Mark Traugott. Durham, N.C.: Duke University Press.

Burgat, François, and William Dowell. 1993. *The Islamic Movement in North Africa*. Austin: Center for Middle Eastern Studies at the University of Texas at Austin.

Campagna, Joel. 1996. "From Accommodation to Confrontation: The Muslim Brotherhood in the Mubarak Years." *Journal of International Affairs* 50, 1 (Summer).

Crenshaw, Martha. 1978. *Revolutionary Terrorism: The FLN in Algeria, 1954–1962*. Stanford, Calif.: Hoover Institution Press.

Davis, S., and J. Hodson. 1982. *Witnesses to Political Violence in Guatemala: The Suppression of a Rural Development Movement*. New York: Oxfam America.

Dekmejian, R. Hrair. 1995. *Islam in Revolution: Fundamentalism in the Arab World*. 2d ed. Syracuse, N.Y.: Syracuse University Press.

Della Porta, Donatella. 1988. "Recruitment Processes in Clandestine Political Organizations: Italian Left-Wing Terrorism." *International Social Movement Research* 1: 155–69.

———. 1992. "Introduction: On Individual Motivations in Underground Political Organizations." Pp. 3–28 in *Social Movements and Violence: Participation in Underground Organizations*, International Social Movement Research, vol. 4, ed. Bert Klandermans and Donatella Della Porta. Greenwich, Conn.: JAI Press.

———. 1995a. *Social Movements, Political Violence, and the State: A Comparative Analysis of Italy and Germany*. Cambridge: Cambridge University Press.

———. 1995b. "Left-Wing Terrorism in Italy." Pp. 105–59 in *Terrorism in Context*, ed. Martha Crenshaw. University Park: Pennsylvania State University Press.

———. 1996. "Social Movements and the State. Thoughts on the Policing of Protest." Pp. 62–92 in *Comparative Perspectives on Social Movements*, ed. Doug McAdam, John D. McCarthy, and Mayer N. Zald. Cambridge: Cambridge University Press.

al-Din, Nabil Sharaf. 1998. *Umara᾽ wa Muwatinun: Rasd li-Dhahirt al-Islam al-Haraki fi Misr Khilal ῾Aqd al-Tis῾inat*. Cairo: Madbouli.

Dix, Robert. 1984. "Why Revolutions Succeed and Fail." *Polity* 16, 3 (Spring): 423–46.

Eckstein, Harry. 1965. "On the Etiology of Internal Wars." *History and Theory* 4, 2: 133–63.

Egyptian Organization for Human Rights. 1992. *The Sectarian Massacre in Dairut*. Egyptian Organization for Human Rights Report, May 7.

———. 1995. *Democracy Jeopardized: The Egyptian Organization for Human Rights Account of Egyptian Parliamentary Elections, 1995*. Egyptian Organization for Human Rights Report, December.

Fahmy, Ninette S. 1998. "The Performance of the Muslim Brotherhood in the Egyptian Syndicates: An Alternative Formula for Reform?" *Middle East Journal* 52, 4 (Autumn): 551–62.

Faksh, Mahmud A. 1997. *The Future of Islam in the Middle East: Fundamentalism in Egypt, Algeria, and Saudi Arabia.* Westport, Conn.: Praeger.

Farhi, Farideh. 1990. *States and Urban-Based Revolutions: Iran and Nicaragua.* Urbana: University of Illinois Press.

Fatah, Nabil Abdel. 1995. *Al-Wajeh wal-Qinaᶜa: al-Haraka al-Islamiyya wal-ᶜAnf wal-Tatbiᶜa.* Cairo: Shishat lil-Dirasat wal-Nashr wal-Tawziᶜa.

Gamson, William A. 1975. *The Strategy of Social Protest.* Homewood, Ill.: Dorsey.

Gamson, William, Bruce Fireman, and Steven Rytina. 1982. *Encounters with Unjust Authority.* Homewood, Ill.: Dorsey.

Gerges, Fawaz A. 2000. "The End of the Islamic Insurgency in Egypt? Costs and Prospects." *Middle East Journal* 4 (Fall): 592–612.

Gerlach, Luther P., and Virginia H. Hine. 1970. *People, Power, Change: Movements of Social Transformation.* Indianapolis: Bobbs-Merrill.

Goldstein, Robert J. 1983. *Political Repression in Nineteenth-Century Europe.* London: Croom Helm.

Goldstone, Jack A. 1991. *Revolution and Rebellion in the Early Modern World.* Berkeley: University of California Press.

Goodwin, Jeff. 1997. "State-Centered Approaches to Social Revolutions: Strengths and Limitations of a Theoretical Tradition." Pp. 11–37 in *Theorizing Revolutions*, ed. John Foran. London: Routledge.

Goodwin, Jeff, and Theda Skocpol. 1989. "Explaining Revolutions in the Contemporary Third World." *Politics and Society* 17, 4: 489–509.

Gupta, Dipak K., Harinder Singh, and Tom Sprague. 1993. "Government Coercion of Dissidents: Deterrence or Provocation?" *Journal of Conflict Resolution* 37, 2 (June): 301–39.

Gurr, Ted Robert. 1970. *Why Men Rebel.* Princeton, N.J.: Princeton University Press.

———. 1986. "Persisting Patterns of Repression and Rebellion: Foundations for a General Theory of Political Coercion." Pp. 149–68 in *Persistent Patterns and Emergent Structures in a Waning Century*, ed. Margaret P. Karns. New York: Praeger.

Gurr, Ted Robert, and Jack A. Goldstone. 1991. "Comparisons and Policy Implications." Pp. 324–52 in *Revolutions in the Late Twentieth Century*, ed. Jack Goldstone, Ted Robert Gurr, and Farrokh Moshiri. Boulder: Westview.

Haddad, Yvonne. 1992. "Islamists and the 'Problem of Israel': The 1967 Awakening." *Middle East Journal* 46, 2 (Spring): 266–85.

Hafez, Mohammed M. 2000. "Armed Islamic Movements and Political Violence in Algeria." *Middle East Journal* 4: 572–91.

———. 2003. *Why Muslims Rebel: Repression and Resistance in the Islamic World.* Boulder: Lynne Rienner.

Hardin, Russell. 1982. *Collective Action.* Baltimore: Johns Hopkins University Press.

Hibbs, Douglas A., Jr. 1973. *Mass Political Violence: A Cross-National Causal Analysis.* New York: Wiley.

Hinnebusch, Raymond A., Jr. 1985. *Egyptian Politics under Sadat: The Post-Populist Development of an Authoritarian-Modernizing State.* Cambridge: Cambridge University Press.

Hoffman, Valerie J. 1995. "Muslim Fundamentalists: Psychosocial Profiles." Pp. 199–230 in *Fundamentalisms Comprehended*, ed. Martin Marty. Chicago: University of Chicago Press.

Horne, Alistair. 1987. *A Savage War of Peace: Algeria, 1954–1962*. Rev. ed. New York: Penguin.

Human Rights Watch. 1993. "Egypt: Human Rights Abuses Mount in 1993." New York: Human Rights Watch, October.

———. 1995. "Egypt: Hostage-Taking and Intimidation by Security Forces." New York: Human Rights Watch, January.

Huntington, Samuel P. 1968. *Political Order in Changing Societies*. New Haven, Conn.: Yale University Press.

Ibrahim, Hasanin Tawfiq. 1996. "Al-Ihtijaj al-Jamaʿai wal ʿAnf al-Siyyasi." In *Haqiqet al-Tʿadudiya al-Siyasiyya fi Misr: Dirasat fi al-Tahawul al-Raʾsmali wal-Musharaka al-Siyasiyya*, ed. Mustapha Kamel al-Sayid and Kamal al- Manoufa. Cairo: Markaz al-Bihouth al-ʿArabiyya, Maktibet al-Madbouli.

Ibrahim, Saad Eddin. 1980. "Anatomy of Egypt's Militant Islamic Groups, Methodological Note, and Preliminary Findings." *International Journal of Middle East Studies* 12: 423–53.

———. 1996. "The Changing Face of Egypt's Islamic Activism." In *Egypt, Islam, and Democracy*, ed. Saad Eddin Ibrahim. Cairo: American University in Cairo Press.

Ismail, Salwa. 2000. "The Popular Movement Dimensions of Contemporary Militant Islamism: Socio-Spatial Determinants in the Cairo Urban Setting." *Comparative Study of Society and History* 42, 2 (April): 363–93.

Jansen, Johannes J. G. 1986. *The Neglected Duty: The Creed of Sadat's Assassins and Islamic Resurgence in the Middle East*. New York: Macmillan.

Jenkins, J. Craig, and Charles Perrow. 1977. "Insurgency of the Powerless: Farm Worker Movements, 1946–1972." *American Sociological Review* 42: 249–68.

Keddie, Nikki R. 1994. "The Revolt of Islam, 1700 to 1993: Comparative Considerations and Relations to Imperialism." *Comparative Study of Society and History* 36, 2 (April): 463–87.

Kepel, Gilles. 1993. *Muslim Extremism in Egypt: The Prophet and the Pharaoh*. Translated by Jon Rothschild. Berkeley: University of California Press.

Khawaja, Marwan. 1993. "Repression and Popular Collective Action: Evidence from the West Bank." *Sociological Forum* 8, 1: 47–71.

Kiernan, Ben. 1996. *The Pol Pot Regime: Race, Power, and Genocide in Cambodia under the Khmer Rouge, 1975–1979*. New Haven, Conn.: Yale University Press.

Kitschelt, Herbert. 1986. "Political Opportunity Structures and Political Protest: Anti-Nuclear Movements in Four Democracies." *British Journal of Political Science* 16: 57–85.

Klandermans, Bert. 1984. "Mobilization and Participation: Social-Psychological Expansions of Resource Mobilization Theory." *American Sociological Review* 49: 583–600.

Korany, Bahgat. 1998. "Restricted Democratization from Above: Egypt." Pp. 39–69 in *Political Liberalization and Democratization in the Arab World*, vol. 2: *Comparative Experiences*, ed. Bahgat Korany, Rex Brynen, and Paul Noble. Boulder: Lynne Rienner.

Kriesi, Hanspeter, Ruud Koopmans, Jan Willem Duyvendak, and Marco G. Giugni. 1992. "New Social Movements and Political Opportunities in Western Europe." *European Journal of Political Research* 22: 219–44.

———. 1995. *New Social Movements in Western Europe*. Minneapolis: University of Minnesota Press.

Kurzman, Charles. 1996. "Structural Opportunity and Perceived Opportunity in Social Movement Theory: The Iranian Revolution of 1979." *American Sociological Review* 61 (February): 153–70.

Lichbach, Mark. 1987. "Deterrence or Escalation? The Puzzle of Aggregate Studies of Repression and Dissent." *Journal of Conflict Resolution* 31: 266–97.

———. 1995. *The Rebel's Dilemma.* Ann Arbor: University of Michigan Press.

Lichbach, Mark, and Ted R. Gurr. 1981. "The Conflict Process: A Formal Model." *Journal of Conflict Resolution* 25 (March): 3–29.

Markaz al-Dirasat al-Istratijiyya fi al-Ahram. 1995a. *Al-Hala al-Diniyya fi Misr.* Cairo: Markaz al-Dirasat al-Siyasiyya wal-Istratijiyya.

———. 1995b. *Al-Taqrir al-Istratiji al-Arabi, 1994.* Cairo: Markaz al-Dirasat al-Istratijiyya fi al-Ahram.

———. 1998. *Al-Hala al-Diniyya fi Misr.* Cairo: Markaz al-Dirasat al-Siyasiyya wal-Istratijiyya.

Martinez, Luis. 2000. *The Algerian Civil War.* New York: Columbia University Press.

Mason, David T., and Dale A. Krane. 1989. "The Political Economy of Death Squads: Toward a Theory of the Impact of State-Sanctioned Terror." *International Studies Quarterly* 33, 2 (June): 175–98.

May, Rachel. 2001. *Terror in the Countryside: Campesino Responses to Political Violence in Guatemala, 1954–1985.* Athens: Ohio University Press.

McAdam, Doug, and Ronnelle Paulsen. 1993. "Specifying the Relationship between Social Ties and Activism." *American Journal of Sociology* 99, 3 (November): 640–67.

Melucci, Alberto. 1996. *Challenging Codes: Collective Action in the Information Age.* Cambridge: Cambridge University Press.

Mishal, Shaul, and Avraham Sela. 2000. *The Palestinian Hamas: Vision, Violence, and Coexistence.* New York: Columbia University Press.

Mubarak, Hisham. 1995. *Al-Irhabiyun Qadimun: Dirasa Muqarana bayn Mouqif al-Ikhwan al-Muslimin wa Jamaᶜat al-Jihad min Qadhiet al-ᶜAnf (1928–1994).* Cairo: Markaz al-Mahrousa lil-Nashr al-Khidmat al-Sahafiyya wal-Mᵓaloumat.

Muller, Edward N. 1985. "Income Inequality, Regime Repressiveness, and Political Violence." *American Sociological Review* 50, 1 (February): 47–61.

Muller, Edward N., and Erich Weede. 1990. "Cross-National Variation in Political Violence: A Rational Action Approach." *Journal of Conflict Resolution* 34, 4 (December): 624–51.

Mustapha, Hala. 1996. *Al-Dawla wal-Harakat al-Islamiyya al-Muᶜaridha: Bayn al-Muhadana wal-Muwajaha fi ᶜAhdi al-Sadat wa Mubarak.* Cairo: Markaz al-Mahrousa lil-Nashr wal-Khidmat al-Sahafiyya wal-Mᵓaloumat.

Oberschall, Anthony. 1973. *Social Conflict and Social Movements.* Englewood Cliffs, N.J.: Prentice-Hall.

Oliver, Pamela. 1980. "Rewards and Punishment as Selective Incentives for Collective Action." *American Journal of Sociology* 85: 1356–75.

Opp, Karl-Dieter. 1988. "Community Integration and Incentives for Political Protest." *International Social Movements Research* 1: 83–101.

Opp, Karl-Dieter, and Wolfgang Roehl. 1990. "Repression, Micromobilization, and Political Protest." *Social Forces* 69: 521–47.

Qandil, Amani. 1995. ᶜAmaliet al-Tahawal al-Dimuqrati fi Misr, 1981–1993. Cairo: Markaz Ibn Khaldun, Dar al-Amin lil-Nashr wal-Tawziᶜa.

———. 1996. "Al-Jamaᶜat al-Mihniya wal-Musharaka al-Siyasiyya." In *Haqiqet al-Tadudiya al-Siyasiyya fi Misr: Dirasat fi al-Tahawul al-Raismali wal-Musharaka al-Siyasiyya*, ed. Mustapha Kamel al-Sayid and Kamal al-Manoufa. Cairo: Markaz al-Bihouth al-Arabiyya, Maktibet al-Madbouli.

Radhi, Muhsin. 1990/1991. *Al-Ikhwan al-Muslimun that Qibet al-Barlaman*. Vols. 1 and 2. Cairo: Dar al-Nashr wal-Tawziᶜa.

Ramadan, Abdel Azim. 1995. *Jamaᶜat al-Takfir fi Misr: al-Usul al-Tarikhiya wal-Fikriya*. Cairo: al-Hayaʾa al-Misriya al-ᶜAlmiya lil-Kitab.

Rubin, Barry. 1991. *Islamic Fundamentalism in Egyptian Politics*. New York: St. Martin's.

al-Shawkabi, ᶜAmru. 1995. "Al-Mᶜaraka al-Intikhabiya: Dhawahir Jadida." In *Al-Intikhabat al-Barlamaniya fi Misr, 1995*, ed. Hala Mustapha. Cairo: Markaz al-Dirasat al-Siyasiyya wal-Istratijiyya.

al-Shourbaji, Manar. 1994. "Al-Qadhaya al-Dasturiya wal Qanuniya fi Fatret Riaʾset Mubarak al-Thaniya." In *Al-Tatawur al-Siyyasi fi Misr, 1982–1992*, ed. Muhammed Sifa al-Din Kharboush. Cairo: Center for Political Research and Studies.

Sivan, Emmanuel. 1985. *Radical Islam: Medieval Theology and Modern Politics*. New Haven, Conn.: Yale University Press.

Skocpol, Theda. 1979. *States and Social Revolutions*. Cambridge: Cambridge University Press.

Smith, Christian. 1991. *The Emergence of Liberation Theology: Radical Religion and Social Movement Theory*. Chicago: University of Chicago Press.

Snow, D. A., L. A. Zurcher, and S. Ekland-Olson. 1980. "Social Networks and Social Movements." *American Sociological Review* 45: 787–801.

Snyder, David. 1976. "Theoretical and Methodological Problems in the Analysis of Governmental Coercion and Collective Violence." *Journal of Political and Military Sociology* 4: 277–93.

Snyder, David, and Charles Tilly. 1972. "Hardship and Collective Violence in France, 1830 to 1960." *American Sociological Review* 37, 5 (October): 520–32.

Springborg, Robert. 1989. *Mubarak's Egypt: Fragmentation of the Political Order*. Boulder: Westview.

Tarrow, Sidney. 1989. *Democracy and Disorder: Social Conflict, Protest, and Politics in Italy, 1965–1975*. Oxford: Oxford University Press.

———. 1994. *Power in Movement: Social Movements, Collective Action, and Politics*. Cambridge: Cambridge University Press.

———. 1996. "States and Opportunities: The Political Structuring of Social Movements." Pp. 41–61 in *Comparative Perspectives on Social Movements*, ed. Doug McAdam, John D. McCarthy, and Mayer N. Zald. Cambridge: Cambridge University Press.

al-Tawil, Muhammed. 1992. *Al-Ikhwan fi al-Barlaman*. Cairo: al-Maktab al-Misri al-Hadith.

Tilly, Charles. 1978. *From Mobilization to Revolution*. Reading, Mass.: Addison-Wesley.

Vatikiotis, P. J. 1987. *Islam and the State*. London: Croom Helm.

Voll, John O. 1983. "Renewal and Reform in Islamic History: *Tajdid* and *Islah*." Pp. 32–47 in *Voices of Resurgent Islam*, ed. John Esposito. Oxford: Oxford University Press.

White, Robert W. 1989. "From Peaceful Protest to Guerrilla War: Micromobilization of the Provisional Irish Republican Army." *American Journal of Sociology* 94, 6: 1277–1302.

Wickham-Crowley, Timothy P. 1991. *Exploring Revolution: Essays on Latin American Insurgency and Revolutionary Theory.* Armonk, N.Y.: M. E. Sharpe.

———. 1992. *Guerrillas and Revolution in Latin America: A Comparative Study of Insurgents and Regimes since 1956.* Princeton, N.J.: Princeton University Press.

Zaki, Moheb. 1995. *Civil Society and Democratization in Egypt, 1981–1994.* Cairo: Konrad Adenauer Foundation and the Ibn Khaldoun Center.

Zimmermann, Ekkart. 1980. "Macro-Comparative Research on Political Protest." Pp. 167–237 in *Handbook of Political Conflict: Theory and Research,* ed. Ted Gurr. New York: Free Press.

Three

Repertoires of Contention in Contemporary Bahrain

Fred H. Lawson

On the morning of November 25, 1994, runners taking part in a charity marathon sponsored by a major Saudi investment company, Round Table Pizza, and the Hash House Harriers set out from Bahrain's capital city, Manama, and headed into the villages that ring the metropolis to the west and south. As men and women, dressed in shorts and T-shirts, wound their way through the narrow side roads inhabited largely by the country's disadvantaged Shiʿi community, they encountered scattered groups of residents who blocked the course and raised banners that proclaimed: "You are guests in our country, but you have no respect for our feelings" and "We are not against sports, just [against] disrobing" (Bahry 1997, 56). Just before 2 PM, the lead runners attempted to shove their way through a crowd of protesters, precipitating a melee that quickly degenerated into rock throwing and fist fights. Security forces descended upon the suburbs that night and took some 20 villagers into custody. The next day, mass demonstrations erupted in several districts in and around Manama. The protests escalated over the following week, culminating in the arrest of a prominent Shiʿi religious scholar, Shaykh ʿAli Salman, on December 5. Authorities charged that his sermons incited the populace to attack the runners.

ʿAli Salman's detention and subsequent deportation, together with two other respected Shiʿi activists, ignited a popular uprising that shook Bahrain for more than four years. On its face, the 1994–1998 uprising bears the hallmarks of an Islamist protest movement. As Gregory Gause (1997, 151) has noted, "The most serious disturbances have been concentrated in Shiʿi neighborhoods and villages. The Shiʿi majority on the island has historically chafed under the rule of the Sunni Al Khalifas [the ruling family], who have been very skillful in framing political dissent in sectarian terms to divide potential

89

opposition movements. [Furthermore,] [s]ome Bahraini Sunnis sympathetic to the cause of political reform have been put off by the violence in Shiʿi communities [that accompanied the rebellion]."

Nevertheless, as Gause recognizes, to label the uprising an Islamist protest movement would be misleading. The objectives articulated by the protesters concerned religion only tangentially. At the heart of the rebellion lay a cluster of secular demands: that the ruler (*amir*) restore the country's popularly elected National Assembly, according to the provisions of the 1973 constitution; that the state of emergency declared in 1975 be terminated and that its draconian restrictions on freedom of expression and association be rescinded; and that the government take concrete steps to reduce unemployment, which had taken a disproportionate, but not exclusive, toll on younger Shiʿis (Fakhro 1997; Darwish 1999).

In short, it is more fruitful to conceive of the uprising as a contemporary instance of what Edmund Burke calls "social movements in Islamic societies." This way of understanding events in Bahrain from 1994 to 1998 highlights not the religious aspects of the rebellion but rather "the social and political structures within which such movements arise, regardless of the cultural idiom in which grievances are expressed" (Burke 1988, 18–19). And in fact, the outbreak of the uprising has most often been explained in terms of four broad trends in the country's political economy:

1. Steadily rising levels of unemployment;
2. The emergence of a glaring gap between the upper middle class—consisting of both "traditional merchant families and a few newly elevated families, particularly Shiʿis of Arab or Persian origins" and "a professional salaried and broker merchant stratum whose power was dependent on income from government-sponsored services"—and the suburban lower middle class and rural poor who, "having benefited from the enlarged education and health services of the state, acquired more political awareness and expectations for development, with no corresponding opportunities" (Seikaly 1996, 5);
3. The spread of exclusive housing and other kinds of conspicuous consumption into less affluent districts surrounding the capital (Seikaly 2001, 191);
4. What Louay Bahry (1997, 51) calls "the unwillingness of the Bahraini government to employ Shiʿa in the lower ranks of the army and the police force, presumably because of doubts about their loyalty to the regime, [which] makes Shiʿa feel they are second-class citizens."

These trends no doubt heightened the overall level of discontent among disadvantaged and disenfranchised Bahrainis in general, and among poorer members of the indigenous Shiʿa in particular, during the early 1990s. But any attempt to account for the 1994–1998 uprising in such terms is likely to have trouble addressing two crucial questions. First, why did simmering popular discontent erupt into mass protest in December 1994, instead of at any other time? Second, why did the rebellion assume the peculiar form(s) it did in subsequent months?

This chapter begins by proposing an explanation for the outbreak of the uprising that focuses on four interrelated developments on the islands toward the end of 1994 that posed a direct threat to powerful forces outside the dominant social coalition (Goldstone and Tilly 2001). It then offers a preliminary overview of the distinctive repertoires of contention that characterized successive stages of the 1994–1998 uprising (Tarrow 1995; Tilly 1995a, 1995b; White 1995a, 1995b). In doing so, the chapter indicates how shifts from one contentious repertoire to another resulted from efforts on the part of the authorities to parry initiatives undertaken by the protesters. Finally, it lays out one important way in which the trajectory of popular contention in this case differed from protest cycles in contemporary Europe.

Rethinking the Origins of the Uprising

There can be little question that underlying trends in Bahrain's political economy alienated important segments of the local population from the Al Khalifah regime after the 1990–1991 Gulf war. Nor is there any doubt that popular grievances assumed an increasingly sectarian cast over time. As one of the country's established Shiʿi merchants told the *Washington Post* (June 13, 1995), "We are totally kept out of all the major ministries. . . . If you switch on the TV, there is not a single program that refers to us, our history, our folklore, our geography. We are nothing." Yet it was only in the context of four more immediate developments that the pervasive discontent generated by relatively long-term political-economic trends exploded into mass protest on the islands during the final weeks of 1994.

In the first place, state officials attempted to curry favor with well-to-do businesspeople in the early 1990s by sponsoring the construction of modern shopping centers. The director of one of these complexes boasted to reporters that "it will house a supermarket, a bank, garment shops, jewelry, and a wide range of other stores so that people can do all their shopping under one roof" (*Gulf Daily News*, October 12, 1994). Such government-supported retail centers proliferated in the suburbs around Manama throughout 1993–1994, diverting a significant amount of business away from older commercial establishments (*Middle East Economic Digest* [*MEED*], September 17, 1993, and April 8, 1994). As a result, sales at many South Asian–owned shops in downtown Manama appear to have dropped during the last quarter of 1994 (*Wall Street Journal*, June 13, 1995).

Furthermore, the new state-sponsored shopping centers posed a direct challenge to private entrepreneurs engaged in similar projects. In the predominantly Shi'i suburb of Sanabis, for instance, the state-affiliated Housing Bank solicited bids in the spring of 1994 to build a 340-shop retail complex on a site adjacent to land on which one of the country's largest private land development companies, the Hajji Hassan Group, had already proposed to build a 28,000-square-meter shopping center (*MEED*, March 11, 1994). Consequently, both well-to-do commercial entrepreneurs and smaller shopkeepers, particularly those who lacked personal connections to the ruling family, found their livelihoods increasingly threatened by efforts on the part of state officials to promote large-scale, capital-intensive shopping centers during the last months of 1994.

Second, government funds allocated to support small-scale manufacturing following the Gulf war ended up financing the operations of companies that employed foreign workers, instead of boosting enterprises that were committed to hiring Bahraini citizens. After acquiring ownership of a major fish processing plant from the Ministry of Agriculture and Fisheries in November 1993, for example, the locally based Banz Group immediately negotiated a contract with an Indian company to operate the facility (*MEED*, November 26, 1993). In June 1994, the local Trans Arabian Investment Bank opened a branch in Bangalore "as a link for Indian industrialists setting up in Bahrain" (*MEED*, June 17, 1994). Two weeks later, the Ministry of Development and Industry announced plans to work with the Japan International Cooperation Agency to encourage local companies to emulate "Japanese-style management practices" (*MEED*, July 1, 1994). That August saw the launching of a Global Technologies Development Corporation, whose stated objective was "to promote and develop small-scale industrial projects initially in the Middle East and the Indian subcontinent," as well as to supervise the construction of a new Pakistani-managed electrical wire plant (*MEED*, August 12 and 19, 1994). Prospects for future employment in light industry, finance, and even commerce therefore dimmed for a sizable number of Shi'is as government policy increasingly favored companies that relied on expatriate labor.

Third, state programs to promote trade and light manufacturing drained the treasury of scarce resources that might instead have been used to modernize Bahrain's rapidly deteriorating heavy industrial sector. Long-standing plans to upgrade the aging Bahrain Petroleum Company refinery at Sitra were scaled back in late 1993, when foreign firms refused to put up the investment capital needed to purchase state-of-the-art equipment (*MEED*, November 5, 1993, and October 14, 1994). Persistent shortages of operating funds led the management of Aluminum Bahrain (ALBA) to ignore efforts by Middle Eastern aluminum producers to implement a coordinated cut in regional production as a means of reviving slumping prices on world markets (*MEED*, February 11, 1994). At the end of March 1994, ALBA announced that it intended to take the unprecedented step of issuing $50 million worth of corporate bonds to cover loans that the company had already taken out to finance a variety of projects (*MEED*, April 8, 1994). Plans to build a new containerized port facility that might have attracted additional work to the Arab Shipbuilding and Repair Yard were once again postponed that fall, while the shipyard's primary competitor, Dubai Drydocks in the United Arab Emirates, continued to expand (*MEED*, November 25, 1994). Even relatively profitable firms like the Bahrain Aluminum Extrusion Company confronted the twin difficulties of insufficient capitalization and heightened competition from more efficient plants in Saudi Arabia and the United Arab Emirates (*MEED*, November 26, 1993).

Consequently, the likelihood of securing satisfactory employment in the heavy industrial sector of the Bahraini economy steadily shrank for growing numbers of disadvantaged Shi'is. Some 200 unemployed laborers tried to push the regime to take steps to address the situation by taking part in a peaceful demonstration outside the Ministry of Labor and Social Affairs at the end of June. When 1,500 workers returned to the ministry three days later and attempted to stage a sit-in, the police released tear gas to disperse the crowd (Human Rights Watch 1997, 29). Popular demonstrations broke out once again at the end of August, organized by a trio of younger Shi'i religious scholars who had gained notoriety as a result of their Friday sermons, which explicitly criticized the regime's economic policies (Stork 1996, 46).

Finally, nonelite women faced tighter restrictions on their educational and employment opportunities. The demand for skilled female employees in local trading companies and banking institutions had increased steadily throughout the 1980s, when the government adopted a series of measures to boost the commercial and financial sectors of the local economy and strongly encouraged companies to replace foreign workers with Bahraini nationals (Lawson 1989; Seikaly 1994). As a result of such programs, younger women, including large numbers of Shi'is from suburban and rural districts, came to constitute a majority of the students enrolled at the National University of Bahrain. May Seikaly (1997, 138) observes that these women, "unlike university male students . . . [were] usually chosen from the top performing students of [the country's] high schools." They tended to be "very ambitious and hardworking" and looked forward to moving into skilled or professional occupations after graduation.

During their time at university, Shi'i women became exposed to a wide variety of ideas. Among these were the notions of social and political reform advocated by Islamist activists. The impact that Islamist scholars and preachers had on university-educated women can be discerned in a noticeable change in the predominant form of dress on campus: by 1993, some 95 percent of female students at the National University were covering themselves in accordance with strict Islamist tenets (Seikaly 1997, 144). Seikaly reports that such students "insist that this new attire is not the traditional *abaya*, but follows particular Islamic prescriptions. In their view it is a modern, educated

Muslim woman's choice. It also signifies a whole spectrum of lifestyle, the understanding of which is also modern in its concern with segregation, education, the family, and woman's role" (139).

Nevertheless, the evident spread of Islamist influence among educated women prompted the authorities to promulgate new regulations governing university life. Admission requirements were raised, preventing applicants from the poorer suburbs from gaining access to the system of higher education unless they found an elite sponsor willing to vouch for them (Darwish 1999, 87). In addition, the Ministry of Labor and Social Affairs organized a cluster of public seminars in October and November 1994 that emphasized women's responsibilities toward their families and neighborhoods. The seminars highlighted effective methods of child rearing and means "to change some of society's ways that have hampered the buildup of strong family infrastructure and to overcome some of the practices and beliefs that harm a marriage" (*Gulf Daily News,* October 18, 1994, and November 3, 1994).

Taken together, these four developments dramatically heightened the degree of threat facing powerful forces outside the dominant social coalition. Small shopkeepers, skilled clerical and commercial employees, workers in heavy industry, and the relatively new class of well-educated female office workers all found their current and future positions in the domestic political economy increasingly jeopardized in 1994. Consequently, when the authorities arrested and deported three outspoken Shiʿi critics of the regime in early December, disaffected Shiʿis from each of these social forces took to the streets in protest.

Repertoires of Contention
and the 1994–1998 Uprising

Popular contention engendered by the threats that galvanized diverse components of Bahrain's heterogeneous Shiʿa to engage in collective action during the last weeks of 1994 assumed a variety of shapes as the uprising proceeded. In any given period, contentiousness gravitated toward one or two specific kinds of activity on the part of protesters. A limited number of significant innovations in contentious action appeared during each time period as well (Tarrow 1998, 102). Taken together, the dominant forms of protest and the most important innovations that were present during particular intervals constituted the distinctive repertoires of contention that characterized successive phases of the 1994–1998 uprising.

Charles Tilly, who originated the concept of contentious repertoires, asserts that the regime's response to initiatives carried out by challengers should be included as an integral component of the repertoire of contention at any given time. This is for two reasons. First, actions undertaken by the authorities often provoke popular challenges to the established order, so it is generally misleading to assume that protesters make the first move. Second, "repertoires of collective action designate not individual performances but means of interaction among pairs or larger sets of actors. A company, not an individual, maintains a repertoire" (Tilly 1995a, 27). The latter claim is patently false, as any pianist knows. The former, on the other hand, represents a profound insight into the dynamics of popular contention, which can provide a basis for answering the key question of why one contentious repertoire comes to be replaced by another.

Existing studies of contentious repertoires deal with the question of why repertoires change by invoking long-term factors that determine the costs and benefits of collective action for those challenging the status quo. Tilly (1995b) argues that contentious repertoires in Britain changed dramatically between 1750 and 1840 due to such things as the gradual expansion of capital-intensive manufacturing, the steady consolidation of the central state apparatus, and the escalating rate of urbanization. As Arthur Stinchcombe (1987, 1249) remarks, in Tilly's view "the repertoire of workable forms of collective action changes in evolutionary correspondence with these great changes in social structure." James White (1995b, 156–60) similarly explains significant changes in repertoires of popular protest in early modern Japan in terms of shifts in national and provincial economic organization, waves of economic prosperity and crisis, and broad transformations in popular consciousness. Mark Beissinger (2002, 49) accounts for variations in the tide of nationalist mobilization during the last years of the Soviet Union by connecting them to a complex "interaction between preexisting structural conditions, institutional constraints, and event-specific processes." Flemming Mikkelsen (1999) explains significant alterations in contentious politics in Denmark between 1914 and 1995 by situating them in the context of changing patterns of international conflict and successive phases of the global business cycle.

This study complements existing analyses of long-term trends by highlighting the short-term efforts that the authorities make to parry challengers' initiatives. Different sorts of regime response have a direct impact on the costs of engaging in collective protest, as well as on the way in which these costs are distributed among actual and potential protesters (Oberschall 1994). Most students of collective action agree that whenever rulers respond to popular protest with tactics that are "more tolerant, selective and softer," the likelihood of subsequent protests increases (Della Porta 1996, 90). On the other hand, to the extent that a regime carries out measures that are highly repressive, comparatively diffuse, and generally "harder," challengers can be expected to have difficulty mobilizing further protest. Empirical tests of these twin propositions have failed to produce clear-cut results (Zimmermann 1980; Lichbach 1987; Opp and Roehl 1990, 522–26; Rasler 1996). Nevertheless, shifts in regime tactics offer a promising way to explain changes from one repertoire of contention to another, regardless of whether such tactical shifts can persuasively be linked to the likelihood that popular protest will be suppressed. In the case of Bahrain, it is clear that the measures adopted by the government to counter initiatives undertaken by its primary opponents played a major role in altering the repertoires of contention that characterized successive phases of the 1994–1998 uprising.

Playing by the Rules:
September 1992–November 1994

When popular protest reappeared in Bahrain in the aftermath of the 1990–1991 Gulf war, it took the form of collective petitions addressed directly to the ruler (*amir*). Such petitions were usually drawn up in formal terms by influential public figures, who were most often former members of the National Assembly, which had been summarily dissolved by amiri decree in August 1975. The petitions were then circulated among the country's social and intellectual elites, a number of whom conspicuously added their signatures to those of the drafters. They generally demanded that the amir take immediate steps to reinstate the National Assembly, as well as to reaffirm the fundamental legal and political rights that were accorded to Bahraini citizens by the 1973 constitution.

One such petition was handed to the ruler in November 1992. Known as the Elite Petition, it was drafted by Shaykh ʿAbd al-Amir al-Jamri (a Shiʿi religious scholar and former member of the National Assembly), Dr. ʿAbd al-Latif al-Mahmud (a Sunni religious scholar and university professor), Shaykh ʿIsa al-Jawdar (a Sunni religious scholar), and Muhammad Jabir al-Sabah (a former leftist member of the National Assembly), and was signed by some 300 local notables (Khalaf 2000, 87). One sponsor of the petition told Human Rights Watch that, in the document, "We called for elections to a restored parliament, release of political prisoners, and permission for [dissident] exiles to return. It was extremely polite and included our fulsome respect for the Al Khalifa" (Stork 1996, 45). The amir accepted the petition and promised to consider its demands. But the government then ordered the security services to break up public gatherings and detain a number of suspected pro-constitution activists.

Confronted with increasing harassment, four opposition groups issued a joint communiqué in April 1994 that reiterated the demands contained in the Elite Petition. The four organizations—the Bahrain Freedom Movement, the Islamic Front for the Liberation of Bahrain, the National Liberation Front, and the Popular Front for the Liberation of Bahrain—represented the full spectrum of active political challengers to the regime, from the comparatively moderate Bahrain Freedom Movement to the more radical Popular Front (Khalaf 2000, 91). When this proclamation was ignored by the authorities, a Popular Petition Committee formed to gather signatures on a revised document to be presented to the amir on the occasion of National Day, December 16, 1994. This second petition, known as the Popular Petition, expressed the people's confidence in the ruler's "wise leadership on the basis of justice, consultation, and faith in the strong foundation which were laid down by our Islamic religion and which had been adopted by your blessed wisdom as stated in the constitution of our dear country." It then appealed to the amir to authorize "the restoration of the National Assembly, and the involvement of women in the democratic process" (Khalaf 2000, 112). More than 20,000 citizens signed the document.

Before the Popular Petition could be delivered to the ruler, however, collective protests broke out in the villages west and south of the capital. The demonstrations, sparked by the marathon incident of November 1994, involved large numbers of younger Shiʿis and centered in the suburban districts where the participants lived (rather than the areas where they worked). At first, the protests appear to have been spontaneous and comparatively unorganized. But immediately after ʿAli Salman was placed under arrest on December 5, large crowds began to gather each day in front of his house in the village of Bilad al-Qadim and outside the Khawajah mosque in downtown Manama, where he led the daily prayers.

The shift from petition writing to street demonstrations reflected the tactics that were adopted by the authorities during the initial phase of the uprising. From September 1992 to November 1994, police and security services closely monitored the activities of leading pro-constitution activists and used tear gas to disperse the small-scale protests that erupted sporadically. In early December 1994, the police upped the ante by launching unannounced raids on the houses of suspected activists and the various mosques where protesters tended to gather. Meanwhile, members of the ruling family replied to the petitions that constituted the dominant form of popular contention during the early months of the uprising by publishing a series of poems that ridiculed critics of the regime and made light of their stated demands (Khalaf 2000, 20).

On the whole, the measures that the authorities implemented during this period effectively undermined the overall legitimacy of the Al Khalifah regime. Disaffected Shiʿi activists consequently took advantage of the country's dense network of neighborhood mosques and mourning houses (*matams*)— which served as meeting places for major religious festivals, most notably the annual ceremonies to commemorate the martyrdom of al-Imam Husain (ʿAshurah)—to mobilize local communities for the large-scale protests that took shape at the turn of the year (Opp and Roehl 1990).

Taking to the Streets:
December 1994–August 1995

Mass demonstrations eclipsed formal petitions as the dominant form of popular protest in the weeks after ᶜAli Salman's arrest and in fact occurred repeatedly in the course of the uprising (see figure 3.1). The rallies and marches that erupted in December 1994 clustered around the major mosques of the capital and its surrounding suburbs. On December 13, protesters marched out of the mosques adjacent to Manama's Old Town and occupied the police station in historic Bab al-Bahrain. Attempts by police officers to seal off the streets leading into and out of the Old Town sparked renewed protests in nearby neighborhoods. Clashes between riot police and stone-throwing protesters became more and more frequent as the month unfolded.

Demonstrators gathered outside the residence of the United States ambassador on January 6, 1995, raising placards written in Arabic and English that demanded a return to a constitutional order. The gathering was immediately followed by a series of coordinated marches in predominantly Shiᶜi neighborhoods. Synchronized demonstrations took place on January 15 and 26 as well, culminating in a cluster of protests to mark the end of Ramadan on March 4. Mass demonstrations became less frequent during the late spring and summer of 1995. But on September 7, some 12,000 people gathered in Nuwaidrat to greet one of the leaders of the uprising, who was scheduled to be released from detention; the authorities quickly postponed his release until the following morning, when some 20,000 returned for the occasion. Police dispersed the crowd by force, but on September 25 the regime freed several key opposition figures, including Shaykh ᶜAbd al-Amir al-Jamri, in an attempt to calm the situation.

Besides organized demonstrations and marches, isolated attacks on facilities associated with the state took place beginning in December. Protesters sacked the Sitra branch of the National Bank of Bahrain on December 14, along with a number of district police stations. Government offices in Sanabis were attacked at the end of January, while the post office in Jidd Hafs was torched at the end of February. On March 4, fires were set at the Sanabis sports club, a shopping center on the western edge of Manama, two electrical substations, and the office of the Bahrain International Exposition. Traffic lights and lampposts throughout the capital and its surrounding suburbs were repeatedly pulled down as well. Branches of the National Bank of Bahrain, electrical transformers, and gasoline stations continued to be frequent targets of sabotage and firebombs throughout the spring and summer of 1995. Attacks on private property, by contrast, were notable for their rarity: a video rental shop in Jidd Hafs was set on fire at the end of March and two furniture showrooms were burned in Sitra in April.

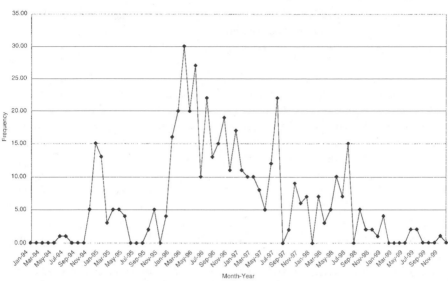

Figure 3.1. Demonstrations and Clashes, 1994–1999

Meanwhile, protests broke out. One hundred students at the National University took part in an antigovernment rally on March 9; twice this number marched to demand the reinstatement of the constitution at the end of April. Six teachers were arrested in mid-April for inciting demonstrations at several girls' secondary schools, and police stormed the girls' high school in ʿIsa Town on May 2 to put down a protest among students there.

Formal petitions did not disappear as means of expressing political demands during this phase of the uprising. In March 1995, 110 notables, both Sunnis and Shiʿis, signed a petition to the ruler; a month later, 320 prominent women affixed their names to a document that demanded an immediate end to the excessive use of force by the police, greater employment opportunities for Bahraini citizens, and the restoration of the constitution. In the same spirit, 11 leading religious scholars faxed a statement to Reuters news agency on April 25 in which they denounced the increasing incidence of acts of sabotage and called on the amir to open a dialogue with his critics and release all political prisoners.

Police reacted by attacking protesters with batons and armored vehicles, as well as by arresting large numbers of suspected antiregime activists. According to Human Rights Watch (1997, 33), "While some of those arrested were picked up for specific offenses involving violence or vandalism, and some for nonviolent activities such as distributing leaflets, writing graffiti, or publicly urging the government to negotiate with the opposition, many arrests were indiscriminate and many of those detained were never formally charged."

The killing of two police officers in late March prompted the authorities to adopt even harsher measures. At the end of April, the police took the unprecedented step of destroying two neighborhood mosques in Sanabis to demonstrate their determination to crush the uprising. Furthermore, the regime conspicuously closed ranks at the highest levels: a major reshuffling of the government in mid-June 1995 removed all cabinet ministers who were not members of the ruling family. Such steps substantially raised the cost of taking part in collective action for anyone who might have been tempted to challenge the existing order. Consequently, the incidence of organized, large-scale public demonstrations fell off sharply in the late spring of 1995.

As mass protests subsided, key government officials made overtures to imprisoned Shi'i notables. The talks produced a tacit agreement between the two sides, whereby influential pro-constitution activists pledged to do their best to restrain the protesters and the authorities committed themselves to "take steps toward satisfying the demands to reinstate the constitution and restore the National Assembly, release political prisoners, and allow exiles to return" (Human Rights Watch 1997, 34). Several prominent Shi'i scholars, including Shaykh 'Abd al-Amir al-Jamri, were subsequently released from detention. Nevertheless, the regime balked at fulfilling its commitments, and by the fall of 1995 al-Jamri and his colleagues once again openly demanded the immediate restoration of the constitution. Police responded by resuming armed raids against antiregime rallies and clashed with worshippers as they emerged from Friday prayer services (35). Popular protest flared once again toward the end of the year after the state appeals court refused to overturn the death sentence that had been pronounced on a man convicted of killing a police officer.

Resorting to Violence:
September 1995 to April 1997

Arson and bombings joined mass demonstrations as a major form of contentious activity on the islands (see figure 3.2). A pair of percussion bombs exploded at Yatim shopping center in Manama on December 31, 1995. Three weeks later, a bomb went off at Le Royal Meridian Hotel in Manama, where an international conference of oil company executives was taking place. On February 11, 1996, a bomb exploded at the Diplomat Hotel in the capital. This attack was followed in quick succession by the detonation of a car bomb outside a newspaper office in Manama, bombings of cash machines at several branches of the National Bank of Bahrain, and explosions at Baisan International Hotel and the shopping complex attached to the Sheraton Hotel in Manama. In June 1996, two more bombs went off outside the Gulf Pearl and Le Vendome hotels in Manama.

Beginning in February 1996, locally owned commercial buildings were in-

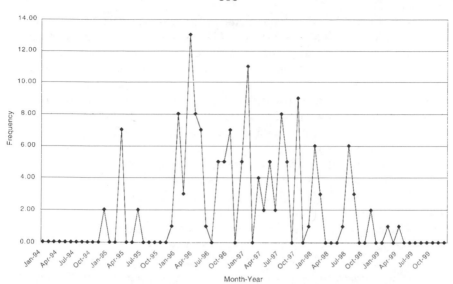

Figure 3.2. Fires and Bombings, 1994–1999

creasingly targeted. That month a car bomb exploded in the commercial center of ʿIsa Town. Three bombs hidden in cigarette packets detonated in April at the Ambassador Music Center, a women's clothing shop near the Sheraton, and a boutique adjacent to Bab al-Bahrain. Similar explosive devices went off at another music shop and boutique a month later. On March 14, Molotov cocktails were tossed into a South Asian restaurant in Sitra, killing not only those eating inside but also a number of expatriate workers who were sleeping upstairs. A South Asian grocery was firebombed in early September 1996.

Mass protests continued to take place throughout this phase of the uprising. When ʿAbd al-Amir al-Jamri announced on October 23, 1995, that he and six other leading Shiʿi scholars intended to begin a hunger strike, hundreds of their supporters gathered outside Zain al-ʿAbdin mosque, across from his house in Bani Jamra, wearing black shirts to express solidarity with the hunger strikers. Some 80,000 massed in Bani Jamra on November 1 to hear the declaration that ended the hunger strike. After al-Jamri addressed a rally at Zain al-ʿAbdin mosque on December 28, several thousand marched with him to a follow-up rally at Quful mosque in downtown Manama; police closed both mosques the next day, precipitating a protest by some 1,000 residents of Bani Jamra. Mass protests erupted throughout the country when al-Jamri was rearrested on January 16, 1996, most notably in Hamad Town, home to many of the ruling family's tribal retainers. Marches spread through Sitra, Dair, Sanabis, Diraz, and Bani Jamra on the occasion of the religious festival of ʿId al-Adha at the end of April, which was designated by the opposition as a Week of Civil Resistance. The first popular demonstration took place on sparsely populated al-Nabi Salih island in late October. That December, a religious procession in Sanabis drew 10,000 marchers, including a phalanx of women displaying banners that condemned the ruling family.

Formal petitions did not disappear. When a member of the new government-appointed Advisory Council (Majlis al-Shurah) visited the hunger strikers on October 25, 1995, al-Jamri and his colleagues asked him to take a statement of their demands to the amir; the delegate demurred. In mid-December, parents of striking students at al-Nuʾaim secondary school presented a petition to the Ministry of Education asking for an end to raids on high schools by armed police. An effort was even undertaken in mid-November 1996 to present the amir with the Popular Petition of 1994.

Key innovations included mass demonstrations in the predominantly Shiʿi villages, organized and undertaken exclusively by women. An example took place on March 21, 1996, when 150 women lined the main Budaʾiyyah highway at the entrance to Daih chanting, "We are not saboteurs; we demand the restoration of the constitution." When a similar women's march was under way in Sanabis, balloons were released into the air carrying pro-constitution slogans. One hundred women gathered in Sanabis cemetery on April 11 to protest continued attacks against women by the police and security forces. Women's demonstrations accompanied balloon releases in Bani Jamra and Sanabis in early May. During the first week of November, a group of women wearing black shawls sprinkled rose water on the grave of a young man who had died in police custody, then raised their fists and chanted pro-constitution slogans. At the end of January 1997, dozens of women rallied in Sitra to demand the release of detained relatives. As a variation on this form of popular contention, a large group of children picketed the main highway at the Sar roundabout on November 16, 1996.

Even more innovative was the emergence of organized boycotts of electricity, water, and telephone service in specific neighborhoods at designated times. One such boycott, which lasted 5 minutes, took place on July 26, 1996; another lasting 15 minutes was carried out on August 8; and yet another occurred on September 15. By mid-October 1996, electricity boycotts had become a regular component of the repertoire of contention in Manama's poorer suburbs. A variant of this tactic was the 10-minute work stoppage that took place at 10:15 AM on November 2 to protest the death sentences given to protesters who were convicted of killing two police officers.

Following the revival of large-scale demonstrations at the end of 1995, the minister of the interior banned all public meetings of more than five persons, while the security forces seized control of the administration of the National University. In addition, military commanders on December 10 ordered units of the Bahrain Defense Force to take up positions at key locations. The deployment lasted only one day. Nevertheless, it sent an unambiguous signal to the population at large that the regime was capable of deploying more forceful instruments to restore order. During the final weeks of the year, the defense minister raised the possibility that Bahrain might go to war with the neighboring state of Qatar to back up its long-standing claim to the disputed waters around the Hawwar islands. In early February 1996, police forcibly broke up a public seminar on democracy and consultation (*shura*) (organized by the prestigious al-ʾUrubah Club in Manama) and arrested the announced speakers, including the well-known Sunni reformer Ahmad al-Shamlan. In mid-March, the State Security Court took over responsibility for prosecuting some 85 offenses against public and private property that had previously been adjudicated in the civil courts.

On June 3, 1996, the government announced the arrest of 44 members of a Bahrain branch of Hizbullah (the Party of God), on charges that these individuals were plotting to overthrow the ruling family and annex the islands to the Islamic Republic of Iran. More important, at the end of September, the prime minister released plans to divide the country into four provinces, each of which would be headed by a military governor. And in early December, the amir and prime minister were shown on local television observing maneuvers carried out by armored units of the Bahrain Defense Force. Such indiscriminate, coercive measures heightened the incentives for disaffected Shiʿis and Sunnis alike to engage in collective protest, since members of both communities faced the prospect of harsh repression and summary punishment, whether they took to the streets or not. At the same time, the policies implemented by the authorities during these months encouraged radical challengers to resort to more desperate measures, such as arson and bombing.

Routinizing the Uprising:
May 1997–March 1998

Bombings of government installations occurred less frequently by the spring of 1997. On March 1, a car bomb was defused on a street adjacent to the Ministries of Justice and Finance; two weeks later, an explosive device was discovered inside the Traffic Department building in ʿAli. Toward the end of the month, a pair of bombs exploded at the Bahrain Phoenicia Hotel and Plaza Hotel in Manama. The Bahrain International Exhibition Center was bombed at the end of October. Thereafter, bombings practically disappeared.

Firebombings, however, continued apace. Arson destroyed a timber and construction equipment warehouse in Jidd Hafs in mid-May, and fires erupted at the Diplomat Hotel and Moonlight Restaurant in Manama, a sweets factory in al-Muharraq, and a cold storage facility in Sitra in early July. Supermarkets, shops, and fast-food restaurants were set on fire throughout the country in August. Large commercial buildings in Manama were torched in

October and December. Several of the establishments that were targeted during this phase of the uprising were owned or operated by South Asians, but many were owned by Bahraini citizens.

At the same time, the coordinated switching off of lights continued in Sanabis, Diraz, Sitra, and Daih. The practice spread to poorer neighborhoods in the predominantly Sunni city of al-Muharraq in early August 1997. Balloon releases and formal petitioning persisted as well, albeit sporadically. A group of notables approached the amiri administration (*diwan*) in late December 1997 to present a letter of protest to the ruler. When the delegation was denied permission to meet directly with the amir, they published the letter in pamphlet form in mid-March 1998. A subsequent petition demanding an end to police raids on mosques attracted more than 5,000 signatures.

Organized popular demonstrations trailed off during the late summer of 1997, but resumed on a more limited scale in October. Sizable marches took place in Bani Jamra and Sitra in early February 1998. The women of Sanabis took to the streets to denounce police abuses later that same month. Residents of Sanabis once again demonstrated in early March to protest the forced dissolution of the Lawyers' Society.

By the fall of 1997, the security services started punishing communities that provided material and moral support to the protesters. Supplies of electricity and water were periodically shut off to predominantly Shiᶜi residential districts. Mysterious fires destroyed the homes and businesses of suspected dissidents. The military commander in charge of the National University abruptly canceled mid-year examinations, disrupting students' progress toward their degrees. On January 16, 1998, the social club in Sar was burned to the ground; state security forces were widely rumored to have carried out the operation to punish the residents of the town for taking part in demonstrations. Less subtle means of persuasion continued to be used as well: on April 19 the regular armed forces were once again ordered to move into positions at strategic points throughout the country. These more discriminating and narrowly targeted punishments gradually drove a wedge between moderate critics of the regime and radical activists. As one Shiᶜi trader told a visiting reporter around this time, "I don't give a damn about parliament, Islamic republic, or Shura. I want to reopen my shop" (Darwish 1999, 86).

Reverting to Demonstrations:
April 1998–January 1999

Mass protests reemerged as the dominant form of popular contention in Bahrain's cities and towns during the spring of 1998. Processions to commemorate the annual religious festival of ᶜAshurah took place in several Shiᶜi districts in early May, followed by pro-constitution demonstrations in Sanabis, Dair, Daih, and Jidd Hafs. Marches continued to spread, culminating in a series of coordinated protests in late July. Large-scale demonstrations occurred once again on September 4, 1998, and January 8, 1999, in Manama, and on December 18, 1998, in al-Muharraq.

Fires continued to be set at warehouses, furniture showrooms, gasoline stations, and retail shops specializing in luxury goods, but they appeared with less and less frequency. Arson destroyed a shopping complex in central Manama in August 1998 and a furniture workshop and office building in ᶜArad in May 1999. On December 21, 1998, a bomb threat prompted the evacuation of the U.S. embassy, but no explosive device was discovered when the building was searched.

Even as the uprising steadily lost momentum during these months, innovative forms of contentious activity continued to appear. It was reported in July 1998 that graffiti was increasingly written in English instead of in Arabic, for the benefit of visiting journalists and other foreign observers. Workers who were dismissed from their jobs at the Bahrain Aluminum Extrusion Company in November 1998 bought an advertisement in one of the local newspapers, expressing thanks to a prominent pro-constitution activist for his legal advice and assistance in their dispute with the company's management.

This final shift in contentious repertoire reflected the return to markedly less coercive and more subtle tactics on the part of the authorities. Police and security units stood by in force but did not try to disrupt the ᶜAshurah processions in May 1998. The police also kept their distance as a wave of demonstrations swept through Shiᶜi neighborhoods over the next two months. In late July, protesters were even permitted to march from Nuᵓaim to the center of Manama, damaging luxury goods shops along the way. Such restraint gradually restored the tarnished legitimacy of the Al Khalifah regime. Popular resentment against the ruling family and its allies slackened further when Amir ᶜIsa bin Sulman was succeeded by his son Hamad, rather than by his brother Khalifah, who was widely believed to be less willing to engage in serious negotiations with critics of the existing order. In his first public address, the new ruler promised that he would not tolerate favoritism or discrimination between the country's Sunni and Shiᶜi citizens. In May 1999, Amir Hamad ordered large quantities of lamb and rice to be distributed at government expense to matams throughout the country for use in the upcoming ᶜAshurah ceremonies, and in early June he ordered the release of 360 leading detainees. The ruler pardoned Shaykh ᶜAbd al-Amir al-Jamri on July 8, after al-Jamri submitted a written statement expressing his regret over the events that had taken place during the course of the uprising. Hundreds of residents of Bani Jamra turned out to welcome him home. On July 13, 1999, Amir Hamad visited several Shiᶜi villages outside Manama for the first time in more than five years. It was under these circumstances that the uprising at last came to an end.

Fred H. Lawson

Violent Contention in Bahrain

Contentious repertoires in Bahrain during the mid-1990s differed in one important respect from a common pattern that has been adduced for cycles of popular protest in contemporary Europe. Donatella Della Porta and Sidney Tarrow (1986, 616) report that in Italy between 1966 and 1973, "Violent forms were . . . part of the protest repertoire from the beginning and their presence tended to grow in total numbers during the whole cycle. But it was when the wave of collective action declined that their percentage distribution increased." In short, "As mass mobilization winds down, political violence rises in magnitude and intensity" (620). Della Porta and Tarrow propose an elegant explanation for this sequence of events: as mainstream challengers steadily lose their capacity to inspire and organize large-scale popular protest, radical organizations and entrepreneurs operating on the fringes of the political spectrum attempt to seize the initiative through the use of violent tactics.

Similarly, in the case of the former Soviet Union, Beissinger finds that "a quantum leap in mass violence occurred in mid-1989, and violence gradually rose from 1989 to 1991. At this very time participation in nonviolent demonstrations declined precipitously, even though attempts to mobilize populations in demonstrations continued apace. Overall, mass violence was concentrated in the latter part of the mobilizational cycle, spilling over into the post-Soviet period and proliferating with great rapidity." In contrast to the Italian case, however, "There is little evidence that the growth in the frequency and intensity of violence can be traced to competition among small factions within the social movement sector. Indeed, in many cases violence was organized by mainstream nationalist movements and by the latter part of the cycle increasingly by governments themselves" (Beissinger 1998, 404–406). In fact, Beissinger concludes that in the former Soviet Union "violent contestation evolved over the mobilizational cycle away from mob violence (pogroms, riots, and communal violence) toward more organized and sustained armed combat" on the part of authorities and challengers alike (409).

Comparative studies of protest cycles in the Federal Republic of Germany and the Netherlands during the 1970s and 1980s discern a parallel trajectory. In these two countries, it was "in the late stages of the [protest] waves" that "heavy violence" emerged as the predominant form of popular contention: "Heavy violence was most common during the second half of the 1980s, when the aggregate number of protests had already declined substantially" (Kriesi et al. 1995, 122). As a general rule, "protests started with disruptive but nonviolent confrontational actions, subsequently entered a phase dominated by more moderate mass mobilization, and ended in a twin process of institutionalization and radicalization" (124). Why this pattern takes shape is not altogether clear—in other words, this question "can be answered only to a limited extent by the protest event data" (122). Kriesi et al.'s best guess is that "repression against nonviolent protest delegitimizes the state's monopoly on violence and strengthens the position of those activists who see reactive violence as legitimate. Moreover, the shift to violence is facilitated because the cost of violence compared to the cost of nonviolent disruption decreases. The final result of these countervailing pressures is an erosion of the middle ground of the action repertoire—nonviolent confrontations—and the simultaneous development of moderation and radicalization" (127).

This broad pattern can be seen in two phases of the 1994–1998 uprising in Bahrain, viz., December 1994–August 1995 and September 1995–April 1997. But it does not accurately reflect the overall trajectory of the Bahrain case. Here, in sharp contrast to European protest cycles, a period characterized by an especially violent repertoire of contention (September 1995–April 1997) was followed by another that featured a markedly less violent repertoire (May 1997–March 1998), which was in turn succeeded by a phase in which comparatively peaceful demonstrations reemerged as the dominant form of contentious activity (April 1998–January 1999). There thus appears to be no inevitable progression from a decline in mass protest to the rise of political violence.

Explaining the contrast between events in Bahrain and trends in contemporary Europe involves a reformulation of Donatella Della Porta's proposed theory about the relationship between policing practices and political opportunity structures. Della Porta hypothesizes that police responses to popular protest have a direct impact on the character of social movement activity. In short, "more tolerant, selective, and softer police behavior favors [orderly, large-scale collective] protest," while "more repressive, diffuse, and hard techniques of policing tend to, at the same time, discourage the mass and peaceful protest while fueling the more radical fringe" (1996, 90). According to this formulation, tolerance, selectivity, and softness constitute one form of police response, whereas repressiveness, diffuseness, and hardness represent another. But it is obvious that these two bundles can be repackaged in a variety of ways: one can easily imagine tactics that are selective yet hard, repressive yet selective, and so on.

In the Bahrain case, the authorities reacted to the pro-constitution petitions that characterized the initial phase of the 1994–1998 uprising by using tactics that were comparatively repressive, diffuse, and soft. As a result, disaffection spread among large segments of the local population and rapidly coalesced into outbreaks of large-scale collective protest. By the spring of 1995, police and security services adopted more forceful tactics to deal with demonstrators, which precipitated a marked rise in violence on the part of radical activists. During the third phase of the uprising, forces loyal to the regime turned to forms of repression that were at once more brutal and more selective. Such tactics diminished the level of public support for acts of violence, while effectively limiting the scale of popular demonstrations. The spring of 1998 saw a shift to relatively softer and more tolerant tactics on the part of the authorities, which selectively targeted individuals and groups operating on the fringes of the political spectrum. Under these circumstances, mass demonstrations regained a predominant place in the repertoire of contention that characterized the last phase of the uprising.

Conclusion

Existing studies of the popular uprising that broke out in Bahrain in December 1994 focus either on the broad political-economic circumstances that set the stage for the emergence of an Islamist protest movement on the islands or on the specific demands that the demonstrators presented to the authorities. Recent scholarship on comparative social movements suggests that such analyses can be expected to have considerable difficulty addressing two crucial questions: why the uprising broke out during the last weeks of 1994, rather than at any other time, and why the rebellion assumed the peculiar form(s) it did.

A more satisfactory explanation for the outbreak of the uprising can be constructed in terms of four short-term trends in the local economy that posed a growing threat to powerful forces outside the dominant social coalition. Highlighting immediate developments that threatened to damage the interests and diminish the future prospects of small shopkeepers, skilled clerical employees, heavy industrial workers, and well-educated women offers a more compelling account of the incentives that led these people to engage in collective protest than do studies that emphasize the opportunity for rebellion. The explanation offered here thus seconds Jack Goldstone and Charles Tilly's (2001, 182) important assertion that "not all mobilization for contentious politics follows rising opportunities; nor do rising opportunities—even with successful mobilization and brilliant framing, as in Tiananmen—always lead to successful contention." What matters more is the nature and extent of the concrete threats that confront actual and potential challengers at any given time.

Explaining the subsequent evolution of the 1994–1998 uprising can best be accomplished through a careful mapping of the successive repertoires of contention that took shape over the course of the rebellion. Instead of following a single trajectory, the uprising occurred in five distinct phases. Each phase was characterized by one or two dominant forms of popular contention and a limited number of significant innovations in contentious activity. On the whole, shifts from one contentious repertoire to another grew out of the specific ways in which the authorities responded to initiatives undertaken by pro-constitution protesters. Reconceiving the fundamental dynamics of the

Bahrain uprising in this fashion not only improves our understanding of this particular case but also contributes to the larger research program that Sidney Tarrow (1999, 55) calls "a progression from the cataloguing of contentious events to a relational analysis of the interactions between contending actors, their allies and enemies of the state."

Note

In addition to the published and unpublished sources cited in the text, this study relies on an extensive body of empirical material drawn from the website of the Bahrain Freedom Movement ("The Voice of Bahrain"), the electronic archive of the Gulf2000 Project at Columbia University, and contemporaneous reports printed in the local and foreign press.

Works Cited

Bahry, Louay. 1997. "The Opposition in Bahrain: A Bellwether for the Gulf?" *Middle East Policy* 5 (May): 42–57.
———. 1999. "Democracy in the Persian Gulf: The Case of Qatar and Bahrain." Paper presented at the annual convention of the Northeastern Political Science Association, Philadelphia.
———. 2000. "The Socioeconomic Foundations of the Shiite Opposition in Bahrain." *Mediterranean Quarterly* 11 (Summer): 129–43.
Beissinger, Mark R. 1996. "How Nationalisms Spread." *Social Research* 63 (Spring): 97–147.
———. 1998. "Nationalist Violence and the State." *Comparative Politics* 30 (July): 401–22.
———. 1999. "Event Analysis in Transitional Societies." Pp. 284–348 in *Acts of Dissent*, ed. Dieter Rucht, Ruud Koopmans, and Friedhelm Neidhardt. Lanham, Md.: Rowman and Littlefield.
———. 2002. *Nationalist Mobilization and the Collapse of the Soviet State*. Cambridge: Cambridge University Press.
Burke, Edmund. 1988. "Islam and Social Movements: Methodological Reflections." Pp. 17–35 in *Islam, Politics, and Social Movements*, ed. Edmund Burke and Ira M. Lapidus. Berkeley: University of California Press.
Dabrowska, Karen. 1997. *Bahrain Briefing*. London: Colourmast.
Darwish, Adel. 1999. "Rebellion in Bahrain." *Middle East Review of International Affairs* 3 (March): 84–87.
Della Porta, Donatella. 1996. "Social Movements and the State: Thoughts on the Policing of Protest." Pp. 62–92 in *Comparative Perspectives on Social Movements*, ed. Doug McAdam, John D. McCarthy, and Mayer N. Zald. Cambridge: Cambridge University Press.

Della Porta, Donatella, and Sidney Tarrow. 1986. "Unwanted Children: Political Violence and the Cycle of Protest in Italy, 1966–1973." *European Journal of Political Research* 14: 607–32.

Fakhro, Munira A. 1997. "The Uprising in Bahrain: An Assessment." Pp. 167–88 in *The Persian Gulf at the Millennium*, ed. Gary G. Sick and Lawrence G. Potter. New York: St. Martin's.

Gause, F. Gregory. 1997. "The Gulf Conundrum." *Washington Quarterly* 20 (Winter): 145–65.

Goldstone, Jack A., and Charles Tilly. 2001. "Threat (and Opportunity): Popular Action and State Response in the Dynamics of Contentious Action." Pp. 179–94 in *Silence and Voice in the Study of Contentious Politics*, ed. Ronald R. Aminzade et al. Cambridge: Cambridge University Press.

Human Rights Watch. 1997. *Routine Abuse, Routine Denial: Civil Rights and the Political Crisis in Bahrain*. New York: Human Rights Watch.

al-Jamri, Mansoor. 1997. "Prospects of a Moderate Islamist Discourse: The Case of Bahrain." Paper presented at the annual convention of the Middle East Studies Association, San Francisco.

———. 1998. "State and Civil Society in Bahrain." Paper presented at the annual convention of the Middle East Studies Association, Chicago.

Khalaf, Abdulhadi. 2000. "Unfinished Business—Contentious Politics and State-Building in Bahrain." *Research Report in Sociology* 1. Lund University.

Kriesi, Hanspeter, et al. 1995. *New Social Movements in Western Europe*. Minneapolis: University of Minnesota Press.

Lawson, Fred H. 1989. *Bahrain: The Modernization of Autocracy*. Boulder: Westview.

Lichbach, Mark I. 1987. "Deterrence or Escalation?" *Journal of Conflict Resolution* 31 (June): 266–97.

Mikkelsen, Flemming. 1999. "Contention and Social Movements in an International and Transnational Perspective: Denmark, 1914–1995." *Journal of Historical Sociology* 12 (June): 128–57.

Oberschall, Anthony R. 1994. "Rational Choice in Collective Protests." *Rationality and Society* 6 (January): 79–91.

Opp, Karl-Dieter, and Wolfgang Roehl. 1990. "Repression, Micromobilization, and Political Protest." *Social Forces* 69 (December): 521–47.

Rasler, Karen. 1996. "Concessions, Repression, and Political Protest in the Iranian Revolution." *American Sociological Review* 61 (February): 132–52.

Seikaly, May. 1994. "Women and Social Change in Bahrain." *International Journal of Middle East Studies* 26 (August): 415–26.

———. 1996. "The Economy of Political Opposition in Bahrain." Paper presented to the annual convention of the Middle East Studies Association, Providence, R.I.

———. 1997. "Bahraini Women in Formal and Informal Groups." Pp. 125–46 in *Organizing Women*, ed. Dawn Chatty and Annika Rabo. Oxford: Berg.

———. 2001. "Kuwait and Bahrain: The Appeal of Globalization and Internal Constraints." Pp. 177–92 in *Iran, Iraq, and the Arab Gulf States*, ed. Joseph A. Kechichian. New York: Palgrave.

Stinchcombe, Arthur L. 1987. "Review of *The Contentious French: Four Centuries of Popular Struggle*." *American Journal of Sociology* 92 (March): 1248–49.

Stork, Joe. 1996. "Bahrain Regime Stages Confessions, Rejects Compromise." *Middle East Report*, no. 200 (July–September): 44–46.

———. 1997. "Bahrain's Crisis Worsens." *Middle East Report*, no. 204 (July–September): 33–35.

Tarrow, Sidney. 1995. "Cycles of Collective Action." Pp. 89–115 in *Repertoires and Cycles of Collective Action*, ed. Mark Traugott. Durham, N.C.: Duke University Press.

———. 1998. *Power in Movement*. 2d ed. Cambridge: Cambridge University Press.

———. 1999. "Studying Contentious Politics." Pp. 33–64 in *Acts of Dissent*, ed. Dieter Rucht, Ruud Koopmans, and Friedhelm Neidhardt. Lanham, Md.: Rowman and Littlefield.

Tilly, Charles. 1995a. "Contentious Repertoires in Great Britain, 1758–1834." Pp. 15–42 in *Repertoires and Cycles of Collective Action*, ed. Mark Traugott. Durham, N.C.: Duke University Press.

———. 1995b. *Popular Contention in Great Britain, 1758–1834*. Cambridge: Harvard University Press.

White, James W. 1995a. "Cycles and Repertoires of Popular Contention in Early Modern Japan." Pp. 145–71 in *Repertoires and Cycles of Collective Action*, ed. Mark Traugott. Durham, N.C.: Duke University Press.

———. 1995b. *Ikki*. Ithaca, N.Y.: Cornell University Press.

Zimmermann, Ekkart. 1980. "Macro-comparative Research on Political Protest." Pp. 167–237 in *Handbook of Political Conflict*, ed. T. Robert Gurr. New York: Free Press.

Four

Hamas as Social Movement

Glenn E. Robinson

The Harakat al-Muqawima al-Islamiyya (Islamic Resistance Movement), better known as Hamas, has elicited distinct reactions from American policymakers and academics. In official circles, Hamas is considered a straightforward terrorist group. Despite Arab protests that Hamas is a legitimate movement of national liberation, this Palestinian group is regularly listed in the U.S. State Department's annual report on terrorist groups. Consistent with this official view, the Bush administration imposed newly authorized sanctions against Hamas in November 2001. Such sanctions, which focus on preventing terrorist groups from engaging in various financial transactions, were promulgated in the aftermath of the September 11, 2001, tragedies. The justification for including Hamas on the terrorist list centers on the actions of the military wing of Hamas, the Izz al-Din al-Qassam Brigades, and its record of purposefully targeting Israeli civilians in violent attacks.

Without regard to the somewhat stale argument about "one man's terrorist is another man's freedom fighter," the official U.S. position is problematic for two reasons. First, by labeling Hamas a terrorist group, the government ignores most of what Hamas actually does. Hamas is a social movement with thousands of activists and hundreds of thousands (perhaps millions) of Palestinian sympathizers, and it engages in extensive political and social activities far removed from suicide bombers. Second, it is always problematic to speak of terrorist groups (or states), as opposed to groups (or states) that periodically use acts of terror for tactical political reasons. By understanding terrorism in tactical terms rather than as a genetic group attribute, rational responses become potentially more effective and less obviously politically hypocritical.

Recent academic work on Hamas has been much more sensitive to these nuances. For example, books by Khaled Hroub (2000), Ziad Abu-Amr (1994), and Shaul Mishal and Avraham Sela (2000) (two Palestinians and two Israelis) have presented a comprehensive picture of Hamas to the English-speaking world. While still recognizing the role of violence, these authors provide much more robust empirical analyses of the totality of Hamas. Indeed, instead of building a wall between Hamas's popular work and its violence, these authors depict the dynamic and often reinforcing relationship between both facets. If there is a weakness to this emerging body of work, it is a lack of conscious theory, whether political sociology or political economy (though building empirical knowledge of Hamas obviously must precede theoretical conclusions).

This chapter attempts to build on the empirical knowledge provided by these authors, as well as my own fieldwork, by interpreting these data through social movement theory. Applying social movement theory allows us not only to understand Hamas better but also to "deorientalize" Hamas by recognizing that it shares the main features of many social movements around the world. Understanding that many—perhaps most—"terrorist" groups are far more complex social movements than typical definitions permit has significant theoretical and policy implications.

This essay is divided into three sections. The first section constitutes a brief overview of the social movement theory framework utilized in this chapter. The second section presents a short history of Hamas since its birth in 1988 in the midst of the first Palestinian Intifada (1987–1993). The third section explicitly applies social movement theory to Hamas through an examination of its political opportunities, mobilizing structures, and cultural framings.

Structure, Agency, and Framing

Social movement theory (SMT) has emerged as a sort of middle ground approach in analyzing episodes of contentious collective actions, falling between structuralist and rational choice schools.[1] As figure 4.1 depicts, the two variables that distinguish these analytical approaches are unit of analysis and level of volunteerism.

In general, these three analytical approaches emphasize different units of analysis. Structural theories tend to have large units of analysis, generally focusing on states and the international system to explain large episodes of collective action. Perhaps the best-known state-centered approach to explaining revolutions is Theda Skocpol's *States and Social Revolutions* (1979). Similarly, changes in the international system have also been employed to explain revolutionary violence, from dependency models to current work on the impact of globalization on collective political violence (Wallerstein 1990; Barber 1995).

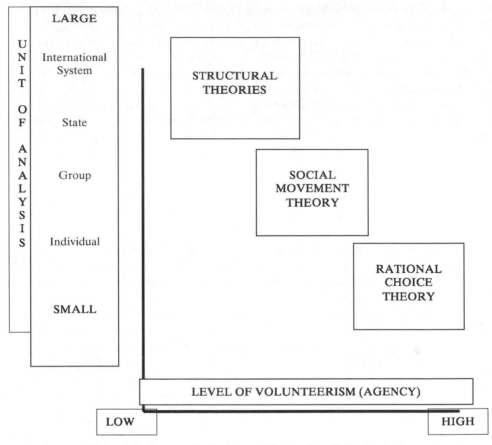

Figure 4.1. Comparative Analyses of Contentious Collective Action

In structural models, understanding large outcomes, such as social revolution, can only be accomplished by analyzing changes in large units.

Rational choice (or public choice) theory is at the other end of the unit of analysis spectrum. In general, rational choice theory denies the explanatory efficacy of units of analysis other than the individual. For rational choice theorists, structural analyses are often viewed as tautological or, perhaps more generously, as frameworks that explain nothing in their attempt to explain everything. For such theorists, states, systems, and groups do not make choices; only individuals do, and modeling individual choices in strategic relationships with other individuals is the preferred analytical approach to understanding collective action, including revolutions. The central analytical question in this school is how collective action overcomes the "free rider" problem through selective incentives and group size.[2]

By contrast, SMT generally focuses on groups as the proper unit of analysis in explaining collective action. While recognizing that individuals make strategic choices, social movement theorists contend that such choices are not made in a vacuum outside of the changing contexts, relations, and networks in which people actually live. Since individual decision making cannot be understood outside of a group-social context, the group is the proper unit of analysis.[3] Similarly, social movement theorists recognize the importance of structural change in creating the conditions necessary for collective action. Indeed, such structural change is a prime component in the creation of political opportunities, one of SMT's triad of variables. However, it is not enough to understand episodes of large collective action only through the lens of structural change. One must also understand how people act within the parameters of such change. In other words, not all similar structural changes lead to similar political outcomes; how groups take advantage of change is critical to understanding the difference in outcomes.

Differences in what is considered the proper unit of analysis in understanding large collective action reflect philosophical differences about the role of agency, or volunteerism, in explaining significant political outcomes. Structuralists generally deny that purposeful human actions account in any meaningful way for large political outcomes. As Theda Skocpol has argued, "The point is simply that no single acting group, whether a class or an ideological vanguard, deliberately shapes the complex and multiply determined conflicts that bring about revolutionary crises and outcomes. The French Revolution was not made by a rising capitalist bourgeoisie or by the Jacobins; the Russian Revolution was not made by the industrial proletariat or even by the Bolshevik party" (1994, 200). As George Lichtheim (1964) argued famously in "From Finland Station," Lenin may have been important when one limits one's views to the events in Russia in 1917 and immediately thereafter, but he made little difference in the larger and historically necessary trend of state-led industrialization in Russia.

Conversely, rational choice theorists understand history as the sum total of millions of strategic choices made by individuals. Such an approach is comparable to understanding a country's total economic output as equal to the sum total of millions of individual transactions. Individual agency, or volunteerism, therefore plays a foundational role in rational choice approaches to understanding collective action (and many other phenomena). There have been only limited academic attempts to find a synthesis between the contrasting logics of decision-making in rational choice theory and structuralism (e.g., Goldstone 1994).

SMT again takes a middle road on the question of volunteerism. It argues that while structural changes outside the control of any individual provide for changing opportunity structures, they do not dictate outcomes. Similarly, SMT accepts that agency is important, but only in the social context in which it transpires. In other words, agency is clearly restricted and must be understood as such.[4]

Social movement theory tends to utilize three variables in its case studies (and SMT is most often applied to individual case studies, such as in this chapter). First, SMT seeks to analyze how changes in political opportunity structures impact the acceleration or deceleration of collective action. Changes in opportunity structures can come from various sources, including changes in international structures (e.g., globalization, the demise of the USSR, attention or inattention by foreign powers), regime or government change at home, domestic policy or legal changes, or changes within the group itself. The second SMT variable focuses on mobilizing structures for the group in question. Mobilizing structures vary from the formal (e.g., political parties) to the informal (e.g., informal urban networks) to the illegal (e.g., underground terrorist cells). It is through these structures that movements recruit like-minded individuals, socialize new participants, overcome the free rider problem, and mobilize contention. The third variable is "cultural framing." Unlike the other two analytical approaches, SMT takes cultural issues seriously, but more in an ideological-tactical sense than is typically found in primordial understandings. In SMT, culture is conceptualized as multitiered. First, every society has a variety of stories, symbols, and histories that make up something of a collective cultural toolbox (Swidler 1986). Different groups privilege different sets of tools, and the various interpretations and uses of cultural tools often directly contradict one another. For example, the political meaning of Hussein's "martyrdom" in Shi'i Islam—its central passion play—has been bitterly contested over the centuries. Some ideologues interpreted it as a call for political quiescence in the face of unjust state power, while others (like Ayatollah Khomeini) asserted an activist interpretation that calls for confrontations with unjust authority no matter the consequences. Different tools are put together in different ways, creating a set of contrasting ideologies and sets of meanings in any given society. The American cultural toolbox can be used to create authentic ideologies as diverse as black nationalism and Christian fundamentalism.

The framing of issues occurs within the context of competing ideologies. In a sense, framing is the bumper-sticker version of how issues get interpreted within a certain ideological context. When done effectively, issue framing can be done with very few words. The U.S. debate on abortion rights can be summarized—framed—in single words that evoke intense emotions on either side: *pro-choice* or *pro-life*. In the Arab world, Islamists have similarly framed their platform with a minimum of verbiage. The most common example is the statement that "Islam is the solution" (*al-Islam huwa al-hall*) to virtually any problem or issue in society. By simply (or simplistically) framing issues, potential recruits need not understand the full ideology of the movement as the leading cadres do. Armed with the Cliffs Notes version of complex ideologies, recruits can effectively do battle in a simpler Manichaean world.

In sum, social movement theory claims a methodological middle ground between structural and rational choice models of contentious collective action. By utilizing groups as the primary unit of analysis, as well as suggesting that volunteerism is important but constrained, social movement theory provides a bridge between structuralism and rational choice. Critics might claim that in so doing, SMT ends up sacrificing theoretical rigor and clarity and ends up as a "laundry list" approach to explaining collective action. Proponents of SMT might counter that this approach actually is a synthesis of the best of structural analysis and rational choice insights, thereby providing a fuller, more robust explanation of contentious collective action.

The Social and Institutional Roots of Hamas

Islamism, including the Hamas variant, is an essentially modern phenomenon. It is strongly urban in its physical orientation; it is led by Western-educated cadres with little clerical involvement; and it is at ease using modern technology to advance its cause. This reality is far different from the popular portrayals of such groups as antimodern movements of rage led by those who are intent on turning back the historical clock to a mythical past. The recent prominence of the Taliban movement in Afghanistan has not helped matters, since it seems to fit a stereotype that is inaccurate in most cases. Islamist cadres are more often than not firmly entrenched in modern society. That is, they have modern, secular educations (often having studied in Europe or North America), live in urban areas (usually capital cities), and are young (generally in their twenties and thirties). Often their studies are in technical fields, such as engineering or medicine. They are almost never students of religious jurisprudence, and most have not studied in religious schools. In other words, leaders of the Islamist movements in the Middle East have virtually the same social profiles as those who, a generation earlier, agitated in favor of Baʿthism, Nasserism, and Arab socialism.

There should be nothing surprising in the fact that Islamist leaders have their roots in modern society. The intellectual vanguards—those who mold the ideology and provide the leadership—of most revolutionary movements, as Michael Walzer has argued, share similar, nontraditional backgrounds: "By and large, while classes differ fundamentally from one revolution to another, vanguards are sociologically similar. They are recruited from middling and professional groups. The parents of the recruits are gentlemen farmers, merchants, clerics, lawyers, petty officials. *Recruitment begins at school,* not in the streets, or in shops and factories, or in peasant villages" (1979, 31).

The Islamist leadership of the revolution in Iran is instructive on this point. It should be remembered that those clerics, such as Ayatollahs Khomeini and Taleqani, who were critical to the success of the revolution had bases of support outside the traditional religious institutions and cities of learning in Iran. Khomeini, of course, had been in exile from 1964 to 1979. Taleqani and other politically active clergy (who constituted a small minority of the ulama before 1978) had built their network of hard-core supporters largely from fellow prisoners in the shah's jails and from alienated university students. It is important to note that the most important revolutionary clerics were based in Tehran, not Qom, Mashhad, or other religious cities in Iran. Nor did they come from provincial capitals.

However, the core cadres of the revolution in Iran were not the ulama but the radical lay Islamists. The social profile of these cadres was often young (twenties and thirties), urban (mostly Tehran), and well educated (studied at secular universities in Iran or the West). Frequently, they were followers of Ali Shariati, an intellectual who blended Marxist concerns for social justice with Islamic themes of authenticity. Thus, while the traditional religious stratum gained much of the credit for the revolution in Iran, the lay Islamists—who are characterized by the same profile described by Walzer above and very much a product of modern society—were the activists, the organization builders, and the bridge to whole strata of society not enamored of clerical politics. The fact that this sociological group splintered after the revolution does not alter the fact of its earlier centrality.

Other examples of the essentially modernist roots of Islamism abound. The Tanzim al-Jihad group in Egypt, responsible for, among other things, the assassination of Egyptian president Anwar al-Sadat in 1981, also fits this description (Guenena 1986; Ansari 1984; Ibrahim 1980). In the 1980s, nearly 70 percent of Jihad's members were either students or professionals. Over 77 percent were between the ages of 20 and 30. And a disproportionate number had studied engineering at secular universities.[5] In Algeria, nearly every leader of the Islamic Salvation Front came from the capital city of Algiers and had a higher degree in a technical subject, such as chemical engineering. Many had studied at top universities in France.

Manfred Halpern was right to suggest 40 years ago that political power in the Middle East was increasingly being seized by a salaried "new middle class" of "managers, administrators, teachers, engineers, journalists, scientists, lawyers, or army officers." It is a "class of men inspired by nontraditional knowledge, clustered around a core of salaried civilian and military politicians, organizers, administrators, and experts" (1963, 52). Clearly, while this class did seize power through the army in a number of Arab countries, the relatively liberal scenarios Halpern forecast have not materialized.

What I am suggesting here is that the Islamist leadership in the Middle East is very much a component of the new middle class that Halpern described. However, its ideological framework runs counter to what Halpern and other proponents of modernization theory predicted. Modern Western education was supposed to breed greater secularization in the new middle class. But, for a number of reasons, significant segments of the new middle class have used Islamist ideologies, not secular-based ones, to address concerns of social justice, political power, and the distribution of resources. Such are the ideologies of authenticity (Ajami 1981).

Even with the exigencies of life under Israeli occupation, the same cleavage was produced in the Palestinian middle classes in the West Bank and Gaza Strip: a dominant secular ideology of nationalism and an influential Islamist rival. It is important to remember that the leaders of both camps came from more or less the same social backgrounds that Walzer described above. There were class cleavages *within* the nationalist and Islamist camps but not *between* the leadership strata. The main fissure in the Palestinian new middle class was along ideological, not class, lines. Ideology, in this case, should not be construed as epiphenomenal or as a mask to advance material class interests. However, how that ideology was put into practice—or, more precisely, *who* put the ideology into practice—within each of the large ideological groupings did often parallel class lines.

Palestinian Islamism emerged for many of the same reasons as other Islamist movements that appeared at the same time. The general reasons are well known and much analyzed elsewhere: the failure of secular Arab regimes to build strong economies and open polities, the demonstration effect of the 1978–1979 Islamist revolution in Iran, and the regional impact of oil money from Saudi Arabia and other conservative Gulf states, all of which were critical in propelling Islamist thought forward.

Causes specific to Israel also helped build Palestinian Islamism, especially the Likud Party's 1977 rise to power with its strong messianic message. In addition to its antagonistic policies in the West Bank and Gaza, the Likud's ideology helped frame the conflict in religious—as opposed to nationalist—terms, coinciding with and bolstering Islamist tendencies. Moreover, Israeli policies beginning in the early 1980s assisted the Muslim Brotherhood organization in the West Bank and Gaza, primarily by providing political space to organize and mobilize. Israel viewed the secular Palestine Liberation Organization (PLO) as its main enemy in the occupied territories and followed a "divide and conquer" strategy of pitting the Islamists against the secularist Palestinians. In this regard, Israel was no different from many other Arab regimes, which initially supported Islamist movements as a counterweight to the more serious secular opposition. Israel's policy was largely effective because Islamist-PLO relations became more strained in the 1980s.

Before Hamas, the Palestinian Islamist movement was dominated by the Muslim Brotherhood organization. Founded in Egypt in 1928 by Hasan al-Banna, the Muslim Brotherhood was an active opponent of many of the secular state policies adopted in the Arab world, in addition to Western colonialism and Zionism (Mitchell 1969). During its first 50 years, the Muslim

Brotherhood was illegal in most countries, including Egypt, and was often harshly suppressed because of its politics and various assassination attempts. In Egypt, the movement was gradually co-opted by the upper stratum of the merchant class, which supported the concept of passive social Islamization and amiable ties with the regime. In part as a response to this trend in the Muslim Brotherhood—strongly encouraged under the leadership of Umar al-Tilmisani in the 1970s—more radical Islamist groups arose in Egypt, seeking to overthrow the state and kill the state's "apostate" leadership.[6] Unlike Egypt, Jordan generally tolerated the Muslim Brotherhood's political activities. In fact, the Muslim Brotherhood was the only continuously legal political organization in the West Bank when Jordan controlled the area from 1948 to 1967.[7] While under Jordanian authority, the Muslim Brotherhood generally limited its political activities to its social agenda. That is, it advocated the gradual Islamization of society through education and adherence to Islamic principles, especially those encoded in the *shariʿa*, or Islamic law.

The differences between Egyptian and Jordanian policies toward the Muslim Brotherhood between 1948 and 1967 go a long way toward explaining the disparate state of affairs for the Islamist movement in the Gaza Strip and West Bank under Israeli rule following 1967. The fact that Nasser outlawed the Muslim Brotherhood gave its activists in the Gaza Strip experience in building decentralized and clandestine organizations. In contrast to the secretive and militant forms of Islamism in Gaza under Egyptian rule, the lawful status of the Muslim Brotherhood in the Jordan-annexed West Bank put no premium on clandestine organizational talents. In addition, since Jordan did not permit cross-border violence against Israeli targets, there was no tradition of armed militancy against Israel in the West Bank, as opposed to the experience of the Gazan branch. Whereas the Gazan Muslim Brotherhood migrated to Fatah in the late 1960s, the West Bank Brotherhood politically stayed put, as that organization was technically illegal but widely indulged by Israeli authorities. Thus, ties between Islamist and nationalist organizations in Gaza have historically been very strong, while those ideologically differentiated organizations in the West Bank have remained isolated.

In part because of these very different histories and orientations, the Muslim Brotherhood in Gaza and the West Bank never formed a common organizational link. Even after the two remaining parts of Palestine were reunited under a common military occupation in 1967, the West Bank Brotherhood members continued to be associated with their colleagues in Jordan, not Gaza, while those in Gaza were generally independent of outside ties.

In spite of both the harshness of military occupation and the persistent rhetorical attacks by nationalists on the seeming ideological acquiescence to the occupation by the Muslim Brotherhood, the leadership of the Brotherhood remained committed to the primacy of social Islamization, not confrontation with Israel. For the ideologues of the Muslim Brotherhood, it was impossible to separate Israel from a larger campaign by the West to discredit and undermine Islam; it was equally impossible to politically differentiate Palestinian Muslims from the greater Islamic world. At base, then, the question of Palestine for the Muslim Brotherhood was essentially an Islamic problem and had to be addressed in those terms. For the Muslim Brotherhood, Palestine had been lost in large measure as God's punishment for turning away from Islam. The logical first step in its recovery was for Palestinians to return to Islam, and only after that could Israel be confronted effectively.

The relatively passive policies adopted by the Muslim Brotherhood leadership vis-à-vis Israel's military occupation of the West Bank and Gaza—the Islamization process could go on indefinitely—put the Brotherhood under intense pressure from the nationalist camp. The Brotherhood was often ridiculed for its inaction in the face of occupation. Such arguments and pressure were especially intense on university campuses, where student elections frequently centered on the subject. Despite its generally strong showing in university elections, the Islamist bloc was clearly on the ideological defensive throughout the occupied territories in the decade leading up to the Intifada. The sharp attacks by the nationalists on the political implications of Brotherhood policies increasingly affected student activists within the Islamist movement.

The Islamist movement began to divide along class and ideological lines in the 1980s, a fissure that pitted the old elite of the Muslim Brotherhood against an activist middle stratum. In terms of social class, the leadership of the Muslim Brotherhood tended to be urban, upper-middle-class merchants. In addition to being generally more well-to-do than their followers, the leaders of the Muslim Brotherhood had very close ties—including financial ones—with a number of conservative Arab states, principally Saudi Arabia, Kuwait, and Jordan.

Because of its economic stake in the status quo, the leadership of the Muslim Brotherhood in the occupied territories could in no way be construed as revolutionary. The Islamist ideology it propagated, unlike those of Ayatollah Khomeini, Sayyid Qutb, or Muhammad Abd al-Salam Faraj, reflected the Brotherhood elite's concern with not unduly disrupting the social and political order. Not surprisingly, the leadership of the Brotherhood constructed various alliances with non-Brotherhood notables and other wealthy businessmen and came to their defense when they were criticized by nationalists for political quiescence.

However, because of the Brotherhood's recruiting strategies in the 1980s, a middle stratum of activists developed that opposed the leadership's policies. Recruitment focused on high school and college students, teachers, and youths from camps and villages, and tended to stay away from the working classes. The middle activist stratum that developed consisted primarily of university-educated men from the lower middle class. In addition, this stratum was primarily based in refugee camps, domains that were formerly bastions of Arab nationalism.

The ideological fissures within the Islamist movement did not center on ultimate goals, since both sides wanted the establishment of an Islamic state in all of Palestine with strong ties to the larger Islamic world. Rather, the question was one of tactics: whether it was better to free the soul or the nation first. Should the occupation be confronted and rolled back first and society purified later, or was successful confrontation with Israel impossible without a genuine Islamic society being created first? Increasingly in the 1980s, the middle stratum of the Islamist movement chose the former "top-down" course, whereas the leadership of the Muslim Brotherhood maintained its long-standing "bottom-up" position, which emphasized prior social Islamization. Thus, the fissure separating the two Islamist camps had overlapping class and ideological implications. The fact that the Muslim Brotherhood was decentralized under Israeli rule delayed a confrontation, at least until the Intifada began.

The first and most important activist-oriented offshoot of the Muslim Brotherhood was the Islamic Jihad, or al-Jihad al-Islami, founded in Gaza in the early 1980s by Shaykh Abd al-Aziz Awda and Fathi al-Shaqaqi.[8] The Islamic Jihad differed from the leadership of the Muslim Brotherhood by advocating immediate confrontation with the Israeli occupation, although the formulation of this line of thought did not fully and clearly emerge until about 1986. Both of the founders had studied at Zaqaziq University in Egypt and were close to the factions of the Egyptian Muslim Brotherhood influenced by Sayyid Qutb. Both leaders were ultimately deported by Israel from the occupied territories in 1988. Shaqaqi was assassinated by Israel in 1995.

Jihad leaders believed in a dialectical relationship between political power and social piety. Because of the intimate relationship between the struggles to obtain political power and purify society, they believed that one challenge should not be undertaken in the absence of the other. Therefore, confronting the occupation and Islamizing Palestinian society should be done simultaneously (Abu-Amr 1990). The use of strikes against Israeli targets as a way of implementing the ideology of Islamic Jihad attracted adherents within the Islamist movement and support from Palestinian nationalists and leftists. It showed that an Islamist ideology could simultaneously fight the occupation and Islamize society. More important, it acted upon this ideology. Islamic Jihad carried out some audacious acts against Israel, including a 1986 grenade attack against members of the Givati Brigade (an elite army unit) while it was gathered in front of the Western Wall in the Old City of Jerusalem during an initiation rite for new recruits, and a 1987 jailbreak from the central Gaza prison (something that had never been done before). Jihad showed the second stratum of the Muslim Brotherhood, indeed all of the Brotherhood, that such action was possible. This prompted greater action against the occupation.

The debate within the Brotherhood sharpened considerably when the Intifada began on December 9, 1987. As Jihad acted, pressures mounted for the Brotherhood to join the uprising and put aside its ideological imperative to purify society before any confrontation. The realization grew that if the Brotherhood did not join in the Intifada, it would lose its political legitimacy within the Palestinian community.

The overlapping class and ideological fissures—in addition to mounting social pressures—finally resulted in a palace coup by the middle stratum of the Muslim Brotherhood against its leaders. The outcome was the establishment of Hamas. In essence, the formation of Hamas constituted an internal coup within the Muslim Brotherhood that brought the middle stratum cadres to the fore of the Palestinian Islamist movement and relegated the old leadership to a more peripheral position (Abu-Amr 1994, 67–68, 134).[9] Hamas rapidly absorbed the mantle and commandeered the institutions of the Muslim Brotherhood. It did not represent a break with the Muslim Brotherhood; rather, it was a reorganization with a new name and mission.

Social Movement Theory Applied to Hamas

In this section, I apply the fundamentals of social movement theory to Hamas in order to show both that SMT can shed important light on the dynamics of Hamas and that Hamas is not an unusual social movement organization (SMO).

Political Opportunity Structures

William Gamson and David Meyer have correctly warned, "The concept of political opportunity structure is in trouble, in danger of becoming a sponge that soaks up virtually every aspect of the social movement environment— political institutions and culture, crises of various sorts, political alliances, and policy shifts. . . . It threatens to become an all-encompassing fudge factor for all the conditions and circumstances that form the context for collective action. Used to explain so much, it may ultimately explain nothing at all" (1996, 275).

In order to avoid this problem, the analyst must show how specific changes in the external environment led to specific changes in the opportunities available to the SMO. In this section, I discuss four specific external (to Hamas) changes that directly enhanced Hamas's opportunity to organize and mobilize: a post-1977 change in Israeli policy toward the Islamist movement, a post-1977 enhanced international demonstration effect of Islamism, the 1987 start of the first Palestinian Intifada, and the 1993 Oslo accords.[10]

The first notable change in the political opportunity structure for the Palestinian Islamist movement came with the election of the Likud Party in Israel in 1977. In response to the growing influence of the PLO in the occupied territories in the 1970s, the Likud implemented a starkly different set of policies toward the Palestinians than had its Labor Party predecessors. Among the numerous policy shifts was a new strategy to contain the PLO by enhancing the position of an anti-PLO alternative. Two groups were identified: rural tribal elders and the Muslim Brotherhood. Enhancing the position of the first group came formally through the ill-fated Village Leagues policy.[11] Enhancing the position of the second group came informally by allowing the Muslim Brotherhood space to organize, space that was not provided to the PLO.

The political space provided to the Muslim Brotherhood (and then Hamas) throughout the 1980s was critical to the development of the Islamist movement in Palestine. Whereas PLO political rallies were banned, those of the Muslim Brotherhood were tolerated. Indeed, the IDF (Israeli Defense Force) looked the other way when demonstrators burned the Red Crescent Society in Gaza during a Muslim Brotherhood rally in 1981. Israel supported the Islamist camp, believing it could use the Islamists as a counterweight to the PLO, which was viewed as the greater threat to Israeli interests and security. While a number of observers claim Israel "created" Hamas—including the former IDF commander in Gaza, Zvi Poleg—that is undoubtedly an exaggeration.[12] Rather, support came in different forms, the most important of which was political and social space (Shipler 1986, 177; Sela 1989).[13] The Brotherhood could organize, demonstrate, and speak with little fear of arrest, whereas their nationalist colleagues were punished for similar actions. Israel's promotion of the Islamist movement as an alternative to the PLO continued during the early part of the Intifada, until Hamas was finally banned in September 1989.

For their part, the Islamists benefited from Israeli assistance in their drive to undermine the PLO and push their own agenda in its place. There was clearly no ideological love lost between Palestinian Islamists and Israel. The cooperation Hamas received from Israel must be considered tactical. In any case, much of this help was not sought by Hamas and was in a form that Hamas could not refuse: space.

Some Hamas officials were relatively open about the Israeli connection. In an interview, Muhammad Nazzal, a Hamas representative in Jordan, objected to the idea that Israel "created" Hamas, but admitted that Hamas was given more room to grow than the PLO. He went on to note that Israel was "playing the game of politics, trying to play off groups. But this does not make us its agents. The Israeli mentality is security first, before politics and everything else. It thought its security was enhanced by allowing us to grow, without thinking what might happen down the road" (Nazzal 1994).

A second change in the political opportunity structure for Palestinian Islamists was the international demonstration effect of Islamist power in the late 1970s and early 1980s. Two specific events had a particularly strong impact. First, the 1978–1979 Islamic revolution in Iran demonstrated that an unarmed but mobilized Muslim population could overthrow a powerful (and hated) regime that was supported by the United States. The Iranian revolution reverberated throughout the Muslim world, enhancing the prestige of—and the ease of recruitment for—Islamist groups everywhere. Virtually overnight the Muslim Brotherhood organization in Palestine was widely seen as a viable means of struggle against Israel's occupation.

The emergence of Hizbullah in Lebanon during the 1980s likewise enhanced the opportunity structure for the Palestinian Islamist movement. In this case, an armed, explicitly Islamist group inflicted serious damage to IDF occupation forces in Lebanon, initially forcing Israel to withdraw to a self-proclaimed "security zone." Mounting IDF casualties eventually compelled Israel to withdraw entirely from Lebanon under Prime Minister Ehud Barak. Hizbullah claimed, with some justification, to be the only group that had ever "defeated" Israel by compelling it to surrender territory it militarily controlled. The Sunni/Shiʿi divide did not prevent Palestinian Islamists from learning a number of lessons from the Hizbullah, most notably the art of suicide bombings—something unknown in Palestinian history.

The third and most important change in the political opportunity structure came with the outbreak of the Intifada in December 1987. As noted earlier, Hamas is best understood as a revolt of the activist second stratum of the Muslim Brotherhood against the more reform-minded first stratum. The Intifada provided the opportunity for the second stratum and its Islamist ideology to come to the organizational fore, leading directly to the creation of Hamas in early 1988. While Hamas did not create the Intifada (contrary to its claims), it is the group that benefited the most from its outbreak. Thus we see where an exogenous event (the start of the Intifada) led to the birth and empowerment of a new SMO.

Finally, the adoption of the Declaration of Principles (the first of the Oslo accords with Israel) by the PLO in September 1993 dramatically restructured and complicated political opportunities for Hamas. The Oslo accords established a Palestinian government (the Palestinian Authority, or PA) with some territorial control in the West Bank and Gaza, thus creating a new reality to which Hamas needed to respond. In general, the seven years of the Oslo process were a mixed blessing for Hamas. Initially, it appeared that Oslo would result in a net loss for Hamas for two reasons. First, the PA had a vested interest in circumscribing Hamas and had the resources to do so. Second, Hamas was cornered ideologically as to whether or not to participate in the governing institutions created by an agreement it rejected. As long as the "peace process" was going reasonably well, Hamas's opportunities were clearly limited. However, as Oslo failed to deliver Palestinian rights, Hamas's star rose and its opportunities for action increased. Israeli reluctance to fully end its occupation of the West Bank and Gaza strengthened Hamas, which had predicted Oslo's failure from the start, and made it the only significant opposition movement in Palestine. The Palestinian Left (primarily the PFLP, DFLP, and PPP) had never recovered from the demise of Marxism and combined could muster only single-digit support, according to numerous public opinion surveys. The political center, Fatah, transformed itself from an oppositional movement (to Israel) to a governing one (over Palestine). Only the Islamist Right, Hamas, constituted a viable opposition. As a result, its membership included not only the true believers but also a large "derivative" element. That is, Hamas became a political home to those who were disillusioned by Oslo. The failure of Oslo is properly seen as an event external to Hamas that significantly altered and ultimately enhanced Hamas's political opportunities.

Mobilizing Structures

One of the leaders of Hamas, Imad al-Alami, stated in a 1992 interview, "Hamas is an institutional movement and is not tied to any one person." He was correct in his assessment. Hamas is a social movement with an institutional base far more important to its success than any individual leader, including Ahmad Yasin, its titular head. Indeed, while Hamas's reputation in the West is that of a terrorist group, its ability to mobilize support in the West Bank and Gaza is tied to its vast institutional network, which supplies many types of social services. In this section, I divide those services into three types: mosque-based institutions (especially the Mujammaᶜ), other medical and educational institutions, and explicitly political institutions.

A common explanation for the rise of Islamist movements everywhere in the Arab world begins with the fact that all Arab states are authoritarian to one degree or another and therefore dominate the public sphere. Since opposition is not allowed to develop in the public sphere, it is pushed into private and semiprivate realms. In most cases, this means the mosque, since it is the one institution that the state dare not challenge directly. Islam, as both physical and discursive space, has become the only consistently legitimate sphere in which to discuss political issues in the Arab world today. The Palestinian case parallels this general trend, almost by default, and the mosque became a key institutional focus for the development of Islamism first in Gaza and then in the West Bank.

The most obvious institutional expression of the growing Islamist movement was the increasing number of mosques found in the occupied territories. Mosques in Gaza more than doubled between 1967 and 1987, with the greatest increase during the decade before the Intifada. The West Bank also experienced a mosque-construction boom, with 40 new mosques built annually. The seven-year Oslo period witnessed another boom, since funding channels for outside monies (e.g., from Saudi Arabia) no longer had to be secret and the financial institutions in Palestine were better able to handle transfers.

Most of the new mosques, as well as many older ones, were controlled by the al-Mujamma^c al-Islami (Islamic Association of the Muslim Brotherhood). Founded in 1973 in Gaza, the Mujamma^c rapidly came to dominate Muslim institutions of all kinds in Palestine. The particular genius of the Mujamma^c was to combine religious and social activities, so that the mosque was not only a place of worship but a provider of social services as well. In fact, the Mujamma^c built mosques, schools, kindergartens, clinics, hospitals, charitable associations, sports clubs, nursing schools, and related institutions. Often, these facilities were located within the mosque, and sometimes they included an activity room for women and girls and a social gathering hall (Abu-Amr 1994, 16; Mishal and Sela 2000, chapter 1 and appendix 1). The Mujamma^c comprised seven specific committees to oversee its institutional network: preaching and guidance, welfare, education, charity, health, sport, and conciliation (Mishal and Sela 2000, 20). While no fieldwork has been done to confirm this hypothesis, it is likely that the Mujamma^c also spawned significant *informal* networks as well, since this has happened in roughly similar circumstances in Jordan, Lebanon, Iran, Egypt, and elsewhere (Denoeux 1993; Wiktorowicz 2001; Singerman 1995). Such informal networks would bind Palestinians together in new (and hard to detect) ways. When the Muslim Brotherhood morphed into Hamas in 1987–1988, the Mujamma^c and all of its institutions likewise went with Hamas.

In addition to these more explicitly religious-based institutions, the Islamist movement in Palestine built numerous other social service institutions, primarily in the medical and educational realms. As above, many of these institutions were also under the control of the Mujamma^c. In the medical realm, for example, Hamas started the Scientific Medical Association in 1997 as a counterweight to the Red Crescent Society. The Scientific Medical Association operates medical clinics, dental facilities, and a blood bank (Mishal and Sela 2000, 157). Hamas's Association for Science and Culture, also started during the Oslo period, provides K–8 education for thousands of Palestinians. Perhaps most significantly in the educational realm, Hamas (through the Mujamma^c) operates the Islamic University in Gaza, where the faculty and student body constitute a hotbed of Hamas support in Gaza. The Mujamma^c took over the Islamic University from Egyptian control following the Egypt–Israel peace treaty and has run the university ever since. Following the lead of all the major PLO factions, Hamas even got into the labor union business when it opened the Islamic Workers Union in 1992.

The PA under Yasir Arafat has had a complex relationship with these organizations. To paraphrase the old saying, Arafat can't live with them and he can't live without them. These institutions, particularly the medical ones, provide invaluable support to the general Palestinian population (Hroub 2000, 241).[14] If these institutions were suddenly removed, thousands would suffer. Indeed, it is estimated that 95 percent of Hamas's annual budget of $70 million went to support these social programs (*Journal of Palestine Studies* 1996, 169). The PA cannot easily replace these institutions on its own. On the other hand, during the Oslo period Arafat came under intense Israeli and American pressure to close down any and all institutions under Hamas control. Periodically, Arafat felt compelled to act, as he did most forcefully in 1997 when the PA closed down more than 20 charitable institutions belonging to Hamas (Hroub 2000, 241). Another significant round of closures occurred in late 2001 and early 2002. Usually, the charitable institutions were allowed to reopen after a period of time and under a new name—further evidence of the PA's need to allow critical social services to remain operational.

Hamas has also built explicitly political institutions of mobilization. By far the most important of these has been the student political parties at Palestinian universities and secondary schools. Throughout the 1980s, Islamist blocs at Palestinian universities garnered significant support. In fact, in the aftermath of the Iranian revolution, Islamist blocs in the West Bank and Gaza gained control of a number of student councils. For the most part, however, alliances of various nationalist and leftist factions enabled the PLO to maintain its hegemony in West Bank universities, even while it relinquished authority to the Islamist bloc in Gaza. In effect, while the PLO—in particular, Fatah—remained the dominant political power at most Palestinian universities in the 1980s, the Islamists represented a powerful counterforce or opposition. In each of the three elections at Birzeit University that immediately preceded the Intifada, the Islamist bloc received approximately one-third of the total vote, second only to Fatah. In the 1985–1986 and 1986–1987 academic year elections at al-Najah University in Nablus, the Islamist bloc won 38 percent and 41 percent of the vote, respectively. In both elections the Islamist bloc finished second to Fatah (which won 49 percent and 48 percent, respectively), but far ahead of the leftist PLO factions. Similar results were seen at Hebron University. At the Islamic University in Gaza, the Muslim Brotherhood won every election in the 1980s. In the 1987 election, the Islamists won three-quarters of the vote, with Fatah gaining most of the remainder. Only at Bethlehem University, with its large Christian minority and official ties to the Vatican, has the Islamist bloc been of marginal importance. Even during the Oslo period when Fatah and the PA had more direct control over student elections, Hamas continued to rival Fatah in university elections, winning majority support in some cases.

In many ways, universities were more important than mosques for the Islamist movement in the occupied territories, principally because the universities had greater autonomy under the occupation (Jarbawi 1989). Many mosques were linked to Islamic endowments, or *waqf*s, whose administration was tied to Israeli and Jordanian authorities. The university-based Islamists, on the other hand, were unfettered by material interests tied to Israeli or Jordanian concerns and thus better able to construct ideologies independent of state interests. Direct Israeli infringement upon Islamist autonomy at Palestinian universities was generally limited to military coercion during periodic confrontations.

While these student blocs were the most important mobilizing political institutions for Hamas, they were not the only ones. Although the National Islamic Salvation Party always maintained that it was independent of Hamas, groups within Hamas supported its formation in preparation for the 1995 legislative elections in Palestine. For its part, Hamas declined to participate in the elections directly, viewing them as little more than a legitimization of Oslo. The formation of the party indicated a split in Hamas's thinking about how to engage PA institutions. Given the absence of elections since 1995, including the indefinite postponement of municipal elections (in which Hamas promised to participate), the importance of the National Islamic Salvation Party as a mobilizing structure has never really been tested.

Hamas has also been cognizant of the importance that public relations play in mobilizing support and framing issues. During the Oslo period, Hamas founded the Supreme Council for Islamic Information in order to disseminate its perspectives in Palestine. It created information bureaus in other countries as well to broaden the reach of its message.

With all of these institutions of mobilization at work over the past three decades, how strong is support for Hamas in the West Bank and Gaza? According to the respected polling institution CPRS in Nablus, the mean level of open support for Hamas between 1993 and 1997 was just over 18 percent of the population. Hroub believes this number is low, citing the high number of "no response" answers and the much higher turnout for Hamas candidates in various professional and student elections. He believes actual support is more likely about 30 percent (Hroub 2000, 229, 233). With the breakdown of diplomatic efforts and the start of the second Intifada in September 2000, other polls suggested Hamas had pulled even with Fatah in overall Palestinian support, although Fatah still controlled "the street."

Cultural Framing

To effectively popularize its ideology, a social movement must be able to provide clear summations of its ideology that resonate with its target audience. Such cultural framings represent the popular, bumper-sticker version of the broader ideology of the movement. While it is unreasonable to expect its hundreds of thousands of supporters (some illiterate) to have detailed knowledge of its ideology, Hamas can expect snippets of its ideological worldview to be known and repeated by all of its followers—indeed to permeate the public consciousness at large. In this way, Hamas can shape the public debate and the popular imagination in its own way. Clearly, the array of tools in the cultural toolbox available to an Islamist movement in a largely Muslim society is far greater than those available to, for example, a Marxist-Leninist group. Hamas has had a relatively easy time shaping the debate through the way it has framed the issues. In this section, I present five of the major frames employed by Hamas to depict its overarching ideology. As noted above, a single cultural toolbox gives rise to multiple competing and overlapping ideologies, which in turn each produce a handful of frames that best capture the essence of that ideological worldview.

1. *Palestine is waqf.* Hamas argues that all of Palestine is a religious endowment (*waqf*) given by God for all time exclusively to Muslims. By extension, therefore, no man or government has the right to negotiate away part of the waqf to non-Muslims. This argument is clearly aimed at denying Arafat the ability to settle for a Palestinian state in only the West Bank and Gaza. It also makes it difficult to recognize Israeli sovereignty over the remainder of historical Palestine. As Hamas put it in Article 11 of its 1988 Charter:

> The Islamic Resistance Movement [Hamas] believes that the land of Palestine is an Islamic waqf endowed to all Muslim generations until Judgment Day. No part of it may be squandered or relinquished. No Arab country, no king or president, no organization—Palestinian or Arab—possesses that right. Palestine is Islamic waqf land consecrated for all Muslim generations until Judgment Day. This being so, who could claim to have the right to represent all Muslim generations until Judgment Day? . . . This waqf will endure as long as heaven and earth last. Any action taken in regard to Palestine in violation of this law of Islam is null and void.

Like most good frames, the "Palestine as waqf" argument puts a new twist on an old institution. It refers to a charitable contribution, usually of productive land for a fixed period of time, for the benefit of the Muslim community, which is administered by the clergy, or ulama. Much of the Old City of Jerusalem, for example, is Islamic waqf property, particularly the area in and around the Haram al-Sharif, or the Temple Mount.

All Palestinians are quite familiar with the institution of waqf; however, Hamas puts a radical new spin on the notion of religious endowment by conflating private property with sovereignty. Traditionally waqf lands were treated as a form of private property (indeed, the benefactor typically received a tax benefit for endowing property). Hamas is not saying that all of Palestine is private property endowed as waqf. Rather, it claims that, in this case, waqf implies sovereignty—God's sovereignty over an entire country. Such an expansive interpretation of waqf has never been so prominently made before in Islamic history. Yet it is the kind of framing that resonates among Muslim Palestinians, very few of whom are historical scholars.

2. *Islam is the solution.* Replicating the most famous frame among Islamist movements in the Middle East, Hamas has employed the powerful phrasing

that "Islam is the solution" (*al-Islam, huwa al-hall*). This phrase is employed on a regular basis by Hamas supporters in Palestine. Indeed, a constant refrain by Hamas is that Palestine was lost, in part, because Arabs turned their backs on Islam, and only by embracing Islam can Palestine be won back. The entire Hamas Charter of 1988 reads this way, with numerous quotes from the Qur'an used to motivate Muslims to return to the fold. A few (non-Qur'anic) samples from the Charter (articles six, eight, and nine) should suffice to highlight the Hamas frame that Islam and only Islam is the right path for regaining Palestinian rights:

> Hamas has evolved at a time when Islam has been removed from everyday life. Thus judgment has been upset, concepts have become confused, and values have been transformed; evil prevails, oppression and obscurity have become rampant, and cowards have turned into tigers. Homelands have been usurped, and people have been expelled and fallen on their faces in humiliation everywhere on earth. The state of truth has disappeared and been replaced by the state of evil. Nothing has remained in its right place, for when Islam is absent from the scene, everything changes. . . . Hamas owes its loyalty to God, derives from Islam its way of life, and strives to raise the banner of God over every inch of Palestine. . . . In the absence of Islam, strife arises, oppression and destruction are rampant, and wars and battles take place. . . . God is our goal, the Prophet our model, the Qur'an our constitution, jihad our path, and death for the sake of God our most coveted desire.

This simple message that "Islam is the answer" or "Islam is the solution" is quite powerful. Needless to say, "Islam" per se has no specific solution to offer. Rather, it is Hamas's interpretation of Islam as it pertains to the conflict that becomes the real answer.

3. *The Jewish conspiracy.* Hamas, like most Islamist groups, is fundamentally anti-Semitic (in the commonly understood sense of the word). This is seen in at least two ways. First, the Hamas discourse refers primarily to "Jews" (*al-yahud*), less so to "Zionists" (*al-sahyuniyun*), and almost never to "Israelis" (*al-isra'iliyun*), thus seeing the conflict in fundamentally religious, not nationalist, terms. On this score, perhaps, Hamas can be forgiven because Israeli Jews themselves quite often refer to "Jews" rather than "Israelis." Think of Benyamin Netanyahu's famous campaign slogan championing himself as "Good for the Jews." However, Hamas is properly termed anti-Semitic for propagating the slander of Jewish control of the world, particularly the world's financial health. Indeed, according to Hamas, Jews are engaged in a grand conspiracy, primarily through the United States, against Palestinians, Arabs, and Muslims. Only this conspiracy has prevented Muslims and Palestinians from acquiring what is rightly theirs. This conspiracy can be seen in

the (rumored) Jewish hidden hand behind the September 11, 2001, attacks on the World Trade Center (Jews, possibly Mossad, were behind the attack, Jews working in the buildings were warned ahead of time to leave the building, etc.), and other events. Again, the Hamas Charter vividly describes this Jewish conspiracy. At one point confirming the validity of the Protocols of the Elders of Zion (article 32), the most sustained discussion of the grand Jewish conspiracy comes in article 22:

> The Jews have planned well to get where they are, taking into account the effective measures in current affairs. Thus, they have amassed huge fortunes that gave them influence that they have devoted to the realization of their goals. Through money they gained control over the world media, such as news services, newspapers, printing presses, broadcast stations, and the like. With money they financed revolutions throughout the world in pursuit of their objectives. They were behind the French revolution, the Communist revolution, and most revolutions here and there that we heard about and are hearing of. With wealth they established clandestine organizations all over the world, such as the Freemasons, the Rotary and Lions clubs, etc., to destroy societies and promote the interests of Zionism. These are all destructive intelligence-gathering organizations. With wealth they controlled imperialist nations and pushed them to occupy many nations to exploit their resources and spread mischief in them. Concerning the local and international wars, let us speak without hesitation. They were behind the First World War in which they destroyed the Islamic Caliphate, picked the material profit, monopolized the raw wealth, and got the Balfour Declaration. They created the League of Nations through which they could rule the world. They were behind the Second World War, in which they grew fabulously wealthy through the arms trade. They prepared for the establishment of their state; they ordered that the United Nations be formed, along with the Security Council, in place of the League of Nations, so that they could rule the world through them. There was no war that broke out anywhere without their hands behind it.

Unfortunately, such anti-Semitism plays well to many common Palestinians, who are ready to believe in the grand Jewish conspiracy. Thus, by framing the conflict as merely a by-product of larger Jewish power, Hamas is able both to produce a message that resonates truth for many people and to absolve Palestinians of their weakness: there is no way such a simple people could have beaten such power. Note, however, that this message is in contradiction with the second frame that Islam is the solution. Implicit in that frame is the notion that had Palestinians and Arabs not abandoned Islam, all would be well today. Consistency is not a requirement in cultural framing.

4. *Patience (*sabr*) is paramount / The peace process will fail on its own.* Hamas has responded to the peace process, begun with the Madrid conference of 1991, with a call for patience (*sabr*) (Mishal and Sela 2000). The concept of sabr has been utilized by Hamas to justify a number of strategic and tactical decisions. Strategically, the notion of sabr underlies the argument that Oslo is fatally flawed and will collapse under its own weight and lack of logic—it is just a matter of time. Hamas leader Musa Abu Marzuq stated this:

> From the outset, Hamas has said that this type of agreement will not work. The Oslo agreement is a very obscure document which, because of its special nature, will never be able to free Palestine from Israeli occupation. It will not put the Palestinians on the road to an independent state. Decisions in Oslo will always be made by the stronger party, which in this instance is Israel. The Palestinians will achieve nothing from the Oslo agreement, and we told Yasir Arafat so from the outset. (1997)

This logic, of course, means that Hamas need not be impatient in trying to hasten the collapse of Oslo since it will happen in any case. Thus, when Hamas is relatively quiescent, sabr explains the inaction. On the other hand, when Hamas's Izz al-Din al-Qassam Brigades undertake an attack, that does not contradict sabr either, as patience certainly does not require complete inactivity.

On the tactical side, the notion of sabr has allowed Hamas leaders to take the apparently contradictory position of rejecting the very legitimacy of Israel while showing a willingness to accept a Palestinian state in only the West Bank and Gaza, next to Israel, as an "interim solution." Through the lens of sabr, they can take the long view and accept such a state as merely an intermediary step in the eventual liberation of all Palestine. This argument is made regularly by Hamas leaders, as in the following statement by Hamas political bureau chief Khalid Mish'al during a 1997 *NPQ* interview:

> We have no problem accepting the Gaza Strip and the West Bank as a transitional solution, but without giving up our right to the rest of the land of Palestine and without giving legitimacy to the state of occupation and aggression [Israel]. This transitional liberation is only one stage in our quest for the total liberation of Palestine. (Question: "You are then ready for an interim solution, but in the long run you refuse to coexist with a Jewish state?" Answer: "Of course.")

The notion of being patient while Oslo fails and taking the long view of generations had undeniable appeal among Palestinians, particularly as year after year of "peace" went by without much to show for it (except more settlements). In other words, as Oslo collapsed, Hamas was in a perfect position to say, "We told you so." This has only enhanced the credibility of Hamas's message.

5. *Hamas offers a more authentic nationalism.* The Palestinian national movement has a long history, and a contender for power in Palestine dismisses nationalist sentiment at his peril. In a philosophical vacuum, Islamism and nationalism share little in common. What Hamas has needed to do, and has done, is to frame nationalism in a different way and then suggest its variant of nationalism is more authentic and powerful. Hamas has come a long way in this regard. In the early 1980s, nationalist parties openly condemned the Muslim Brotherhood as a prop for the occupation. The framing of the nationalism question has thus had to be done very carefully so as not to raise these old ghosts. The Charter is Hamas's first attempt to praise Palestinian nationalism and the PLO while staking out a somewhat different vision. Much of the Charter praises the legitimate role that nationalism has played in the Palestinian struggle (articles 12 and 14):

> Nationalism,[15] from the point of view of the Islamic Resistance Movement, is part of our religion. Nothing in nationalism is more significant or important than waging jihad when an enemy treads on Muslim land. While other nationalisms are concerned just with material, human, and territorial causes, the nationalism of the Islamic Movement has all this in addition to the more important divine qualities that give it soul and life. The question of the liberation of Palestine is bound to three circles: the Palestinian circle, the Arab circle, and the Islamic circle. Each of these circles has its role in the struggle against Zionism.

Parallel with its acceptance of nationalism, Hamas also gave due credit to organizations that espoused nationalism, principally the PLO (articles 25 and 27):

> The Islamic Resistance Movement respects the Palestinian nationalist movements and appreciates their circumstances and the conditions surrounding and affecting them. It encourages them as long as they do not give their allegiance to the Communist East or the Crusading West. The Movement assures all the nationalist trends operating in the Palestinian arena for the liberation of Palestine that it is there for their support and assistance. The Palestine Liberation Organization is close to the heart of the Islamic Resistance Movement. The PLO counts among its members our fathers, our brothers, our cousins, and our friends, and the Muslim does not estrange himself from his father, brother, cousin, or friend. Our homeland is one, our situation is one, our fate is one, and the enemy is a joint enemy to all of us.

However, Hamas argued that the reason the PLO adopted a secular, nationalist ideology was not through informed choice but rather because of "the ideological confusion prevailing in the Arab world as a result of the ideological invasion under whose influence the Arab world has fallen since the defeat of the Crusaders" (article 27). It was only because of the purposeful confusion perpetrated by "Orientalists, missionaries, and imperialists that the PLO adopted the idea of the secular state." While such misperceptions by the PLO can be understood in their historical context, Hamas argued in article 27, they cannot be reconciled with the true nature of Islamic Palestine:

> Secularism completely contradicts religious ideology in its attitudes, conduct, and decisions. That is why, with all our appreciation for the Palestine Liberation Organization—and what it can develop into—and without belittling its role in the Arab-Israeli conflict, we are unable to reconcile Islamic Palestine and secularism. The Islamic nature of Palestine is part of our religion. The day the Palestine Liberation Organization adopts Islam as its way of life, we will become its soldiers and fuel for its fire, which will burn our enemies. Until such a day, and we pray that it will be soon, the Islamic Resistance Movement's stand toward the PLO is that of a son toward his father, a brother toward his brother, a cousin toward his cousin: We will suffer his pain and support him in confronting our enemies, wishing him to be wise and well guided.

By accepting Hamas's vision of the proper interpretation of nationalism, a Palestinian can simultaneously support the Islamist Hamas and still view himself as a Palestinian patriot. Thus, Abu Marzuq could legitimately claim to be a Palestinian nationalist because "Hamas now carries the Palestinian hope and will fight to achieve Palestinian identity and achieve independence" (1997). Alternatively, Hamas spokesman Ibrahim Abu Ghawsha could declare, "History shall record that Hamas is the Palestinian group which safeguarded the fabric of Palestinian society. The picture would have been different had the Islamists been in power and the secular Fatah movement in the opposition" (1998). Nationalism is a great thing, but only within the context of Hamas's interpretation of what nationalism actually means.

Conclusion

I have attempted to show that social movement theory can shed valuable light on Hamas and that Hamas is intelligible as a social movement, similar to other social movements around the world. This would achieve two goals. First, it would continue the recent trend in Middle East studies to be self-consciously theoretical in our treatment of data, either through the generation of new theory or, as in this case, the application of existing social science theory to a Middle East case study. Second, it would make the point contra-Orientalism (which exists more in the press and policy worlds than it does anymore in the academy) that Islamism, like other things Muslim, can be understood through the application of general concepts and does not exist in a parallel explanatory universe where a completely different set of theoretical tools is necessary to make sense of it.

Moreover, I have argued that SMT is best understood as a middle path between structuralist and rational choice theories of collective action, which recognizes the constraints under which choices are made as well as the partial efficacy of purposeful action. The analytical tools available to social movement theorists can construct a more powerful conceptual understanding of groups like Hamas than competing analytical approaches.

Finally, I have suggested that the relationship between "terrorist group" and social movements is far more complex and problematic than simplistic categorizations can account for. The dynamic relationship between tactical violence and a social movement has profound policy and theoretical implications.

Notes

1. The following discusses these schools in terms of ideal types. Although I recognize that there are important attempts to bridge the micro/macro division, for analytic purposes I highlight the distinctive tendencies in the different approaches.

2. An excellent collection of essays that explicitly use rational choice theory to explain rebellion can be found in *Rationality and Revolution* (Taylor 1988).

3. Some rational choice theorists have begun to apply their model to strategic *group* decision-making. This would seem to deny the fundamental theoretical underpinnings of rational choice theory.

4. Perhaps the most sophisticated statement to date on why SMT provides a better explanation of volunteerism and its relationship to structures than either rational choice or structural theories is Jeffrey Berejikian's "Revolutionary Collective Action and the Agent-Structure Problem" (1992).

5. There is some evidence to suggest that in Egypt in the 1990s the profile of a typical radical Islamist changed somewhat to a younger, less educated individual. According to the Ibn Khaldun Center's statistics on arrested Islamists, the "typical" Islamist was younger (the median age going from the upper twenties to the lower twenties since the 1970s), less educated (four out of five Islamists in the 1970s went to university; only one out of five in the 1990s did), and less urban (55 percent from large cities in the 1970s; only 15 percent in the 1990s).

6. The ideological arguments for such views were most famously articulated by Sayyid Qutb in a book (entitled *Ma'allim f'il-Tariq*, literally "Signposts on the Road") that indirectly called for the overthrow of Nasser's regime. Qutb, who sought to take the Muslim Brotherhood in a more confrontational direction, was hanged for his views.

7. While its charter called exclusively for social and cultural activities, the Brotherhood in Jordan was clearly a political organization as well. The Brotherhood was used as a counterweight by the regime against both pan-Arabists and more radical Islamists.

8. In his 1990 *Intifada*, Don Peretz has suggested that there were eight offshoots of the Muslim Brotherhood in the 1980s in Gaza alone (103).

9. There is some debate over interpreting the creation of Hamas. Ziad Abu-Amr, in his *Islamic Fundamentalism in the West Bank and Gaza* (1994), argues that the formation of Hamas did not represent a break in the Muslim Brotherhood but was rather a logical continuation of Brotherhood policy, made by longtime Brotherhood leaders (67–68). His analysis denies the kinds of internal pressures that had built up in the Brotherhood, in part because of the changing nature of its recruitment in the 1980s. At the same time, Abu-Amr admits that a radicalization of the Islamist movement occurred (134), but gives no sociological explanation for the change. The model employed above corrects this deficiency.

10. For clarity, I refer to Hamas throughout this section without trying to differentiate between pre-1987 Muslim Brotherhood and post-1987 Hamas.

11. In the late 1970s and early 1980s, Israel helped set up a system of "Village Leagues," local Palestinian organizations designed to act as intermediary institutions between the local Palestinian populations and the Israeli authorities. Most Palestinians viewed those who participated in the Leagues as collaborators.

12. Poleg served as commander of the IDF in Gaza from July 1988 to March 1990 and was later elected mayor of Natanya. In an interview published December 15, 1994, in the *Mideast Mirror,* he stated: "Hamas was set up by us, in the mid-1980s, as a competitive movement to the PLO. The idea was that Hamas would carry out cultural, educational, and humanitarian activities. Within a few months the movement became more militant and began leading the violent resistance, including the use of guns against the IDF" (5–6). Marwan Muasher, Jordan's first ambassador to Israel and former spokesman for Jordan's delegation to the Washington peace talks, likes to tell a story that confirms this suspicion among public policymakers. When the delegation went to meet with President Bush, a delegate commented that Israel had "created" Hamas. Surprised, Bush turned to advisor Dennis Ross and asked if this was true. Ross replied affirmatively (interview with Marwan Muasher, April 11, 1994, Amman).

13. Funding support also occurred (see Shipler 1986, 177). Michel Sela, a respected Israeli journalist, reported that assistance also included arming certain Islamists, although this was certainly a less common form of support. See her article "The Islamic Factor," *Jerusalem Post,* October 25, 1989.

14. The World Bank noted that, before Oslo, Palestinian NGOs (including the Hamas NGOs) provided 60 percent of the costs of primary health care and 50 percent of the costs of secondary health care in the West Bank and Gaza.

15. Hamas uses the Arabic *wataniyya,* not *qawmiyya.* The former is usually employed in Arabic to represent state-based nationalism (e.g., Egyptian nationalism), while the latter has a communal or ethnic sense and is used in the phrase "Arab nationalism" (*al-qawmiyya al-ʿArabiyya*).

Works Cited

Abu-Amr, Ziad. 1990. Interview. East Jerusalem and Ramallah, January 20.
———. 1994. *Islamic Fundamentalism in the West Bank and Gaza.* Bloomington: Indiana University Press.
Ajami, Fouad. 1981. *The Arab Predicament: Arab Political Thought and Practice since 1967.* Cambridge: Cambridge University Press.

al-ᶜAlami, ᶜImad. 1992. Interview. *Filastin al-Muslima*, August.

Ansari, Hamied N. 1984. "The Islamic Militants in Egyptian Politics." *International Journal of Middle East Studies* 16: 123–44.

Barber, Benjamin. 1995. *Jihad vs. McWorld: How Globalism and Tribalism Are Reshaping the World*. New York: Ballantine Books.

Berejikian, Jeffrey. 1992. "Revolutionary Collective Action and the Agent-Structure Problem." *American Political Science Review* 86, 3 (September): 647–57.

Denoeux, Guilain. 1993. *Urban Unrest in the Middle East: A Comparative Study of Informal Networks in Egypt, Iran, and Lebanon*. Albany: SUNY Press.

Gamson, William, and David Meyer. 1996. "Framing Political Opportunities." Pp. 275–90 in *Comparative Perspectives on Social Movements: Political Opportunities, Mobilizing Structures, and Cultural Framings*, ed. Doug McAdam, John D. McCarthy, and Mayer Zald. New York: Cambridge University Press.

Ghawsha, Ibrahim Abu. 1998. *al-Urdun* (Jordan), October 24. Cited in *Foreign Broadcast Information Service*.

Goldstone, Jack. 1994. "Is Revolution Individually Rational? Groups and Individuals in Revolutionary Collective Action." *Rationality and Society* 6, 1 (January): 139–64.

Guenena, Nemat. 1986. "The Jihad: An Islamic Alternative in Egypt." *Cairo Papers in Social Science* 9, monograph 2 (Summer).

Halpern, Manfred. 1963. *The Politics of Social Change in the Middle East and North Africa*. Princeton, N.J.: Princeton University Press.

Hroub, Khaled. 2000. *Hamas: Political Thought and Practice*. Washington, D.C.: Institute for Palestine Studies.

Ibrahim, Saad Eddin. 1980. "Anatomy of Egypt's Militant Islamic Groups, Methodological Note, and Preliminary Findings." *International Journal of Middle East Studies* 12, 4 (December): 423–53.

Jarbawi, Dr. Ali. 1989. Interview. Ramallah, September 27.

Lichtheim, George. 1964. "From Finland Station." *New York Review of Books*, December 17.

Marzuq, Musa Abu. 1997. *al-Hayat*, January 19. Cited in *Foreign Broadcast Information Service*.

Mishᵓal, Khalid. 1997. Interview. *NPQ*, Fall.

Mishal, Shaul, and Avraham Sela. 2000. *The Palestinian Hamas: Vision, Violence, and Coexistence*. New York: Columbia University Press.

Mitchell, Richard P. 1969. *The Society of Muslim Brethren*. London: Oxford University Press.

Nazzal, Muhammad. 1994. Interview. Amman, Jordan, April 13.

Peretz, Don. 1990. *Intifada: The Palestinian Uprising*. Boulder: Westview.

Sela, Michel. 1989. "The Islamic Factor." *Jerusalem Post*, October 25.

Shipler, David. 1986. *Arab and Jew: Wounded Spirits in a Promised Land*. New York: Times Books.

Singerman, Diane. 1995. *Avenues of Participation: Family, Politics, and Networks in Urban Quarters of Cairo*. Princeton, N.J.: Princeton University Press.

Skocpol, Theda. 1979. *States and Social Revolutions*. New York: Cambridge University Press.

———. 1994. *Social Revolutions in the Modern World*. New York: Cambridge University Press.

Swidler, Ann. 1986. "Culture in Action: Symbols and Strategies." *American Sociological Review* 51 (April): 273–86.

Taylor, Michael, ed. 1988. *Rationality and Revolution*. New York: Cambridge University Press.

Wallerstein, Immanuel. 1990. "The French Revolution as a World-Historical Event." Pp. 117–49 in *The French Revolution and the Birth of Modernity*, ed. Ferenc Fehér. Berkeley: University of California Press.

Walzer, Michael. 1979. "A Theory of Revolution." *Marxist Perspectives* 2, 1: 31.

Wiktorowicz, Quintan. 2001. *The Management of Islamic Activism: Salafis, the Muslim Brotherhood, and State Power in Jordan*. Albany: SUNY Press.

PART II

NETWORKS AND ALLIANCES

Five

The Networked World of
Islamist Social Movements

Diane Singerman

Understanding Islamic activism is an urgent concern in the aftermath of September 11, 2001. A wider audience now focuses on groups like al-Qaeda and Egypt's Islamic Group and strives to understand the meaning, motives, and organization of these movements. Some do so simply to understand a phenomenon that has emerged as a seemingly new, significant actor in world politics; others do so for the express purpose of responding to the attacks of September 11 and undermining future operations planned by such organizations. Whether one's goal is insight or eradication, our understanding of Islamic activism can be greatly enhanced by seeing such phenomena as a form of social movement activity and thus availing ourselves of the large and ever-growing body of theory and scholarship on social movements in general.

It may appear problematic to some readers to draw comparisons between radical Islamist activism and other popular social movements such as the women's movement or the civil rights movement in the United States. As I hope to show, however, a comparative lens explains the similarities between movements across time and space and also suggests their distinctiveness. At the same time, a comparative lens challenges the all-too-common position, articulated by many throughout the media, government, academia, and the policy world, that Islamist activism is "exceptional" and somehow unique due to religious, ethnic, regional, or cultural factors.

In this chapter, I want to suggest that Islamic activism is not unique but rather has elements common to all social movements. The organizational structures, repertoires of contention, collective identity, and so forth of Islamic movements are similar to those of other movements throughout the world. However, what is specific to Islamic movements is the political context within which they operate. Many regimes in the Middle East rely upon political exclusion and repression to maintain rule. Citizens, under such conditions, are forced to organize through informal networks and build collective identities through these networks; and it is this character of the Islamist movement which makes it distinct from other social movements. The networked world that constitutes associational life in the Middle East is what explains the emergence and organizational power of these movements and also the capabilities of such extreme elements as al-Qaeda in executing complicated, costly, and ultimately horrific attacks.

I will begin by discussing the political landscape of the modern Middle East and its exceedingly repressive nature. The costs of political participation in the region are high, and thus conventional forms of political expression are unavailable. As an alternative, people turn to informal networks to organize and advance their interests. The complex web of associability sits at the heart of Islamic movements and is fundamental to understanding them. Networks are not only the most viable means of building movements within the current political environment. They are also key transmission belts of collective identity, drawing the ideas, sensibilities, reflexivity of people together while crisscrossing social, economic, and political hierarchies. I then explore the dynamism between networks and the sense of solidarity they inspire. In particular, I suggest how collective identities are forged out of the sensibilities and ties that are cultivated by networks. Social movement theory helps us to understand the construction and significance of these identities, as activists draw upon nascent but invisible communities of sympathizers. I conclude by noting that the transnational dimension of Islamist activism, particularly its most militant variety such as the al-Qaeda network, is premised on a collective identity forged by the types of repression and informal networks commonly found at both the domestic and regional levels in the contemporary Middle East.

Families, Dynasties, Monarchies, and Contentious Politics

Social movements emerge out of specific local contexts, and this political environment is key to an understanding of an Islamist movement's agenda and trajectory. The Middle East, as a region, is characterized by political exclusion and extremely limited practices of citizenship. Monarchy, dynastic rule, and the military dominate political life, plain and simple. Families, with a hereditary right to rule, govern 14 Middle Eastern states outright, including the Kingdom of Morocco, the Hashemite Kingdom of Jordan, the Kingdom of Saudi Arabia, Kuwait, Bahrain, Qatar, the Sultanate of Oman, and the seven federation members of the United Arab Emirates (Abu Dhabi, Dubai, Sharjah, Ajman, Umm al-Qaiwain, Ras al-Khaimah, Fujairah). Even in some of those states where elected opposition parties participate in parliament and prime ministers wield some power, most notably Morocco and Jordan, legislative bodies remain subject to the pleasure of the monarch and political parties, and other groups suffer from legal and extralegal constraints on fund-raising, mobilization, and freedom of association (Posusney 2001). While some of the dynastic regimes, such as Bahrain, have recently restructured their governments toward a constitutional monarchy with promises of greater autonomy, at the same time they reaffirm their monarchical character (see Herb 1999 for a thorough discussion of the differences and commonalities of Middle Eastern monarchies).

In addition to the monarchies and sultanistic regimes of the Arabian Gulf, dynastic succession is de rigueur even in avowedly secular, nationalist regimes such as Ba°thist Syria, and the sons of secular rulers such as Saddam Hussein in Iraq (prior to the U.S. invasion in 2003), Qadhafi in Libya, Mubarak in Egypt, and Ali Abd Allah Salih in Yemen are rumored to be "in contention" for succession. In these regimes, ideological, developmental, and nationalist ideologies serve as the basis for legitimacy and authority, yet kinship seems to be trumping the ideologies of Arab nationalism and Ba°thi politics. The principle of dynastic succession was so firmly rooted, for instance, in Hafez al-Assad's mind that after the heir apparent, Basil al-Assad, died in a car crash in 1994 he whisked his other son, Bashar al-Assad, back from Europe (where he was studying ophthalmology), gave him a crash course in Alawi/Ba°thist dominance, and rapidly promoted him in the military.

It is too early to tell if Egypt, Libya, or Yemen will follow in the footsteps of Syria and create dynasties with the outward appearance of nationalist, secular, authoritarian political systems, but such a trajectory would be consistent with other regimes in the region. For example, in Egypt Hosni Mubarak has ruled since 1981 in four successive terms without participating in a competitive election. Rumors of a "succession crisis" surround his presidency, particularly as he ages and continues to prevent competitive presidential elections, but there is strong evidence that, like other Middle Eastern monarchs (both of the republican/secular and conventionally dynastic kind), he is grooming his wealthy son, Gamal Mubarak, to be his political heir.[1] Ann Lesch (1996) has appropriately labeled Egypt a presidential monarchy, and rumors of a dynastic succession only reinforce the monarchical tendencies of this centralized, bureaucratized state. In short, when considering the possible emergence of social movements and oppositional politics, it must be remembered that the political climate throughout the Middle East offers extensive power and authority to *anyone* who occupies the ruler's office, whether a king, shaykh, amir, or president, and this authority often gets passed down through the ruling family. The modern state, as such, continues to thrive with little transparency, financial accountability, legislative or judicial autonomy, or rule of law.

Islamist activists must not only contend with the concentration of power around the family at the elite level. Their organizational efforts are also deeply constrained by the military and its proximity to the center of power. Whether one adopts a historical or contemporary perspective, the military has often sat either at the heights of power or just below dynastic rulers. The Ottoman sultan utilized the military institution of slave-soldiers, or *mamluks*, collected from the outer reaches of the Ottoman Empire to conquer, protect, and eventually rule the sultan's territory. The officer corps of the military emerged not from the notable, aristocratic, or religious classes but rather from slave-soldiers who were loyal and dependent on the sultan for their power. While some Ottoman mamluks were eventually able to establish an independent dynastic rule, for the most part the officer corps was a cosmopolitan professional elite, which offered rags-to-riches opportunities for loyal, gifted, obedient soldiers, including sinecures in the Empire's administration. Even before World War I and the dismemberment of the Ottoman Empire, officers and soldiers in Egypt, Syria, Turkey, and Algeria were already beginning to dabble in nationalism and express anticolonial and anti-Ottoman politics. Local nationals were finally admitted to national military academies in the 1930s, and the future leaders of nationalist regimes in the Middle East emerged from the first generations of graduates, who cut their teeth on anticolonial movements and the 1948 war with Israel.

The problem with militaries is that their coercive power and their increasingly national reach make them dangerous to rulers who do not have strong bases of support and legitimacy. As war making or preparations intensify, rulers must raise large standing armies that they or their notables or mercenaries can lead. But when armies become national and recruit ordinary soldiers and the middle class from their nations, they are in an advantageous position to take over their country. In some places in the Middle East, this is exactly what happened (Tarrow 1994, 59).

The first military coup d'état in the region and in Africa took place in Iraq in 1936, and during that same year the graduating class of the Egyptian military academy included Gamal Abdel Nasser and Anwar Sadat. Successful military coups followed in Egypt in 1952; Iraq in 1958; Algeria in 1965; Libya in 1969; Sudan in 1958, 1969, and 1989; and Syria in 1970 (only the latest coup). Originally motivated by nationalist, anticolonial, and modernist ideologies, the military coups did not become the "change agents of modernization" expected by some social scientists. In fact, Middle Eastern leaders have to constantly "check their back" and police their own military and security forces to avoid new coup d'états by challengers.

By the 1960s, Richard Bulliet (1999, 191) writes, "Most of the Middle East had become subject to autocratic regimes increasingly addicted to the use of police-state methods to maintain power. Indeed, after the fall of the Soviet empire in 1991, the Middle East became the world's foremost arena of despotic, non-participatory government, whether in monarchical or military guise." Bulliet uses the term *neo-Mamluk* to describe Middle Eastern military regimes that are embedded in secular or monarchical regimes.

[The term *neo-Mamluk*] stresses important continuities with the pre-imperialist past. Mamluks—professional military officers bound to one another by strong ties of training and camaraderie, but substantially divorced from the general populace in outlook and career path—had been a pervasive force in Middle Eastern governance for 600, if not 1,000, years prior to the onset of Westernization in the nineteenth century. The system, in a variety of forms, had consistently provided excellent soldiers, and it was often receptive to new ideas of a technical sort emanating from the West. But the system had been unrelenting in its tendency toward tyranny: government of the officers, by the officers, for the officers. . . . The term puts an emphasis on autocracy and the officers' self-serving exclusion of the general populace from political participation, relegating issues of declared ideology to a subordinate role. Many have argued, for example, that the failure of these regimes to defeat Israel or secure the material blessings of modernization sapped their ideological legitimacy and made an Islamic resurgence possible. I would point not to these undeniable failures, but to the regimes' success in instituting brutal and all-pervasive internal security structures as a root cause of Islamic opposition. (191–92)

In a similar fashion, Amira El-Azhary Sonbol argues that twentieth-century military regimes, such as in Nasserist Egypt, "should be seen as a resurrection of traditional military power" found among the *khassa* or special class holding power, which includes the ruling elite, the military, and the business classes (2000, xxiii–xxix). It is not that any military leader can become president or that ideologies, reputation, support, and luck do not play a role. The state depends upon the military and security forces to maintain the regime and public order. These institutions have certainly been the breeding grounds for presidents.

Within the Arabian Gulf, the royal family neutralizes the potential threat from the military by appointing family members to powerful staff positions, keeping armies small (which has its own risks), hiring foreign mercenaries, and relying on foreign military alliances (the Gulf war in 1990–1991 demonstrated some of the benefits and pitfalls of this approach; see Owen 1992, 50). Again, it is not that the military trumps the presidency, but it is the basis and means for regime stability. Only one supreme leader is allowed, and if the ruler discovers that his loyal servants are developing their own popularity, charisma, or power, they are quickly deposed, transferred to less important positions, or suffer "accidents" (see Hammoudi 1997 for a discussion about the entrenched master/disciple relationship in the Arab world).

Furthermore, while several Middle Eastern countries, including Jordan,

Morocco, Egypt, and Turkey, faced privatization pressures amid the growth of capitalism, they experienced a horizontal expansion of the military into the national economy. In regimes that owe their power to the military, even after the heydays of the 1960s and 1970s, the "officer-politicians continue to use these institutions to perform a variety of functions, becoming at once military commanders and civilian technocrats, ideologues, and commercial producers. . . . Hegemony within these states continues to lie with the armed forces, even if the state has assumed a civilian character more than ever before" (Kamrava 2000, 80).

Oppositional forces, whether democratic, Islamist, or leftist, can certainly ridicule the ideological (anti-imperialist, modernist, or nationalist) pretensions that militaries once espoused, but there are great risks in challenging the coercive, economic, political, and bureaucratic might of the militaries since they are now clearly stakeholders. The unusually powerful role of the military can be seen even in the most democratic countries of the Middle East, Israel and Turkey, where challenges by Palestinians and Islamists, respectively, have provoked severely "illiberal" policies. In these "military democracies," despite a tradition of electoral competition, vibrant oppositional politics, political turnovers, and peaceful succession, "civil military interactions are cemented either by institutional devices (the National Security Council in Turkey) or international geopolitical realities or tradition (retired Israeli officers becoming politicians). [The] military is a highly visible and integral feature of the political system [and] the legitimacy of the military's political influence is seldom questioned by the electorate" (ibid., 70–73).

In an effort to retain power, by the 1990s authoritarian military regimes had "been reduced to autocratic *mukhabarat* (intelligence) states, and in a number of instances, notably in Algeria, Iraq, and Sudan, they had also become instruments of random terror and bloodshed" (ibid., 81). Absorbing the limited resources of even wealthy Gulf countries, the Middle East remains the most militarized region in the world by virtually every measure. NATO countries spend approximately 4.5 percent of their GNP on military expenditures. Developing countries on average spend about 5.5 percent of their GNP on similar outlays. In contrast, countries in the Middle East devote 17 percent of their GNP on military expenditures, while North African nations spend about 8 percent of their GNP (Algeria, Morocco, Tunisia, Libya, Egypt, Chad, Mauritania, and Western Sahara) (Cordesman 2001, 34, 37). International actors such as Russia, the United States, France, and the United Kingdom are key supporters of foreign military aid and private arms sales to the region.

The collusion among monarchical, dynastic regimes, the military, and intelligence forces has suffocated a wide range of mediating structures and formal organizations throughout the region, whether they are professional associations, regional clubs, neighborhood and community organizations, political parties, women's associations, human rights groups, youth groups, etc. The power and organizational vitality of society has been diminished by draconian laws of association and assembly, limitations on fund-raising, a censored press, and regulatory overkill (see, e.g., Amnesty International 2000). This has left the state, kinship, and religious institutions in place, offering few rights of citizenship, representation, voice, or political freedoms in return. Thus, the ground for activism—no less Islamic activism—is littered with risks and formidable obstacles (Ibrahim et al. 1996). Whether one follows descriptive accounts of political life in the post-1967 order in any single country in the Middle East, analytic single-case studies by social scientists and/or indigenous intellectual critics, official government publications, human rights reports, or reports from such institutions as the World Bank, UNESCO, and the European Union, the prognosis on representative, open, participatory politics in the region is bleak (though important concessions to collective life occur occasionally in certain countries) (see, e.g., the UN *Arab Human Development Report 2002* for further analysis).

Informal Networks and Islamist Movements

Monarchy, familial rule, the military, and intelligence services retain a strong hold on citizens of the Middle East and stifle civil society. This would explain the weakness of social movements in general and opposition groups in particular. Nonetheless, as is well known, the region is replete with domestic (often illegal) political activism and provides a base for transnational activist forces. Why is this the case? And why have Islamist activists, as opposed to liberals, democrats, socialists, or communists, been able to build and sustain a regional, if not international, movement? The diverse trends within social movement theory and arguments about contentious politics, collective identity, and informal networks are quite useful for understanding the rise of Islamist movements, their limitations, and the predicaments they continue to face. At the same time, the universality that implicitly underpins many strands of social movement theory has obscured some of the more distinctive elements of Islamist movements.

Like other social movement theorists, McAdam, Tarrow, and Tilly's view of contentious politics as "public" unintentionally narrows the scope of social movement activity within the historical and cultural context of the Middle East, even though they claim to "challenge the boundary between institutionalized and non-institutionalized politics" and "insist that the study of politics has too long reified the boundary between official, prescribed politics and politics by other means" (2001, 6). They define contentious politics as "episodic, *public,* collective interaction among makers of claims and their objects when (a) at least one government is a claimant, an object of claims, or a party to the claims and (b) the claims would, if realized, affect the interests of at least one of the claimants" (5, emphasis added). They make a further distinction between transgressive contention, which fulfills these first two criteria, and contained contention where two additional criteria are fulfilled: "(c) at least some parties to the conflict are *newly* self-identified political actors, and/or (d) at least some parties employ *innovative* collective action" (emphasis added). Collective action is defined as innovative in the above definition if it "incorporates claims, selects objects of claims, includes collective self-representations, and/or adopts means that are either unprecedented or forbidden within the regime in question" (7–8). Islamic activism is best described in terms of "contained contention."

What marks the innovative style of Islamist movements is twofold: first, they challenge most reigning regimes in the Middle East by rearticulating the boundary between the "public" and "private" itself to propose a less secular and autonomous vision of the "good life" and governance. This rejection of secularism and a Westernized version of "the public" threatens almost every Middle Eastern regime, albeit in different ways. Even in nations which claim religious legitimacy or whose laws are heavily influenced by Islam, such as Morocco, Jordan, and the Kingdom of Saudi Arabia, religious authorities are subordinate to dynastic rulers and/or the military. Islamists wish to change this formula. For example, despite the fact that Article 1 of Saudi Arabia's "Basic Law of Government" states, "The Kingdom of Saudi Arabia is a sovereign Arab Islamic state with Islam as its religion; God's Book and the Sunnah of His Prophet, God's prayers and peace be upon him, are its constitution, Arabic is its language and Riyadh is its capital," Islamists attack the government for its monarchical rule, which they condemn as un-Islamic (see chapter 10 by Gwenn Okruhlik in this volume).[2]

We see that across Islamist movements in the region, the contours of public and private spheres, state and society, are themselves contested. As Seyla Benhabib has argued, "All struggles against oppression in the modern world begin by redefining what had previously been considered private, non-public, and non-political issues as matters of public concern, as issues of justice, as sites of power" (1992, 84).[3] Struggles over the boundaries between the public and private are contested issues in Western democracies (abortion, education, school prayer), and they remain at the heart of debates about rule and power in the Middle East. The Islamist vision of the "good life" is "not simply about 'religion' or 'politics,' but is part of a cultural battle over the very definition of these terms" (Wuthnow 1991, 16). Islamist movements have framed their agenda around fundamental questions about the meaning of life and how Islamic beliefs and practices should inform daily life, law, morality, the economy, and governance. While Islamist groups have certainly targeted their governments, made claims against regimes, and established mass organizations and political parties, they have more commonly and successfully directed their message and organizational strategies toward changing practices and the meaning of everyday life. Battles over dress, morality, marriage, celebrations, entertainment, sexuality, and faith as well as conflicts over governance and law are at the center of Islamist oppositional frames that have attracted sympathetic support. The Islamist movement reshapes how "people understand themselves as creators and practitioners of their world" (Escobar 1997, 63).

On more conventional political grounds, Islamists point to the model of the prophet Muhammad when he created an Islamic state in the seventh century and argue that his example is relevant for the twenty-first century as well. Even more moderate religious movements and authorities, such as the Muslim Brotherhood or state-supported religious institutions such as al-Azhar in Egypt, argue that Islam and its laws, morals, and practices should serve as the ideological and authoritative basis of the polity.[4] These theocratic positions clearly challenge the legitimacy and authority of the nationalist, authoritarian, developmentalist, and liberalizing regimes of the region.

Second, Islamists are innovative because they utilize informal and less visible means to mobilize supporters and build movements (see, e.g., Wiktorowicz 2001a). The use of informal networks, in addition to formal, bureaucratized, mass organizations, definitionally displaces Islamist movements from the "contentious politics" framework, since their collective action is often not "public" in a conventional sense. Their strategies of mobilization and their ideological vision often rely upon informal, personal networks and religious and cultural associability to build movements. Wiktorowicz (2001b) has argued that al-Qaeda "members" act not according to organizational dictates but rather according to the accepted Salafi method of religious interpretation that joins al-Qaeda supporters together in a loose transnational network of Muslims as they continue to dispute, revise, and transform religious understanding. (The Salafi school in Islam argues that the *salafs* or original companions and followers of the prophet Muhammad in the seventh century created what should stand as the model for any Islamic society and polity.)

The vague call that "Islam is the solution" resonates on so many levels in the Muslim world, and as a result it influences multiple social and political fields and encourages a collective identity. Purchasing a cheap pamphlet from a street vendor on proper Islamic dress for women, visiting a medical clinic attached to a mosque, attending study circles with clerics, making the pilgrimage to Mecca, veiling, or reading a religious magazine links an individual, indirectly perhaps, to a larger social phenomenon. In this context, Melucci's understanding of collective action as a phenomenon rooted in identity construction, contingent upon culturally and historically constructed notions of "the public" and "the private," and based on informal networks as a strategy for mobilization and a conduit for the constant regeneration of a "meaning machine," seems more appropriate than the conventional approach to contentious politics, which subscribes to the notion that collective action must be "public" (and thus misses the heart of the Islamist phenomenon). Wearing a particular type of dress or praying in a radical mosque can get one arrested in neighborhood sweeps by internal security forces, but it also enhances the feelings of belonging to a distinct group. Melucci's approach thus allows for a wider definition of an "activist," since as collective identity is constantly constructed and reconstructed, the plane of action and the definition of the actor shift as well.

> Collective identity as a process involves cognitive definitions concerning the ends, means, and field of action. These different elements or axes of collective action are defined within a language that is shared by a portion or the whole of a society or that is specific to the group; they are incorporated in a given set of rituals, practices, cultural artifacts; they are framed in different ways, but they always allow some kind of calculation between ends and means, investments and rewards. (Melucci 1995, 44–45)

For purposes of emphasis, a collective identity is something that is shaped, intentionally and unintentionally, by movement entrepreneurs and cultural producers, such as religious and intellectual authorities, poets, essayists, journalists, cartoonists, and even movie producers. In a region that forbids so much formal political participation and constrains and harasses governmental associations and civil society in general, participating in "given sets of rituals, practices, and cultural artifacts" can themselves be "evidence" of commitment to the Islamist movement and signs of shared beliefs that resonate among fellow travelers. Identifying movement adherents by these processes of signification can be much harder for outsiders than reading membership lists of formal organizations, but nevertheless these movement "adherents" convey their interests without risks of visible, political, formal collective action. The ability to "flip" a sympathizer into an activist is a main preoccupation of any movement, and a shared collective identity is a prerequisite to providing additional resources, labor, money, or facilities to the movement (see McCarthy and Zald 1977). Tarrow (1994, 3) notes that particularly in repressive systems, symbolic politics and collective identity build movements characterized as "discursive communities." Furthermore, as Aminzade and Perry (2001, 159, 161) point out,

> Religious groups have a unique institutional legitimacy that gives them distinct advantages; it is harder to repress them; and they feel "safer" to confront and discuss issues that no one else can. . . . Religious leaders do not have to rely only on rational persuasion since their followers can be "moved by the spirit" rather than persuaded by rational arguments. Given the highly salient nature of these beliefs and their imperviousness

to falsification, they often sustain the level of commitment required for high-risk activism and violent challenges to secular authority.

A range of social movement theorists have noted the important links between collective identity, mobilization, and activism. As Melucci argues, a collective identity can develop long before mobilization. It produces solidarity and a shared moral investment in a set of issues (Melucci 1995, 52–53). This sense of collective identity forges links among sympathizers to the movement while making them internally and externally distinctive. Northern white students, for example, who joined Freedom Summer in 1964 in Mississippi adopted blue jeans and overalls, "liberated" sexual mores and behavior, and manners of speech to signify their solidarity with African Americans in the South, their membership in the civil rights movement, and their rebellion against white Northerners and Southerners (McAdam 1988, 93). In similar ways, young women in Egypt reject "Western" clothing and adopt Islamic dress that covers the body, hair, and face. Men and women join religious study groups, attend prayers at mosques regularly, engage in charitable associations and services organized by mosques, and read the newspapers and books of the religious groups and publishing houses. These types of behaviors signify to others that such individuals subscribe to a more religious way of life which often, but not necessarily, communicates adherence to the goals and vision of an Islamist movement.

In the language of rational choice theory, movements overcome the free-rider problem by developing programs that offer collective incentives of group solidarity and commitment to moral purpose (Jenkins 1983), something that Carrie Wickham discusses in chapter 9 in this volume. A strong sense of collective identity promotes a reflexive feeling of solidarity among like-minded travelers, who become more entwined through ideological, educational, cultural, political, or social networks. Individuals join movements, but movements are built through networks of associations that ultimately build and cultivate a collective "we." People who know each other can "vouch" for, motivate, comfort, and challenge one another and use their shared history in the face of political and social risks. Knowing someone who is already involved is one of the strongest predictors of recruitment into the membership of a social movement (McAdam and Paulsen 1997, 146). Dense interpersonal networks exclusive to group members, particularly in a situation where the group feels challenged by authorities or the status quo (as in the racist South of the 1960s), means that the group represents a "mobilization potential" (Klandermans 1984, 1988) for activists. Movement entrepreneurs can recruit already existing networks of people with a strong sense of collective identity in blocs much more easily than random individuals (see McAdam 1988; Morris 1997).

Here again, it is important to emphasize the critical role of nurturing a collective identity, which can then draw people together in interpersonal networks. These networks may be cemented through a particular mosque, migration, school, work, prison, repression, or an ideological vision, but they also reinforce shared identities, create group feeling, solidarity and distinctiveness, and make mobilization easier while reducing its uncertainty (McAdam and Paulsen 1997, 146–47). As Mueller (1997) notes in her explanation of the rise of the women's movement in the United States in the late 1960s, submerged networks become "cultural laboratories" within civil society, only emerging in confrontation with the state at a later point in public policy debates. Islamists have also created "cultural laboratories" that have influenced oppositional strategies and changed the behavior of elites themselves.

As mentioned earlier in this chapter, social movement theorists have long noted the importance of "social networks." For example, Tarrow's (1994, 27) four-part inquiry into the dynamics of social movements suggests that we examine (1) opportunity structures that create incentives for movements to form; (2) the repertoire of collective action they use; (3) the social networks on which they are based; and (4) the cultural frames around which their supporters are mobilized. Tarrow also suggests that the major *external* resources of social movements are the social networks in which collective action occurs and the cultural and ideological symbols that frame it (44–45). Melucci (1995, 45) argues that "collective identity as a process refers thus to a network of active relationships between the actors, who interact, communicate, influence each other, negotiate, and make decisions. Forms of organizations and models of leadership, communicative channels, and technologies of communication are constitutive parts of this network of relationships." And Tilly has argued that movements are built through lateral moves of categories of networks (of personnel of movements from one group to another). Following Harrison White (n.d.), Tilly (1978, 63) suggests that "catnets" are sets of individuals that form both a category because they share some common characteristic (education, neighborhood, migration, worship, kinship, collegiality, occupation, or prison) and a network. Tilly argues that "catness" times "netness" (or how extensive a network may be) equals organization. Network multiplicity is a key to mobilization, and particularly weak or loose ties created by newspaper, print, and informal social networks make coordinated collective action possible across groups, diffusing collective action and making coalitions possible (Granovetter 1995; Gould 1997, 133–34).

While social movement theory has focused on "social" networks as critical to the growth and base of social movements, networks have long been an important component of political life in the Muslim world, though perhaps this has not been typically recognized by many Western social scientists, since these networks tend to be informal and relatively invisible. Networks need to be understood within the context of specific political structures and environments. More than a question of semantics or a tug-of-war over the terrain of the disciplinary boundaries between sociology and political science, networks take on political meaning and political utility in circumstances where formal, bureaucratized, visible, legal collective action is systematically repressed. Under these conditions, informal networks constitute a parallel site of political life, connecting disparate and varied individuals, families, and communities to larger places and centers of power and political contestation. Elsewhere, I have used the term *informal* rather than *social* to describe networks in Cairo, since it calls attention to the extremely sensitive and politicized nature of associational life in contexts where the state closely and minutely supervises any formal, legal, public associations (Singerman 1995). "Informal activities," whether economic or political in nature, are those which escape licensing, regulation, and even enumeration by the state and thus have an illegal or quasi-legal status (see Hart 1973; Abdel-Fadil 1980, 15; de Soto 1989; and Singerman 1995). Despite the lack of formal, legal, political space for citizens in Egypt and elsewhere throughout the region, these networks articulate and further the demands of their members for such things as jobs, houses, cheap food, public goods, community order, conflict resolution, and public morality. The preponderance of informal networks provides an organizational grid in these communities, a type of associational life that remains outside the surveillance of the state, precisely because it is informal, invisible, unregulated, and unlicensed in nature. In Egypt, these networks are ubiquitous among the residents of lower income communities within both the older popular quarters of Cairo and the newer, informal housing areas that ring central Cairo, and they exist in similar locales throughout the Middle East.[5]

Networks clearly have macro implications as they spread transnationally and regenerate throughout society and the polity. Thus, it is not surprising that familial, mosque, occupational, educational, clerical, and village networks of activists that already crisscross the globe and connect such disparate locales as New York City, Cairo, Jerusalem, Paris, London, Kabul, Hamburg, Khartoum, and Boston should serve as a significant structural characteristic of Islamist movements. These heterogeneous, informal networks must be considered in any assessment of the phenomenon of Islamist movements, since they provide a vehicle for recruitment, facilitate the consolidation of their material and social bases, and offer general support and solidarity. Islamist movements do not necessarily produce these networks, but they rely on them, since the networks are deeply embedded in society. Furthermore, informal networks transcend both the spatial boundaries of neighborhood, work, and state institutions, as well as cultural, class, and gender boundaries, incorporating men and women, different social classes, and various status groups into complex networks. Teachers, religious leaders, artisans, bureaucrats, police officers, engaged couples, and leaders of informal credit associations maintain links and networks to each other to further their interests.

Networks also have a material dimension or value in that they facilitate the production and distribution (and redistribution) of goods and services. Though many of the goods and services procured through informal networks are technically illegal (private tutorials from schoolteachers, bribes for bureaucrats, currency exchanges, black market food, informal housing) but not always illicit (drugs and prostitution, for example), their engagement in the economic sphere enhances their utility and reinforces their popularity in the community.[6] Networks facilitate access to knowledge and resources, whether in the sense of finding the right people who can present one's case to the police or housing authorities, directing poor women and men to someone who will initiate an informal savings association on their behalf, or finding a cleric to advise young people on morality, marriage, or religious observance. The integration of informal networks in the local and international economy reinforces their authority in the community.

Informal networks constitute an organizational grid in the community, which *may* be enlisted to support clandestine activities or collective repertoires of action, so essential to social movements. Since networks are designed to aggregate the interests and demands of individuals and groups, many, though not all, of the constituents of a network know and trust each other, and these networks can be easily exploited for the purposes of more visible and direct resistance to the state and its institutions. Putnam defines social capital as "features of social organization . . . that can improve the efficiency of society by facilitating coordinated actions" (1993, 167). I would argue that "efficiency" is not quite the right term to use in describing the value of these networks because it strips the political dimension from our attention. In Egypt, people rely on social capital, in the context of networks, because, in part, they are objects of rule rather than true citizens of their state with full political rights. Western analyses of Islamist movements often dismiss the key role played by political exclusion in the region, which obscures not only the role of networks in movements themselves but also the weight and legitimacy they carry within society at large.

As political activists in Islamist movements grow bolder and more organized, informal networks are essential for activities such as mobilizing supporters, raising funds, promoting symbolic protest, smuggling arms, hiding and feeding people, eluding the police, dispersing propaganda, and organizing mass protests. Throughout the Middle East, the level of Islamist violence and government repression has steadily increased since the mid-1980s. Yet, even though governments increased repression and Islamists countered with more violence, movements were able to sustain themselves and perhaps even grow throughout the 1990s, particularly in heavily populated urban areas, provincial cities, the countryside, and transnational communities (as September 11 clearly demonstrated) (see Fandy 1994; Toth 1998). Despite this growth, however, popular support for radical Islamists in Egypt declined after the horrific massacre of tourists in Luxor in 1997 by a faction of the Islamic

Group. In addition, increased use of military and security courts in the 1990s kept Islamists in jail or in exile.

Transnational Islamist Activism

Due to limitations of space, I cannot address sufficiently the obvious transnational dimensions of contemporary Islamist movements. Nonetheless, there are clear links between the domestic and regional dimensions of Islamic activism (discussed above) and the broader transnational expressions that now garner so much attention in the post–September 11 period. For this reason, let me simply concentrate on how the three themes of this article—informal networks, political exclusion and repression, and a strong collective identity—affect, and are effected by, the transnational dimensions of Islamic activism. In this final section, my analysis compares Islamist movements with other social movements.

The ubiquity of informal networks in Islamist movements and the regional tradition of political exclusion, as well as the presence of a strong Islamist collective identity, brings us to a particular appreciation of the goals and vision of the more radical and extreme expressions of Islamic activism, exemplified by the al-Qaeda network. It has been extensively reported since September 11 that Egyptian Jihad leader Ayman el-Zawahri formed a new joint operation with Osama bin Laden in 1998 called the International Islamic Front to Combat Jews and Crusaders. This operational merger between some of the al-Jihad leaders in Egypt and the networks, resources, and labor of Osama bin Laden's al-Qaeda produced a more powerful network with enhanced organizational capabilities (Rashwan 2000). The new umbrella organization also included three Islamist groups from Pakistan and Bangladesh. It was this alliance which explained the phenomenal "success" of al-Qaeda's growth under the protection of the Taliban. In isolation and security, this organization could then plan the attacks on U.S. installations in Saudi Arabia, Yemen, Kenya, and Tanzania and plan for the September 11 attack in the United States and Europe. The transnational dimension of this movement is obvious, since it was quite capable of moving its operatives, weapons, communication capabilities, and other resources across national boundaries with ease. The thousands of Muslims from Sudan, Egypt, Palestine, England, France, Algeria, and other countries who went to protect Muslims in Bosnia, Afghanistan, and Chechnya (often at the urging of Middle Eastern governments and religious institutions) constituted a labor force and set of activists whose experiences of violence, brutality, and oppression obviously radicalized them. (The United States also recruited Muslims for the jihad against the Soviets in Afghanistan.) In addition, many returned to Europe or the Middle East with greater ideological commitments, deeper loyalties to a particular community, and military experience.

In the 1980s and 1990s, these same young men (and it was primarily men who went abroad in the name of the Afghan or Bosnian "jihad" to defend their fellow Muslims) largely returned to domestic economies with limited opportunities and to highly charged political environments where the "Afghans," as they were called, were immediately deemed politically suspect and suspicious due to their travels. Some of these men returned several times for further training in Afghanistan or education and employment in Europe, and their networks and sense of collective identity grew. The "white heat" of the war in Afghanistan and Bosnia was a transforming, radicalizing experience that is not dissimilar to the effects of the violence of the American South in the 1960s on black and white civil rights activists. In Mississippi and elsewhere the brutality of racism produced a generation of activists who worked together in the early 1960s (most notably during Freedom Summer in 1964) and then went on to form other movements such as the Free Speech movement in Berkeley, the antiwar movement, the student movement, and the women's movement in the late 1960s and early 1970s (McAdam 1988). By way of analogy, such solidarity-building, in response to what were seen as intolerable and repressive conditions, took place in the Middle East as activists from groups such as al-Gamaᶜa al-Islamiyya or al-Jihad in Egypt enhanced their sense of collective identity and commitment through their prison experiences and the general experience of operating in an authoritarian environment. Again, we see the cumulative and cyclical consequences of political repression and state violence against challengers in the region, as activists burrow deeper into subterranean and invisible places.

The dynamic between informality, repression, and networks can also lead to greater fragmentation within movements. Arrests or prison may destroy the movement's leadership, and cells are left to operate on their own with increasingly desperate and hardened leaders in control. As David Smilde comments about al-Qaeda's attacks on September 11, great historical moments are created by individuals, and the actions of one can create turning points that alter everything that comes "after." "Social movements are effective precisely to the extent that the actions of a relatively small group of people are successfully projected as representing a much larger collectivity. That representation may or may not be true, but whether it is true rarely has much relation to the movement's impact" (AMSOC list-serve e-mail, October 10, 2001).

Conclusion

Reasonable reflection on the kind of collective identity that Islamist movements cultivate, the informal character of their organizations, and the general dynamics of how such movements emerge and operate might reveal that Islamist movements are less effective than they would otherwise be. If such groups pursued more formal types of organization or joined official types of representation (however limited), perhaps they would be better able to advance their aims. This is the point of social movement theorists who employ a quasi-modernist understanding in which social movements do best when they engage the state, become part of its organs, and win major concessions. While such strategies may be effective for some movements in some settings, there is strong evidence that *informal* organizational strategies—which can take advantage of nascent support communities and concomitant fervor—may provide greater instrumental benefits.

Piven and Cloward (1979) have long argued that movements often lose steam and are co-opted by elites and thus are ultimately compromised as they concentrate on building permanent, centralized, bureaucratized mass-membership organizations. From this perspective, disenfranchised groups, reacting to widely experienced social dislocation and galvanized by consciousness-raising and greater feelings of efficacy, should take advantage of "moments of madness" that the movements produce. As collective defiance mounts, they can exert leverage by causing or contributing to "dealignments" among elites and escalating, not compromising, their demands. Popular insurgency, Piven and Cloward argue, "flows from its own structure, logic, and direction and is historically specific" and should not always be stuffed into a Leninist strategy of building a disciplined, bureaucratic party structure (1979, xii).

It is important to reiterate that Islamist movements cannot easily organize mass, centralized, bureaucratic organizations; their governments will not let them. Their sympathizers may increase, but the resources for repression at the hands of the Egyptian, Syrian, or Saudi governments are huge. Thus, some movements have turned away from local insurrection to destabilizing their enemies and producing fear, crises, and uncertainty. The consequences of violent political actions, often associated with Islamist movements, are not uniform or predictable. Nonetheless, they often cause the status quo to change by exposing vulnerabilities and challenging established wisdom and practices.

In the aftermath of September 11, observers of all stripes struggle to understand the character of Islamist movements. In this chapter, I have attempted to contribute to this understanding by employing conceptual categories from social movement theory in the context of the contemporary Middle East. The unique element of the Middle East is the extreme repression and political exclusion practiced by regimes, and this most marks social movement activity by forcing associational life to go underground, as it were, thus creating and sustaining enduring collective identities and networked action.

If there is a political prescription embedded in the chapter, it is that the most effective way for Middle East regimes to address the interests and grievances of Islamist movements is to open up their polities and allow for political inclusion. Whether one abhors or embraces these movements is immaterial. What is clearly necessary is to allow people to make these decisions as citizens rather than as objects of rule. This will both blunt the violent strains of Islamist aspirations and enable Islamist movements to conceive of themselves as full, invested citizens. The lessons we can learn from this study are not merely academic but will hopefully highlight the enduring costs of political exclusion and constrained civil societies in the Middle East that produce funnels of political violence. The "criminalization of politics" produces activists and sympathizers who create their own political world, with different rules and norms where the transcendental end justifies the means. Dualistic rhetoric of good and evil not only blot out the place for complexity in our analysis but also distract us from our mutual responsibility in how we make the world.

Notes

I would like to thank students in my seminar at American University on social movements in spring 2002 for indirectly influencing this essay as well as the AMSOC list serve following September 11. I also appreciate the assistance and advice received from Paul Wapner, Steven Cook, Suzanne Hitchman, Nida al-Aḥmad, and Seda Demiralp.

1. Many observers have suggested that the recent prosecution and imprisonment of Dr. Saʿad Eddin Ibrahim, the founder of the Ibn Khaldun Center for Development Studies, was motivated by the Mubarak administration's severe displeasure over an article by Dr. Ibrahim and his comments on television, which suggested sarcastically that "the Arab world's contribution to political science" was a term that he coined *gumlukiyya*. This term is a pun that combines the Arabic words for republic (*gumhuriyya* and *malakiyya*). He used the term to describe how the new president of Syria, Bashir al-Assad, had assumed office automatically after his father died, even though the country hadn't been a hereditary kingdom for centuries. He was also making a pun, because *gumlukiyya* rhymes with *mulakhiyya,* a word for a viscous vegetable soup that Egyptians use to describe a mess. When pressed by a call-in questioner, Dr. Ibrahim reluctantly suggested that President Hosni Mubarak, marking his twentieth year in power, might be grooming his son Gamal as his successor. Seventeen days later, armed State Security policemen stormed into Ibrahim's home and arrested him. He was eventually acquitted.

2. "Basic Law of Government," 1993, Kingdom of Saudi Arabia, <http://www.oefre.unibe.ch/law/icl/sa__indx.html>, accessed July 3, 2003.

3. In the Middle East, this politicization of the "private" due to struggles against injustice, exclusion, and patriarchy is further complicated by European colonialism in the Middle East, which entailed the adoption of foreign legal codes. Civil and criminal codes were borrowed from Belgian, French, British, or Swiss legal jurisprudence, greatly reducing the jurisdiction of *shariʿa,* or Islamic law. Only matters of "personal status" remained within the realm of shariʿa, and Islamic family courts and religious authorities jealously guarded any further encroachment upon their reduced authority. These affairs of marriage, divorce, child custody, and inheritance seemed, particularly according to Western tradition, "private" concerns, yet in Islam they are central concerns of Islamic law and crucial to the morality of the community of believers.

Like feminist organizations in the West, women's rights activists have waged controversial campaigns to change Personal Status Law, with moderate success (see Sonbol 1996 and Charrad 2001). Islamists have been particularly antagonistic to women's groups and others who support a woman's right to divorce and enhanced rights in marriage, child custody, and inheritance. Arguments about the gendered division of labor, female employment, birth control, child-rearing practices, sexuality, and morality are at the center of public debate and Islamist discourses.

4. After coming to power in Egypt in 1970, Anwar Sadat altered the Egyptian constitution, under Article 2, to state that "Islam is the religion of the state and Arabic its official language. Islamic jurisprudence is the principal source of legislation." <http://www.sis.gov.eg/eginfnew/politics/parlim/html/pres0303.htm>, accessed March 28, 2003.

5. One government report in 1993 estimated there were 23 informal settlements in the Greater Cairo Region (GCR) of 5.88 million people, while another survey from the Ministry of Local Administration estimated that 4.52 million people live in 171 informal housings areas in the GCR (Arandal and El-Batran 1997, 1–2). According to the 1996 population census, 10 million people inhabited the GCR (Electronic Atlas of Cairo 1998).

6. The post–September 11 investigation of al-Qaeda, for example, revealed the complex mix of primarily informal financial networks that supported the conspirators.

Works Cited

Abdel-Fadil, Mahmoud. 1980. "Informal Sector Employment in Egypt." *Series on Employment Opportunities and Equity in Egypt*, no. 1. Geneva: International Labour Office.

Aminzade, Ron, and Elizabeth J. Perry. 2001. "The Sacred, Religious, and Secular in Contentious Politics: Blurring Boundaries." Pp. 155–78 in *Silence and Voice in the Study of Contentious Politics*, ed. Ronald R. Aminzade et al. Cambridge: Cambridge University Press.

Amnesty International. 2000. "Egypt: Muzzling Civil Society." AI-index: MDE 12/021/2000. London, September 19.

Arandal, Christian, and Manal El-Batran. 1997. "The Informal Housing Development Process in Egypt." Centre Nacional de la Recherche Scientifique (CNRS), Working Paper no. 82, Bordeaux, France (July).

"Basic Law of Government." 1993. Kingdom of Saudi Arabia. <http://www.oefre.unibe.ch/law/icl/sa00000_.html>, accessed March 28, 2003.

Benhabib, Seyla. 1992. "Models of Public Space: Hannah Arendt, the Liberal Tradition, and Jurgen Habermas." Pp. 73–99 in *Habermas and the Public Sphere*, ed. Craig Calhoun. Cambridge: MIT Press.

Bulliet, Richard W. 1999. "Twenty Years of Islamic Politics." *Middle East Journal* 53, 2 (Spring): 189–200.

Charrad, Mounira M. 2001. *States and Women's Rights: The Making of Postcolonial Tunisia, Algeria, and Morocco*. Berkeley: University of California Press.

Cordesman, Anthony H. 2001. *The Military Balance in the Middle East: Executive*

Summary: Region-Wide Trends. Washington, D.C.: Center for Strategic and International Studies, January.

de Soto, Hernando. 1989. *The Other Path: The Invisible Revolution in the Third World.* Translated by June Abbott. New York: Harper and Row.

Electronic Atlas of Cairo. 1998. Cairo: Centre d'études et de Documentation Economique, Juridique et Sociale.

Escobar, Arturo. 1997. "Cultural Politics and Biological Diversity: State, Capital, and Social Movements in the Pacific Coast of Colombia." Pp. 201–26 in *The Politics of Culture in the Shadow of Capital,* ed. Lisa Lowe and David Lloyd. Durham, N.C.: Duke University Press.

Fandy, Mamoun. 1994. "Egypt's Islamic Group: Regional Revenge?" *Middle East Journal* 48 (Autumn): 607–25.

Gould, Roger V. 1997. "Multiple Networks and Mobilization in the Paris Commune, 1871." Pp. 133–44 in *Social Movements: Readings on Their Emergence, Mobilization, and Dynamics,* ed. Doug McAdam and David A. Snow. Los Angeles: Roxbury.

Granovetter, Mark. 1995. *Getting a Job: A Study in Contacts and Careers.* 2d ed. Chicago: University of Chicago Press.

Hammoudi, Abdalla. 1997. *Master and Disciple: The Cultural Foundations of Moroccan Authoritarianism.* Chicago: University of Chicago Press.

Hart, Keith. 1973. "Informal Income Opportunities and Urban Employment in Ghana." *Journal of Modern African Studies* 11: 61–89.

Herb, Michael. 1999. *All in the Family: Absolutism, Revolution, and Democracy in the Middle Eastern Monarchies.* Albany: SUNY Press.

Ibrahim, Saʿad Eddin, et al. 1996. "An Assessment of Grassroots Participation in the Development of Egypt." *Cairo Papers in Social Science* 19, 3 (Fall).

Jenkins, J. Craig. 1983. "Resource Mobilization Theory and the Study of Social Movements." *Annual Review of Sociology* 9: 527–53.

Kamrava, Mehran. 2000. "Military Professionalization and Civil–Military Relations in the Middle East." *Political Science Quarterly* 115: 67–92.

Klandermans, Bert. 1984. "Mobilization and Participation: Social-Psychological Expansions of Resource Mobilization Theory." *American Sociological Review* 49: 583–600.

———. 1988. "The Formation and Mobilization of Consensus." Pp. 174–96 in *From Structure to Action: Comparing Movement Participation across Cultures,* ed. Bert Klandermans, Hanspeter Kriesi, and Sidney Tarrow. International Social Movement Research, vol. 1. Greenwich, Conn.: JAI Press.

Lesch, Ann Mosely. 1996. "Comparative Politics Today: Egypt." Pp. 608–67 in *Comparative Politics Today: A World View,* ed. Gabriel A. Almond and G. Bingham Powell Jr. New York: HarperCollins.

McAdam, Doug. 1988. *Freedom Summer.* New York: Oxford University Press.

McAdam, Doug, and Ronnelle Paulsen. 1997. "Specifying the Relationship between Social Ties and Activism." Pp. 145–57 in *Social Movements: Readings on Their Emergence, Mobilization, and Dynamics,* ed. Doug McAdam and David A. Snow. Los Angeles: Roxbury.

McAdam, Doug, Sidney G. Tarrow, and Charles Tilly. 2001. *Dynamics of Contention.* New York: Cambridge University Press.

McCarthy, John, and Mayer N. Zald. 1977. "Resource Mobilization and Social Movements." *American Journal of Sociology* 82: 1212–41.

Melucci, Alberto. 1995. "The Process of Collective Identity." Pp. 41–63 in *Social Movements and Culture*, ed. Hank Johnston and Bert Klandermans. Minneapolis: University of Minnesota Press.

Morris, Aldon D. 1997. "Black Southern Student Sit-in Movement: An Analysis of Internal Organization." Pp. 90–109 in *Social Movements: Readings on Their Emergence, Mobilization, and Dynamics*, ed. Doug McAdam and David A. Snow. Los Angeles: Roxbury.

Mueller, Carol. 1997. "Conflict Networks and the Origins of Women's Liberation." In *Social Movements: Readings on Their Emergence, Mobilization, and Dynamics*, ed. Doug McAdam and David A. Snow. Los Angeles: Roxbury.

Owen, Roger. 1992. *State, Power, and Politics in the Making of the Modern Middle East.* London: Routledge.

Piven, Francis Fox, and Richard A. Cloward. 1979. *Poor People's Movements: Why They Succeed, How They Fail.* New York: Vintage Books.

Posusney, Marsha Pripstein. 2001. "Multi-Party Elections in the Arab World: Institutional Engineering and Oppositional Strategies." *Studies in Comparative International Development* 36 (Winter): 34–62.

Putnam, Robert D. 1993. *Making Democracy Work: Civic Traditions in Modern Italy.* Princeton, N.J.: Princeton University Press.

Rashwan, Diaa. 2000. "Life after El-Zawahri." *Al-Ahram Weekly*, February 17–23. <http://weekly.ahram.org.eg/2000/469/op3.htm>, accessed July 3, 2003.

Singerman, Diane. 1995. *Avenues of Participation: Family, Politics, and Networks in Urban Quarters of Cairo.* Princeton, N.J.: Princeton University Press.

Sonbol, Amira El-Azhary. 2000. *The New Mamluks: Egyptian Society and Modern Feudalism.* Syracuse, N.Y.: Syracuse University Press.

———, ed. 1996. *Women, the Family, and Divorce Laws in Islamic History.* Syracuse, N.Y.: Syracuse University Press.

Tarrow, Sidney. 1994. *Power in Movement: Social Movements, Collective Action, and Politics.* New York: Cambridge University Press.

Tilly, Charles. 1978. *From Mobilization to Revolution.* New York: McGraw-Hill.

Toth, James. 1998. "Beating Plowshares into Swords: The Relocation of Rural Egyptian Workers and Their Discontent." Pp. 66–87 in *Directions of Change in Rural Egypt*, ed. Nicholas Hopkins and Kirsten Westergaard. Cairo: American University in Cairo Press.

United Nations Development Programme. 2002. *Arab Human Development Report 2002.* New York: Arab Fund for Economic and Social Development.

White, Harrison. n.d. "Notes on the Constituents of Social Structure." Manuscript, Harvard University.

Wiktorowicz, Quintan. 2001a. *The Management of Islamic Activism: Salafis, the Muslim Brotherhood, and State Power in Jordan.* Albany: SUNY Press.

———. 2001b. "The New Global Threat: Transnational Salafis and Jihad." *Middle East Policy* 8, 4 (December): 18–38.

Wuthnow, Robert. 1991. "Understanding Religion and Politics." *Daedalus* 120 (Summer): 1–20.

Six

Islamist Women in Yemen
Informal Nodes of Activism

Janine A. Clark

Diane Singerman's chapter in this volume helps us reconceptualize movements, especially Islamic movements, as large, amorphous networks. This largely arises out of recognition that the formal organizations operating in the name of a social movement do not operate in isolation and cannot always encapsulate the fluid "boundaries" of a movement. Social movements, especially in less open political systems, often do not operate in a hierarchical fashion with an identifiable leadership, system of order, or "direction." Rather, movements comprise numerous organizations (each with its own agenda), networks of participants, and informal institutions. In expanding our understanding of social movements to incorporate the myriad components of collective action, social scientists are increasingly interested in relationships between elements of a social movement. In particular, there is greater interest in the relationship between social movement organizations (SMOs) and the social networks that connect these organizations to one another and to communities of movement participants. According to social movement theory, the networks of linkages—primarily social—that connect SMOs provide crucial resources to the formal movement organizations. Most important, they are a primary source of both membership and financial support. While the formal organizations with head offices and boards of directors may be the most visible manifestation of a social movement—the tip of the iceberg above the water—they could not survive or expand without the social networks that foster recruitment and resource extraction from supportive communities. Preexisting social networks not only provide recruits and resources; they also provide the glue that holds the movement together. Solidarity to the movement and its cause is strengthened by preexisting ties of friendship and loyalty.

While social movement theory has effectively detailed how social networks provide organizations with the tangible and intangible means to operate, less is known about how SMOs adapt and/or create networks to foster mobilization, how this impacts collective action, and how networks operate beyond recruitment and other institution-building processes. This chapter therefore seeks to address the following questions: How do SMOs use and/or create social networks? What impact does this have on preexisting social networks? And what significance does this have for the SMO and collective action as a whole?

In answering these questions, this chapter examines Islamist women in Yemen and finds that the relationship between social networks and SMOs is far more complex than is generally understood in social movement research. Social networks cannot simply be considered providers of various services and resources—as umbilical cords providing sustenance for SMOs. In the process of recruiting and utilizing social networks, Islamist SMOs in Yemen break down preexisting social networks and create new ones to foster supportive communities that are not necessarily formally tied to the organization through membership. Rather than simply sustaining the organization, activists use social relationships to create what Alberto Melucci (1989) terms "networks of shared meaning"—communities that accept, internalize, and promote a particular set of values.

Among women Islamists, this is primarily accomplished through Qur'anic study groups—nadwas—as informal intermediary institutions between the formal organization and the general public, which would not normally have access to the SMO or be receptive to its message. The most important utilization of nadwas is indirect and is largely conducted by SMO members as individual acts of da'wa (propagation of the faith), which is central to the Islamist worldview, rather than as organization representatives. Nadwas provide a forum for recruitment and message dissemination in an environment and manner that accesses deeper layers of society than is possible via the formal mechanisms of the SMO. Because they are embedded in both the social fabric of society and preexisting social networks, nadwas provide SMOs a seemingly nonpolitical, socially reinforcing institution through which organization members engage women on an ad hoc, regular, or consciously committed basis in the name of da'wa activities. The informal and embedded nature of nadwas not only grants SMO members access to new audiences; it also enables women to participate in Islamist activities without formal membership.

The degree to which women consciously or unconsciously participate in Islamist activities, however, becomes relatively irrelevant. What is at stake is not membership but social values and change. By using nadwas as a tool, SMO members reconfigure these social networks to support their values and goals. Women slowly enter Islamist networks, often gradually detaching themselves from previous networks of family and friends. Islamists thus break down preexisting ties and reconstruct new social networks supportive of their ideology. The potential for widespread social change lies precisely in this reconfiguration of social networks through informal nodes of activism such as nadwas.

Networks and Social Movement Organizations

Resource mobilization theory has effectively documented the flow of resources from social networks to SMOs. Networks, depending on their strength (the degree of resource transfer) and breadth (the extensiveness of linkages), provide SMOs with a membership base, legitimacy, money, prestige, information, and power (Aveni 1978, 188–90). Theorists generally conceptualize networks as playing their most significant role at the stage of movement recruitment: "Individuals are drawn into participation not by the force of the ideas or even the individual attitudes but as the result of their embeddedness in associational networks that render them 'structurally available' for protest activity" (McAdam 1994, 36–37).[1] Numerous studies have found that social networks—usually composed of homogeneous, like-minded people—constitute the primary source of recruits (Snow, Zurcher, and Ekland-Olson 1980, 791), and social networks make people available for recruitment, more inclined to join (particularly if large numbers of friends and family are already members), and the targets of recruitment (Kitts 1999). People are thus structurally predisposed to join SMOs (Klandermans and Oegema 1987, 530). As McAdam and Paulsen argue, interpersonal ties encourage the extension of an invitation to participate and ease the uncertainty of mobilization (1993, 644). Social bonds also aid potential joiners in overcoming the various perceived costs of joining a social movement (Klandermans and Oegema 1987, 530).

But recruitment does not occur simply through structural availability, ideological congruity with movement values, or word of mouth. It is part of a conscious effort by movement activists to selectively target prospective participants in sympathetic social networks and communities. Klandermans and Oegema's study of the 1983 peace demonstration in The Hague, for example, demonstrates that without exception every person who intended to participate in the demonstration had in one way or another been a target of a mobilization attempt and that informal recruitment links were far more important than formal ones (1987, 526). Similarly, McAdam and Paulsen's research on the 1964 Mississippi Freedom Summer Project finds that the occurrence of a specific recruiting attempt is an important limiting condition that determines whether or not an individual participates in a movement (1993, 662). In some instances, particularly for organizations with high costs and low resources, this selectivity is further narrowed to target individuals whose contributions to the organization would be greatest (Marwell, Oliver, and Prahl 1988, 528–29).

Studies of recruitment and "selective targeting" through social networks, however, generally emphasize how such efforts impact the size of the relevant social networks of activists and concomitant consequences for mobilization. Greater numbers of demonstrators or associations, for example, clearly create greater pressure for policy change. But this does not explain the dynamics of expansion and how it may affect preexisting social relationships or engender new social networks. In utilizing social networks and targeting recruitment, are SMOs simply expanding preexisting social networks? Is this a process that merely "taps" those potential members with concurrent beliefs through direct mailings, posters, face-to-face recruitment, and the like? Or is there a deeper effect on preexisting networks? Does this impact the social values of network members? What are the implications for the social movement as a whole?

Some insights into these questions are offered by Schennink in his study of the Interchurch Peace Council (IKV) in the Netherlands. He found that IKV developed its own networks for recruitment and the diffusion of the peace movement message (1988, 250). Core peace movement activists were encouraged to create new local groups in order to attract new members and organize local events. Networks were thus seen as important in building the bridge between the mobilization potential and the protest participant. Once established, these newly created networks could be used for action mobilization. However, while Schennink profiles the types of people who joined the networks, he does not examine the actual network building process beyond attempts by local groups to contact what they believed to be sympathetic institutions and audiences. More important, for the purposes of this chapter, he does not examine the impact of this targeted recruitment upon preexisting social networks.

Stark and Bainbridge provide one of the only studies that explicitly examines an SMO's concerted manipulation of social networks in detail. In their study of Mormon recruiting strategies in the United States, they note that Mormon missionaries are exhorted to use their existing social networks to create new friendships as part of their strategy toward gaining new recruits. Mormon recognition of the importance of social bonds for successful recruitment is evidenced by the fact that activists are advised to give personal testimony to their faith only after a strong friendship bond is created. Indeed, of the 13 steps for recruitment (published in a widely read Mormon magazine), activists are repeatedly admonished to refrain from discussing religion until completion of 10 prior steps aimed at developing tighter social relations (Stark and Bainbridge 1980, 1379–89). Stark and Bainbridge provide an excellent example of the targeted creation of social networks for SMO purposes, yet their observations need further corroboration and comparative analysis. The "ripple" effect of this expansion upon preexisting social networks—in other words, within the broader societal picture—remains unexplained.

Greater research of how social networks are utilized by SMOs and the impact of this manipulation on the social networks themselves is of particular importance in terms of understanding not only the spread of a social movement but also how it effects widespread grassroots value changes. It furthermore contributes toward a larger attempt within social movement theory at theoretically reconceptualizing social movements to capture both the organizational and nonorganizational elements of social movements and the relations among them (Oliver 1989, 1).

Islamism: The Centrality of Daʿwa

This chapter examines how SMO members utilize nadwas in the fulfillment of SMO objectives. The usefulness of nadwas to SMOs, however, can only be understood within the context of the meaning of Islamism and the centrality of daʿwa to the Islamist worldview and lifestyle. An "Islamist" is a Muslim who attempts to re-Islamize society by encouraging individuals to practice Islam in daily life and bridge the gap between religious discourse and practical realities.[2] In other words, he or she is a Muslim who seeks to actively extend and apply Islam beyond what is commonly regarded as the private realm to affect the public realm. In doing so, Islamism promotes the idea that Islam is a complete system or body of values, beliefs, and practices encompassing all spheres of life (Roald 1998, 17n1).

The Islamist challenge is rooted in what Dale Eickelman and James Piscatori refer to as the "invention of tradition" (building on Eric Hobsbawm). Islamists generally regard the period of the prophet Muhammad and his first four successors, the "rightly guided caliphs," as one in which there was little divergence between ideals and reality. It is therefore a period of ideological inspiration or guidance. Islamists' appropriation of what they believe to be this tradition includes the assertion that Islam is *din wa dawla*, religion and state. From this perspective, Islam is a comprehensive system encompassing all things material, spiritual, societal, individual, political, and personal (Eickelman and Piscatori 1996, 46). By allowing the separation of religion from public life, traditional Muslim authorities failed the Muslim community. Islamists are thus committed to implementing their vision of Islam as a corrective to current un-Islamic practices in the prevailing political and social establishments and status quo.

In this "invention of tradition," the concept of daʿwa becomes central (Eickelman and Piscatori 1996, 35–36). Beyond simply proselytizing or preaching, daʿwa becomes the very act of "activating" Islam through deed in all spheres of life. As stated by Egyptian Muslim Brotherhood Member of Parliament Ahmad al-Bis, for example, working for politics is working for Islam (Abed-Kotob 1995, 332). Da°wa becomes a vital component of practicing Islam. Indeed, da°wa can include joining a political party, hosting a nadwa, or working in a free medical clinic—actions that are incumbent upon all Muslims.

For Islamist women in Yemen, therefore, there exists a seamless web between religion, politics, charity, and all forms of activism. All of these realms should reinforce each other and promote public virtue and personal piety. In this regard, the deed or act of da°wa is as important as the word of Islam. The act of da°wa itself promotes an environment in which Islam and Muslims can flourish. Indeed, the act of da°wa and the activities involved in fulfilling da°wa are what make nadwas such potent tools for Islamists. Through their personal fulfillment of da°wa, of which hosting and attending nadwas are an integral part, SMO members promote the Islamic movement message.

Why Nadwas?

Strictly speaking, nadwas are Qurʾanic study or discussion groups. Groups of women gather together in homes to read and discuss passages from the Qurʾan and themes important to the study and practice of Islam. They generally focus on how to apply Islam to everyday life and be a better Muslim. Subjects, for example, may include a discussion of the meaning of Ramadan or the evils of jealousy.

In the larger sense, nadwas are informal social gatherings that bring friends together or link several social networks on a regular basis. There is no formal membership. Women attend these gatherings as often or as little as they wish. Furthermore, as a social gathering, women of different degrees of religious conviction are in attendance. While many of the women are deeply pious, the social nature of the gatherings draws together women with differing attitudes toward Islam (or different degrees of identification with Islam). Islamist women may host nadwas or attend ones sponsored by non-activists.

Nadwas form an important part of women's informal networks. These Qurʾanic study groups provide religious solace and guidance, an education in reading and in Islam, an emotional outlet, a social life outside of the home, and a support group for the women who attend them. They also provide an arena where a woman can go for advice or find out where (or to whom) she can go to alleviate her problem. Nadwas furthermore form an important link in the transmission of knowledge and education from female religious scholars to the next generation. While girls generally learn about Islam at home, those with a desire for broader knowledge seek out a nadwa in someone's home.

Nadwas are therefore rooted in the fabric of Yemeni society; and as an integral "organization" of women's social networking they provide ideal institutions for the Islamist movement. As intermediary institutions between Islamist SMOs and the public or "crowd," nadwas are useful in several regards. First, as a social gathering they bring Islamist women (women who are formal members of Hizb al-Islah or the Islah charity) in regular contact with nonactivists. They thus facilitate the communication of ideas for the Islamist movement and provide opportunities for direct contact with numerous social networks. Second, much like the "bull sessions" of the university student demonstrations in the 1960s in the United States, nadwas provide a micromobilization context in which cognitive liberation and the process of collective attribution can occur. It is here that the rudiments of organization needed to translate attributions into concrete actions are found. And third, nadwas provide the necessary established structures of solidarity and interpersonal rewards that assist in overcoming the "free rider" problem in collective action (McAdam 1988, 135–36). They also provide a "ready" mobilization potential: because many women who attend nadwas are religious, they are potentially predisposed to Islamist interpretations of Islam. They thus serve as a single forum for providing SMO access to overlapping and linked social networks and concomitant benefits for activism.

Nadwas also offer a "free space" for Islamists. In other words, nadwas provide an ostensibly nonpolitical forum that can serve as a setting where SMOs can recruit without raising substantial suspicions from authorities. They also foster a protective function in that the repression of such socially accepted religious institutions would prompt a public outcry that could erode regime legitimacy and control. In this sense, the role of nadwas is similar to black churches in the early stages of organizing during the civil rights movement in the United States (McAdam 1988, 135).

Nadwas are also an excellent tool for Islamists because they are replicable. They are a tool that can be emulated and reproduced. Not only do SMO members indirectly use preexisting nadwas as a source of recruitment through social networks; they also create and host new nadwas in targeted areas, such as close to the university, where they feel they can draw in large numbers of women. Much like the above-mentioned case study of the Mormons, they thus create new centers or nodes where different women are brought together in an effort to create new effective social networks. These networks act as conduits for the Islamist message and help to structurally dispose women toward activism on behalf of the SMO's goals and values, even if they are not formal members.

Finally, and perhaps most important, nadwas act as a nonverbal model of the Islamist message. Nadwas themselves are an act of daʿwa, much like volunteer work, education, and other forms of activism. In this sense, the nadwa hosts and attendants who discuss their daʿwa activities elsewhere act as models for emulation by other women. They represent the ideal of a pious Muslim woman.

The centrality of the activist's understanding of da'wa is pivotal in understanding nadwas and how they are utilized by Islamists. This understanding is not just an ideological construct; da'wa is an act or deed. As such, the act of da'wa itself is ideologically and politically significant even if undertaken in isolation from the larger (verbal) political message. In other words, the act speaks as loudly as the words. Da'wa, such as volunteer work or hosting a nadwa, need not be explained in terms of its relevance to the Islamist ideology or agenda, because the very act is a concrete example of what it means to be a good Muslim. For Islamists, an activist Muslim engaged in consistent da'wa is a good Muslim.

Indeed, the case study of Islamist women in Yemen indicates that the act speaks louder than words where SMOs are pursuing a political agenda. In attempting to access supporters, SMOs are hampered by the social context within which they operate. The violent political history in Yemen, the conservative tribal customs, and women's relatively small role in public life all serve to dissuade women from overt political activity. Overt references to political parties or ideologies hamper Islah's success at recruitment. Da'wa, however, is a religious act. As forums that focus on the Qur'an and Islam and do not discuss politics, nadwas foster religious acts and more readily facilitate women's participation on their own terms. As Snow, Zurcher, and Ekland-Olson argue, people seldom initially join movements per se; rather, they typically participate in movement activities and only gradually become members (1980, 795). Da'wa activities (which can be the nadwa itself or activities conducted via nadwas) offer women precisely this gradualist opportunity.

The ease with which women are able to participate in da'wa activities, as opposed to political events sponsored by the Islamists, is furthered by the fact that the political significance of da'wa activities is ambiguous. A woman donating money to the Islamist charity once a year and a woman hosting a charity fund-raising event are both contributing, but the meaning the two women attribute to these acts can differ substantially. It may be a simple act of charity, a concerted effort to "live" Islam in all aspects of one's life, or a political act aimed at demonstrating the viability and superiority of the Islamic alternative. The act of da'wa as a political expression or as a religious act does not force a woman to either state her position publicly or overtly challenge social norms. Yet this very "flexibility" creates the potential for tremendous social change.

Having explicated the usefulness of nadwas to Islamist SMO and their members, the chapter now details the two dominant Islamic SMOs in Yemen —the Islah party and the Islah Charity—and explains how they are linked to nadwas. It will then focus on how Islamists indirectly and directly use nadwas and their related social networks to foster the movement's goals.

Moderate Islam in Yemen:
The Dominant SMOs

Moderate Islamic activism or Islamism has been present in Yemen since the beginning of the twentieth century. Although a number of Islamic groups and trends have coexisted since the unification of the two Yemens in 1990, two organizations tend to dominate: the Yemeni Congregation for Reform, or Hizb al-Islah, and the Islah Charitable Society, or the Charitable Society for Social Welfare.

The establishment of democratic party politics facilitated the emergence of Hizb al-Islah in January 1991. Islah as a political party essentially brings together several conservative (not always Islamist) currents in Yemeni society. These include prominent tribal leaders, businessmen, the Muslim Brotherhood, a pro-Saudi Wahhabi group, and several prominent ideologues with their own personal followings. Composed mostly of Northern-based conservatives, members share a common pro-Northern regime stance and conservative social objectives, such as shari^{c}a as the sole basis of law, although there are differences over strategy and religious interpretations.

In Yemen's first democratic elections in 1993, the Islah party won 62 out of 123 seats in the newly created parliament (Majlis al-Nawab), making it the third and junior partner in a governing coalition with the General People's Congress (GPC) and the Yemeni Socialist Party (YSP) (Carapico 1993, 2–6; Associated Press, May 1, 1997). The coalition established after the 1993 elections was not to last long. Four years after unification and one year after the elections that brought the coalition to power, a war between the armies of the former North and South broke out. The upshot of the war was the destruction of the YSP and the consequent rise of Hizb al-Islah in the power vacuum that ensued. A new cabinet was formed, based on a new GPC–Hizb al-Islah ruling coalition, and Hizb al-Islah was given a number of ministries, including education. During the 1997 elections, Islah did not fare as strongly and dropped from 62 to 47 seats in parliament.[3] However, Islah retained control of several ministries, and the head of the Islah party (al-Ahmar) remained Speaker of the Parliament.

In conjunction with the political party, the Islah Charitable Society, formed in May 1990, constitutes the second major Islamic SMO in Yemen. While technically independent from the Islah party, anecdotal evidence strongly indicates that the two overlap in terms of membership and financial funders. The Islah Charitable Society is the most successful humanitarian, nonprofit, nongovernmental organization helping the poor in Yemen. The headquarters of the Society is located in Sana^{c}a, attached to a large mosque near the new campus of Sana^{c}a University. While the Society is based in Sana^{c}a, it operates throughout the country with extensive services located in Sana^{c}a, Aden, Ibb,

Thmar, Hodeidah, Hajja, Taiz, Mukalla, and Say²oon. It is one of the few NGOs that operate in every governorate of Yemen, urban and rural (Dorman et al. 1996, 13).

The Society is largely a charitable organization and does not focus on development per se. Its stated goals are to provide social services in the form of financial, educational, health, and counseling assistance to six identified groups: the economically deprived and needy; the orphaned; the handicapped; the mentally and psychologically disturbed; women, children, and the elderly; and victims of economic or natural disaster. In order to address these needs, the Society is divided into six committees: the Neighborhood Activities Committee; the Special Projects Committee; the Orphanage Care and Sponsorship Committee; the Basic Health Services Committee; the Emergency Relief Committee; and the Women's Committee.[4]

Women are represented in both the party and the charitable society. In Hizb al-Islah, they are represented by the Women's Sector. Theoretically speaking, the Women's Sector in Hizb al-Islah operates as a parallel organization to the main party (the "male" part). The departmental divisions within the party as a whole are technically present within the Women's Sector.[5] The women therefore have their own representatives for social affairs, political affairs, and economic and budgetary matters. In this organizational sense, women in Hizb al-Islah are independent. Since 1998, seven women have also served on the party's highest executive council, the Majlis as-Shura.[6]

Similarly, the Women's Committee of the Islah Charity and its headquarters are separate from its "male" counterpart. In Sanaᶜa there are three branches of the Women's Committee, including the central headquarters located near Sanaᶜa University. Based in extremely modest buildings, the women conduct activities that parallel those conducted by men in their own committees.[7] While the Women's Committee does offer a limited number of services for the poor, on the whole it concentrates on collecting and distributing charity (food, clothing, money), reflecting the overall thrust of the charity's activities.

The women in both organizations tend to be in their twenties, although many in leadership positions are in their thirties. In general, most of the women are well educated, with university ambitions or degrees, and are from the middle class, although there are exceptions. They have generally attended state schools or private Islamic schools rather than Westernized private schools. Their relative affluence and education and the fact that many of them live in an extended family situation enable these women to conduct activities on behalf of others outside the home.

The women in both SMOs are deeply religious and share an activist understanding of Islam. Working for the Charity or party (in other words, activism) is seen as a religious duty. Having stated this, many women join the party for the same reasons that people join politics throughout the world: to participate in the democratic process and to improve and develop their societies. In the long term, women view the improvement of their country in terms of educating the population about Islamic rights and duties and facilitating the eventual application of Islamic law.

The profile of Islamist women in both the Charity and the party is important. These are the women with the time and education to work on behalf of the party and/or Charity. They also represent women and social networks with the socioeconomic means to donate resources to the party and/or the Charity. They thus form relatively homogeneous social networks from which the Charity and party draw their recruits. It is also through these very same social networks that party and Charity members conduct work, consciously or unconsciously, on behalf of their organizations.

Women's Social Networks and Nadwas in Sanaᶜa

As largely social events, nadwas form an important "node" within Islamist and other women's social networks in Sanaᶜa. To a large degree, socializing in northern Yemen is conducted in the late afternoon and early evening in the form of *qat*-chewing sessions and other forms of get-togethers.[8] Women are no exception. While women have more household and child-rearing duties and, as a result, cannot chew qat as often or for long periods like men (more women than men are also opposed to the chewing of qat), the afternoon is a time to meet for a tea party, chew qat, or go to a nadwa.

Throughout Sanaᶜa, pious women gather on a weekly or biweekly basis to read the Qurᵓan and discuss passages. These nadwas are usually held in one woman's home and can be as small as 4 women or as large as 40, with women of all ages in attendance. In some nadwas, passages are read from a learned scholar's book and then discussed. In other cases, a speaker is brought in to talk or "preach" on a religious topic. Nadwas vary in the level and amount of discussion. Many women have a regular nadwa they attend; however, they may drop in to attend a nadwa on a more casual basis. Some nadwas are clearly "closed" and not intended for uninvited drop-ins or guests, while others are much more open. In general, while a certain core group of women may be "regulars," the women at a nadwa may not know everyone. Women may learn about nadwas at universities or at charity events, or a "regular" may bring a guest.

While they are open to all women, the social nature of the nadwas generally dictates that women of similar status in terms of education, families, and education gather together. In general, they are found in social circles of educated, middle-class, and upper-middle-class women, not among the poor, and this social categorization reinforces itself as new members join. This is not to say that uneducated or poorer women never attend. Occasionally, for example, poorer women from various charity events may be encouraged by someone in the Society to come to a nadwa as a means of learning more about Islam. In general, however, the networks are based on educated women from the middle classes. Nadwas thus draw upon and overlap with the same socioeconomic class as the majority of women in Islamist SMOs.

In bringing various networks of women together in fairly large numbers, nadwas create a tight community of overlapping, generally like-minded social circles, where women can socialize, establish friendships, and learn about Islam. As such, they not only unite the dominant Islamist SMO members and link them with other social networks. They also offer SMO members a tool that can be consciously or unconsciously utilized to the SMO's advantage. These women may act as individuals at nadwas, but in promoting their religious beliefs they promote the SMO message.

Nadwas and the Islah Charitable Society

The Women's Committee of the Islah Charity is largely independent of the rest of the Charity. While the Charity as a whole (the "male" part) does offer services designed for women, the Women's Committee is largely responsible for designing programs to meet poor women's needs.[9] While the Charity does support various services for women, such as sewing lessons or literacy classes, most volunteers are devoted to raising donations and distributing charity such as Ramadan meals or clothes for the poor,[10] and it is largely through informal social networks that they are able to do so.[11]

During Ramadan in 1996, for example, the women hosted their first fund-raising event for the Sanaᶜa elite and women from the ambassadorial community. The event, loosely modeled on Western fund-raisers, was a relatively elegant affair. Entertainment and food were provided, and an appeal was made for donations. Most of the Sanaᶜa female elite attended. Indeed, as word spread of the event, even those women opposed to any Islamist political platform attended for social reasons, such as the desire to support a friend's efforts, curiosity, and recognition of the good work the Society is performing. Through the various contacts of women in the Charity, a wide variety of social circles were brought together in an effort to raise money.

Far more commonly, however, members enlist large numbers of women through more informal face-to-face contact. The number of women working full-time for the Society is relatively small, but through their efforts large numbers of women assist the Committee on an irregular basis. They may be students at an Islamic university, for example, and may know someone in the Society—a friend or teacher—and decide to help with an event. Or during Ramadan someone may negotiate on behalf of the Committee to buy material at the wholesale price from a friendly retailer. Another woman on the Committee may then find a seamstress who agrees to sew clothing for orphans for free as a Ramadan gift. Through similar methods, Committee women approach individuals and business persons for new and used books in order to hold book sales at the university and raise funds. Committee members also arrange to sew school uniforms.[12] In this way, the Committee raises money and engages networks of women from a variety of backgrounds, skills, education, ages, and commitment to provide for Yemen's poor.

Nadwas play an important role in the raising and distributing of such charity. SMO members are able to access women at nadwas in support of an SMO cause, such as Ramadan clothing for orphans, through several means. At the end of the nadwa, an SMO member may tell the story of a woman and her family in particular distress and ask people in the room to donate whatever they can. Alternatively, members of the Charity may discuss their efforts on behalf of the Charity while socializing with other women. Or it may be at a nadwa that SMO members learn of a retailer or seamstress, for example, who would be amenable to donating time and goods. Nadwas furthermore present a meeting place for Charity members to finalize plans and distribute materials among themselves.

Nadwas thus offer SMO members direct and indirect means for enlisting people and gaining participants. Charity members do not have to explicitly or directly "use" nadwas by openly encouraging women to join the SMO or making announcements on its behalf. There is rarely any type of pressure, and the process is far more natural and subtle—through regular socializing among like-minded women and through the emulation of doing good work in the name of Islam, SMO members are able to achieve their goals. Through nadwas, Islamist women provide an example and an environment where daʿwa is actively practiced.

Nadwas and Hizb al-Islah

Much like the Charity, the Islah party does not have a specific program for women per se. The Women's Sector of the party largely determines the most appropriate means and programs for women. To a large extent, the Women's Sector focuses its efforts in two related directions. The first is expanding the female membership of the party. The second is educating women about their rights and duties according to Islam and its laws, an example of daʿwa. This may include lectures on health education or women's right to work according to Islam. The Sector is thus trying to create a new picture of society, change traditions, and enact social change.

The Sector uses nadwas in two ways. First, the SMO may send a speaker to a nadwa or qat session in someone's home, or it may host a nadwa, usually at the university or at the Sector's headquarters. Although hosting nadwas at the university or the headquarters enables the SMO to target large numbers of women, sending speakers to homes to talk at nadwas or, less frequently, qat chews enables the Sector to target or select women with education, professional skills, financial resources, and personal contacts. Since the 1997 elections, women within the party have indicated an increased focus on attracting women with resources and personal ties.[13]

Nadwas are very popular on university campuses and in the dormitories. Islahi women come to the dorms on a regular basis, and word spreads that a nadwa will be held at a specific time. Some of these are relatively spontaneous; others are conducted at a regular time and place. Special nadwas are also organized and announced ahead of time in honor of specific events and often draw in large numbers.

Hosting nadwas is an explicit party strategy, but it cannot be said that women who lead nadwas at the university or act as guest speakers at nadwas within the home are necessarily acting on behalf of the party as part of a larger attempt to usurp nadwas for party purposes. The very nature of daʿwa creates an almost indistinguishable line between activities on behalf of the party and those forming part of an individual's personal fulfillment of daʿwa. The promotion of Islam, which lays the foundation for the Islamist message, is an important part of these women's lives, regardless of whether or not they are formal members of the party or under the directives of Islah.

Indeed, at the nadwas and lectures within the university and headquarters, Islahi women rarely mention the party directly (with the exception of election times). Rather they focus on Islam as the proper and comprehensive path. Educating women in Islam, regardless of whether or not they become party members, is a useful strategy. By doing so, party members are creating a sympathetic environment in which Islah's ideas and political ascent become increasingly possible. The focus on education, furthermore, serves to provide access for women who would normally shy away from political discussion or activities.[14] Finally, SMO members create an intermediate step for women between noninvolvement and membership.

Women in the Islamist SMOs thus use nadwas in direct and indirect ways in order to gain members and to create an environment in which Islamist ideology can take root. By hosting and attending nadwas, they work within the fabric of society and within social networks to create social change. In doing so, the social networks themselves are affected, as explained below.

The Impact of SMOs on Social Networks

We find in Sanaʿa overlapping networks of women's circles. Women educators and students and their social, religious, political, and family circles overlap at school, university, lectures in mosques, Qurʾanic study groups, social occasions, the Islah Charitable Society, party meetings and activities, and work. Members of the Charity Society find volunteers (and/or donations) from among the women present at the nadwas they attend. A teacher at an Islamic university may ask one of her students to lead a nadwa. A friend active in giving nadwas in the dorms on behalf of Hizb al-Islah may be invited to host one in a home. A woman attending one nadwa may be invited to visit another. Or women attending a lecture at the Society's headquarters learn about a nadwa or meet someone from the party. These uncoordinated networks overlap in activities, memberships, and friendships.

These networks, and particularly nadwas, are vital to the expansion of the middle-class membership of the Islamist movement. Through informal and formal means, Islamist women are able to access and recruit women through all these gatherings. While at the universities Islahi women may overtly recruit members and voters, in other parts of the network, such as nadwas in the home, the influence of Islah is more subtle and far more effective. Nadwas in the home provide SMOs with an indirect process of introduction and possibly recruitment to the Islamist movement. This indirect process of recruitment occurs as women participate—even if on an irregular basis—in Islamist work or activities for the Charity or party. Through their activities, Islamist women engage large and different social networks of women in the process of daʿwa.

Depending on women's degree of involvement, new bonds of friendship develop between women as they work together to achieve a goal, whether it is sewing clothing or donating books. New circles of women developing a common activist understanding of daʿwa and engaged in daʿwa (whether it be for the Society, the party, or themselves) are created. While women generally do not mix party politics into their nadwa discussions, after the discussions and during the social segment of the nadwa an Islahi woman may quietly approach others and suggest they join her at another nadwa on another day.[15] At this second nadwa they may be introduced to a social group that is more openly in support of Islah or Islamist goals. Women who become engaged in charity or party activities thus develop new and strong friendships with one another. They may even find a husband via the party or Society networks who supports and encourages her activities.

Girls and women thus slowly enter new Islamist networks that encompass many aspects of life—networks that eventually lead them to withdraw from their previous childhood friends. It may also alienate them from their families. As they become more involved in daʿwa, including nadwa activities, they spend increasing amounts of time with new friends engaged in similar activities. This reconfiguration of social circles or clusters thus both breaks down and builds upon existing social networks to create new clusters or subgroups bound by an activist understanding of Islam and a commitment to daʿwa activities. While women often enter Islamist networks precisely because they are familiar and built upon existing friends, as Carrie Rosefsky Wickham demonstrates in her chapter on Islamists in Egypt in this volume, the end result is one that may take them away from these familiar faces—particularly if they marry an Islamist as opposed to a man their respective parents would have chosen. Within these new social groups and networks, the Islamist ideology is reinforced through deed and word. Whether these women become formal members of Islah is relatively irrelevant, since their active support for Islamist ideology has a far bigger impact than simply garnering votes for Islah. As social networks based on an activist understanding of Islam develop and expand, they are engaged in a grassroots process of social change that further expands networks of shared meaning.

These newly established bonds are solidified not only by the satisfaction of jointly working for Islam but also by the various personal benefits women receive. Islamist activities, whether they be for the party or the Charity, involve a variety of functions, including lecturing, preaching, writing a newsletter, organizing events, learning about one's social and political rights, helping others, fund-raising, and participating in the democratic process, thereby providing women with broader skills.[16] They thus give women a strong sense of satisfaction and self-worth—something women do not generally receive elsewhere, especially at a young age. Quite simply, these activities involve a great deal of self-growth and ultimately grant women a gratifying role outside the home. Fulfilling daʿwa via the party or Charity provides meaning and direction for young women. It gives a sense of self-worth as members are encouraged to be active and take on challenging projects and creates a tremendous feeling of solidarity as friends jointly engage in creating a new society.

As they increasingly conduct activities outside the home, members and participants remain consistent with the dominant cultural norms. For example, attending a nadwa or working for a charitable society is considered a legitimate reason for going outside the home alone, and therefore it does not challenge local social norms that provide little room for women in public space.[17] Indeed, the importance of nadwas for the Islamist movement lies precisely in the fact that they do not challenge prevailing cultural norms. Nadwas are furthermore not perceived as political work per se, and in this sense they are also useful to the Islamist movement. In a conservative and largely tribal society, such as Yemen, families regard politics and public roles for women as inappropriate, and many women shy away from overt political participation. It is precisely the nonthreatening nature, socially and politically, of the activities of the Charitable Society and of nadwas, as well as the tremendous personal benefits participants reap, that make the associated networks so effective at social change, something Wickham indicates with regards to Islamists in Egypt in chapter 9 of this volume.

Islamist success at creating new and supportive social groups thus rests in the personal fulfillment of daʿwa and in the sense of joint purpose and solidarity it creates among women. Women bond together by actively and concretely working toward a new social vision. The key to Islamist success lies in the fact that their methods, primarily nadwas, are informal and are firmly rooted in the social fabric of women's lives in Yemen. Yet, in doing so, they seek to break down and rebuild that very same social fabric in accordance with their religious vision.

Conclusion

Social movement theory generally views social networks in terms of how they provide resources and recruits for SMOs and link together disparate organizational elements of a movement. Yet the case study of Islamist women in Yemen indicates that the relationship between networks and formal organizations is more complex and that the impact of SMOs upon social networks is profound—one that extends far beyond the issue of formal recruitment. SMOs actively target and utilize social networks. In doing so, they are able to access larger numbers of women with different degrees of commitment, including those women normally found outside of the counterculture or mobilization potential.

In accessing large numbers of women, Islamists slowly bring new members into the movement through various degrees of SMO commitment. As women become more involved in SMO activities, they gradually break away from their previous social circles and create new social ties based on Islamist ideology and rooted in an activist concept of daᶜwa. In other words, SMOs do not simply grow out of friendship networks. The reverse can happen: friendship networks emerge from recruitment efforts.

As daᶜwa activities reconfigure social networks, Islamist women are creating and reinforcing a worldview that ultimately envisions dramatic social change. The potential for grassroots social change is all the more powerful given that many of the women targeted by SMO members may participate in SMO activities without consciously acknowledging that they are, in essence, working on behalf of a political party or ideology by supporting its interests. As the Islamist "invention of tradition" slowly takes root through social networks, political parties, regardless of ideological persuasion, will have to take note of the groundswell of support for an Islamist-inspired, conservative social and political agenda.

Notes

I am indebted to the Social Science and Humanities Research Council of Canada, the American Institute for Yemeni Studies, and the University of New Hampshire for enabling me to conduct this research. Special thanks must also be extended to Quintan Wiktorowicz, Charles Kurzman, and Paul Kingston for their help in the research and writing of this chapter.

1. There is some recent dissent concerning recruitment patterns. Jasper (1997), for example, speaks of the "moral shock" that induces members to join a movement.

2. Adapted from Ask and Tjomsland (1998).

3. The shift was due in part to the elimination of the YSP from the political scene after its defeat in the 1994 civil war. As Jillian Schwedler argues in chapter 8 of this volume, the war ironically weakened the political standing of the Islah party because President Salih no longer needed the Islah party to offset the strength of the YSP and its challenge to the Northern elite. Thus by the time the 1997 elections rolled around, the Islah party saw its relative influence in political affairs decrease dramatically.

4. As stated in the Society's literature, the Neighborhood Activities Committee establishes Assistance Centers through which it collects donations and assists the needy in designated neighborhoods. The Special Projects Committee engages in projects that do not fall under the purview of the other committees. It plans, for example, to initiate local credit systems whereby the poor can establish their own income-generating projects. The Orphanage Care and Sponsorship Committee supports orphanages and provides monthly allowances to identified orphans. The Basic Health Services Committee runs Primary Health Care Food Distribution Centers, particularly in rural areas. It also established Yemen's first hospital for mentally ill women. The Emergency Relief Committee primarily devotes its energies to assisting emigrant returnees from the 1990–91 Gulf war and addressing their housing, clothing, and food needs. The Women's Committee works with the other committees and runs centers for women and children where they develop reading, writing, and sewing skills.

5. Among other responsibilities, the General Convention votes for the president and vice president of the Supreme Board, the members of the Majlis al-Shura (the Consultative Council), and the president of the Judicial Department. Organizationally, the party is composed of the Majlis al-Shura, the Supreme Board, the Secretariat General, the Judicial Apparatus of the Organization, and the Councils and Apparatuses of the Local Organizational or Executive Units. The Secretariat General comprises nine executive bodies or departments: Political; Mobilization and Recruitment; Information and Propaganda; Education and Culture; Economics; Social Affairs; Labor Unions and Organizations; Financial and Administrative Affairs; and Planning, Statistics, and Research. The party structure is basically replicated in the form of local units at various administrative levels throughout the country: at the capital and provincial level, in provincial capitals and their districts, and in villages, neighborhoods, and wards.

6. In 1998, the General Assembly/Congress voted in favor of allowing women to be on the Majlis as-Shura. Seven women were nominated and subsequently elected. As of yet, the party has never allowed female members to stand as candidates in the country's elections; consequently, no Islamist women are represented in parliament.

7. The Society as a whole, dominated by men, also runs some events on behalf of women. For example, the Society conducts weekly lectures for women on the Qur'an. They are conducted in the basement of the mosque attached to the main Society headquarters. As many as 500 women attend the lectures of the shaykh. When

the basement is full, the women spill into an upstairs room where they watch the lecture on a television screen. This upstairs room also offers women the opportunity to remove their head coverings (*hijab*) and veils (*lithma* or *niqab*).

8. Qat is a mildly narcotic shrub that is (legally) chewed in afternoon social gatherings for its stimulating effects.

9. The Committee is hampered, however, by a lack of funding from the general Charity; and due to its relatively small size, limited funds, and lack of relative influence within the Charity, it is circumscribed in what it can do.

10. The Women's Committee also financially supports widows and their families or assists in finding employment for widows. The Committee conducts hospital and prison visits and hosts a limited number of training sessions in women's prisons. Lectures on health-related issues are also offered by the Committee. Much of this work is relatively ad hoc, addressing needs as they arise.

11. There are some exceptions. For example, the Committee has organized fundraising events at Sana°a University by selling donated books and handicrafts made by the poor. For other events, they may simply post notices throughout the university campus announcing events and asking for volunteers and donations for orphans.

12. The Women's Committee in Hodeidah, for example, has a program to teach girls to sew. One of the students' projects is to sew school uniforms, which are then sold by local retailers for profit.

13. In interviews with members of the Sector, party women indicated that the primary lesson they learned from the electoral losses of 1997 was the need to target women with wide-ranging and influential personal ties in terms of prospective members and resources (interviews conducted by author, November 1998, Sana°a).

14. Tribal tradition generally prevents women from entering politics. In addition, given the history of political violence in Yemen, many women are wary of formally joining a party.

15. The degree to which a nadwa becomes political is also dependent upon the interests and education of the women in attendance. For example, a discussion concerning cleanliness could potentially evolve into a discussion of health policies and institutions.

16. In her work on female dervishes in Turkey, Catharina Raudvere (1998) notes that women's associations provide benefits to women beyond the spiritual. She finds that these associations provide, for example, networks of economic contacts as well as a basis for other important relations.

17. In her study of Islamist women in Egypt, Soraya Duval (1998, 63) notes that Islamic duties such as nadwas are deemed by both husband and wife to take precedence over other issues.

Works Cited

Abed-Kotob, Sana. 1995. "The Accommodationists Speak: Goals and Strategies of the Muslim Brotherhood of Egypt." *International Journal of Middle East Studies* 27, 3 (August): 321–39.

Ask, Karin, and Marit Tjomsland, eds. 1998. *Women and Islamization: Contemporary Dimensions of Discourse on Gender Relations*. New York: Berg.

Aveni, Adrian. 1978. "Organizational Linkages and Resource Mobilization: The Significance of Linkage Strength and Breadth." *Sociological Quarterly* 19 (Spring): 185–202.

Carapico, Sheila. 1993. "Elections and Mass Politics in Yemen." *Middle East Report*, no. 185 (November/December): 2–6.

Dorman, Deborah, Ahmed No³man al-Madhaji, Mohammed Aidarus, Sharon Beatty, Zarina Ismael, and Marina de Regt. 1996. *Yemeni NGOs and Quasi-NGOs: Analysis and Directory*. Part II: *Directory*. Sanaᶜa: Embassy of the Netherlands.

Duval, Soraya. 1998. "New Veils and New Voices: Islamist Women's Groups in Egypt." Pp. 45–72 in *Women and Islamization*, ed. Karin Ask and Marit Tjomsland. New York: Berg.

Eickelman, Dale, and James Piscatori. 1996. *Muslim Politics*. Princeton, N.J.: Princeton University Press.

Jasper, James M. 1997. *The Art of Moral Protest: Culture, Biography, and Creativity in Social Movements*. Chicago: University of Chicago Press.

Kitts, James A. 1999. "Not in Our Backyard: Solidarity, Social Networks, and the Ecology of Environmental Mobilization." *Sociological Inquiry* 69, 4 (Fall): 551–74.

Klandermans, Bert, and Dirk Oegema. 1987. "Potentials, Networks, Motivations, and Barriers: Steps towards Participation in Social Movements." *American Sociological Review* 52 (August): 519–31.

Marwell, Gerald, Pamela Oliver, and Ralph Prahl. 1988. "Social Networks and Collective Action: A Theory of the Critical Mass. III." *American Journal of Sociology* 94, 3 (November): 502–34.

McAdam, Doug. 1988. "Micromobilization Contexts and Recruitment to Activism." Pp. 125–54 in *From Structure to Action: Comparing Social Movement Research across Cultures*, ed. Bert Klandermans, Hanspeter Kriesi, and Sidney Tarrow. Greenwich, Conn.: JAI Press.

———. 1994. "Culture and Social Movements." Pp. 36–57 in *New Social Movements: From Ideology to Identity*, ed. Enriquez Laraña, Hank Johnston, and Joseph Gusfield. Philadelphia: Temple University Press.

McAdam, Doug, and Ronnelle Paulsen. 1993. "Specifying the Relationship between Social Ties and Activism." *American Journal of Sociology* 99, 3 (November): 640–67.

Melucci, Alberto. 1989. *Nomads of the Present: Social Movements and Individual Needs in Contemporary Society*. Edited by John Keane and Paul Mier. Philadelphia: Temple University Press.

Oliver, Pamela E. 1989. "Bringing the Crowd Back In: The Nonorganizational Elements of Social Movements." Pp. 1–30 in *Research in Social Movements, Conflict, and Change*, vol. 11, ed. Louis Kriesberg. Greenwich, Conn.: JAI Press.

Raudvere, Catharina. 1998. "Female Dervishes in Contemporary Istanbul: Between Tradition and Modernity." Pp. 125–45 in *Women and Islamization*, ed. Karin Ask and Marit Tjomsland. New York: Berg.

Roald, Anne Sofie. 1998. "Feminist Reinterpretation of Islamic Sources: Muslim

Feminist Theology in the Light of the Christian Tradition of Feminist Thought." Pp. 45–72 in *Women and Islamization,* ed. Karin Ask and Marit Tjomsland. New York: Berg.

Schennink, Ben. 1988. "From Peace Week to Peace Work: Dynamics of the Peace Movement in the Netherlands." Pp. 247–79 in *From Structure to Action: Comparing Social Movement Research across Cultures,* ed. Bert Klandermans, Hanspeter Kriesi, and Sidney Tarrow. Greenwich, Conn.: JAI Press.

Snow, David, Louis Zurcher, and Sheldon Ekland-Olson. 1980. "Social Networks and Social Movements: A Microstructural Approach to Differential Recruitment." *American Sociological Review* 45 (October): 787–801.

Stark, Rodney, and William Sims Bainbridge. 1980. "Networks of Faith: Interpersonal Bonds and Recruitment to Cults and Sects." *American Journal of Sociology* 85, 6: 1376–95.

Seven

Collective Action with and without Islam
Mobilizing the Bazaar in Iran

Benjamin Smith

Although most "old" social institutions in Iran were destroyed or significantly weakened during the Pahlavi dynasty (1926–1979), the bazaar survived, even flourished, despite numerous challenges by central state authorities and shifting economic and political conditions. During the 1977–1979 revolution, the bazaar was a crucial component of the social movement that brought down the monarchy, providing both material and mobilizing resources. The bazaar's close cooperation during the revolution with the *ulama* (Shi'a Islamic leadership) engendered scholarly claims of a historic "bazaar and mosque" alliance. Indeed, outside of the ulama itself, no group in Iran has been as consistently labeled "Islamic" as the bazaaris—the merchants, shopkeepers, employees, hawkers, and other urban Iranians who make their living inside the bazaar or depend upon it for a living (Thaiss 1971; Ashraf 1988; Keshavarzian 1996). Bazaaris have been nearly uniformly described as conservative, traditional, devout Muslims who joined the revolution either out of cultural-ideological affinity with the ulama or out of a sense of outrage at the late Pahlavi secular modernism. While it has been established that the bazaar-mosque alliance was central to the success of the revolutionary movement against the shah in 1978, this alliance is often used to make ahistorical generalizations about bazaari political behavior.

Those generalizations often run afoul of the historical record, even as close to the revolution as 1977, during which time Iranian bazaaris were engaged in a series of collective protests with secular intellectuals rather than with their religious allies in the Shi'a clergy. In addition to questioning the bazaar's external alliance with the clergy, the 1977 protests suggest a strong internal capacity for mobilization in the bazaar itself and a set of motivations

185

for political action that are independent of any external alliances. The generalizations run into further trouble when the issue of bazaar-state relations under the Islamic Republic is raised, and the analytical response has often been either to neglect the changing relationship or to explain the changes in an ad hoc manner. In general, scholars have, with few exceptions (see, e.g., Parsa 1995), been willing to presume that the mobilization of the bazaar during the revolution could be explained by the ideological outcome of the revolution itself.

In this chapter I argue, first, that we must be careful about assuming that the constituent social components of a broad-based Islamic movement like the Iranian revolution are uniformly motivated to action by religion. While there was certainly a segment of the bazaar in Iran that sided ideologically with Khomeini during and after the revolution, the evidence suggests that merchants joined the revolutionary movement for diverse reasons and through a spectrum of political organizations, from Khomeini supporters in the ulama to Marxist groups. Moreover, we must give greater attention to the fact that resources mobilized in support of the movement, like those of the bazaar, remain internal to the group, even though they may be "borrowed" by political entrepreneurs during movement periods. The bazaar's Islamic activism during the revolution, then, was temporally contingent and does not necessarily define a trend. The ulama's successful attempt to "reach into" and utilize bazaari social networks was crucial to the success of the revolution, but the temporary nature of that alliance becomes much clearer when bazaar-mosque relations are traced into the Islamic Republican period.

Second, as an important corrective to prevalent social movement theory developed from Western European and American cases, the mobilization of the bazaar highlights the importance of informal networks as mobilization resources in authoritarian settings. Whereas formalized organizational structures may increase the likelihood of movement success in a democratic polity, in an authoritarian setting they mark movements or groups as targets for state repression. In such environments, well-established informal networks are likely to be the most successful means of mobilization. Informal networks such as the ones in the bazaar in Iran are not inherently oriented to political action. They are primarily social and economic strategies of survival that have become institutionalized, and thus their potential as resources for political mobilization is secondary. In addition, networks like these make a strong sense of community identity possible for the bazaar, even in the face of serious ideological and cultural divides within the community itself, and suggest that what has been termed a sense of "shared fate" is the strongest communal bond between bazaaris of varying religious and class backgrounds.

Third, social groups like the bazaar, which are not movements per se and thus not inherently inclined toward overt political action, are often, perhaps mostly, politically reactive. Under authoritarian rule, they are inclined to remain apolitical when state leaders do not threaten their social autonomy. However, bazaaris are liable to mobilize if the state infringes upon their economic or social interests. Given a consistent potential for mobilization, whether such groups in fact mobilize depends heavily on their ongoing relations with the state. As I argue below, it is crucial to study closely such patterns of state-society interaction over time, as it is state action that has largely driven the bazaar's political action rather than any innate motivation to protest. Rather than focus on political opportunity *structures*, therefore, I argue for a closer concentration on authoritarian states as strategic actors in their own right, whose specific policies can make it too costly for groups like the bazaar *not* to protest.

Why the Bazaar Rebels

Existing analyses of Iran's bazaar that seek to find a coherent logic for its involvement in politics tend to start with the 1977–1979 revolution and infer backwards to make implicit assumptions based on the religious aspects of the bazaar. As I outline below, these macro-theories tend to explain bazaari political behavior by reference to a very limited time frame, the 1978–1979 protests. By focusing only on the last year of the revolution, scholars have attempted to grant a historical logic to the "bazaar-mosque alliance," asserting that this coalition is at the center of all major political events in modern Iranian history (Skocpol 1982; Arjomand 1986; Ashraf 1988). By focusing exclusively on religion as a mobilizing ideology, others have been forced to presume that bazaaris and others were primarily motivated to challenge the state on religious grounds (Arjomand 1986; Saleh 1988; Moaddel 1993), despite the sizable documentary and interview evidence suggesting that economic concerns were foremost for many of the bazaaris who joined the opposition (Atiqpur 1979; Parsa 1995, 2000; Kurzman 1996).

Indeed, one of the constants in the bazaar in Iran is that there is a noted lack of ideological uniformity. During the 1977–1979 revolution, merchants mobilized in support not only of Khomeini but also of the National Front and other secular groups (Parsa 1989, 105–25). Moreover, well into the revolutionary crisis itself bazaaris showed a willingness to work with the shah's government. In October 1978, for instance, merchants met with government minister Manouchehr Azmoun to discuss price controls and the status of bazaar guilds (115). That the Islamic Republic executed many bazaari supporters of the National Front and other groups after the revolution further suggests a marked disconnect between the "bazaar-mosque" alliance theory and the reality of pre- and postrevolutionary bazaar-state relations.[1]

Some scholars do note the political diversity present in the bazaar and the periodic tension between bazaar and mosque (see Keddie 1981, 245; Mottahedeh 1985, 346–47); however, even these more nuanced accounts grant analytic primacy to the religiocultural and institutional ties between the two groups. According to Keddie (1981, 245), "the 'traditionalist' bazaar attitude, along with the close family, financial, and cultural ties of the bazaar with the ulama, help explain the bazaar-ulama alliance that has been responsible for so much revolutionary activity in Iran since 1891." Similarly, Mottahedeh (1985, 346–47) acknowledges that the religious spheres in the bazaar retained substantial autonomy from the mosque, such as *hay'at* or "association" meeting groups, but maintains that, on balance, "the mosque and the bazaar actually acted to give each other shape and sustenance." Among the members of the bazaar community there are doubtless many individuals for whom these characterizations are accurate and for whom this cultural affinity explains much of the willingness to engage in antistate collective action. However, the equally frequent collaboration of the bazaar with radical secular intellectuals across many of the same episodes of contention suggests that it may be the convergence of *interests* rather than ideologies that drives the formation of alliances between the bazaaris and other groups.[2]

There are thus two primary problems with existing approaches to studying the bazaar. The first is that they mesh poorly with the record of bazaari political activity during the late Pahlavi period. The reality is more complex: the bazaari-ulama alliance during the revolution was contingent on the political exigencies of the 1978–1979 period; before then one coalition partner or the other often sided with the monarchy. The second is that, unless we are willing to overlook the complexity of bazaar-state relations in postrevolutionary Iran, we must move beyond the assumption that there exists any permanent alliance between mosque and bazaar. Rather, even now that the bazaar has "captured" a part of the state under the Islamic Republic, as it periodically did to a lesser degree in the monarchic period, the same tensions are exhibited. What remains is to flesh out a theoretical account of bazaar-state relations that can explain conflict under both monarchic and Islamic Republican governments.

Social Movement Theory and Bazaar-State Relations

Theorists of social movements and collective action have outlined external constraints on the mobilization of groups in terms of political opportunity structures and theorized the capacity to mobilize in terms of internal structure (Tilly 1978, 98–142; McAdam, McCarthy, and Zald 1996; Tarrow 1998). While it is certainly true that potential collective action resources are likely to become actual resources only given certain external conditions (Kurzman 1994), it is less clear from theories of opportunity structures how to make sense of them systematically. Absent greater specification, "[political opportunity structure] threatens to become an all-encompassing fudge factor for all the conditions and circumstances that form the context for collective action"

(Gamson and Meyer 1996, 275), a concern also raised by Hafez and Wiktorowicz in chapter 2 of this volume.

If the focus is on the relationship between a specific group, such as the bazaar in Iran, and an authoritarian state, it seems reasonable to make patterns of accommodation and protest the center of analysis. Theories of state-society relations from the comparative study of state formation in the developing world offer a model based on struggles over social control that can help to complete the "other side" of the equation—the role of the state (Migdal 1988, 2001; Migdal, Kohli, and Shue 1994). One major focus in these theories is how social structure plays a major role in determining the capabilities of states to enact and enforce policy: "The disparity [between state aspirations and achievements] demands an approach that focuses attention on the sources of resistance to the state's efforts at achieving predominance" (Migdal 1988, 24). To describe the political atmosphere in which social movements exist in this way, we must look closely at the roots and subsequent patterns of conflict between state elites and powerful groups that mobilize to protect social interests and autonomy.

For the question at hand, the other and more important focus is on the state-building project itself. External expectations of what states should be capable of and the internal exigencies of consolidation impose powerful incentives to establish state authority over social spheres. A number of scholars working in the state-in-society tradition have described the conflict as one in which expectations of the nation-state, both domestically and in the international arena, compel elites to strive for a Weberian authority not just over the means of violence but also over economic life within national borders (Chaudhry 1993; Vitalis 1995; Vitalis and Heydemann 2000). *focus on state-building*

Authority over the national market has been one of the most crucial tests for the success or failure of state-builders. When, for instance, Sidney Tarrow describes the early eighteenth century as the beginning of a "new and more general repertoire of collective action in Western Europe" (Tarrow 1994, 78), it is important to remember the powerful incentives that emerged during this period for merchants and early capitalists to stake their claims for a role in deliberating state policy and limiting state authority over emerging markets (Habermas 1989). Those new patterns of collective action were a response by primarily economic actors to a state intent on extending the reach of "public" authority deeper into the economy. A similar process took place in Iran during the twentieth century, and in my view, it is in this process that external incentives for bazaar mobilization are to be found. As outlined above, prevalent interpretations of bazaari politics have tended to cast it in terms of cultural/religious opposition to the secularizing tendencies of the Pahlavi state-building project. While I do not intend to suggest that either religion or culture is unimportant to bazaaris, the record of bazaar protest suggests a more prevalent motivation to challenges to the state.

During the twentieth century, the bazaar in Iran found itself uncomfortably caught between two groups for whose support various states have vied: the working classes and peasantry, on the one hand, and foreign investors and traders, on the other. Particularly in the late twentieth century, political exigency led state leaders to target the bazaar in order to support other domestic groups. Thus, I suggest here that the roots of bazaari protests lie in a determined effort to resist state encroachment on the bazaar's market autonomy.

Autonomy for the bazaar can be defined along a number of indicators—fair market standing relative to foreign capital, freedom to set prices internally, and freedom from forced competition with state-subsidized cooperatives are arguably the three most important—and interference by the state in any of these arenas is likely to be seen as arbitrary and thus resisted, regardless of the type of government. Arbitrary state intervention in the market, defined as (1) subjection of merchants to unfair foreign competition; (2) the establishment of state-run cooperatives to compete with the bazaar; or (3) the imposition of price controls, is likely to meet with protest by the bazaar. Bazaar mobilization, then, is a function of external factors (particularly state policy) and mobilizing structures internal to the bazaar itself. These factors go far to explain the timing of bazaar protest across a wide range of episodes and under both monarchic and Islamic Republican governments.

bazaar mobilization = f (external/state policy ; internal/structures)

Informal Networks as Mobilizing Structures

Nearly every scholar who has written about modern Iranian history has highlighted the solidarity of the bazaar community (Thaiss 1971; Bonine 1981; Ashraf 1988; Parsa 1989, 91–125; Kheirabadi 1991, 62–84, 95–104). While much has been made of the homogeneity of the bazaar as a social organization, the potential for collective action is a relatively new phenomenon. It began in the late nineteenth century and was primarily a result of two factors: the modernization of communication and transportation in Iran and the country's gradual integration into the European global economic system. The first made it possible for geographically dispersed bazaaris to communicate and spread information quickly, and the second raised the likelihood of both state fiscal crises and subsequent state efforts to target the bazaar as a means of revenue during the crises. During this period, as Abrahamian notes, the penetration of a formerly internally oriented economy by British and Russian commercial interests "induced the scattered regional commercial interests to coalesce into one cross-regional middle class that was conscious for the first time of its own common grievances" (1982, 50). Placing the emergence of the bazaar on the political scene in historical context highlights its twentieth-century political potency and incentives for collective action as a direct result of conflict with a consistently encroaching state intent on penetrating domestic markets.

In using collective action theory to get at the social characteristics of the bazaar, it is important to note the role of norms and informal institutions in enhancing merchants' reputations, regulating price levels, reinforcing communal solidarity, and maintaining a network for quickly transmitting information among bazaaris. The bazaar became a socioeconomic sphere adept at reducing information, social, and transaction costs for merchants and customers alike. As we shall see, the array of social institutions that emerged also served to strengthen the bazaar's independence from the state.[3] These were not networks "designed" to mobilize protests; rather, they developed to promote smooth interaction between economic actors (for a common dynamic in other regions, see Greif 1989). The parallel trends of increasing tension between bazaar and state, on the one hand, and a web of social networks that produced and reproduced contact and trust among bazaaris, on the other, laid the basis for conflict and all but guaranteed that the bazaar would maintain the capacity to mobilize against the state.

Reputation

For the bazaar merchant in Iran, reputation as an honest member of the community was central not only to social status but also to economic viability. A reputation for honesty derived, in large part, from customers' sense that the merchant set prices fairly. Freedom to set those prices daily, depending upon availability of a given good (including road conditions between bazaar and suppliers, growing season, weather, etc.), and to offer a sliding price scale for varying degrees of "friend" (Rotblat 1972, 154–64) was the foundation of individual economic viability in the bazaar. Price levels were thus embedded in an interactive relationship between character and reputation. By offering varying price levels, with the lowest paying clients—the "good friends"— forming the smallest group of one's total clientele, bazaaris were able both to augment their reputations and to retain a profitable and continuous clientele. Reputation also affected a range of other factors, including the ability to obtain credit and the terms on which it was offered (164–67, 169–79, 189–208). As Rotblat notes, "character and reputation are the main bases of competition in these bazaars" (161).

A different sort of reputation issue emerged during my research in the Isfahan bazaar in July 1998. My primary informant there, Hossein, had taken great pains to employ carpet sellers who spoke English, Spanish, Japanese, and German. (Isfahan is a major attraction for increasing numbers of European and Japanese tourists.) He had built a reputation as an informal go-to man for foreign travelers and as someone who could call on friends to arrange transportation around or out of Isfahan, visa extensions, hotel accommodations, and other services on short notice and as a last resort. I was sitting in his shop drinking tea when two English women arrived from a sightseeing trip around the city. They had stopped in his shop the day before. He casually asked them how much they had paid for the taxi ride around the city, and when they told him the amount (too high), he went running out of his shop after the taxi. He yelled at the driver for several minutes, then returned with the balance of the women's money over the "fair" fare. To demonstrate again how salient these reputation concepts are for bazaaris, Hossein told me, unsolicited, how bad things might have been for him if word had leaked out among other merchants that he was incapable of looking after travelers.

Religion

While scholars have pointed to the bazaar as a last bastion of traditional Islamic values in Iran (Bonine 1981; Ashraf 1988), in reality its religious views seem to be less homogeneous. Howard Rotblat's long-term sociological study of the Qazvin bazaar[4] suggests that many bazaaris' outward piety was aimed at maintaining their reputations and, thus, their profits. Community acclaim as a faithful Muslim could enable a merchant, for instance, to call on divine authority that his prices were fair.[5] Furthermore, outward religiosity legitimized the public display of wealth that might otherwise be thought pretentious, and thus the sight of a bazaar merchant or shopkeeper fingering worry beads would be unsurprising but might indicate less piety than first glance would suggest.[6] Another important aspect of religiosity in the bazaar is the distinction made by many bazaaris between their own beliefs and the legitimacy of clerical rule in postrevolutionary Iran. During a 1980 conflict between bazaaris and the ruling Islamic Republican Party, one merchant complained about the ulama's ignorance of economic matters, claiming, "If you shake hands with a mullah you will notice that his hands are as soft as those of a 14-year-old girl because these people never do anything useful" (*Christian Science Monitor,* November 18, 1980). In my own research in the Tehran and Isfahan bazaars in 1998, I encountered many self-identified devout merchants and shopkeepers who passed slow periods by telling their favorite or latest mullah jokes. This practice, along with frequent declarations that one could be a good Muslim while disapproving either of specific policies or of a state run by mullahs, suggests that, even for those bazaaris who consider themselves devout, there is a conscious distinction between Islam and the politicization of the ulama.

Absent the assumption of piety, we might be left wondering whether bazaaris shared any common beliefs. However, the fact that bazaaris from all class levels—from the richest merchants to the most meager wandering street hawkers—have acted in concert against common threats suggests a more general interest: the survival of the bazaar as an institution. Supporting this assertion are the patterns of interaction between bazaaris, aimed at reinforcing social and reciprocity networks within the bazaar. Although we might profitably describe these relationships as "shared interests" (Lamborn 1983, 131–33; Parsa 1989, 92), such an understanding undervalues the strong collective normative commitment merchants have to the bazaar itself.[7] This commitment means that despite ideological diversity among bazaaris, solidarity in response to a threat to the bazaar was and is something on which all could agree.

Reciprocity

Merchants were also customers, and they not only shopped in other bazaaris' shops but also on occasion sent their customers elsewhere when they didn't have the desired item in stock. In 1995, Arang Keshavarzian (1996, 35), for instance, observed a shopkeeper taking a customer to another shop for an item he did not carry. When asked why, the shopkeeper replied that the practice not only "keeps customers happy" but also "uses and strengthens the various channels of communication." I experienced similarly purposive maintenance of social networks in the Tehran and Isfahan bazaars in 1998. On one occasion, I was taken across the whole of the Tehran bazaar (a walk of about two kilometers) to shop at a specific luggage seller whom my carpet seller guide had not seen in some time, mostly so my merchant guide could say hello.[8] On another occasion, an employee of one shop in the Isfahan bazaar took me a considerable distance (again) to look for something his employer did not sell. He explained to me the importance of frequent communication, suggesting that in addition to friendship and reciprocity there is an active realization among bazaaris that these norms serve their common interests by keeping them in touch with one another.

Credit and Dispute Resolution

Norms of behavior such as reciprocity, by all counts, have gone far to maintain the bazaar as a viable sector in Iran's economy, despite the late shah's conviction that "the bazaaris are a fanatic lot" whose "time is past" (Pahlavi 1980, 156). In addition, the bazaar community fostered a number of other informal institutions that served to reinforce the community itself. Among the most important were the credit process and internal mediation. Most commercial exchange in the bazaar took the form of credit transactions in the 1970s, either in the form of straight loans or postdated checks. Despite the availability of commercial bank loans at a frequently lower interest rate, in-house lending between merchants remained viable because of the "relative easiness with which the merchants themselves get credit" (Rotblat 1972, 203). Merchants were sometimes hesitant to use bazaar moneylenders because of the high interest rates, but again reputation entered the picture: "The moneylender will discount a merchant's signature at rates which vary according to the reputation of the person seeking the cash" (207). Credit-based transactions between merchants became institutionalized as a way to avoid using state-run banks, to reinforce reputations, and to maintain reciprocity and communication networks. Even in the tightly knit bazaar community, however, economic and legal disputes were inevitable.

What is notable about the bazaar, though, is the degree to which it remained independent of the state legal system to resolve these disputes. Even as the "rationalized" state court system expanded under the reign of Reza Shah and then under his son Mohammed Reza Shah, bazaaris continued to rely on internal arbitration and mediation. Why? Gustav Thaiss (1971, 190) offers two answers. First, "the recourse to traditional forms of conflict resolution is less expensive and less time-consuming and avoids the corruption and bribery that are often associated with the courts." In short, bazaaris trusted the state considerably less than they trusted each other. Second, by relying on mediation and arbitration, merchants, as with their reciprocity arrangements, continually strengthened both the institutions of conflict resolution and their own communal solidarity: "Thus, the persistence of 'traditional' behavior . . . coincides to a high degree with what is rational to do with the means available."

The pattern of informal institutions in the Iranian bazaar of the late twentieth century served not only to reinforce community solidarity but also to maintain autonomy from the state. The process of modern state-building under the Pahlavi dynasty began in 1926 under Reza Shah, and its history is replete with attempts to wrest social control from other centers of authority (Hooglund 1982; Mottahedeh 1985; Keshavarzian 1996). The bazaar was one such center of authority, but it was able to resist state encroachment better than even the ulama, in part because of its continued independence from the state largesse brought by oil revenues (Parsa 1989, 91–125). That the state could rely on oil revenues for well over half of its budget by about 1960 meant that it no longer needed to expend resources to extract significant taxes from the bazaars, which even further enhanced the latter's autonomy. Thus, the evolution of Iran's political economy into an oil-rich rentier state augmented the social autonomy and solidarity made possible by the bazaar's social institutions.

Bazaar-State Relations under
Monarchy and Theocracy

Between 1975 and 1977, before the January 1978 ulama-led protests that most analyses use to mark the "beginning" of the revolution, a modernizing monarchy confronted a coalition of radical students and bazaar merchants in a protest movement that to a large degree was bankrolled by the bazaar. In the postrevolutionary period, despite its close involvement in the consolidation of the revolutionary government, the bazaar has consistently opposed the popu-list economic policies of the Islamic Republic. Tracing bazaari involvement in Iranian politics from the late Pahlavi through the recent Islamic Republican periods suggests that there may be underlying interests that created conti-nuity in bazaar-state relations, regardless of whether the country was run by kings or ayatollahs.

Bazaaris, the State, and the Rastakhiz Party, 1975–1977

In late 1974 the regime announced that Majlis (parliament) elections would be held the following spring, and the shah apparently was sufficiently confi-dent of his political position to allow opposition parties to participate for the first time in 12 years. The result was vibrant political participation in the election campaign, and the sanctioned opposition party Hizb-e Mardom (Party of the People) won several by-elections before the main parliamentary balloting. The surprise showing by Mardom threw into doubt the national victory of the pro-state Iran-i Novin (New Iran) party and raised questions about the control commanded by the regime. This political setback, coincid-ing as it did with a bout of inflation and a drop in oil revenues, also apparently spurred the shah to announce the creation of the Rastakhiz (Resurgence) party on March 2, 1975, as a means of extending the control held by the regime in economic planning into societal mobilization (Afkhami 1985, 70; Abrahamian 1989, 22–28; Alam 1991, 415–16; Milani 2000; 275–79).

What the new party meant for the bazaar was soon made clear. The Ras-takhiz party became an instrument of invasion beginning in August 1975 as 10,000 party recruits were sent into the bazaars to enforce new price controls (returned to January 1975 levels) on 16,000 goods and a profit margin ceiling of 14 percent, roughly half the inflation rate (Zabih 1979, 30–31; Abrahamian 1982, 442–43, 498; Bashiriyeh 1984, 93–95; Parsa 1989, 103; Chehabi 1990; 94). When crackdowns on industrialists and the richest bazaar merchants failed to ameliorate the problem, middle-class merchants and shopkeepers be-came the next targets (Green 1982, 56–59). By early August, 10,000 shop-keepers had been fined, over 7,500 had been arrested, and more than 600 shops had been shut down by the Rastakhiz Youth, who were described by Prime Minister Amir Abbas Hoveyda as "the instruments of Iran's develop-ment" (*Kayhan International* 1975; Abrahamian 1982, 498). The antiprofiteer-ing campaign was directed not by a preexisting institution of the state, but by a special "task force" of the Rastakhiz party (Ashraf 1988, 557), tying the attack on the bazaars to official party policy, which identified bazaaris as "enemies of the state." The shah went so far in October 1975 as to call the antiprofiteering campaign an Iranian "cultural movement," and he decreed antiprofiteerism the fourteenth principle of the White Revolution (*Kayhan*, October 8, 1975).

In addition to the antiprofiteering campaign, the Rastakhiz party also "opened branches in the bazaars, forced donations from small businessmen, and required shopkeepers and workshop owners to register their employees with the Labor Ministry and pay monthly contributions for their medical insurance. . . . *The government had rushed into a territory in which previous regimes had feared to tread*" (Abrahamian 1982, 443, emphasis added). Finally, the Rastakhiz party began two policies that directly endangered bazaaris on both an individual and collective level. First, all merchants and shopkeepers who were arrested or who had their shops forcibly closed were publicly vilified in party posters hung in the bazaars as dishonest merchants and unsavory members of the community who had engaged in profiteering (Parsa 1989, 103–104). Recalling the centrality of a merchant's reputation to his economic viability, these intentional character attacks by the party were immensely threatening to individual bazaaris.

While the campaign against the bazaar was notable on a purely socioeconomic level—the degree of state encroachment was unprecedented in Iranian history—the political significance made the writing on the wall even clearer for bazaaris: they were to be the scapegoats in a populist appeal to the poor (Abrahamian 1982, 498). Bazaaris complained to Western journalists that the "Shah-People Revolution" was starting to sound more "red" than "white," and they openly accused the regime of shifting the blame to the bazaar to cover its own corruption (Rouleau 1976; Cage 1978).

Second, in early 1976 the shah's government announced the establishment of the Urban and Rural Consumers' Cooperative, aimed at providing subsidized competition for basic goods previously available only in the bazaar. Shortly after that, the regime announced plans to tear down large portions of the Tehran bazaar in order to make room for a freeway and "modern" market, endangering the bazaar's survival as an institution. One merchant's response to the new policies was telling: "If we would let him, the shah would destroy us. . . . The bazaar will be flattened so new buildings can go up" (*New York Times* 1978). As Houchang Chehabi (1990, 94) noted, "The bazaaris interpreted the creation of the [Rastakhiz] party and the antiprofiteering campaign as a declaration of war."

Other groups in society felt the regime's pressure and repression as well. In March 1977, the government announced that it would move Aryamehr University from Tehran to Isfahan, most likely to distance it from the capital and thus from the center of Iranian politics. Students and professors protested, and during the demonstrations the entire Tehran bazaar remained closed. After the protest, when the regime cut salaries to punish professors, bazaar merchants "quickly established funds to pay faculty salaries in full" (Parsa 1989, 109).

Intellectuals flooded the regime with demands for increased freedom of expression. In May, a group of lawyers wrote a highly critical letter to the government, the first time since 1963 that the regime had been so publicly and strongly criticized. In June, the Writers' Association of Iran wrote a public letter to the Prime Minister and Rastakhiz Secretary General Hoveyda (Karimi-Hakkak 1985). In July, another group of lawyers wrote a public manifesto criticizing the regime's control of the judiciary (*Ettela'at*, February 7, 1980).

In early August, the government continued its attack on the bazaaris by levying heavy new taxes on the bazaar in an attempt to balance the budget and by placing political conditions on the availability of commerce licenses (Parsa 1989, 103). Later in the month, the government decried tax evasion by bazaaris not simply as an economic problem but as a problem "of the [Rastakhiz] party," to be dealt with politically (*Ettela'at*, August 23, 1977). Shortly after that, bazaar representatives met with party officials to object to the taxes, and the bazaars formally protested the Rastakhiz party's price-control campaign (Abrahamian 1982; Parsa 1989, 109).

From October 10 until October 19, 1977, a Writers' Association poetry meeting gathered some 10,000 participants at the Irano-German Cultural Society (also called the Goethe Institute) in Tehran (Karimi-Hakkak 1985, 208–11). When the shah's police broke it up, students and teachers responded by shutting down nearly all of Tehran's universities for a full ten days (the Ten Nights). Government attorneys previously loyal to the regime acquitted all of the demonstrators who were arrested after the poetry reading was broken up. In support, the Tehran bazaar closed throughout the protests.

The magnitude of the Ten Nights indicates that by late 1977 a large portion of Iran's bazaar and intellectual communities had turned against the state. Throughout 1978, the bazaars remained closed for several months, communicating, as closures always did, "to other groups in society that some sort of conflict [was] underway" (Parsa 1989, 93). Interviews with bazaaris who closed their shops reveal a strong community component to the decision to protest in this way: "When everyone is shutting down [their shops], the rest shut down, too" (Kurzman 1996, 167).

Several years earlier, the same bazaaris did not take action in support of a major demonstration led by theological students in the Madraseh-e Faizieh-e Qom, Iran's most important center of religious training. On June 5, 1975, the twelfth anniversary of the arrest of the Ayatollah Khomeini during the June 1963 protests (Parsa 1989, 100–102; Kurzman 1997), a three-day protest began that ended with a military siege of the Madraseh. Khomeini issued a statement from exile in Iraq strongly supporting the students, but no bazaar support emerged. This incident raises not only the question of why the bazaaris failed to support a demonstration by their "permanent" allies, but why they did not seize on this event as an opportunity to resist the regime. The evidence suggests that the timing of the event is the reason. Although the Rastakhiz party had been in existence for three months, it had directed none of its energy yet toward attacking the bazaar, and given the latter's continued economic viability and social autonomy, no incentive existed to challenge the state.

While by mid-January 1978 the supporters of the Ayatollah Khomeini had taken a leadership role in the protest movement, albeit one that they would expand as the movement grew, the vitality of the 1977 protests is striking. Equally notable is the frequent economic motivation noted by bazaaris in their specific complaints against state policies. The bazaar-mosque coordination of the majority of the major demonstrations in 1978 is well documented, and by no means do I seek to question it here. I do want, however, to highlight the fact that the coalition, powerful as it was, is sandwiched between the 1975–1977 period, in which the bazaar mobilized independently of the ulama, and the postrevolutionary period, in which the bazaar mobilized *against* the ulama.

Bazaar-State Relations under the Islamic Republic

One major empirical assumption that I question in this chapter is that Iran's bazaar and Shiᶜa leadership communities form a "natural" alliance. Even given their close coordination of protests throughout 1978 and the increased role of bazaaris in the Iranian economy after the revolution, tensions remain. Simply put, the arguments by a number of scholars about the "bazaar-mosque alliance" have not withstood the test of time. Bazaar-state relations under the Islamic Republic, in which the "mosque" rules, have been nearly as antagonistic as they were under the monarchy. What is striking is the similarity of circumstances surrounding bazaar protest during the monarchic period and postrevolution Iran. Below, I briefly analyze two cases of protest by the bazaar in Iran since 1979, stressing the common chronology: economic or inflationary crisis, government intervention against the bazaar, and resultant bazaar protest.

In 1980, before the revolutionary government was consolidated, a split emerged between supporters of the new Islamic Republic Party (IRP) and followers of Dr. Abol Hasan Bani-Sadr, the first elected president. Bani-Sadr's foreign minister, Sadeq Ghotbzadeh, had been imprisoned by the IRP, and the Tehran bazaar collected signatures to petition for his release on November 8. The next day the bazaar in Qom submitted a similar petition. After his release from prison, Ghotbzadeh chose the Tehran bazaar as the site of his first public appearance, and the gathering grew into a substantial protest challenging the IRP's intervention in the market. Bazaaris specifically targeted the regime's command economic policies, noting that, while they had opposed the shah, "everything was easier before. The shah supported capitalism and private enterprises. [We] hoped that everything would be better. Instead we have lost our capital and gained nothing" (*Christian Science Monitor,* November 18, 1980). The bazaaris also threatened to mobilize a broader strike if their concerns were not heeded, despite their support for national unity during the war with Iraq: "We are convinced that if we close the bazaar the workers will support us as they did during the revolution. The Imam [Khomeini] is aware of the effect of a strike in the bazaar on the rest of the country." In response to the show of support for Bani-Sadr, the IRP staged a mass meeting on November 17 in the Imam Khomeini mosque in the Tehran bazaar, but failed to attract much of a turnout. Two weeks later, hundreds of young *komiteh* members armed with clubs ordered the bazaars in Tehran, Mashhad, and Qom to close following street clashes between IRP and Bani-Sadr supporters.

In late 1989, President Ali Akbar Hashemi Rafsanjani made a serious effort to reform Iran's largely command economy by relaxing import restrictions. However, his first Five-Year Plan opened the country's foreign exchange system and encouraged heavy increases in private consumption without an accompanying political opening that would have made access to foreign markets for Iranian exporters easier. The resultant inflation by the early 1990s spurred a number of demonstrations against the rising prices of consumer goods and public transportation (Pesaran 1998, 5; Smith 1999). In response, in December 1994 Rafsanjani announced a new state-owned cooperative supermarket chain, called Refah (Welfare), to provide heavily subsidized goods in direct competition with the bazaar. Declaring that 1,000 of the stores would ultimately be built, he took aim politically at produce sellers in the bazaar, declaring that "the leech-like elements standing between production, distribution, and consumption [must] be eliminated" (*Christian Science Monitor,* February 22, 1995). Bazaaris in Tehran organized major street demonstrations to protest the Refah stores. Although the government proclaimed victory in the dispute and went ahead with Refah while analysts predicted widespread bazaari bankruptcies, as of mid-1998 most of the stores had been built well outside urban centers and in dramatically smaller numbers than had been planned,[9] posing little threat to the bazaar's near monopoly on produce or other goods.

The same economic distortions that had led to price inflation in the early 1990s had by 1996 compelled the Iranian government to look to tax revenues as a means of balancing the budget. Given the ease of locating bazaaris, and the lucrative carpet trade, carpet sellers faced the heaviest burden under the new tax plan. In July 1996, the carpet bazaar in Tehran, the largest sector of the bazaar writ large, went on strike (*Xinhua,* July 24, 1996; Associated Press, July 25, 1996).

Conclusion

The history of bazaar-state relations in Iran during the past 25 years suggests a different kind of relationship with the ulama than the one that is often described and a need to examine the political fallout of mass-based Islamic movements like the 1977–1979 revolution in Iran. Even though prominent members of the bazaar community have successfully "captured" large sectors of the Iranian economy through the leadership of revolutionary foundations, and the bazaar (at large) maintains closer ties to the leadership of the Islamic Republic than it did to the Pahlavi monarchy, economic crisis under both regimes has tended to produce similar state policy responses. These policies have, in turn, elicited bazaar challenges.

While another mass-based movement like the one in 1978–1979 that brought down the shah is unlikely, it is likely that the pattern of state-bazaar contention will continue (and probably intensify). President Mohammed Khatami's economic plan in 1999 called for significant structural adjustment in an effort to attract foreign investment, and many of those policies will directly threaten the privileged position of the bazaar. However, merchants with significant capital do stand to gain from the economic changes due to their position as "early comers" in an increasingly internationally oriented market (Smith 1999, 6). But bazaar merchants remain divided on whether to support Khatami's economic reform program, tending to favor the relaxation of restrictions on exports while opposing the opening of the domestic market to foreign competition (*Business Week,* June 7, 1999).

In addition to economic conflict, bazaar-state relations continue to be politicized over religion, in ways that are hard to foresee. For instance, in April and May 1998, bazaaris and university students in Qom, Najafabad, and Isfahan staged collective protests against the arrest of the Ayatollah Ali Montazeri, siding with Montazeri and his reformist supporters against what were rumored to be the direct orders of the religious leader Ali Khamene³i (Associated Press, April 30, 1998). Yet despite this initial support for the reformers, the Tehran bazaar closed to support a government-organized rally decrying student uprisings after the summer 1999, apparently siding with conservatives against a reform-minded student movement (*International Herald Tribune,* July 15, 1999).

In a major contribution to the study of social movements in the Islamic world, Edmund Burke (1988, 26) draws a distinction between studies that examine cases like the bazaar in Iran as "a history of Islamic political movements" and those that view such instances of collective action in terms of "the history of collective action in Islamic societies." Central as it was to the success of the Iranian revolutionary movement, the bazaar fits better into Burke's latter category.

Moreover, the bazaar contributes significantly to our understanding of the role of Islam in motivating protest movements. While it is certainly true that many bazaaris joined the protest movements discussed above for religious reasons and, further, that many who joined for other reasons remained devout, it is imperative that analysis of the outcomes of such movements not become behavioral assertions of motivation. These cases of bazaar protest, combined with field research in the bazaar spanning nearly 30 years, suggest that (1) state economic policy plays the crucial role in determining when the bazaar *as a whole* will mobilize; and (2) individual bazaaris demonstrate a willingness to separate their religion from their politics, even under theocracy.

These cases also present two findings pertinent to social movement theory more generally. First, the role of the state, conceptualized not only as a set of institutions but as a set of leaders with their own interests, helps greatly to specify how and when external conditions—or political opportunity structures—are likely to lead to the activation, or actualization, of strong but potential mobilizing structures (see Boudreau 1998; Wiktorowicz 2001). Islamic activism, if bazaari mobilization is representative, is more likely to succeed when it can tap into the social networks of powerful groups with their own grievances against authoritarian governments. Convergence of grievances, thus, is likely to be a key to the success of such movements. Second, tracing patterns of relations and episodes of contention over time—a process termed "dynamic interaction" by McAdam, Tarrow, and Tilly (2001)—can highlight the variant underlying motivations in cases like the 1978–1979 protests in Iran and shed valuable analytic light on the causes of recurrent contentious movements. Where social movement theory traditionally leaves off, state-in-society theories of struggle over arenas of social control can help to fill in the analytic gaps.

Notes

1. The British Broadcasting Corporation (BBC), July 15 and 17, 1981, reported the mobilization of the Tehran bazaar for a strike in response to the executions of two merchants convicted of contact with the National Front.

2. Keddie (1981), for example, notes that it was not merely a bazaar-ulama alliance but a tripartite bazaar-radical-ulama alliance that was central to the Tobacco Rebellion of 1891 and the Constitutional Revolution of 1905–1906. As I discuss below, that tripartite alliance of the 1978–1979 revolution in Iran was preceded by a bazaar-radical alliance in late 1977, during which time the ulama was almost entirely absent.

3. It is important to note here that, since the revolution in 1978–1979, the social organization of the bazaar has become more hierarchical and somewhat less autonomous of the state. I am grateful to Arang Keshavarzian for his discussions on this and other issues.

4. Qazvin is a provincial capital northwest of Tehran.

5. Rotblat (1972, 185) notes an example of this. A customer in the Qazvin bazaar questioned the price of an article in his presence, to which the merchant's apprentice replied, "The Haji says only one word." The title Haji is reserved for those Muslims who have made the pilgrimage to Mecca, and the reference indicates special piety on the merchant's part for which his prices were not to be questioned or haggled.

6. Worry beads were still ubiquitous in the bazaar in the late 1990s, even among those younger merchants who professed to me to be more secular.

7. It should be noted here that the bazaar's hierarchical class structure—with merchants at the top—probably made (and makes) nearly complete solidarity possible, even given vertical discord.

8. The merchant pointed out to me the importance of keeping up these sorts of social ties, although he did not specify why. Author's interview, August 12, 1998.

9. There are a handful of Refah stores in greater Tehran, but nothing to indicate the 1,000 stores nationwide that were promised at the announcement of the chain's establishment. I saw only one Refah store in Isfahan, located several kilometers outside of the city on the highway to the airport. I could find no centrally located Refah stores in Tehran, Isfahan, Mashhad, Ardabil, Rasht, or Tabriz during my research in July–September 1998.

Works Cited

Abrahamian, Ervand. 1982. *Iran between Two Revolutions.* Princeton, N.J.: Princeton University Press.

———. 1989. *The Iranian Mojahedin.* New Haven, Conn.: Yale University Press.

Afkhami, Gholam 1985. *The Iranian Revolution: Thanatos on a National Scale.* Washington, D.C.: Middle East Institute.

Arjomand, Said Amir. 1986. *Turban for the Crown.* New York: Oxford University Press.

Ashraf, Ahmad. 1988. "Bazaar-Mosque Alliance: The Social Basis of Revolts and Revolutions." *Politics, Culture, and Society* 1: 538–67.

Atiqpur, Muhammad. 1979. *Naqshi-i Bazar va Bazariʾha dar Inqilab-i Iran.* N.p.

Bashiriyeh, Hossein. 1984. *The State and Revolution in Iran, 1962–1982.* New York: St. Martin's.

Bonine, Michael. 1981. "Shops and Shopkeepers: Dynamics of an Iranian Provincial Bazaar." Pp. 233–58 in *Modern Iran: The Dialectics of Continuity and Change,* ed. Michael Bonine and Nikki Keddie. Albany: SUNY Press.

Boudreau, Vincent. 1998. "Styles of Repression and Mobilization in Southeast Asia." Manuscript, City College of New York.

Burke, Edmund, III. 1988. "Islam and Social Movements: Methodological Reflections." Pp. 17–35 in *Islam, Politics, and Social Movements,* ed. Edmund Burke III and Ira M. Lapidus. Berkeley: University of California Press.

Cage, N. 1978. "Iran: The Making of a Revolution." *New York Times,* December 17.

Chaudhry, Kiren Aziz. 1993. "The Myths of the Market and the Common History of Late Developers." *Politics and Society* 21, 3: 245–74.

Chehabi, Houchang. 1990. *Iranian Politics and Religious Modernism: The Liberation Movement of Iran under the Shah and Khomeini.* Ithaca, N.Y.: Cornell University Press.

Gamson, William, and David S. Meyer. 1996. "Framing Political Opportunity." Pp. 275–90 in *Comparative Perspectives on Social Movements: Political Opportunities, Mobilizing Structures, and Cultural Framings,* ed. Doug McAdam, John D. McCarthy, and Mayer Zald. New York: Cambridge University Press.

Green, Jerrold. 1982. *Revolution in Iran: The Politics of Countermobilization.* New York: Praeger.

Greif, Avner 1989. "Reputation and Coalitions in Medieval Trade: Evidence on the Maghribi Traders." *Journal of Economic History* 59: 857–82.

Habermas, Jürgen. 1989. *Structural Transformation of the Public Sphere.* Translation by Thomas Burger. Cambridge: MIT Press.

Hooglund, Eric. 1982. *Land and Revolution in Iran, 1960–1980.* Austin: University of Texas Press.

Karimi-Hakkak, Ahmad. 1985. "Protest and Perish: A History of the Writers' Association of Iran." *Iranian Studies* 18, 1–4: 189–229.

Keshavarzian, Arang. 1996. "From Holy Alliance to Enemy of Islam." M.A. thesis, University of Washington.

Kheirabadi, Masoud. 1991. *Iranian Cities: Formation and Development.* Austin: University of Texas Press.

Kurzman, Charles. 1994. "A Dynamic View of Resources: Evidence from the Iranian Revolution." *Research in Social Movements, Conflicts, and Change* 17: 53–84.

———. 1996. "Structural Opportunity and Perceived Opportunity in Social-Movement Theory: The Iranian Revolution of 1979." *American Sociological Review* 61: 153–70.

———. 1997. "The Qum Protests of 1975 and 1978." Manuscript, Georgia State University.

Lamborn, Alan C. 1983. "Power and the Politics of Extraction." *International Studies Quarterly* 27: 125–46.

McAdam, Doug, John D. McCarthy, and Mayer Zald, eds. 1996. *Comparative Perspectives on Social Movements: Political Opportunities, Mobilizing Structures, and Cultural Framings.* New York: Cambridge University Press.

McAdam, Doug, Sidney Tarrow, and Charles Tilly. 2001. *Dynamics of Contention.* New York: Cambridge University Press.

Migdal, Joel S. 1988. *Strong Societies and Weak States.* Princeton, N.J.: Princeton University Press.

———. 2001. *State in Society: Studying How States and Societies Transform and Constitute One Another.* New York: Cambridge University Press.

Migdal, Joel S., Atul Kohli, and Vivienne Shue, eds. 1994. *State Power and Social Forces.* New York: Cambridge University Press.

Milani, Abbas. 2000. *The Persian Sphinx: Amir Abbas Hoveyda and the Riddle of the Iranian Revolution.* Washington: Mage.

Moaddel, Mansoor. 1993. *Class, Politics, and Ideology in the Iranian Revolution.* New York: Columbia University Press.

Mottahedeh, Roy. 1985. *Mantle of the Prophet.* New York: Pantheon.

Pahlavi, Mohammed Reza. 1980. *Answer to History.* New York: Stein and Day.

Parsa, Misagh. 1989. *Social Origins of the Iranian Revolution.* New Brunswick, N.J.: Rutgers University Press.

———. 1995. "Conversion or Coalition: Ideology in the Iranian and Nicaraguan Revolutions." *Political Power and Social Forces* 9: 23–60.

———. 2000. *States, Ideologies, and Social Revolutions.* New York: Cambridge University Press.

Pesaran, M. H. 1998. "Economic Trends and Macroeconomic Policies in Post-Revolutionary Iran." Manuscript, Cambridge University.

Rotblat, Howard. 1972. "Stability and Change in an Iranian Provincial Bazaar." Ph.D. dissertation, University of Chicago.

Rouleau, Eric. 1976. "Iran: Myth and Reality." *Guardian*, October 31.

Saleh, M. M. 1988. *Insurgency through Culture and Religion: The Islamic Revolution of Iran*. New York: Praeger.

Skocpol, Theda. 1982. "Rentier State and Shiᶜa Islam in the Iranian Revolution." *Theory and Society* 11: 265–83.

Smith, Benjamin. 1999. "Old Markets and New Politics: The Politics of Economic Reform in Late Twentieth-Century Iran." Manuscript, Gadjah Mada University, Yogyakarta, Indonesia.

Tarrow, Sidney. 1998. *Power in Movement: Social Movements and Contentious Politics*. 2d ed. New York: Cambridge University Press.

Thaiss, Gustav. 1971. "The Bazaar as a Case Study of Religion and Social Change." Pp. 45–75 in *Iran Faces the Seventies*, ed. Ehsan Yar-Shater. New York: Praeger.

Tilly, Charles. 1978. *From Mobilization to Revolution*. Reading, Mass.: Addison Wesley.

———. 1985. "Models and Realities of Popular Collective Action." *Social Research* 52: 717–47.

Vitalis, Robert. 1995. *When Capitalists Collide*. Berkeley: University of California Press.

Vitalis, Robert, and Steven Heydemann. 2000. "War, Keynesianism, and Colonialism: Explaining State-Market Relations in the Postwar Middle East." In *War, Institutions, and Social Change in the Middle East*, ed. Steven Heydemann. Berkeley: University of California Press.

Wiktorowicz, Quintan. 2001. *The Management of Islamic Activism: Salafis, the Muslim Brotherhood, and State Power in Jordan*. Albany: SUNY Press.

Zabih, Sepehr. 1979. *Iran's Revolutionary Upheaval: An Interpretive Essay*. San Francisco: Alchemy Books.

Eight

The Islah Party in Yemen
Political Opportunities and Coalition Building in a Transitional Polity

Jillian Schwedler

Long before the September 11 attacks, scholars and policymakers sought to understand the motives, objectives, behavior, and ideological bases of Islamist groups, ranging from underground extremist cells to formal political parties working within pluralist systems. One of the central (but often unspoken) assumptions has been that Islamists—actors that seek to apply Islamic law to all spheres of social, political, and economic life—consistently represent radical or revolutionary challenges to existing regimes. Instances where Islamist groups ally themselves with distinctly non-Islamist ruling elites or where regimes actively court Islamists to widen the base of support are less well studied and undertheorized. In transitional polities, such topics become increasingly important as Islamist movements create political parties that interact with other political actors through coalitions and parliamentary politics. Despite this lacuna, these issues can be fruitfully explored through the concepts and insights of social movement theory, particularly notions of coalition building and mobilization within changing political opportunity structures. At the same time, such studies contribute to social movement theory by examining the dynamics of contention as strongly ideological movements transform into formal parties. The Yemeni Islah Group (often called the Islah party) provides a rich case study.

The Islah party was formed in 1990 in an effort to take advantage of the new political opportunities that emerged with Yemeni unification in 1989 and subsequent political liberalization. By 1993, the party had joined the ranks of the ruling coalition government, and within less than a year its rival, the Yemeni Socialist Party (YSP), was defeated in a brief civil war. In the first postwar cabinet, an Islah member was appointed first deputy prime minister and the number of Islah-controlled ministries increased from six to nine. The defeat of the YSP in 1994 should have marked the rapid ascent of Islah, yet the party's influence diminished a few years later to such an extent that it no longer held a single ministry. By that time, the party had a well-established institutional structure and still enjoyed a close alliance with the ruling elite, but it was a party in decline. Why did the defeat of the YSP mark the decline of the Islah party, when all indications suggested a contrary trajectory?

This chapter argues that the Islah party *as a formally institutionalized political party* was useful to President Salih and the ruling General People's Congress party (Al-Mu'tammar al-Sha'bi al-'Amm) only within the context of a North-South struggle for political domination. With the YSP virtually defeated, GPC leaders maintained personal ties with prominent Islah leaders, but no longer needed Islah as a third party to offset the potential influence and mobilization capacity of the YSP at the polls. In this context, the relative strength of the Islah party witnessed a rapid decline as the broader field of alliances (not only those between the GPC and Islah) altered the structure of political opportunities.

Political Opportunities, Elite Alliances, and Yemeni Unification

Much of the literature on social movements has focused on political opportunity structures: the organization of the broader political system and how it shapes possibilities for mobilization. Key areas of concern regarding political opportunities include the level of state repression, relative openness of the system (including the opportunities for mobilization to take on particular forms), the stability of elite-level alliances, and relations between state and social actors (see, e.g., Seidman 1994; McAdam, McCarthy, and Zald 1996; Della Porta and Diani 1999). Where changes in any of these factors occur, one can expect opportunities for mobilization to change as well.

Perhaps one of the most dramatic shifts in the structure of opportunities occurs during political liberalization. If an authoritarian regime decides to initiate a process of limited political liberalization, the new opportunities increase the likelihood that new forms of mobilization will emerge to take advantage of changing political conditions. When opposition groups are permitted to organize and campaign as political parties, for example, it provides political actors with the opportunity to expand their support bases and convey alternative political visions to a wider audience. Similarly, regimes may open the political system by allowing civil society organizations to function freely, therefore changing the structure of the public sphere to allow for an increased level of political debate.

In Yemen, political liberalization formally began in 1990 as part of a negotiated unification of North and South Yemen, neither of which had a strong history of democratic or electoral politics. The Yemen Arab Republic (YAR, or North Yemen) was established in 1962 through a military coup against a theocratic state ruled by a hereditary line of Zaydi Imams. The move started a civil war that lasted most of the decade, with Egyptian troops backing the republicans and Saudi Arabia supporting the royalists. After Egypt withdrew its forces in 1967, the republic survived several final pushes by royalists, and a split within the republicans resulted in the defeat of divided leftist elements by tribal-backed conservatives, who led the new government.

South Yemen also underwent a revolution in the 1960s, but one of a very different character. The port of Aden had been part of the British Empire since 1839, but following World War II various nationalist groups opposed to a British presence on the peninsula gained strength. These groups ranged from leftist revolutionaries inspired by Marxist and Arab Socialist ideologies to conservative tribal elites. After the North's 1962 revolution, southern nationalists found ready allies among the northern republicans, who along with Egyptian troops were eager to aid fellow Arabs in their struggle against the British. The nationalists finally won independence from Great Britain in November 1967. Conservative tribal elites, merchants, and politicians who had cooperated with Britain fled the country (Schmitz 1997, 14–15), leaving the new state in the hands of the victorious socialists, who formally established the People's Republic of South Yemen, later renamed the People's Democratic Republic of Yemen (PDRY, or South Yemen).

North and South Yemen might have moved toward unification at that time, had it not been that conservatives and tribalists emerged victorious in the North while leftists triumphed in the South. Over the next few years, both countries supported opposition groups in one another's territory. Leftists from the North found refuge and support in the South, while some southern conservatives fled to the North. In 1972, southern exiles based in the North sought to overthrow the South's socialist regime, but failed. And in 1979, the northern regime was attacked by a southern-supported group of leftists, which called itself the National Democratic Front. As Halliday (1995) argues, this history of fighting not only makes the unification of the 1990s seem remarkable; it also makes the 1994 civil war (discussed below) seem all the more inevitable. These shifting alliances across territorial boundaries prove essential for understanding post-unification politics.

The 1980s marked a period of reflection and limited reorganization for both regimes. In the North, President Ali Abd Allah Salih, who had ruled since 1978, sought to provide an alternative to multiparty politics by creating a national assembly called the General People's Congress, which first met in 1982. This representative body reflected the first significant change in opportunity structures in the North since the revolution and represented an effort by Salih to formalize his base of support. Initially comprising 700 elected and 300 appointed representatives, the GPC brought together virtually every prominent individual who had supported the regime, thus gathering the elite from diverse hierarchies of power in one formal assembly. Many of these individuals had even taken up arms to defend the regime during its ongoing struggles against the National Democratic Front in the 1970s. The establishment of the GPC thus set the stage for unification by institutionally linking the most powerful political forces under one umbrella organization, reinforcing and formalizing patronage ties, and offering government positions to influential supporters. For the South, the 1980s witnessed struggles among a number of shifting factions, and victorious leaders often did not survive to enjoy the victory (Halliday 1990). Among these clashes was a push by some to democratize the southern regime, thereby marking the first moves toward representative governance in either Yemen.

The mounting political and economic problems in both North and South Yemen led both regimes to explore the possibility of unification. The option was attractive because each side believed it could secure significant support among the population of the other. The leaders of the South's ruling party, the Yemeni Socialist Party, also recognized that the decreasing remittances from the Soviet Union necessitated a fundamental rethinking of their economic policies, since the state-centered economy could no longer rely on external rents. In many ways, the North's vast resources and the South's modern market infrastructure made unification a logical choice.[1] And with the discovery of oil in lands straddling the border, the stakes increased for both sides.

In 1989, the North's President Salih and the South's President Ali Salim al-Baydh negotiated the unification of the two Yemens in virtual secrecy. Although other southern leaders were angry that they had not been consulted, the idea of unification proved popular in both countries, and formal negotiations led to an agreement that the new state would have a representative democratic government. This was in part because both sides viewed democracy as an institutional outlet for the anticipated continuance of a long-standing rivalry, but it was also because each side believed it could mobilize support in the other's "home" territory. The South's YSP, for example, immediately sought to create an electoral base in the North "by portraying itself as a collection of national reformers of a modernist bent, playing upon the considerable existing opposition to the military rule of the North" (Schmitz 1997, 9–10). At the same time, the northern political elite sought to appeal to the more conservative and traditional elements in the South that had been alienated during British control and the subsequent period of socialist rule. In this regard, prominent tribal leaders in the North—many who enjoyed formal and informal alliances with the North's political elite—reached out to their southern counterparts. The South seemed considerably disadvantaged in the unification arrangement, given that it was home to less than a fifth of the population of united Yemen. In the interim government, Salih and Baydh held the presidency and vice presidency, respectively.

The initial period following unification was as popular as it was remarkable. Liberalization brought significant shifts in political opportunity structures, creating new paths for formal mobilization and political contestation. As Carapico (1998, 136) argues, "The relaxation of security, political, financial, and legal controls, the issuance of legal-constitutional guarantees to personal, press, and political freedom, and the unleashing of pent-up desires to travel within the country, publish, organize, and hold public debates were all unprecedented."

The change was particularly dramatic because the entire process unfolded practically overnight. Dozens of newspapers appeared in the major cities, and more than 20 political parties were quickly organized even before the political parties law was passed in late 1992. The North's GPC and the South's YSP both registered as political parties, thus institutionalizing the rivalry of the northern and southern elites in competitive party politics. The assemblies of the North and South merged to form an interim parliament of 301 seats and immediately debated the new constitution, a draft national charter, and a number of laws codifying the new liberalizations. The whole process culminated in the 1993 elections for the unicameral parliament, which produced a genuinely pluralist assembly (Detalle 1994; Glosemeyer 1993). The North's GPC won the largest bloc, with 123 seats (less than a majority). The South's YSP came in third with only 56 seats. The "newcomer" Islah party won 62 seats, and five other parties won a combined 12 seats.[2] There were an additional 48 independents in the new parliament. The three largest parties formed a coalition government, with Islah and the YSP acting as junior partners to the GPC. The three divided the cabinet portfolios (though not without considerable disagreement) and set about negotiating the final transition to full unity.

The negotiations did not get very far. Just months after the elections, the leaders of the GPC and the YSP remained in fundamental disagreement on a number of issues. The YSP was concerned that the GPC had come to dominate the government too quickly, particularly given that leaders of Islah were closely tied to the North's political elite. Indeed, some of Islah's leaders are themselves key figures in the ruling elite, notably Islah party chair Shaykh Abd Allah ibn Hussein al-Ahmar, the head of the large Hashid tribal confederation, which includes the Sanhan tribe from which President Salih hails.[3] The political and military rivalry between the YSP and the GPC escalated, and they failed to reach agreement on the unification and central command of the two militaries. The South was reluctant to allow the process to continue in the face of what it believed to be rapid northern dominance, particularly since it was not convinced that the government would continue along a democratic course. The ensuing armed conflict lasted from May to July 1994. After a failed secession attempt, the southern leadership fled the country. The northern-dominated government later tried and convicted many of them in absentia for treason (Dresch 2000).

Islamists, the Islah Party, and
the Northern Regime

One of the more interesting questions for social movement theory is why certain movements opt to take advantage of political liberalization by forming political parties while others do not. As Wiktorowicz (2001) illustrates in his study of Islamist movements in Jordan, organizing as a political party holds different advantages and disadvantages for different groups, depending on resources, objectives, ideological orientation, and—importantly—relations with the ruling elite. Particularly in transitional polities, the trade-off is not insignificant for groups that are unsure whether regimes will honor the liberalization bargain and negotiated pacts. For groups with close ties to the ruling elite, the risks are somewhat reduced. But without regime connections, other movements may feel more vulnerable and less willing to step into the political field through a party. While organization as a political party enables a group to establish infrastructure such as regional offices, publicize their agenda, distribute literature, and reach a wide audience, it also opens the movement to a level of state control and monitoring that may not be desirable for all movements (see, e.g., Gamson 1975; Tarrow 1994; McAdam et al. 1996; Della Porta and Diani 1999). The value of the "movement-into-party" decision entails careful consideration of the group's resources (including alliances) and ultimate objectives. The creation of the Islah party made sense for its founders given the context of elite-level alliances at the time of Yemeni liberalization.

The Yemeni Reform Group (the Islah party) was formally established on September 13, 1990, just months after the unification of Yemen. Because it did not emerge from a single cohesive movement, the party's internal dynamics are more complex than those of more cohesive Islamist political parties such as Jordan's Islamic Action Front, Lebanon's Hizbullah, and Turkey's Virtue Party. As a result of internal differences, it is somewhat of a misnomer to identify the Islah party as merely an "Islamist" party, though the character of its political agenda has been overwhelmingly and consistently Islamist. In this regard, elucidating the origins of the coalition that emerged as the Islah party in unified Yemen is essential for a nuanced understanding of the development and location of the party within the broader political field.

Before the 1962 revolution in North Yemen, a number of Yemenis claimed membership in the banned Muslim Brotherhood. Although the group had roots in Yemen dating to the 1930s, it did not play a prominent role on the political scene nor was it well organized, in contrast with Muslim Brotherhood branches in Jordan and Egypt.[4] After the revolution, Muslim Brotherhood leaders formed the group's first formal consultative council under the leadership of Shaykh Abd al-Majid al-Zindani, a conservative and charismatic speaker who enjoyed strong Islamist credentials, a modest personal following, and ties to Saudi Arabia's Wahhabi movement (Weir 1997; Saʿid 1995). Following the 1962 revolution, the group joined with other conservative trends in supporting the new republican leadership against the more left-leaning members of the revolutionary guard. Thus from the earliest days of the Yemen Arab Republic, the Muslim Brotherhood had close relations with the North's conservative and tribal political elite (Saqqaf 1997).

In the late 1970s, after more than a decade under Zindani's guidance, a number of younger Muslim Brotherhood members felt it was time for a change in leadership and mounted what several of them described as an internal coup against Zindani.[5] They felt that Zindani was developing his own cult of personality at the expense of the teachings of Hassan al-Banna, the Egyptian who founded the Muslim Brotherhood in 1928. Shaykh Yasin Abd al-Aziz al-Qubati became the new head of the organization (a position he is widely acknowledged to still hold unofficially, despite the formal absorption of the Muslim Brotherhood within the Islah party).[6] Zindani went to Saudi Arabia, reportedly in a fit of anger. During his self-imposed exile from Yemen, he strengthened his ties with Saudi's Wahhabi government and led a powerful Islamic scientific institute. Around this time, several prominent leaders from Yemen's Zaydi movement joined with the Muslim Brotherhood to expand Islamist influence in the country. As a Shiʿite group, the Zaydi movement had confrontational relations with Wahhabis and Wahhabi-minded thinkers like Zindani.

In 1979, the southern-based National Democratic Front (NDF) launched border skirmishes with the northern regime, in part with the widespread though secret support of some northerners, particularly Shafiʿi sharecroppers, workers, and students from the southern regions of the North (Carapico 1998, 36). The northern army defeated the NDF, however, in part due to the support of an informal group of conservatives and Islamists known as the Islamic Front. This interesting coalition included members of the Muslim Brotherhood, conservative tribal leaders, and a few smaller Islamist groups. The willingness of Islamic Front members to fight for the regime stemmed from their ties to the political establishment and their view of the South's socialists as a common enemy. The armed struggles also cemented the Islamic Front's relationship with the North's President Salih, who had taken power in 1978. When Salih inaugurated the General People's Congress in 1982, Islamic Front members were prominent among its numbers.

Following unification, the core members of the Islamic Front joined with others who shared a conservative social vision to form Islah as a coalition political party. These groups pooled their strengths not out of a commitment to political liberalization, but because a party was the institutional form necessary to serve as an ally of the northern regime and lessen potential YSP victories at the polls. Given that the party's Islamist and tribal bases were distinct from those of the GPC, an Islah–GPC alliance would certainly prove important in weakening the YSP's position in the new government. At its inception, the Islah party thus showed little concern with whether Salih himself was genuinely committed to political liberalization. At that time, its goal was to work through existing institutional channels to promote its conservative programs and weaken potential YSP influence in the new united country.

The Islah party is often said to consist of two primary wings, religious and tribal, along with a small number of prominent business leaders and conservative intellectuals. While this picture is generally accurate, labels such as "tribal" and "Islamic" are problematic in that they create assumptions and expectations about why the party behaves as it does. Such broad strokes also tend to suggest a level of cohesiveness among the various branches that does not reflect the group's internal dynamics, as reflected by competition among various party leaders (Clark and Schwedler 2003).

The most powerful and prominent member of Islah is Shaykh Abd Allah ibn Hussayn al-Ahmar, head of the Hashid tribal confederation, to which Salih belongs. Ahmar was a supporter of the republican government of North Yemen from the time of the 1962 revolution and a strong defender of the government against dissenters throughout the 1970s and 1980s. He has served as speaker of North Yemen's national assembly, a position he has also held under two parliaments in unified Yemen. But Ahmar is not the lone tribal leader within Islah. Shaykh Naji Abd al-Aziz al-Shaʿif is a prominent leader of the Bakil tribal confederation, and the two have not consistently presented a united "tribal" front within the party.[7] Nevertheless, Ahmar is widely recognized as one of the most powerful individuals in all of Yemen and, as such, the key to Islah's power as a political party.[8]

What has been called the ideological wing of Islah may be more accurately described as an assemblage of Islamist activists, including members of the Muslim Brotherhood; adherents to a more conservative, Salafi brand of Islam; the largely Wahhabi personal following of Zindani; and Wahhabis who do not follow Zindani. Zindani remained in Saudi Arabia from 1979 (after he was ousted as head of the Muslim Brotherhood) to 1993, when he was persuaded by Salih and other powerful actors to return to Yemen with the promise of a seat on the powerful five-person Presidential Council. Much of his power is derived not only from his personal following but from his lucrative business investments as well. Like Ahmar and Salih, Zindani has found close ties with the Saudi government to be an important source of power, political as well as economic. Also prominent within the party is Abd al-Wahhab al-

The Islah

Anisi, who has complex   Islamic, and leftist lines.
The point to emphas-   ppearances, Islah does not
comprise a cohesive tri   ideological wing, and this has
significant implications fo   alition maintenance, both within
the party and with other gro

The fact that Yemen's ruling   re themselves part of the field of political competition, contesting elections as the GPC, has important implications for the role of the Islah party, its leadership, and its political strategies. During political liberalization, strong groups were brought into the same sphere as the ruling elite, using "agreements among leaders of political parties (or proto-parties) to (1) divide government offices among themselves independent of election results; (2) fix basic policy orientations; and (3) exclude and, if need be, repress outsiders" (Przeworski 1991, 90). The various Islamist groups that became part of the Islah party were thus effectively partners with the northern political elite in common opposition to the southern elite, a coalition that made the transition from movement into party logical, despite the seeming appearance of "competition" with Salih's GPC.

In social movement theory, one key element of political opportunity structure is the arrangement of elite alliances, and the close personal ties of many of the Islah party's leaders to Salih and the GPC were significant in bringing the coalition together. The purpose of mobilizing the group to form a single political party, however, was also a strategic move aimed at exploiting the opportunities created under liberalization. These groups were not proto-democrats looking for a political opening but elites seeking to preserve (and perhaps expand) their authority and their conservative social visions. The interests that formed Islah viewed the political party as a mobilizing structure that would enable a deeper reach into other parts of Yemen (particularly the South) to promote conservative values and adherence to Islam.

For its part, the GPC sought to use the Islamists against the southern leaders. As an "independent" third party, the Islah party played an important role in tipping the power struggle between the political elites of the former North and South Yemen. With its formal Islamist bent, the Islah party appealed particularly to the fears of its conservative social bases throughout the north, which opposed the progressive and liberal programs promoted by the YSP. In effect, the Islah party further offset the potential bases of support for the YSP in northern Yemen. Although the ruling coalition that emerged following the 1993 elections included the Islah party as a junior partner, the de facto balance of power relegated the YSP to a junior position while the northern alliance of the GPC and the Islah party dominated. This formulation, however, had a significant impact on the Islah party following the 1994 war when Salih's regime no longer needed the Islamists to play the role of a third political party.

A Party Is Born

This section examines the ways in which the Islah party sought to exploit the political opportunities that expanded with unification in 1990, focusing in particular on the institutionalization of the party and the group's formal interactions with and participation in state institutions. Although its founders embraced the party as a means of promoting their interests and not because of commitment to democratic reform, its experiences during this process of institutionalization illustrate an interesting process of political learning. Of particular note here is the extent to which the structure of the group and the modes of contestation evolved in response to the shifting political opportunities associated with political liberalization. Likewise, broader power struggles also structured political opportunities and therefore impacted the role played by Islah in political contestation. All of this must be understood within the context of elite-level alliances that shaped decisions by various movements to form the Islah party.

Institutionalization

Often the first visible evidence of the impact of political liberalization on political actors is the emergence of new bodies within the public political sphere. Yemen witnessed a rapid proliferation of civil society organizations in the form of political parties and special-interest groups, although the North in particular was characterized by a vibrant public sphere even before unification (Carapico 1998). The Islah party itself emerged from existing social movements and power bases, a characteristic typical of the other political parties to emerge in Yemen in the 1990s (Manea 1994). Yet even groups that were relatively well established adopted new processes of institutionalization, including registration with the appropriate government agency, the establishment of a formal office or headquarters, and efforts at increasing local presence through regional offices.

The processes of institutionalization serve as a first glimpse at the ways in which groups adopted new modes of political contestation within a changing public political sphere. Before liberalization, political parties were banned in both countries and their public spheres were highly restricted. As the structure of the public political sphere expanded with institutional change to accommodate new modes of organization, existing groups as well as new movements fashioned themselves to take advantage of new resources and opportunities. Once party officials were selected, office space rented, letterhead printed, and telephones connected, groups experimented with new modes of mobilization while adapting familiar modes to new circumstances.

The first action by the Islah party was to establish a formal structure within the party, including eight administrative divisions of the headquarters office, an executive committee, and a consultative council. This model closely followed the internal structure of the Muslim Brotherhood, particularly the well-developed branches in Jordan and Egypt. The next step was to negotiate a distribution of power among the various power bases within the party. Few disputed that Ahmar, the powerful Hashid tribal shaykh, would become the chair of the party, particularly given his powerful position and his close relationship with Salih. Ahmar also served as the speaker of the interim parliament immediately after unification, providing the party with an immediate high profile. Abd al-Wahab al-Anisi, a moderate ideologue with tribal ties, became the party's first secretary-general, a position that entailed direct oversight of the activities and daily functioning of the party. The various administrative offices were largely staffed by moderate ideologues with ties to the Muslim Brotherhood.

The next step was the routinization of operations, the organization of public events to expand visibility, and preparation for national elections. The Islah party began organizing meetings and conferences; some were organized around current issues (such as proposed constitutional amendments) and others were organized as regular gatherings of party committees. The group also initiated a process of convening large-scale member gatherings at two-year intervals. The party's first general congress was held September 20–22, 1994, in Sanaᶜa, during which the party elected its leaders and adopted the weekly *Al-Sahwah* newspaper, formerly a Muslim Brotherhood publication, as its official mouthpiece.[9] In September and November 1996, Islah held its second general congress, where members discussed and reported the activities of the party since 1994.[10] Following the November session of that meeting, the party issued a statement that summarized the conference's proceedings and outlined its views on a number of local, regional, and international issues.[11] The meeting was open to the press, which received folders containing conference agendas and statements, and the Islah party took the opportunity to reiterate its stance that democratization is the appropriate path of political reform for Yemen and that the party is dedicated to working within a democratic framework.

An additional aspect of this routinization of operations entailed the formulation of official party positions on a variety of issues. Policies were debated, published, and distributed; numerous statements to the press were issued in response to specific social, political, and economic developments; and electoral programs were prepared before each national election. Members and nonmembers alike debated the party's political program or weighed its performance against its declared goals and principles. On occasion, the articulation of official party policies may have constrained the group by pressuring the leadership to act in accordance with the party's stated principles.

The media has also provided important loci for the dissemination of party policies and debates over public issues. Yemen has a lively and relatively free press, especially compared with other Middle Eastern and Third World countries. Many of the weekly papers, in particular, are associated formally or informally with various political parties and trends. While *Al-Sahwah* is the official mouthpiece of the Islah party, the party has been associated with other publications as well, including *Al-Islah* and *Al-Balagh*, which are no longer published regularly.

In addition to newspapers, magazines, press releases, and formal party platforms, the parties in Yemen occasionally publish books and pamphlets on topics of economic, political, and social concern. A number of these publications appear in English as well as Arabic, underlining the extent to which parties seek to ensure the availability of firsthand information about their activities and agendas for a foreign readership. The Islah party has taken an additional step of forming a research institute, the Yemeni Center for Cultural and Strategic Studies (YCCSS), inaugurated in 1996 by Prime Minister Abd al-Aziz Abd al-Ghani. Although the YCCSS is not formally linked to Islah, it acknowledges its close relations with the party.

A final aspect of institutionalization includes the establishment of mechanisms to challenge specific government policies and respond quickly to pressing social, economic, and political developments. The Islah party has organized rallies, demonstrations, and innumerable local gatherings to mobilize Yemenis around certain issues. As Carapico (1998) argues, this practice is not an exclusive phenomenon of recent years: a range of public gatherings, including tribal conferences, increased in popularity during the 1980s, although large-scale gatherings were restricted. The liberalization of the political system in 1990 facilitated the reemergence of such modes of mobilization. At least 25,000 citizens attended an Islah-sponsored rally before the 1993 parliamentary elections, and thousands more attended similar GPC- and YSP-sponsored gatherings.

Electoral, Parliamentary, and Cabinet Participation

The groups that united under the banner of the Islah party were active on the political scene of North Yemen for years prior to Islah, a political presence that intensified during the late 1970s. This included roles as cabinet ministers and seats in other appointed government bodies; influential positions of employment within various ministries; and, with liberalization, popularly elected members of the lower house of parliament. The most public role has been its direct participation in state institutions, such as the Presidential Council, the cabinet, parliament, and the appointed consultative assembly (established in May 1997 and formalized through a referendum in February 2001). Because many Islah leaders emerged from within the ranks of the GPC in pre-unification North Yemen, they held a number of seats in the newly unified parliament from the onset of unification until the first post-unification elections.

Islah won 62 seats in parliament during the first post-unification multi-party elections on April 27, 1993. The new assembly elected Ahmar as speaker with 223 votes. The GPC, the YSP, and Islah formed a coalition government, with the YSP and Islah as junior partners. When Prime Minister Haydar Abu Bakr al-Attas announced his new government following those elections, the Islah party was given control of six portfolios: legal affairs, local governance, health, religious affairs and endowments, supply and trade, and deputy prime minister.[12] Islah leaders complained that it was initially offered only four portfolios compared with the YSP's eight, despite Islah's greater electoral victory. Two additional portfolios brought Islah's total to six, including one that went to Anisi, making him the highest-ranking Islah member within the government. The ministries opened more direct channels for the Islah party to influence public policy, though the new Islah ministers—like the YSP ministers—soon learned that the government bureaucracies were so bloated that efforts to implement change were restricted at every turn. In October 1993, Islah gained a seat on the Presidential Council with the appointment of Abd al-Majid al-Zindani, chair of the party's consultative council, who returned from Saudi Arabia for the occasion.

YSP leaders had little choice but to agree to GPC demands to include Islah in the coalition, even though Islah leaders were antagonistic and spoke out against the YSP and the "evils" of socialism. Although the Islah party formally accepted the right of socialists to organize (so long as they did not advocate atheism, which South Yemen's socialists had in any case never done), it has criticized leftist groups on the basis that they oppose the central tenets of Islam. In this regard, Zindani, chair of Islah's consultative council, has consistently criticized the YSP on ideological grounds, arguing that as Muslims, Yemenis are called upon by God to fight against communists and socialists. Daylami, another of Islah's hard-line ideologues, even issued a formal religious opinion (*fatwa*) in the summer of 1994 in which he justified the war as a confrontation between infidels (the YSP) and pious Muslims. The more moderate Islah members who staffed the central party offices did not share the extremist views of Zindani and Daylami, and many even have cordial relationships with prominent YSP members.

The 1994 Civil War and the Defeat of the YSP

Early on, Yemen's transition to democracy looked promising. The 1993 elections produced a genuinely pluralist parliament in which no party commanded a majority. The YSP and GPC shared ministries with the Islah party. The YSP gained more ministries than Islah because of the conditions of the previously negotiated unification pact, even though Islah won more seats. Within the public sphere, civil society organizations rapidly emerged, some two dozen political parties remained fairly active, publications appeared in major urban centers, and democracy was widely debated.

With the civil war of 1994, a significant element of political opportunities shifted: elite-level alliances. While the GPC and the Islah party remained close, the logic of the alliance immediately changed in a manner that introduced constraints on Islah's ability to mobilize and wield power. With the virtual disappearance of the YSP from the political scene, the GPC (under the leadership of President Salih) granted additional power to the Islah party, but with some caveats. The goal was not to alienate the Islah party but to place limits on its ability to challenge the GPC's primacy. The new cabinet of GPC member Abd al-Aziz Abd al-Ghani gave nine posts to Islah members,[13] including Anisi's promotion to first deputy prime minister. With Islah's expanded role in the cabinet, newspapers and public opinion focused on the implications of the party's rise to power, particularly the extent to which it would implement a "radical" Islamist agenda. But the GPC's offerings were strategic, and the Islah party did not fail to notice that it had been given primarily service ministries, including health, supply and trade, electricity and water, and education. While the party was pleased with the opportunity to effect change in areas considered of great importance, considerable speculation arose both within the party and in the media as to whether Islah had been set up to fail. Indeed, reform in the troubled service industries proved exceptionally difficult and economically painful, making reforms unpopular among the Yemeni citizenry.

Meanwhile, a number of disputes arose between Islah and GPC ministers. One widely debated issue concerned the level of corruption within the ministries and the extent to which reform was virtually impossible without a fundamental overhaul of the staff.[14] Tensions increased as GPC and Islah officials both tried to staff the ministries with their own party members. Several ministers argued about the rate at which currency was transferred among ministries before the rial was floated in 1996.[15] And several Islah ministers complained that GPC members branded their every move as "Islamist" to mobilize partisan opposition against Islah attempts at implementing reform and combating corruption. One Islah minister noted correctly that President Salih tended not to send Islah ministers abroad, particularly to non-Islamist countries, because Yemen was striving to improve relations with a number of Western and secular nations. The regime feared that conservative religious ambassadors might not be well received.[16] Ten years after unification, no Islah member had yet served as an ambassador.

The Islah ministers quickly realized they would not be able to effect much change, and beginning in 1995 several resigned their posts. Muhammad al-Jubari resigned as minister of supply and trade and was initially replaced by Islah member Muhammad al-Afandi. In December 1995, Afandi also resigned, as did Abd Allah al-Akwa, minister of water and electricity. Both complained that they were unable to do their jobs and that they were being prevented from taking steps to reduce corruption within their ministries. Each was replaced by a GPC member. Akwa felt he had been personally targeted, evidenced by a series of cartoons lampooning him that appeared in an official newspaper over the course of several weeks.[17] Abdu Ali al-Qubati resigned as minister of education in October 1996, replaced by Islah member Abd al-Majid al-Mikhlafi.[18]

One of the most interesting aspects of Islah's role within the ministries concerns the party's selection of members for accepted cabinet posts. With the exception of Abd al-Wahab al-Daylami, who served as minister of justice, all of the Islah ministers were relative moderates. Most had long-standing but informal ties with the Muslim Brotherhood, and half were educated in Western institutions and spoke English, French, or both. BaFadl, for example, was educated in Paris and speaks French at home with his family. By his telling, he was living in Jeddah as a businessman in 1993 when an Islah official called to tell him that he would be announced as minister of supply and trade the next morning. He returned to Yemen to take up the position.[19] Akwa states that he was not close to the Muslim Brotherhood until his campaign for a parliamentary seat in 1988 (in pre-unification North Yemen, at which time political parties were illegal). The Muslim Brotherhood supported his candidacy, he says, because of the similarities in their conservative platforms. Following unification, he was courted by the Islah party, which he then formally joined.[20] Islah's selection of moderates to fill ministerial positions is meaningful because it suggests that the leadership realized that to maximize the party's influence, Islah needed to present moderate ministers who would receive wide government support as well as popular acceptance.[21] This tactic was clearly a response to the particularities of the broader political context and the constraints contained therein. The selected individuals were also chosen to facilitate the maintenance of alliances with the GPC because many had personal ties to key regime figures. This highlights the extent to which Islah leaders sought to preserve their access to the highest level of power.

Yet while the defeat of the YSP in the 1994 conflict seemed to have created a new opportunity for an increased Islah role in governing, in practice the opposite happened. The explanation for this is best understood within the context of alliances that stretched across the whole political field and not only between two parties. By 1996, Islah had witnessed a considerable decrease in its power as a political party, though prominent Islah leaders remained close to Salih. While a consensus emerged among former ministers and leaders of Islah that their biggest mistake had been trying to implement reforms too quickly, particularly in challenging corruption,[22] they also recognized that GPC officials no longer looked at them as ready allies. As the April 1997 elections approached, an agreement fell apart between the GPC and Islah concerning who would campaign for which seats. The GPC realized that it no longer needed Islah's support to win a majority of the 301 seats,[23] setting the stage for Islah's declining political power.

1997 Parliamentary Elections

In light of the deteriorating GPC–Islah relationship, the leaders of Islah's central bureaucracy were concerned with the party's prospects in the 1997 parliamentary elections. When the GPC announced in June 1996 that it would strive to obtain a majority of seats in the next elections, a number of columns and articles in *Al-Sahwah* charged that the GPC was seeking to undermine Yemen's multiparty system. Members of the YSP remaining in Yemen were already discussing a boycott, and a number of Islah members expressed the same possibility through various channels. Officially, Islah leaders were struggling to reach an agreement with the GPC to ensure that prominent candidates from each party did not run against each other. By August, however, the GPC–Islah negotiations had not moved forward.

Although discussions with the GPC continued, Islah representatives held several meetings with Yemen's organized opposition bloc, the Supreme Coordination Council of the Opposition. The SCCO includes several parties traditionally hostile to Islah, but leaders believed that the political expediency of cooperation outweighed other differences, since Islah's position near the top of Yemen's political hierarchy was slipping. On August 27, the Islah party and the SCCO jointly issued a statement of cooperation, which was published in several newspapers. The document expressed "grave concern for the direction of democratic development in Yemen" and emphasized the role of the state in fragmenting the political opposition. It is notable that the statement did not name either President Salih or the GPC and instead only criticized abuses by the "state." In October, Muhammad Alawi, a member of Islah's consultative council and a representative to the talks with the SCCO, lamented Islah's years of isolation from the opposition parties:

> Lack of dialogue with other parties was a gross error. Islah has now taken an historical step by talking to other parties. . . . It is rumored that Islah has started talking to the opposition for political gains. I say this is not so. Islah has a democratic aim, especially after the Islamist movement in Yemen changed its attitudes and mechanisms.[24]

Indeed, Islah had changed, though primarily as a result of its relative decline in power since 1994 and the subsequent need to pursue alternative means of ensuring its place within various hierarchies of power. The tentative Islah move toward cooperation with the opposition political parties as a political strategy was motivated by the desire to gain as much power as possible. If the move failed to scare the GPC into bringing the Islah party back into the fold, then pooling resources with the opposition bloc might prove a viable alternative.

Yet Islah did not abandon hope that an agreement could be reached with the GPC to coordinate candidates for the April 1997 elections. On October 24, 1996, its consultative council issued a statement in which it expressed a desire to maintain a strong relationship with the GPC, noting that their coalition had been established on "basic national foundations unstained by any narrow interests." The language of the document lacked the harsh criticism that characterized the articles published in *Al-Sahwah* or the broad criticism of the "state" that appeared in the Islah-SCCO cooperative statement. Still, tensions between the parties continued to escalate. On December 4, for example, the remaining Islah ministers walked out of a cabinet meeting after heated discussions about the 1997 budget.[25] By January 1997, the GPC and Islah agreed that GPC candidates would run uncontested by Islah candidates in 100 constituencies, and Islah would run uncontested by the GPC in 50. In the remaining 151 constituencies, the parties would freely compete. As early as February, each side accused the other of violating the agreement by supporting third-party candidates and by secretly running candidates as "independents" in districts where they had agreed to withdraw candidates. It is difficult to know how much of the agreement held in the end, but there is considerable evidence that, in broad terms, it simply fell apart.[26] The result was a landslide for the GPC, which won 187 seats, as compared with Islah's 53.[27]

With its dramatic victory in the 1997 elections, the GPC had no need to form a coalition government, and no Islah members were offered cabinet portfolios under the new leadership of Prime Minister Faraj ibn Sa'id ibn Ghanim. Ahmar was reelected speaker of parliament, an outcome that likely has less to do with his leadership of the Islah party than with his position as head of the Hashid tribes and his personal relationship with the president. President Salih did finally follow through on his promise to create an appointed consultative council in May 1997, although this body is not constitutionally an upper house of parliament. Islah members were given about 10 seats, including 3 to former cabinet members.[28] One minister in the Ghanim cabinet described this move as a concession to the Islah party, a means of keeping the party from joining the opposition following its electoral losses, which it had informally threatened to do.

Further Deterioration

As the 1999 presidential elections approached, the relationship between the Islah party and the GPC deteriorated even further. Contacts between certain Islah leaders (such as Muhammad Qahtan, the head of the political section, and the secretary-general, Muhammad Yadumi) and YSP leaders (notably Jarallah Umar, the party's deputy secretary-general) were still sporadic but more frequent. YSP and Islah leaders sat together on panels and at public debates and participated together in a workshop on democratization organized by the National Democratic Institute's local office in Yemen. The Islah party did not field its own candidate for the presidential elections, choosing instead to join the GPC in endorsing Salih's candidacy. The move signaled the Islah party's continued reluctance to break away from the GPC and join the opposition, though tensions with the GPC continued. GPC officials reportedly accused Islah of not fully participating in the presidential elections, to which Islah officials replied that the outcome was a foregone conclusion. One Islah official further accused some GPC officials of pocketing money earmarked for the transportation of voters to the polls (*Yemen Observer*, October 1999, 4).

The following August, the GPC and Islah blocs within parliament agreed to pass a resolution to extend the presidential term from five to seven years and the parliamentary term from four to six years. The resolution also introduced a mechanism whereby the constitution could be altered in the future without a referendum. The joint-sponsored amendments were formally approved by the parliament on November 14 amid vocal dissention from the opposition parties. On January 3, with the elections just six weeks away, the Islah party held a general meeting with the entire executive committee to discuss whether to participate in the elections at all. The meeting was quite contentious, and the consensus of the group appeared to be leaning toward boycotting the elections, but then President Salih showed up. In comments widely reported in the press, Salih reaffirmed the strategic coalition between the two parties: "We were all together under the umbrella of the GPC before 1990. Since then, political pluralism was adopted as a system for the country according to the constitution and the law. But this does not mean separation between the GPC and other parties, including Islah."[29]

The country was not ready for the local elections, Salih admitted, but he had decided to proceed for financial considerations (combining the referendum and local elections was cheaper than holding two separate elections). The referendum concerning the constitutional amendments had to be put to the people immediately to ensure that in the event the measure was defeated, there would be sufficient time to prepare for the parliamentary elections. Salih argued that while the government would have preferred to separate the issues and hold the local elections at a later date, each election would cost Yemeni 3.9 billion rial. Consequently, the government was forced to move forward with the local elections for financial reasons.

Just two weeks later, GPC-Islah tensions were again high. In an interview with Islah's official newspaper, *Al-Sahwah*, Muhammad Qahtan, head of Islah's political section, charged that the Supreme Election Committee was displaying bias against the opposition and the Islah party. *Al Rai Al Aam* reported that GPC members in the Sa²fan province in the Sana°a governate charged that Islah members had rounded up arms and fired live rounds to disrupt the local elections in that region. The independent paper also reported "tens of violent confrontations" between the GPC, Islah, and opposition candidates, and numerous contentious articles appeared in each party's publications.[30] GPC mouthpiece *Al-Mithaq* accused the Islah party of creating common electoral lists in provinces in Hadramout, Shabwa, Ta²iz, and Abyan, suggesting that some YSP members believed this was a ploy by the Islah party to gain YSP votes without actually supporting YSP candidates.[31] *Al-Sahwah*, meanwhile, quoted an interview with Muhammad Yadumi in *Al Sharq Al Awsat* in which the Islah secretary-general stated that the numerous promises of the GPC to improve Yemen's economic conditions had been unrealized.[32]

In February 2001, Yemenis went to the polls. The constitutional amendments passed with 75 percent voting in favor of the amendments, thus extending Salih's "legal and constitutional" rule until 2013, when his son will be of eligible age to run for the position. At the time Salih steps down (if indeed he does), he will have ruled North Yemen and united Yemen for 35 years, including 24 years of "democratic" politics. Meanwhile, Yemenis themselves remain subject to worsening economic conditions, not to mention arbitrary arrests, summary judgments (often with formal charges filed), and torture. Deliberalization tendencies indicate that Yemen's regime is democratic in name only (Schwedler 2002).

Conclusion

The purpose of recounting experiences regarding Islah's participation in parliament and the ministries is to demonstrate both the extent to which the party strives to maximize the political opportunities created by political liberalization and the manner in which formally participating *as a party* introduces new dynamics (and constraints) to the coalition party's political strategy. The parliamentary and cabinet experience of the Islah party signaled shifts in Yemen's political opportunity structures. But while the YSP's virtual disappearance from the political scene following the 1994 civil war initially appeared as a boon to the Islah party, the result was in fact a lopsided political environment monopolized by Salih's GPC. Ironically, the victory over the YSP initiated a weakening of Islah. *As a political party*, Islah witnessed a relative decline in significance.

While these shifts in political opportunities have produced considerable antagonisms between Islah and the GPC, personal ties between elites from both parties remain strong. In this regard, the formal party structure adopted by the movement outlived its usefulness to the GPC and was weakened by exclusion from the highest offices. Under current opportunity structures, the logical step for Islah to remain powerful *as a party* would be to join the opposition, which has thus far remained extremely weak. But Islah clings to its position as a "coalition" partner, hoping to be brought back into the fold rather than discarded as part of the opposition.

One of the relevant conclusions from examining Islah as a case study for social movement theory is the importance of shifting alliances as a part of political opportunity structures, something social movement theory has long recognized. This study, however, draws attention to regime-movement alliances as distinct from personal alliances among a broad range of social, political, and economic elites. The logic of the GPC-Islah alliance was sustained only as long as a third party challenged the ruling party. With the YSP defeated, certain personal elite alliances remained strong while the institutional weight of the Islah party rapidly deteriorated. This is a particularly important insight given that Islamist parties, like other strongly ideological parties, are frequently analyzed in terms of the content of their beliefs, worldviews, and agendas, rather than in terms of the dynamics of political alliances and changing opportunity structures. Thus to understand the motives, objectives, behavior, and ideological bases of a wide range of Islamist movements, much is to be gained by analyzing these diverse groups first as social movements and only later (if ever) in terms of their particular beliefs.

Notes

Original research for this chapter was supported by the Social Science Research Council, the Fulbright Commission, and the American Institute for Yemeni Studies. I would like to express my sincerest thanks to Sheila Carapico, Janine Clark, Pete Moore, Lisa Wedeen, and Quintan Wiktorowicz for comments on earlier versions of this chapter as well as other long conversations on Yemen and social movement theories.

1. Although South Yemen had been ruled by a Marxist regime since 1967, it had retained much of the modern economic infrastructure developed by the British when Aden served as a major port city.

2. The Baʿath Arab Socialist Party won seven seats; the Zaydi Islamist Party, al-Haqq, two seats; the socialist Nasserist Unionist Party, one; the socialist Nasserist Democratic Party, one; and al-Tashih, one.

3. The Hashid tribal confederation is smaller than the Bakil, who are also located in the North. The Hashid are more powerful, however, due to a relative lack of intratribal conflict about lines of authority. Whereas Hashid tribes all recognize Ahmar as the top figure, Bakil tribes have reached no such consensus. See, for example, Dresch (1989) and Dresch and Haykel (1995).

4. For a history of the Muslim Brotherhood in Yemen, see Saʿid (1995). For the role of early Muslim Brotherhood members in the Free Yemeni Movement (which

challenged the Imamate in the 1930s and 1940s), see Douglas (1987). For the Muslim Brotherhood in Egypt, see Mitchell (1969) and Kepel (1984); in Jordan, see Boulby (1999).

5. Interviews with Yasin Abd al-Aziz, Muhammad Yadumi, Faris Saqqaf, Zayd Shami, Nasr Taha Mustafa, and Muhammad al-Afandi, 1995 to 1998, Sanaʿa.

6. Qubati was elected the vice chair of Islah's consultative council in 1993.

7. Numerous other tribes exist, and it should not be inferred that all tribes fall under the Hashid and Bakil umbrellas.

8. For an amusing (in its creativeness with historic details) and almost hagiographic biography of Ahmar, see Hadrami (1997).

9. Ahmar was elected chair of the party and of the 15-member executive council; Shaykh Yasin Abd al-Aziz al-Qubati, the chair of the formally disbanded Muslim Brotherhood's consultative council, was elected vice chair; Zindani was to lead the 100-member consultative council, the central committee of the party; Abd al-Wahab al-Daylami was elected chair of the judicial council; Muhammad Yadumi was elected secretary-general; Abd al-Wahab al-Anisi moved from secretary-general to assistant secretary-general; and Faris Saqqaf was elected director of information and public relations. The newspaper *Al-Sahwah* continued to reflect the views of the Muslim Brotherhood branch of the party and not the extremism of other party ideologues such as Zindani.

10. The official programs from both the 1994 and 1996 conferences describe each gathering as Islah's "first" general congress. For clarity, I call the 1994 meeting the first general congress and the 1996 meeting, held in two sessions, the second general congress.

11. Members were urged to pay their dues and to contribute to the party as generously as possible. The statement went on to demand that the constitution and the law be implemented fully and routinely and that the distribution of authority between the executive, legislative, and judicial be formalized to ensure democratic governance.

12. Abd al-Salam Karman was named minister of legal affairs; Abd al-Wahab al-Anisi, deputy prime minister; Muhammad al-Dammaj, minister of local governance; Najib al-Ghanim, minister of health; Ghalib Abd al-Kafi al-Qurashi, minister of religious affairs and endowments (*Awqaf*); and Abd al-Rahman BaFadl, minister of supply and trade. In a statement to the newspaper *Al Wahdah*, Karman said that he was not a member of Islah. Islah secretary-general Muhammad al-Yadumi refuted this in a statement to the newspaper *Sitta-Ashrin Uliu* September 13, 1993, saying that Karman had not expressed himself well.

13. New Islah appointments included Muhammad al-Jubari, minister of supply and trade; Abd al-Wahab al-Daylami, minister of justice; Abdu Ali al-Qubati, minister of education; and Abd Allah al-Akwa, minister of electricity and water. Ghanim, Dammaj, and Qurashi retained their portfolios of health, local governance, and religious affairs, respectively. BaFadl was later given the portfolio for the newly revived Ministry of Fisheries, charged with reforming and reviving Yemen's fishing sector.

14. Within Yemen's government bureaucracy, corruption is facilitated not only by ministers who wish to gain their share but also by the vast number of positions that, though unnecessary, cannot be eliminated for patronage reasons. Ministers from all political trends complain about their inability to fire employees, despite the fact that many never show up to work (many of those who do are not needed). In 1997, for

example, the Ministry of Health had seven assistants to the minister's secretary: one to sort incoming mail; one to handle outgoing mail; one to screen appointments; two to fetch coffee and tea; one for general errands; and one to inform the minister's driver when the minister was on his way. Such arrangements are apparently typical.

15. BaFadl reported that as minister of supply and trade in 1993 he was pressured to accept highly unfavorable rates and was not free to explore alternate means of exchange, such as purchasing currency on the open market (interviews with author, October 9–10, 1997, Sanaᶜa). Other Islah and GPC ministers have recounted similar stories and noted that the head of the central bank is a highly political appointment.

16. Interview with author, October 1997, Sanaᶜa. Name withheld by request.

17. Interview with author, October 5, 1997, Sanaᶜa.

18. BaFadl resigned from his post on January 27, 1997, but for a different reason. Ministers who wish to stand in the elections must resign three months before the polling. BaFadl was successful in the May 1997 elections and took up the position of heading the Islah bloc in the lower house.

19. Interview with author, October 9, 1997, Sanaᶜa.

20. Interview with author, October 5, 1997, Sanaᶜa. Akwa's case is particularly interesting in that he has, on occasion, publicly opposed Islah positions. For example, he voted against accepting the new constitution, a move that was popularly seen as a vote against unification. Islah leaders did not share his view that it was the act of voting, and not the content of his vote, that signaled participation and thus support for unified Yemen.

21. Salih personally approves all ministry appointments, though in theory the prime minister makes such decisions.

22. This view was repeatedly expressed to the author from July through November 1997 during interviews conducted in Sanaᶜa with Yadumi, Anisi, Afandi, Akwa, BaFadl, Muhammad Qahtan (head of Islah's political section), Zayd al-Shami (head of Islah's education section), and others.

23. Interview with a GPC minister and a GPC official, August and November 1997. Names withheld by request.

24. *Yemen Times*, October 7, 1997.

25. *Yemen Times*, December 9, 1996. The disagreement revolved around an ongoing debate concerning the operation of a network of "scientific institutes" currently controlled by Islah. The GPC and others have long argued that they should fall under the domain of the Ministry of Education.

26. There are signs that the dispute went to the highest level, between Salih and Ahmar. A short article in the London-based daily newspaper *Al-Hayat* reported that Ahmar was considering withdrawing his candidacy for a seat in the April elections. The editor of *Al-Hayat*, Khairallah Khairallah, was close to both Salih and Ahmar, and he occasionally served as a conduit through which the two would send delicate messages to each other. Several current and former ministers believe that Ahmar leaked the story to Khairallah to push Salih to honor the agreement. In the end, Ahmar did not withdraw his candidacy. See *Al-Hayat*, March 17, 1997.

27. Prominent ideologues within Islah who were unsuccessful in the elections included Muhammad Ali Ajlan, Mansur al-Zindani (brother of Abd al-Majid al-Zindani, who heads the consultative council), former minister Muhammad al-Afandi, Abd Allah al-Maqalih, and Muhammad al-Sadiq Abd Allah. Every tribal candidate on Islah's list was successful in his bid.

28. They were Anisi, Dammaj, and Afandi.
29. *Yemen Times,* January 8–14, 2001.
30. January 30, 2001, as summarized in the *Yemen Times,* February 5–11, 2001.
31. February 1, 2001, as summarized in the *Yemen Times,* February 5–11, 2001.
32. Ibid.

Works Cited

Boulby, Marion. 1999. *The Muslim Brotherhood and the Kings of Jordan, 1945–1993.* Atlanta: Scholars.

Carapico, Sheila. 1998. *Civil Society in Yemen: The Political Economy of Activism in Modern Arabia.* New York: Cambridge University Press.

Clark, Janine Astrid, and Jillian Schwedler. 2003. "Who Opened the Window? Women's Activism in Islamist Parties." *Comparative Politics* 35, 3 (April): 293–312.

Della Porta, Donatella, and Mario Diani. 1999. *Social Movements: An Introduction.* Cambridge: Blackwell.

Detalle, Renaud. 1994. "Les elections legislatives du 27 avril 1993." *Monde Arabe Maghreb-Machrek,* no. 141: 3–36.

Douglas, J. Leigh. 1987. *The Free Yemeni Movement, 1935–1962.* Beirut: American University of Beirut.

Dresch, Paul. 1989. *Tribes, Government, and History in Yemen.* Oxford: Oxford University Press.

———. 2000. *A History of Modern Yemen.* New York: Cambridge University Press.

Dresch, Paul, and Bernard Haykel. 1995. "Stereotypes and Political Styles: Islamists and Tribesfolk in Yemen." *International Journal of Middle East Studies* 27, 4 (November): 405–31.

Gamson, William. 1975. *The Strategy of Social Protest.* Homewood, Ill.: Dorsey.

Glosemeyer, Iris. 1993. "The First Yemeni Parliamentary Elections in 1993: Practising Democracy." *Orient* 34, 3. 439–51.

Hadrami, Abd al-Rahman. 1997. *Al-Rajal alathi Ahabbu al-Haram wa al-Haram: Batal al-Jumhuriyyah al-Shaykh Abd Allah bin Hussein al-Ahmar* (The Man Beloved to the Holy [Mecca] and the Pyramids: Hero of the Republic Shaykh Abd Allah bin Hussein al-Ahmar). Sanaᶜa: Dar al-Shawkani.

Halliday, Fred. 1990. *Revolution and Foreign Policy: The Case of South Yemen, 1967–1987.* Cambridge: Cambridge University Press.

———. 1995. "The Third Inter-Yemeni War and Its Consequences." *Asian Affairs* (June): 131–40.

Kepel, Gilles. 1984. *Muslim Extremism in Egypt: The Prophet and Pharaoh.* Berkeley: University of California Press.

Manea, Ilham. 1994. *Al-Ahzab wa al-tanthimat al-siyasiyyah fi al-Yaman, 1948–1993* (Parties and Political Organizations in Yemen, 1948–1993). Sanaᵓa: Kitb al-Thawabit 2.

McAdam, Doug, John D. McCarthy, and Mayer N. Zald, eds. 1996. *Comparative Perspectives on Social Movements.* New York: Cambridge University Press.

Mitchell, Richard P. 1969. *The Society of the Muslim Brothers.* Oxford: Oxford University Press.

Przeworski, Adam. 1991. *Democracy and the Market: Political and Economic Reforms in Eastern Europe and Latin America.* Cambridge: Cambridge University Press.

Saᶜid, Abd al-Karim Qasim. 1995. *Al-Ikhwan al-muslimun wa al-harakat al-ᶜusuliyun fi al-Yaman* (The Muslim Brotherhood and the Fundamentalist Movement in Yemen). Cairo: Maktabat Madbuli.

Saqqaf, Faris. 1997. *Al-Islamiyun wa al-Sultah fi al-Yaman* (Islamists and Power in Yemen). Sanaᶜa: Maktab Dirasat al-Mustaqbal.

Schmitz, Charles Paul. 1997. "State and Market in South Yemen." Ph.D. dissertation, University of California, Berkeley.

Schwedler, Jillian. 2002. "Yemen's Unlikely 'Emerging Democracy.'" *Journal of Democracy* 13, 4 (October): 49–55.

Seidman, Gay W. 1994. *Manufacturing Militance: Workers' Movements in Brazil and South Africa, 1970–1985.* Berkeley: University of California Press.

Tarrow, Sidney. 1994. *Power in Movement: Social Movements, Collective Action, and Politics.* Cambridge: Cambridge University Press.

Weir, Shelagh. 1997. "A Clash of Fundamentalisms: Wahhabism in Yemen." *Middle East Report*, no. 204 (Fall).

Wiktorowicz, Quintan. 2001. *The Management of Islamic Activism: Salafis, the Muslim Brotherhood, and State Power in Jordan.* Albany: SUNY Press.

PART III

CULTURE AND FRAMING

Nine

Interests, Ideas, and Islamist Outreach in Egypt

Carrie Rosefsky Wickham

The rise of Islamic activism among urban, educated youth in Egypt in the 1980s and early 1990s poses something of a puzzle for students of collective action. Under the shadow of Egypt's authoritarian state, even nonviolent reformist Islamist groups like the Muslim Brotherhood remained technically illegal and subject to surveillance and harassment by the security police. An open affiliation with the Islamist cause entailed real risks, while the prospect of affecting positive change was at best uncertain. Yet despite such seemingly unpropitious conditions, Islamist groups in the 1980s and early 1990s did manage to attract a substantial number of the country's bright, ambitious, and upwardly mobile university graduates.

Puzzle: What explains the success of Islamist outreach to Egypt's university-educated youth? This question is best answered by addressing the broader social movement literature on the "micro-mechanisms of mobilization" (see McAdam 1988)—that is, on how movement leaders forge and sustain linkages with potential recruits. The mobilization literature contains at least two major theories of recruitment, which draw on different assumptions about the motives that drive collective action. One strand of the literature, informed by a "rational actor" model of human behavior, contends that movements attract new members by appealing to individual interests (see, e.g., Olson 1965). Movements do this by providing "selective incentives"—material, psychological, and/or emotional benefits that are contingent upon participation. From this viewpoint, *access to benefits* motivates potential participants to join a group or movement, and these benefits explain their continued involvement over time.

Another strand of the literature on mobilization contends that individuals

231

often join groups or movements to express deeply held commitments, values, and beliefs and are thus frequently motivated by more than narrow self-interest and a desire to obtain benefits (e.g., see Laraña, Johnston, and Gusfield 1994). Hence movement leaders are able to mobilize individuals into politics by issuing a "call to arms" or normative rationale for collective action—a process described by Robert Benford and David Snow as "motivational framing" (2000). A movement may thus elicit participation as a response to a perceived moral duty or obligation, whether driven by "moral shock" or by deeply held values and beliefs, irrespective of the costs and benefits likely to affect those involved (Jasper and Poulsen 1995; Jasper 1997).

This chapter argues that both interests *and* ideas motivate collective action and that the relative causal weight of each can shift over time, especially as participants become increasingly integrated into movement networks. A close investigation of Islamic patterns of recruitment among high school and university graduates in three *sha'bi* ("popular" or urban, lower-middle-class) neighborhoods in Cairo demonstrates that while *both* interests and ideas help account for the success of Islamist outreach, their relative importance as motivating factors changed over time. Most graduates initially joined Islamic networks because of various social, psychological, and emotional benefits conferred by participation, much as "rational actor" models of mobilization would predict. But while such benefits help explain involvement in initial, low-risk forms of activism, they alone cannot explain an eventual progression to riskier, more overtly political forms of Islamic activity.

To facilitate a progression toward high-risk activism, Islamists framed activism as a moral "obligation" that demands self-sacrifice and unflinching commitment to the cause of religious transformation. Such a frame encouraged graduates to view political participation as a religious duty. The positive reception of the Islamist message by Egypt's educated *shebab* (young adults), however, was not a function of the frame's "intrinsic" appeal. Rather, it hinged on a set of conditions external to the message itself, including (1) its close "fit" with the life experiences and beliefs of those graduates targeted for recruitment; (2) the credibility and effectiveness of its agents and modes of transmission; and (3) its reinforcement through intensive, small-group solidarity at the grassroots level. The framing "success" helped set the groundwork for riskier political contention.

Networks and Selective Incentives

Many graduates first got involved in the Islamic movement by participating in social or cultural activities sponsored by a neighborhood mosque or Islamic student association. Such activities included attending religious lessons at a nearby mosque, joining an informal study group, or accompanying a friend or neighbor to special prayer services in observance of an Islamic holy day. Several factors diminished the perceived risks and increased the perceived advantages of these initial forms of participation. Islamic lessons, seminars, and prayer meetings offered some of the few socially sanctioned venues for graduates of both sexes to congregate outside the home. In addition, the religious character of these activities elevated their respectability and prestige. When asked to describe people active in local Islamic networks, the residents of sha'bi areas typically replied that they were "strongly attached to religion." The small activist mosques and those involved in them were referred to as *sunniyyin,* meaning those who follow the Sunna (path) of the Prophet and his companions. The term thus had the positive connotation of exemplary behavior and closeness to God.

Recruitment into these activities drew upon preexisting ties among relatives, friends, and neighbors (Wickham-Crowley 1992, 138–40). This enabled Islamists to absorb graduates into their circle on the basis of pre-established familiarity and trust, thereby avoiding the kind of suspicion aroused by a dependence on strangers. The presence of Islamist networks at the local level where people lived, studied, and worked made them highly accessible and minimized the social distance between participants and nonparticipants. In sha'bi neighborhoods, most residents had a brother, cousin, friend, or neighbor involved in Islamic prayer circles or study groups, and Islamist participants frequently maintained close social relationships with non-activist peers. Joining Islamist activities did not necessarily require a rupture from prior social ties, thus lowering the initial costs of participation. For example, one of my interviews with a young woman who wore the *niqab* (the full veil covering the face and body) and gloves was interrupted by the unexpected arrival of a close female friend from the university, dressed in a T-shirt and jeans. The result of such relationships was that many neighborhoods viewed Islamist activities and the heightened religiosity they were presumed to reflect as a normal and unremarkable feature of local community life.

The social embeddedness of Islamic networks also permitted a certain amount of flexibility and experimentation, enabling graduates to "try out" different levels and forms of participation without initiating a break from their social circles. Furthermore, such networks provided opportunities for participation detached from the realm of *al-siyasa* or high politics. It was well known in sha'bi neighborhoods that young people suspected of involvement in militant Islamic groups were vulnerable to the threat of arrest, detention, interrogation, torture, and even death. Moreover, state authorities were seen as often failing to discriminate between reformist and militant Islamist groups, lumping those active in the Brotherhood, say, with those in al-Jihad. With their emphasis on incremental change at the local level rather than direct confrontation with the regime, Islamic communal networks were perceived by potential recruits and their families as less risky venues for social activity.

Islamic networks not only provided opportunities for comparatively low-risk forms of participation that were sanctioned by the surrounding community; they also offered graduates a range of selective incentives (Gamson 1975, 66–71; Friedman and McAdam 1992, 161; McAdam 1982, 45–46; Richards and Waterbury 1996, 349–50). For instance, such networks served as channels for the distribution of goods and services and the exchange of favors and protection. Some Islamists I interviewed mentioned that they could turn to peers in the movement for help in securing a job or a visa to work abroad. An individual's participation in Islamist networks might also increase his/her chances of securing work within the Islamic parallel sector or enhance his/her family's access to the funds distributed by mosques, subsidized day care, or health services. Involvement in Islamist circles could even increase marriage opportunities. Islamist peers could vouch for the morals of unmarried men and women and expand their range of eligible mates by drawing upon family contacts beyond the neighborhood or even Cairo. Indeed, several of the graduates I interviewed indicated that they had met or planned to meet a spouse through the mediation of their Islamist circle.

In addition to these tangible benefits, participation in Islamic networks conferred a range of psychological and emotional rewards that social movement scholars refer to as "solidary incentives" (McAdam 1982, 45). Participation promoted a feeling of belonging and an intimacy with peers based on shared commitments and routines. Graduates commonly referred to others in their Islamic circle as *ikhwa*, brothers and sisters, and the close bonds were evident in warm embraces between members of the same sex, exchanges of personal secrets and confidences, and the readiness to assist one another in times of need. Beyond this, participation offered recruits a sense of psychic empowerment, transforming poorly skilled graduates with bleak economic prospects into fellow-soldiers in the noble task of Islamic reform.

While providing positive incentives for participation, Islamist networks and outreach also created powerful pressures for social conformity, thereby increasing the social and psychological costs of nonparticipation. Critics of the Islamic movement have emphasized the role of coercion and argue that young people in many sha'bi communities face intense peer pressure to conform to Islamic moral and social codes. Critics have also noted the marginalization of contesting viewpoints and point to the fact that the Islamists have been indoctrinating younger students, shifting from the university and secondary (grades 9–12) levels to the preparatory schools (grades 7–9). Several leftists I interviewed in one sha'bi neighborhood witnessed this early indoctrination firsthand. As one observed, "The Islamic groups get to the students now when they are young—in preparatory school and in high school. They get them when they are young and impressionable, telling them this is *haram* (forbidden) and that is *halal* (permitted)." In 1994, Islamist activities in the lower levels of the schools system prompted the Ministry of Education to punitively transfer thousands of teachers for allegedly disseminating "extremist" Islamic views in the classroom.

In a December 2, 1992, article entitled "From Here Extremism Begins: The Independent Mosques," the Egyptian weekly *Akhir Sa'a* forcefully articulated the claim that Islamists were "trapping" innocent youth through indoctrination:

> The private mosques have become the biggest snare of the youth, who comes originally to pray, but who, upon being ready to leave, is seized by an extremist as his next victim, who sits him down and whispers at him, and his nice-sounding, honeyed words have an effect, who promises him a straight path to heaven if he obeys the rulings of Allah (and the extremist takes it upon himself to interpret what they are), and warning of the suffering in hell if he disobeys. Then he suggests that the youth start attending daily religious lessons and listen to the Friday sermons, and invites him to eat dinner at his home, where the other members of the extremist group are waiting for him in order to complete his mobilization.

In this way, the article concludes, the "unsuspecting youth, who started out just wanting to pray, ends up a member of a Shawqiyya or Ikhwaniyya or Gihadiyya or Salafiyya extremist group, which are enemies of the state."

One need not take the appraisals of critics at face value to recognize that under certain conditions Islamist ideology can be difficult to resist. In a social context in which a majority of the population are devout Muslims and where other interpretations of Islam are not authoritatively presented, it may be difficult for a young man or woman to withstand the argument that Allah requires you to pray, or veil, or fast or that Allah requires you not to drink, or smoke, or interact with members of the opposite sex, or socialize with non-Muslims.

Although less common, there were also instances when Islamists attempted to prohibit ostensibly non-Islamic behavior by force. The majority of Islamists active at the grassroots level rejected the use of physical force, emphasizing that true religious conduct must stem from inner conviction rather than external pressure. But more militant Islamist groups and factions were less hesitant about using force to achieve goals.

Cases of physical coercion by Islamists were, not surprisingly, reported in detail in the official Egyptian press. For example, in the 1992 article quoted above, *Akhir Sa'a* published the names of several mosques in Greater Cairo and Upper Egypt where Islamic militants allegedly issued *fatwas* (Islamic legal rulings) banning the enjoyment of photography, music, films, and television. During the 1980s and early 1990s, radicals bombed video stores, nightclubs, and other leisure establishments viewed as promoting moral decadence, and assassinated movement critics, including the well-known secular intellectual Farag Fawda. Such episodes make it clear that at least some Islamists were ready to punish those seen as deviating from radical visions of Islamic belief and practice.

In sum, a range of positive and negative inducements facilitated the entry of graduates into Islamic communal networks on the periphery. And yet, while easing their initial entry into the movement, such interest-based appeals cannot explain their progression from lower-risk to higher-risk and more overtly political forms of Islamic activism. The risks associated with participation increased as a graduate proceeded from attending a collective prayer session or religious study group in his dorm or neighborhood to campaigning for an Islamist candidate or participating in sit-ins, strikes, or demonstrations. In such instances, the "costs" of participating could be absolute, and a strictly "rational" or instrumental explanation for involvement does not suffice. Furthermore, a focus on individual costs and benefits does not capture the ways in which participation in Islamic networks is subjectively experienced. In interviews, graduates involved in the movement repeatedly stressed the *normative* basis for their own actions, explaining that they were obligated to participate in the task of Islamic reform. While selective incentives and social networks facilitated initial recruitment, ideas seemed to become increasingly important in laying the groundwork for high-risk activism and concomitant movement commitment.

Ideational Factors and Framing

A central goal of Islamist outreach was to instill graduates with a new ethic of civic obligation, one that emphasizes the duty of every Muslim to participate in the task of Islamic reform *regardless of the benefits and costs to those involved.* Why were so many graduates ready to embrace—and act upon—an ideology that stressed the primacy of the public good over the pursuit of private self-interest? This section argues that movement frames tapped into the grievances of graduates and resonated with their life-experiences and prevailing themes in Egyptian popular culture. The credibility and efficacy of the agents and methods of transmission enhanced frame reception.

Many graduates from urban, lower-middle-class communities had profound grievances concerning their own limited prospects for advancement as well as what they perceived as the breakdown of fairness and accountability in society at large. Yet their search for solutions took different forms. Some graduates sought to emigrate, temporarily or permanently; others tried to develop the personal or social connections (*wasta*) needed to obtain a better job. Hence some (and perhaps even most) graduates confronted their circumstances with a hard-knocks pragmatism, disinclined to explore the causes of their diminished prospects or the policy changes needed to revive them.

Yet graduate dissatisfaction also triggered a broader existential search for meaning that, in some instances, culminated in the embrace of Islam. Gamal, a graduate involved in a militant Islamic group, explained: "Most people have problems and are looking for a solution. In the end, many find the solution in Islam." Muhammad, another young Islamist, explained that Islamist books and tapes "spoke" to him. He recalled the period after he graduated from college:

> I felt lost. . . . After graduating, I had no goals, no direction. Actually, I felt it even during my years at the university. I didn't know my purpose in life. Before I became committed (*multazim*), I read Naguib Mahfouz, Taha Hussein, Tawfiq al-Hakim, and they all increased my confusion. They didn't speak from an Islamic point of view but from a Western conception of things.

Muhammad began to read Islamic books, listened to tapes on the *daʿwa* (propagation), and started attending lessons at the Gamʿiyya Shaʿriyya mosque on Galaa Street in Ramses:

> I began to attend services at the mosque and to listen and read, and there were doubts and questions inside of me. I looked for answers to them. Questions about God. For example, why worship God? He doesn't need us. The beginning and the end, my aim and my purpose in life—what was it?

Muhammad found the answers he was seeking in Islam. "There is a major difference between the committed and the uncommitted youth," he explained. "The committed youth has a goal and a purpose; he wants to be a servant of God."

By providing a sense of purpose, Islamic ideology built upon—and responded to—the "culture of alienation" that prevailed among educated, lower-middle-class youth. Many graduates were struck by the juxtaposition of acute poverty and great wealth. They read about drug dealers in parliament and allegations of corruption implicating senior government officials and their family members. They or someone they knew had been passed over for a job, despite their qualifications, because they did not have the right *wasta* (connections). Many had witnessed a high school teacher distribute an exam in advance to students who paid for it. Some witnessed wealthy motorists violate traffic laws with impunity. Some had even been arrested without committing any crime. For many, the single greatest problem facing Egyptian society seemed to be its *normlessness*.

According to many lower-middle-class graduates—including those with no political affiliations whatsoever—this crisis of morals (*azmat al-akhlaq*) was at the root of the country's malaise. Unfettered by conscience, wealthy and powerful elites manipulated the system to their own advantage with little concern for the less fortunate. As one graduate put it, "Here the rich eats the poor, the strong eats the weak." For graduates who had been socialized to view themselves as a meritocratic elite, perhaps the greatest source of bitterness was the perceived erosion of the link between merit and reward. The exhaustion of Egypt's statist economic model and the introduction of market reforms diminished the force of graduate entitlements and augmented the importance of marketable skills and social connections linked to class background. To graduates without social connections or sufficient resources to acquire foreign language and computer skills, the distribution of jobs and incomes in the liberalized economy appeared strikingly unfair. At the same time, many graduates perceived the political system as dominated by Westernized politicians and military officials who were indifferent to popular suffering and—in the absence of effective mechanisms of oversight—both able and willing to exploit their offices for private gain.

The Islamist da‘wa tapped into these grievances and portrayed Islam as the means to fundamentally transform the existing order. Indeed, with its emphasis on collective adherence to a God-given moral code and collective responsibility for the public welfare, the da‘wa projected a vision of Islamic rule that stood out as a striking reverse-image of the status quo. Against the perceived reality of state elites preoccupied with self-enrichment and removed from popular needs and concerns, the da‘wa projected the image of a leadership animated by its religious duty to safeguard the well-being of the Islamic *umma* (community). Against the perceived reality of a society of atomized individuals pursuing selfish aims, it offered the image of a moral community living in accordance with God's precepts. Perhaps most important, against the perceived reality of a society in which power and circumstance determined life-chances, Islamist ideology projected the image of a society in which merit—both moral/spiritual and practical/professional—would be justly acknowledged and rewarded. Such diagnostic and prescriptive dimensions—capable of revealing the causes of societal malaise and pointing the way for solution—resonated with new graduates faced with growing socioeconomic marginalization and a sense of alienation. With its emphasis on fairness and social justice, Islamic ideology gave voice to the moral outrage felt by graduates who perceived themselves as unjustly deprived of their due rewards as an educated (i.e., meritocratic, as opposed to class) elite. At the same time, it offered graduates a new conceptual language for understanding the predicament of contemporary Egyptian society, a vision of a better alternative, and an agenda for change—all in a single package. In Snow and Benford's terms (1988, 200–204), the da‘wa succeeded in accomplishing diagnostic, prognostic, and motivational framing tasks.

But the success of the frame was not due only to the resonance of the da‘wa; the efficacy of agents and methods of transmission also contribute to mobilization. First, let us consider the agents or "social carriers" of the da'wa. What qualities contributed to their mobilizing success? As Brysk argues, "Since the credibility of information is judged in part by the credibility of the source, we would expect speakers with greater social legitimacy to succeed more often at persuading others." Legitimacy is particularly strong for those "to whom society has already allocated a special protective or interpretive role" such as mothers, priests, warriors, or doctors (Brysk 1995, 577).

In Egypt, the Islamists' successful appropriation of the authority to interpret sacred texts—an authority formerly monopolized by the state-appointed *ulama* (religious scholars)—paved the way for graduates' acceptance of their message. Several other factors enhanced the credibility and prestige of Islamist activists as well. First, those activists who gained political skill and sophistication as Islamist student leaders in the 1970s became active in broader arenas of Egyptian public life in the 1980s and early 1990s. By then in their thirties and early forties, this "middle generation" of Islamic activists included several charismatic leaders who offered compelling role-models for younger activists and provided intellectual, logistical, and moral support to outreach efforts. Second, while the country's senior military and technocratic elites were generally of upper- or middle-class origin, this emerging "Islamic counter-elite" had its roots in the neighborhoods of Egypt's cities and provincial towns. Drawn from the same class and cultural background as potential recruits, the middle generation of Islamists helped bridge the divide between elite and mass political culture because they spoke the same language and shared the same deprivations as their target audience.

Graduates' internalization of Islamist values was further reinforced by their integration within the local Islamist networks that transmitted the frame. As McAdam, Tarrow, and Tilly observe (1996, 16), "The cultural construction of collective action is invariably a network—that is to say, a structural—process." The Islamic networks of Egypt's sha'bi neighborhoods constituted the structural pathways for the transmission of Islamist ideas. At the same time, they facilitated the rise of new forms of intensive, small-group solidarity that reinforced graduates' new Islamist commitments while simultaneously detaching them from the conventional socializing influences of family, neighbors, and peers. Islamic communal networks thus constituted a crucible for both the transmission of Islamist ideology and the development of new kinds of collective practice through which it was reinforced.

The Transvaluation of Values

The integration of graduates into Islamist social networks heightened their receptivity to an Islamist perspective on everything from the nature of the political system to such issues as veiling, education, marriage, sex, and death. Hence the most fundamental change produced by Islamic outreach efforts is what I call a "transvaluation of values"—that is, a reordering of the priorities that guide individual action.

This transvaluation of values had numerous manifestations. For example, in a social milieu in which aspiring students coveted a secular university degree (*shahada*) as both a status symbol and an instrument of career advancement, the Islamist subculture diminished the relative value attached to secular knowledge gained through formal education. Instead, greater priority and status were given to religious knowledge gained informally through self-study and group lessons at private mosques. My conversations with a group of young veiled women in one shaᶜbi neighborhood illuminate this trend. As one young woman explained, "Knowledge for us is knowledge of religion. Religion includes and encompasses all other kinds of knowledge." Another added, "That's right. Did you know that all of modern scientific knowledge was already known and can be found in the Qurʾan?"

When asked what kind of books they read, several of the women replied that they only read religious books. Two sisters were especially proud of their extensive Islamic book collection. As one of them explained:

> We read what we respect—religion only. It is a question of priorities. Rather than waste time reading novels or other books, we read religious books. Novels and other nonreligious books can be read, too, as long as they don't contain anything against religion—stories about sex are forbidden, for example. If there was time after religion, we'd read other books, but there's never enough time for religion, is there?

Another woman later commented, "Why waste time going to a film when we can go to the mosque and take religious lessons?"

A parallel change involved the devaluation of a university education and white-collar employment, either for oneself or a spouse. Young women in particular began to question the pursuit of a university degree, which would only equip them for jobs that, by strict Islamist standards, were inappropriate. The young veiled women cited above shared a widely held Islamist view that a woman's first priority is at home. As one of them explained, a woman should only work if four conditions are met: she is not needed at home, the work has an inherent value, her husband approves, and the job does not require mixing with members of the opposite sex. Examples of "appropriate work" for women include jobs in the health and teaching fields that entail the provision of services to women and children only.

The devaluation of secular university degrees enabled lower-middle-class graduates to rationalize their decision to opt out of a system that seemed to relegate them to the lower rungs. Reflecting the debilitated state of public schooling in urban, lower-middle-class neighborhoods, many of the veiled young women I interviewed had received low scores on their college entrance exams, limiting their career options. As Amina recalled:

I originally intended to go to university, but when I received my *magmu* (exam score), the only thing it allowed me to enter was Commerce. So I refused. Why go into Commerce, a field for which there is no need? Only in medicine and teaching, where women can teach girls, is there a need for women to work. So I gave it up.

Similarly, young women began adjusting their expectations regarding the education level and jobs of potential husbands. For decades, urban, lower-middle-class women and their parents favored suitors with white-collar jobs, which they associated with job security and higher social status. Yet from an Islamist perspective, the premium attached to white-collar work was unwarranted. As one young woman explained:

Why does the ordinary youth want to wait for a government job? For the social status. But now even he is forced to find work elsewhere. In Islam, work is obligatory. But it can be any work, as long as it is honest. My cousin is a law graduate, but he sells perfume at a kiosk on the street. There's no shame in that. The important thing is not how much prestige is involved or how much he earns. The important thing is to earn a living legitimately, not earn it through stealing, drugs, or other illegal activities.

Among the jobs some Islamists considered religiously prohibited were positions in banks that charge interest and employment in the tourism industry.

In all three of the sha°bi neighborhoods where I conducted fieldwork, graduates active in Islamic networks spoke of adjusting their expectations. For example, Mona, who wears the *khimar,* explained that five years ago she had hoped to go to university. Now that she had finally completed secondary school (it took her several extra years because she left school and later returned), she would like to continue learning. "But not necessarily for a degree. Degrees aren't what matter. What counts is learning. I could study at home, and Ahmad (her fiancé) could bring me books." What about her fiancé? Mona responded:

Ahmad, who never even finished °adadi (junior high school), knows so much about Islam! I am constantly amazed. I ask him, how did you learn so much? He learned from the mosque, from lessons, from other people who are committed. I respect that more than people who have degrees. I'd rather have someone like Ahmad than an engineer or doctor who didn't know anything about Islam.

In addition, those graduates involved in Islamic networks asserted their self-conscious rejection of the materialist values pervading the surrounding secularized Egyptian society. As Amina explained, "The ordinary Muslim needs to earn more money than the committed Muslim, because his needs for material things (*istilzamatu*) are greater." Respondents frequently contrasted the lavish dowries, furniture, and consumer durables expected by ordinary brides and grooms with the far more modest requirements of partners committed to Islam. (For a comparison, see Wiktorowicz and Taji-Farouki 2000.) As Muhammad observed:

> For us to get married, we need only the simplest things—for example, a little room in our parent's apartment is enough. The pressure to get everything at once is not present in a *multazim* family. The truly Muslim woman knows she is like a queen in the house; she doesn't need material things. If a woman sets a fixed amount of money for the engagement gift as a condition of marriage, how can that be love?

As their expectations regarding higher education, career advancement, and material wealth diminished, graduates' feelings of disappointment and frustration abated as well. When graduates active in Islamic networks were asked what problems they faced as young adults, most responded that they did not have any problems. As one veiled woman explained, "We don't consider ourselves to have any problems. You should talk to the ordinary youth if you want to know about problems." Several young women nodded in agreement, but one expressed a different view. Acknowledging the difficulties of daily life, she noted, "We struggle, but we regard it as a test of our faith."

Leaders within the Islamist movement echoed the idea that society's main problems were not a matter of resources but of values. In the spring of 1990, I interviewed Kamal Habib, an Islamic militant who had been imprisoned for his leadership role in the Jihad organization, which, he proudly reminded me, "was the one that assassinated Anwar Sadat."[1] His comments in this regard were striking:

> I as a graduate don't have any problems. We need very little, take life in simplicity, don't need fancy cars and apartments and all that. I married a woman from the university. We lived very simply, but we didn't feel the poverty. Society imposes shackles on people; it pressures them to worry about clothes and apartments and money.
>
> We in the organization do not need to have dowries or expensive parties or anything like that to get married. I found an apartment in [a sha°bi neighborhood]. From the organization, I had 21 volunteers helping me find a cheap apartment. That's the meaning of Islamic solidarity (*al-takaful al-Islami*).
>
> The problem is that we are not living an Islamic reality. The definition of a society's problems depends on the nature of that society. It's not just a question of resources. In the 1970s, there were many private luxury apartments that remained vacant, while other people could not find

housing. That was during Sadat's time, may Allah destroy him. People's values got all shaken up (*zalzilit qiyam in-nas*).

In their deliberate rejection of values widely held within their own communities, young Islamists often confronted intense opposition from their parents. Several graduates mentioned that their parents initially balked at their decision to adhere to a strict Islamic way of life. For example, several young women noted that their parents had opposed their decision to cover their faces with the niqab or to wear gloves; others mentioned their parents' strenuous resistance to the idea of marriage without a generous dowry. In order to proceed with their plans, graduates were often forced to defy parental authority. Nevertheless, graduates stressed that respect for one's parents was still important. As one female graduate explained, "We can't blame them for thinking as they do, because they grew up in a different environment." Or as Muhammad noted, "If my parents told me to do something which went against God's laws, I wouldn't do it. But I wouldn't curse them for it."

One solution to parental resistance was to encourage parents to come to the mosque and talk things over with the imam. Salma, who wears the niqab, noted that her mother objected to the idea at first but later agreed to attend the prayer services led by the charismatic young imam at the "Sunni" mosque in her neighborhood. After hearing the imam's sermons, her mother reconciled herself to Salma's decision. In effect, the Islamist subculture occasioned a subtle reversal of authority relations within the family, encouraging adolescents—backed by self-trained Islamist authorities at the local level—to challenge and correct their parents' faulty understanding of Islamic dictates.

The Islamist rejection of values dominant in Egyptian popular culture occurred under a distinct set of circumstances. It occurred at a time when many students failed to receive the scores needed to enter the academic field of their choice, when formal education no longer guaranteed permanent employment, and when "respectable" jobs were in increasingly short supply. Furthermore, it occurred at a time when the lifestyle many residents in sha'bi communities sought for themselves or their children—a lifestyle associated with the possession of expensive consumer goods—was increasingly out of reach. Rather than promising the satisfaction of material needs, the Islamist movement promoted detachment from them as an emblem of moral superiority.

This reordering or "transvaluation" of values indicates that the Islamic movement lessened graduate frustration not by providing the means to satisfy their aspirations for middle-class status, jobs, and lifestyles but by promoting goals more readily fulfilled within existing resource constraints. By redefining what was to be valued, the Islamists offered many young Egyptians a "solution" to the problems they faced in everyday life. This solution extended to the most basic of human needs. For example, Muhammad explained that for men with few resources, who wanted to get married, Islam offered a cure for sexual frustration—fasting and prayer were advised as ways to "decrease the longing." Islam was thus offered as a way out of psychic distress, a solution that took into account existing structural constraints (in this instance, the limited opportunities for sexual expression outside marriage and the financial hurdles to getting married in the first place).

Islamic outreach also enhanced the relative position of graduates within existing social and political hierarchies of power. First, the embrace of Islamic commitments augmented graduates' sense of their own moral authority vis-à-vis non-Islamist parents, neighbors, and peers. Paradoxically, by adopting the strict behavioral code of the "committed Muslim," graduates were freer to flout the strictures of traditional sha'bi social conventions that limited their choice and autonomy in other ways. This type of empowerment was particularly significant for young, lower-middle-class women, whose freedom of movement and control over education, career, and marriage decisions were often sharply restricted by conservative social codes. By adopting "correct" Islamic behavior, young women gained an aura of respectability that enabled them to move more freely in public spaces without fear of social sanction. In addition, they were able to invoke their "rights in Islam" as a means to mobilize social pressure against parents or spouses who mistreated them.[2]

Islamic outreach also reshaped popular political culture by altering graduates' relationship to the authoritarian state. Islamist ideology challenged the prevailing climate of fear and passivity by exhorting graduates to obey a higher authority, regardless of the risks they would incur as a result. The embrace of Islamist commitments was thus a form of psychic empowerment. "The committed Muslim is not afraid of anything except God," Muhammad noted. "He doesn't fear death." Moreover, struggles in this life were viewed as a test of faith to be welcomed by the believer. The point to be made here is not that all graduates active in the Islamic movement were ready to sacrifice their lives for the cause, but rather that a firm belief in the righteousness of their mission and its backing by God enabled many of them to overcome the paralyzing fear that impedes protest in authoritarian settings. By stressing the fleeting and ephemeral nature of life on earth in comparison with eternal life in the world to come, the Islamist message reduced the potency of regime threats to citizens' physical and material comfort and well-being, perhaps more than leftist and other secular ideologies.

In addition to helping graduates overcome fear, the da'wa (particularly in the version propagated by the Muslim Brotherhood) challenged the dominant trend of noninvolvement in public life. Against the "rational" idea that voting and other forms of political action were a "waste of time," the Brotherhood da'wa asserted that every Muslim is obligated to contribute to the task of Islamic social and political reform. As one young activist explained, "The young person who is religious is the one who is interested in the affairs of society—Islam requires it." Or as another put it, "An observant Muslim will

not be quiet when she sees oppression or wrongdoing going on around her."
By promoting a *new ethic of civic obligation*, the daʿwa helped convert a passive
political stance into an active one.

Islamic outreach also generated a widespread sense of optimism about the
future. In interview after interview, graduates involved in the Islamic movement stressed that the committed Muslim is positive thinking (*igabi*), a term
connoting optimism and faith in the future. As a young man working in an
Islamic bookstore explained to me, "If you talk to ordinary youth, you will
find that they are negativists (*salbiyyin*); they are miserable and they complain a lot and they feel that nothing can be done. But the Muslim youth is
positive-thinking." Notwithstanding the hardships and difficulties Islamists
face, they believe that the influence of Islam as a global force is destined
to expand. As Kamal Habib predicted, "The future is with us. The shaʿbi
neighborhoods are our base, because they didn't change when the upper
classes began to imitate the West. . . . American society is in decline. All societies pass through phases; they rise and fall. Now is a period of transition.
Soon Islam will be resurgent." Asked whether he meant that those in prison
would one day take power, he responded, "Yes, exactly. When I get out, we
can talk about it some more."[3]

Other Islamic activists, including militants and reformists, expressed the
same faith in the inevitable advance of Islam. Western societies were in a state
of decay, as demonstrated by their high rates of crime, teen pregnancy and
drug use, the breakdown of the family, and the presence of homelessness and
poverty amid great wealth. Only Islam could offer humankind the moral
and spiritual framework it needed, and in time this would be obvious to all.
As one young Islamist journalist put it, "First Islam will spread through the
neighborhoods, and then to Egyptian society as a whole, and then to the
Egyptian state, and then to other Muslim countries, and then to countries in
which Muslims were formerly the rulers, and then to other parts of the world,
including Europe and the United States." I had already moved to another
question when I realized he had not finished. "And then it will spread to other
planets in the solar system, and eventually it will encompass the entire universe."

"Breaking Out of the Circle": A New Islamist Critical Consciousness

Islamist ideas provided Egyptians with a radically different vantage point
from which to view the political system and their role within it. This break in
consciousness was one of the Islamist movement's main goals and, to the extent that it succeeded at the collective level, one of its greatest achievements.
Zeinab, a female Islamic activist, makes the point quite clearly:

The government keeps people running after a morsel of bread. Therefore, they aren't free to think, to question, to challenge anything. Most
people never escape from that circle. They are too busy running after
money or lurching from one crisis to another. But we [Islamists] stand
outside the circle and are trying to bring other people out of it as well.

In a second interview, Zeinab returned to this theme, noting that "most
people lack the means to think critically" and that "the Muslim Brotherhood
gives them those tools."

Zeinab's idea of "breaking out of the circle" exhibits some striking parallels with Vaclav Havel's notion of "living within the truth" (Vladislav 1986,
36–122). To both Zeinab and Havel, ruling elites had implicated citizens in
their own domination by sapping them of the capacity to challenge dominant
beliefs and norms. Both held the view that a change in consciousness—in how
individuals perceive and relate to the world—was necessary before they could
aid in their own liberation from oppression. Before conditions are ripe for
broader social change, both Zeinab and Havel stressed, the individual must
live in accordance with his or her own inner convictions. "At a minimum the
Muslim must be honest," Zeinab stated, echoing Havel's call for living as
close to the truth as possible.

Yet here the similarity ends. While Havel wrote of "truth" with a small
"t" and viewed liberation as freedom from the constraints of all ideologies,
Zeinab and other Islamists in Egypt retained their belief in the existence of
a transcendent Truth with redeeming power. While Havel and the other
"antipoliticians" of Eastern Europe aimed to liberate the individual from the
noose of a suffocating orthodoxy, the Islamists promised relief from moral
anarchy through the establishment of a community united in adherence to
God's laws.

To establish this community and live within the truth, graduates involved
in Islamic networks consciously sought to separate themselves from secularizing and Westernizing influences in society. As one explained, "We isolate
ourselves from bad people." Other graduates active in the movement told
me they had been advised not to associate with Egyptian Copts; others had
been warned against contact with foreigners. Several graduates stressed that
Egypt's leaders, laws, and social customs had all been shaped by imported
ideas and institutions that are unsuitable for a Muslim society. Muhammad
pointed out that many of Egypt's laws were borrowed from France and the
United States; Zeinab noted that most of the country's leaders were trained
in foreign schools. The solution, they stressed, was to achieve greater self-
sufficiency within the Islamic community. As one veiled young woman noted,
"If I had a disagreement with a friend, I wouldn't consult the French laws
which prevail in this country; instead, I would approach someone from our

circle." Islamist ideals thus promoted nothing less than a "countersociety," detached from the mainstream social and political order.

Conclusion

The debate concerning whether "interests" or "ideas" constitute the main set of factors behind the rise of Islamic activism in Egypt cannot be definitively resolved in favor of one explanation or the other. An investigation of Islamist strategies of recruitment in three urban, lower-middle-class neighborhoods of Cairo reveals that both "selective incentives," emphasized by rational-actor models of collective action, and "frames" of moral obligation, highlighted by scholars interested in the mobilizing role of ideas, helped motivate educated youth to participate in the Islamic movement. Such research highlights the critical importance of the Islamist daʿwa, or project of ideological outreach, in generating motives for the higher-risk forms of Islamist activism associated with the movement's bid for political power. More generally, such research suggests that it was on the plane of ideas that the Islamists achieved their greatest success.

While Islamist mobilization did not overturn existing relations of economic and political domination in Egypt, it did foster the creation of a new subculture detached from the values and orientations of the country's state institutions and elites. This new subculture supplied the ideational framework for new kinds of political activism, encompassing various forms of opposition (both violent and nonviolent) to authoritarian rule. Yet it was not Islam per se that led to political activism. Rather, the springboard to activism was a particular ideologized form of Islam, transmitted through grassroots networks and reinforced through intensive small-group solidarity facilitated by prior family, friendship, and neighborhood ties. This brand of Islam resonated with the values and experiences of potential recruits and ensured that the ideas of the mobilizers were embraced by the mobilized as well.

Notes

This chapter is adapted from chapter 7 of *Mobilizing Islam: Religion, Activism, and Political Change in Egypt* (New York: Columbia University Press, 2002). It is based on fieldwork conducted in Cairo in 1990–1991 and during shorter research trips in 1993 and 1997. The names of all respondents have been changed in order to protect their identities.

1. Kamal Habib was permitted on several occasions to visit the campus of Cairo University under armed guard to meet with his advisor while he was writing in prison. I interviewed him during one of these visits.

2. In one instance, a group of young Islamist women in one sha ͨbi neighborhood responded with indignation to a neighbor's report that her husband had beaten her and threatened to throw their colicky infant out the window. "He has no right to treat you like that," said one of the Islamists. "Tell him to read this!" And here she picked up a book on the rights and duties of women in Islam. If he didn't shape up, the Islamist women promised the neighbor, they would contact the local imam and have him issue a stern warning to her husband.

3. Kamal Habib was released from prison several years later. Since that time, he has renounced the use of violence and is working to form a political party calling for the application of Islamic law.

Works Cited

Benford, Robert D., and David A. Snow. 2000. "Framing Processes and Social Movements: An Overview and Assessment." *Annual Reviews in Sociology* 26: 611–39.

Brysk, Alison. 1995. "Hearts and Minds: Bringing Symbolic Politics Back In." *Polity* 27 (Summer): 559–86.

Friedman, Debra, and Doug McAdam. 1992. "Collective Identity and Activism: Networks, Choices, and the Life of a Social Movement." Pp. 156–73 in *Frontiers in Social Movement Theory*, ed. Aldon D. Morris and Carol McClurg Mueller. New Haven: Yale University Press.

Gamson, William. 1975. *The Strategy of Social Protest.* Homewood, Ill.: Dorsey.

Jasper, James M. 1997. *The Art of Moral Protest: Culture, Biography, and Creativity in Social Movements.* Chicago: University of Chicago Press.

Jasper, James M., and Jane Poulsen. 1995. "Recruiting Strangers and Friends: Moral Shocks and Social Networks in Animal Rights and Anti-Nuclear Protests." *Social Problems* 42, 4 (November): 493–512.

Laraña, Enrique, Hank Johnston, and Joseph R. Gusfield, eds. 1994. *New Social Movements: From Ideology to Identity.* Philadelphia: Temple University Press.

McAdam, Doug. 1982. *Political Process and the Development of Black Insurgency, 1930–1970.* Chicago: University of Chicago Press.

———. 1988. *Freedom Summer.* New York: Oxford University Press.

McAdam, Doug, Sidney Tarrow, and Charles Tilly. 1996. "A Comparative Synthesis on Social Movements and Revolution: Towards an Integrated Perspective." Paper presented at the annual meeting of the American Political Science Association, September.

Olson, Mancur. 1965. *The Logic of Collective Action.* Cambridge, Mass.: Harvard University Press.

Richards, Alan, and John Waterbury. 1996. *A Political Economy of the Middle East.* Boulder: Westview.

Snow, David A., and Robert D. Benford. 1988. "Ideology, Frame Resonance, and Participant Mobilization." Pp. 197–217 in *From Structure to Action: Comparing Movement Participation across Cultures, International Social Movement Research*, vol. 1, ed. Bert Klandermans, Hanspeter Kriesi, and Sidney Tarrow. Greenwich, Conn.: JAI Press.

Vladislav, Jan, ed. 1986. *Vaclav Havel: Living in Truth*. London: Faber and Faber.

Wickham-Crowley, Timothy. 1992. *Guerrillas and Revolution in Latin America*. Princeton, N.J.: Princeton University Press.

Wiktorowicz, Quintan, and Suha Taji-Farouki. 2000. "Islamic Non-Governmental Organizations and Muslim Politics: A Case from Jordan." *Third World Quarterly* 21, 4 (Summer): 685–99.

Ten

Making Conversation Permissible
Islamism and Reform in Saudi Arabia

Gwenn Okruhlik

We are only beginning to understand how a social movement emerges under conditions of political authoritarianism and stringent social norms that militate against speaking out. In this chapter, I seek to explain the dynamics of mobilization where associations are prohibited; the voices of opposition where civil society has been subverted; and the taking of risk in the face of overwhelming concern for privacy and the protection of familial reputation. Even under such constraints, a powerful and articulate Islamist social movement emerged in Saudi Arabia to challenge the regime. How can we explain the politics of contention under such conditions? Resource mobilization theorists would be frustrated in their search for answers. The emphasis on organization, structure, rational decision-making, recruitment strategies, and garnering of resources leads to explanatory dead-ends under such sociopolitical conditions. Scholars who seek to "rationalize contention" argue that participation is a calculated response to objective conditions of political and economic exclusion (e.g., Oberschall 1973; McCarthy and Zald 1977; Jenkins 1983). In this approach, material resources—such as money, communications, facilities, volunteers—are the keys to social mobilization and the development of movements. The leaders of social movement organizations offer incentives to potential recruits, and movement entrepreneurs then direct the action of followers. Most attention is focused on formal organizations, though increasingly informal networks are being given their due.[1] Given much less attention, however, are the broader social processes in which any decision making is deeply embedded and the critical roles of ideological debate and symbolic resonance in the formation of political preferences.

Fortunately, analyses derived from the framing perspective have added the cultural dimensions of struggle to the structural and organization foci of resource mobilization theory. This is a much needed enhancement. Frames are tools that lend order and sense to an otherwise confusing world by providing language that captures or constructs the meaning of problems. Social movement activists frame political struggle in ways that resonate with publics and mobilize sympathizers. For a frame to resonate among a population, Benford and Snow (2000) argue, it must have empirical credibility, experiential commensurability, and narrative fidelity. That is, the frame must "fit" with a person's previous beliefs, experiences, and cultural narratives. For Swidler (1995), social movements are able to choose vocabulary and symbols from a "cultural tool kit" so that they can provide common scripts to people. In their volume on culture, Johnston and Klandermans (1995) argue that social movements arise out of what is culturally given but that they are also a fundamental source of cultural change.

The work of Williams and Kubal, in particular, extends framing literature to provide a powerful tool to explain the particular form that contention has assumed in Saudi Arabia. They argue that the contours of the cultural repertoire both constrain and facilitate contention because the repertoire demarcates what is acceptable or unacceptable. There are boundaries to what is considered legitimate behavior. A social movement finds its niche in the political terrain by tapping into recognizable rhetoric and symbols (1999, 229). Their concern, then, is with the fit between a frame and the wider cultural environment, rather than the fit between a frame and the experiences of an individual. That fit determines the resonance of a social movement. This perspective is refreshing in that it allows for change in cultural repertoires; its boundaries shift over time. What is appropriate at one moment may give way to new, innovative forms of contention.

Examining the relationship between frame and culture in this manner allows us to capture the complex struggle over symbolic politics in Saudi Arabia. It gives shape and meaning to such political struggle and thus provides a way to talk about the politics of contention in Saudi Arabia that moves beyond mere description. In this chapter, I demonstrate how this fit between culture and frame produced innovative collective action and agency under conditions of authoritarianism and self-censorship. In doing so, I highlight the nuanced differences within the Islamist social movement in Saudi Arabia in order to tweak and expand the applicability and power of social movement theory, without stretching concepts beyond their recognizable meaning.[2]

In the case of Saudi Arabia, a "loose" definition of a social movement is an appropriate starting point: a solidarity network with potent cultural meaning (Melucci 1985). Communal identities and cultural frameworks are far more relevant than are formal organizations, hierarchies, or membership lists. Social movements reflect and are transmitted across familial and regional networks, the most potent "national organizational forms" (McAdam, McCarthy, and Zald 1996). Organization itself is largely prohibited by law and also frowned upon socially. Thus, an analytical focus on the embedded social structure is necessary in order to capture the fluid, amorphous nature of the Islamist social movement in Saudi Arabia. My explanation, then, is less contingent on material resources and more contingent on the power of ideas and cultural resources. It is about the collective construction and articulation of a new (or redefined) relationship between self (as believer, citizen, and member of the community) and authority (as clergy, state, and ruling family). It is an effort to find meaning as a nation.

I examine the emergence of the Islamist social movement with the stationing of U.S. troops on Saudi Arabian soil during the first Gulf war (1990–1991). In the birth of this movement, I pay special attention to the holistic framing of grievances that resonated broadly across the country; the power of the embedded social structure; and the centrality of (re)writing historical narratives to counter established canons. This case is especially interesting because of the condition of authoritarianism and the social concern to protect the familial reputation, both of which inhibit collective action. Yet this articulate movement still emerged to challenge the status quo. I demonstrate that the repertoire of contention "fit" the culture, and I argue that the clergy assumed the risk of collective action for the larger population. A further nuance to this case is that formal social movement organizations arose in exile—disconnected from the movement they would normally be expected to lead. Finally, Saudi Arabia is an interesting case in which to evaluate measures of movement success or failure, since this is an Islamist movement in a country already governed by religious law (*shariᶜa*).[3]

God, Kings, and the Rise of the Religious Right

The al-Saud base their claim to legitimacy on the success of military conquests in the 1920s and 1930s and on their alliance with religious authorities. The al-Saud rule is in an uneasy symbiosis with the clergy. This relationship dates back to the 1744 alliance between Muhammad ibn Abd al-Wahhab and Muhammad ibn Saud, a merger of religious legitimacy and military might that has been lionized in the civic mythology. The descendants of Al-Wahhab still dominate the official religious institutions of the state. But Islam remains a double-edged sword for the al-Saud. It grants them legitimacy as protectors of the faith, yet it constrains their behavior to that which is compatible with religious law. When members of the family deviate from that straight path, they invite criticism, since the regime's "right to rule" rests largely on the alliance with the Al-Wahhab family.

In the last decade or so, the "alliance" between the regime and official clergy (both its contemporary manifestations and its historical roots) has been contested by Islamist dissidents because the parties no longer serve as independent "checks" on each other. The official clergy are said to be dependent upon the al-Saud for their existence. They are co-opted, or "in the pocket of the al-Saud." The official clergy regularly issue *fatwas* (religious judicial opinions) that justify the policies of the al-Saud in Islamic vocabulary, even when they are deplored by the populace (e.g., the fatwa to justify the presence of U.S. troops during the first Gulf war). While the ruling family still needs the legitimation conferred by the clergy, the clergy have become subservient and bureaucratized in the last 25 years (Krimly 1992; Piscatori 1983).

There are two important historic moments of opposition that provide striking parallels with the contemporary Islamist movement. These are the 1929 Ikhwan rebellion and the 1979 seizure of the great mosque in Mecca by Juhaiman Al Utaibi. In both instances, the Islamic legitimacy of the al-Saud family was seriously challenged by movements that emanated from the heartland of traditional al-Saud support, the Najd. This meant that both movements were composed of *muwahidun* (or unitarians, inappropriately called Wahhabis by detractors), a particularly austere and puritanical school of thought. Both times, opposition was justified because the regime deviated from the straight path of the Qur'an and Sunna (traditions of the prophet Muhammad). Corruption was a common theme, as was dependence on the West.

During the conquests of the peninsula in the early part of the twentieth century, the founder of Saudi Arabia, Abdulaziz, depended on the formidable fighting force of the Ikhwan, tribal muwahidun warriors, to extend the borders of his kingdom. When the strength on which he had depended turned against his leadership (due to deviation from Islam, corruption, and dependence), Abdulaziz crushed the Ikhwan as a military force at the Battle of Sabalah in 1930.

In 1979, Juhaiman Al-Utaibi forcibly took control of the sacred mosque in Mecca in an effort to topple the ruling family (Kechichian 1986). He was the grandson of an Ikhwan warrior. He charged King Fahd with corruption, deviation from the straight path of Islam, and dependence on the West. He echoed his grandfather's charges against Abdulaziz. Al Utaibi did not garner much popular support because he chose a holy venue rather than a palace, but the incident exposed the vulnerability of the regime. It took several weeks and the assistance of French special units to root the rebels from the mosque.

The takeover of the Great Mosque in 1979 was coupled with other tumultuous events, which led to great political sensitivity on the part of the regime. In particular, the Islamic Revolution in Iran had just toppled the shah's government and initiated new institutions in the country. The long-oppressed Shi'a community in the eastern province of Saudi Arabia, organized open demonstrations in the streets of several towns in support of the new Iranian government. These uprisings led to greater surveillance over the population, more power for the *mutawwaʿ* (for lack of a good translation, the morals police), and new constraints on mobility and expression (despite simultaneous promises of reform).

The regime's response to the deteriorating conditions produced two decades of political paralysis and social stagnation. The regime first executed the rebels who had taken over the Grand Mosque and then instituted tighter controls over social and political life in the country. Rather than confronting the religious right, King Fahd wrapped himself in the mantle of Islam, changing his title from "Your Majesty, King Fahd" to "Custodian of the Two Holy Mosques, King Fahd." He sought to bolster the legitimacy of the ruling family by appropriating the power of Islam.[4]

Since they had been accused of deviating from Islam, the regime sought to justify itself also by allowing the religious right even more maneuver in Saudi Arabian life. There were new restrictions on women's mobility and employment. Working women lost their jobs in shops, salons, and at Aramco (the national oil company). They covered more, ventured forth less, and were prohibited from appearing in papers or on television. Gender segregation was profound and enforced in any public space. Restaurants and amusement parks instituted separate sections for men and for family (inclusive of women). The mutawwa^c were granted more leeway in their oversight of behavior of the public realm. Tiny shops and fancy malls closed several times a day during prayer. Music could only be played in the privacy of homes. The heavily censored media became a mouthpiece for the government. Always and everywhere, the mutawwa^c were prowling. A narrow and intolerant interpretation of Islam (known as Wahhabism in the West) dominated the national discourse. Sulaiman al Hattlan, a Saudi scholar and journalist, explained, "Different groups ended up competing with fundamentalists over who can appear more conservative in the public eye" (*Arab News*, May 20, 2002). Islam, of course, has always been empowered and central to life in Saudi Arabia. The difference after 1979 was that only one very particular practice of Islam was empowered. Excluded from public discourse were the many Sufi, mainstream Sunni, and Shi^{c}a populations.

During the 1980s, an Islamic education system fostered a new generation of shaykhs, professors, and students. The state provided generous funding for the expansion of Islamic universities, even during the oil bust when other projects were scaled back, and sought to legitimize the regime during hard times by institutionally binding religion and the state. Imam Muhammad bin Saud University in Riyadh, the Islamic University in Medina, and Umm al Qura University in Mecca continued to grow, even as other programs were cut back. By 1986, more than 16,000 of the kingdom's 100,000 students were pursuing Islamic Studies. By the early 1990s, one-fourth of all university students were enrolled in religious institutions. They had ideas and resources: intellectuals, computers, fax machines, libraries, and everything necessary for mobilization.[5] This generation of students serves as bureaucrats, policemen, mutawwa^c, shari^{c}a judges, and preachers in some of the 20,000 mosques in the country.

An Islamic resurgence swept the country. It was not about politics nor was it directed against the regime. This resurgence was about private belief systems and the comprehensive message of Islam, a phenomenon noted by Diane Singerman in chapter 5 of this volume. Several nonviolent, nonpolitical Islamist groups took root during this time, and the embrace of Islam they advocated was about a spiritual awakening. They were not formal organizations, but they did inculcate a sense of group identity. What began as small, closed circles gradually grew into large, loose underground groups.

The resurgence was also propagated by the newly returned Arab Afghan *mujahidin* (holy warriors). About 12,000 young men from Saudi Arabia went to Afghanistan to fight the Soviets; perhaps 5,000 were properly trained and saw combat. At the time, no one ever thought the mujahidin would fight their own regime; indeed, they were supported by the regime.

All of this cultivated a fertile field for dissent, which culminated in the rise of an Islamist opposition movement during the first Gulf war. Its grievances and justification echo historic predecessors in 1929 and 1979.

The Gulf War and the Birth of a Social Movement

The Gulf war of 1990–1991, and particularly the stationing of U.S. troops in Saudi Arabia, ushered in a decade of turmoil. With the entrenched stationing of troops, what had been mostly an inchoate resurgence of Islam that was private was transformed into an organized and explicitly political movement; that is, many Wahhabi believers became Salafi activists.[6] The religious resurgence in the previous decade had been largely private, inwardly focused, and concerned with religious practice and social norms. Believers were identified by short *thobes* (the customary dress for men), beards, and the lack of an *agal* (rope) to hold their *ghutra* (head cloth) in place. The women of their families likely covered more and were strictly segregated, often even within the home. Wahhabism has existed in Saudi Arabia for centuries and is most prevalent in the Najd, the central region of the country. It is an offshoot of the Sunni Hanbali school of Islam, which assumed a local specificity. They are antagonistic toward extreme Sufism, saint worship, and folk religious traditions.

With the stationing of U.S. troops during and after the Gulf war, Wahhabism was transformed into a Salafi movement that was now explicitly political.[7] The private became public; the spiritual became political; intrafamilial norms were increasingly enforced on others; individuals became organized; and the formerly inward focus on the just believer became an outward vision of the just state and just society.

Opposition groups took shape in the country and abroad largely under the rubric of Islamism. For decades, there had been sporadic resistance, but with the Gulf war resistance became continuous and individuals emerged as symbols of opposition to the corruption of the al-Saud. The war accelerated debates that had long been under way in private. A new generation of clerics voiced strident political opinions in Friday sermons, calling for the removal of U.S. troops and the overthrow of the ruling family. Opposition to the presence of U.S. military bases reached a feverish pitch.[8]

Although the universities remained closed for much of the war, the mosques became centers of political sermons, ideological debate, and opposition. Both mosques and private homes served as safe havens for opposition activists during this turmoil (Fantasia and Hirsch 1995). In these sanctuaries, narratives were woven that provided people with a vocabulary to utilize in distilling their discontent. These safe sites of contention allowed people to construct oppositional alternatives to the dominant history, status quo dogma, and prevailing ideology. Social intercourse and sermons provided alternative historic narratives that resonated among people and empowered them to confront the overwhelming power of state institutions (Swidler 1995). Secret tapes of sermons and underground leaflets were circulated in the streets, schools, and mosques.

In the wake of the Gulf war, the state-appointed ulama were supplemented by an increasingly empowered popular-level alternative clergy that was vocal and articulate,[9] and the division between the official and popular clergy grew. Popular imams offered fatwas that effectively countered the fatwas of the official clergy. For example, when the state-appointed clergy issued a fatwa that justified the presence of U.S. troops in Islamic vocabulary, the popular ulama responded with fatwas that condemned the presence of U.S. troops, also grounded in Islamic vocabulary and reasoning. These oppositional fatwas often carried more credibility than did the official opinions because they were issued by scholars who were "independent" of the government. Al Faqih explained, "The previous al-Saud regimes had legitimacy conferred on them by one religious establishment [the state-appointed clergy]. The current regime has two religious establishments to contend with." The multiple clergy complicated governance for the al-Saud.

Several of these oppositional scholars were jailed. Salman Al Awdah, an influential leader in Buraydah, was arrested by police for criticism of government policy during the Gulf war and prohibited from delivering sermons. In Riyadh, a popular preacher, ʿAidh Al Qarni, was detained for criticizing the foreign military presence. Safar Al Hawali, an intellectual from Imam Muhammad bin Saud University, was harassed and eventually jailed for publicly arguing that the al-Saud had deviated from the straight path of the Qurʾan and Sunna.

Around the same time, societal disruption grew dramatically. Several societal groups presented King Fahd with petitions demanding political change. There were street demonstrations, an unusual occurrence under authoritarian regimes. Women, weary of strictures on their mobility, drove through the streets of Riyadh after kicking their foreign male drivers out of the front seat of their cars. In the midst of severe domestic turmoil, King Fahd, who had ruled since 1982, suffered a stroke in 1995, which incapacitated him. The price of oil plummeted to a 12-year low in 1998, straining all development projects. Unemployment soared to more than 30 percent among recent male university graduates. Per capita income declined drastically, dropping to less than half of the 1981 high. New social problems of guns, drugs, and crime appeared. The once-fabulous infrastructure began to crumble. This was especially true in hospitals, schools, and municipal services, things that touched everyday life. Mostly, there was a convergence of dissent for the first time. Ordinary Saudis grew weary of ad hoc and arbitrary governance—whether male or female, urban or rural, rich or poor, Sunni or Shiʿa. People shared a common desire for the rule of law. The decade was a time of crisis and socio-economic distress.

The forms in which contention manifested itself appeared rather innocuous. Formal petitions presented to a king, women driving cars, and clerics delivering sermons did not appear to threaten the status quo. But, in fact, they were the genesis of a powerful social movement that began to reconstruct the discourse and create political openings.

Symbolic and Material Grievances:
A Holistic Framing of Contention

Social movement mobilization in Saudi Arabia is made difficult by both the abundance of rent (oil wealth) and the reality of authoritarianism. It is further complicated by the overwhelming concern for privacy and discretion. How can we explain the politics of contention under such conditions? An episode of contention will not become a sustained social movement unless leaders are able to tap into some reservoir of collective identity, sense of (in)justice, or solidarity (Benford and Snow 2000). The integration of both ideological and material concerns in the framing of grievances against the regime accomplished that important task. The convergence of dissent—on ideational and material criticism of the regime—lent credibility, power, and authenticity to Islamism in Saudi Arabia. This is the rather holistic framing of contention that resonated broadly and garnered sympathy.

First, the ideational critique is that the regime, of which the official ulama are a part, has deviated from the straight path of Islam. The historic parallels are obvious. Movement activists assert that the official clergy are a serious problem because it is they who have convinced people that the al-Saud are Islamic. Al Fawwaz argues, "The corrupt scholars show only the good side of the al-Saud. There is much misinformation in our society. We must follow the true Islam as the Prophet and his companions understood it, not as the corrupt scholars say. The point is not how miserable you are, but how far the regime has deviated from Islam." Al Mass²ari explained, "The Wahhabi in contemporary Saudi Arabia do not name the exact ancestors to which we should refer because it would undo their own arguments about authority and obedience. If we really read the early stuff, we would see that the ancestors do not advocate blind obedience to unjust rule, but rebellion. . . . Their writing undermines the position of the al-Saud, so they have been conveniently dropped from the discourse." For Al Faqih, the differences between the old clergy and the new generation of clergy are profound: "The old clergy believe that the ruler is the shadow of God on earth and cannot be publicly criticized. For the new clergy, the ruler is not God's vice-regent. The clergy is duty-bound to criticize the ruler, to work for change, and to take risks to correct injustices." All grieve repression, authoritarianism, and the absence of representation in the political system.

Second, in material terms, there has been a fundamental abrogation of the pact—or the social contract—in Saudi Arabia that traditionally defined the relationship between state and society. Saudis refer to specific historic moments as pacts, and there are three pacts that are most often recounted by contemporary Saudis: the pacts made between Abdulaziz and representatives of major families; between Abdulaziz and the clergy; and between Abdulaziz and the Hijazi notables. These pacts were thought to protect private citizens and clergy from the reach of the state by providing a separate space for them. In the eyes of many Saudis, all three agreements have been violated.

Islamist activists all respond to this perceived abrogation by calling for a separation of the public and political from the private and commercial. There is shared resentment at the corruption and commissions that many princes have received. All call for a halt to the intrusion of the ruling family into private life, especially land registrations in the names of royalty and the penetration of private businesses. Al Mass²ari notes that the princes have even penetrated the small businesses, and people are fed up. The al-Saud now control the tailoring shops, grocery stores, and car repair shops. In a more general sense, all deplore the mismanagement, maldistribution, and waste of national assets. Enormous expenditures on military purchases, for example, proved worthless. One dissident noted, "So rampant has corruption become that ordinary people are as revolted by it as scholars and reformers" (*Middle East Mirror,* June 30, 1999). Another activist echoed a common argument: "It is the princes who run drugs, guns, and prostitution! Those are princely fields."

What has made inequitable material conditions salient is that they are not compatible either with the straight path of Islam or with social contracts forged in the early years of the country. Maldistribution and authoritarianism do matter, but what resonates among people is less the objective condition and more that *it was not supposed to be this way.* The Islamist social movement effectively captured this sentiment, and the holistic critique centered on a renegotiation of the social contract and a redefinition of the rules of the game.

Framing History: Dominant and Alternative Constructions

Brysk explains that counterhegemonic narratives are a form of political consciousness-raising, used to open hearts and to change minds. Ultimately, they may change political behavior. To deconstruct the canon, or received wisdom, history is rewritten to link personal and social history. Brysk argues that successful symbolic politics must be culturally appropriate, have historical precedent, be reinforced by other symbols, and signal a call to action. She writes, "Reframing leads to renaming, and renaming leads to reclaiming" (1995, 57).

The dominant narrative or canon in Saudi Arabia is recounted in history textbooks, the national museum, and in the state-run media. It tells a glorious history of state formation under the wise leadership of Abdulaziz, who unified diverse tribes and regions. He married into all defeated tribes in order to confer "voice" on them and to instill a sense of nationhood. City after city "opened its gates" to his military forces, and Islam was embraced by the al-Saud.

All of the Islamist opposition activists contest this historical narrative, and alternative constructions of history are every bit as carefully woven as the dominant version. Oppositional histories are coherent narratives, intricate and internally consistent, and woven from a fabric of cultural symbols and language that resonate among people across cleavages such as region, gender, status, and class. Recounting the same period as the official history, this narrative is one of conquering rather than unification; violence rather than wisdom; massacres rather than opened gates; and the abuse of Islam rather than its embrace. One activist argued that marriage "was a trinket extended to the tribes, like graft. It was un-Islamic." Further, the movement activists all draw careful analogies from history in order to articulate parallels in contemporary Saudi Arabian politics. These include historical episodes with good and corrupt ulama, previous reform movements, problems with foreign intervention, and the lessons of Afghanistan and Iran.[10] Alternative histories also speak eloquently about the early social contracts, that is, the agreed-upon separation of politics from commerce. Finally, they describe the deleterious social, economic, and political consequences of the oil boom rather than focus on the technological glories of exploration. One activist said, "We must appreciate history, but it is different from the one being told." This is echoed by a Shiʿa who was told as a child, "Ibn akhi [son of my brother], do not believe anything that is written, especially anything about religion." The Shiᶜa, of course, were largely written out of official histories of the country.[11]

Transmitting Frames: Power of the Embedded Social Structure

All movement activists recognize the power and persistence of the embedded social structure in Saudi Arabia. It is evident in their language and in their strategies. Islamists explicitly acknowledge that the embedded social structure serves as a constraint on their activities and as a source of strength. The point is that opposition leaders work within this social structure, rather than trying to dismantle it. One commented, "We must work within this framework until we have domination, then we will work for the bigger picture."

The opposition activists based in London recognize the importance of connecting to this structure. One individual emphasized the village level of mobilization. He is plugged into the villages, and his network closely listens to and utilizes sermons each week. Village-level activists communicate with him in London about local developments. Another individual drew distinctions between bedu and settled communities in terms of sustaining a commitment to change. Bedu communities, he suggested, are temperamental; settled communities are more reliable and consistent in terms of belief and more reliable in terms of action. Villages, he argued, are more reliable than cities. And like his colleague, he says that he finds sustained support there.

Several examples illustrate the power of this embedded social structure. These opposition activists, who are living abroad, remain cognizant of the origin and relative status of families. Their damning political critique of the ruling family is enhanced by devaluation of their familial origins. For example, the "al-Saud are just a minor branch of minor tribe," "the family has no status or respect as a unit," "the al-Saud are definitely going away," and "they are on the periphery of the tribe." Further, all the activists in London made reference to the importance of family networks in mobilizing support in the country. One even commented on the relative status of other opposition activists, saying, "His family, you know, is from slaves."

All these leaders recognize the current norms of behavior that are derived from the Saudi social structure. Behavior in the public realm (any place outside of the home) is regulated by well-defined codes of conformity, and the privacy of the family unit is always "protected." Not only is collective action against the law in Saudi Arabia, but the potential for collective action is further inhibited by the extraordinary social concern with discretion. Massʾari explains, "Society was much looser and more open 60–70 years ago. Abdulaziz and his sons have weakened civil organizations and prohibited free speech." He argues that the origins of this overwhelming concern with privacy and discretion are political, not social. Conformity, discretion, and limitations on expression are enforced by the state. The problem is that they have now been ingrained socially and internalized by the people. This is difficult to change and creates significant logistical and strategic problems in movement mobilization that somehow must be overcome for Islamic activism to be effective on a mass scale.[12]

Agency by Proxy: The *Nasiha* as Collective Action

In spring 1991, 52 religious scholars, judges, and university professors used strong and direct language to call for a restoration of Islamic values. The petition explicitly called for 12 reforms of political life, including a consultative assembly, fair judiciary, redistribution of wealth, an end to corruption, and the primacy of religious law (Dekmejian 1994).

Later, in July 1992, 107 religious scholars signed a "memorandum of advice" (*muzakharat al nasiha*) and then gave it to King Fahd. At first, he refused to receive the 46-page document. It was an even bolder and more defiant petition than the one drafted the previous year. Its tone was straightforward; its charges were specific. The petitioners deplored the "total chaos in the economy and society . . . widespread bribery, favoritism, and the extreme feebleness of the courts." They criticized virtually every aspect of domestic and foreign policy, and demanded a more rigorous application of Islamic law. The government was shaken because the very people thought to be pillars of regime support had endorsed such sweeping changes. The ruling family was upset not only by the content but also by the very public way in which it was circulated. The petition made the rounds at schools and mosques before the king saw it. Because it abrogated the norm for privacy in political discussion, the Supreme Council of Scholars condemned the publication and circulation of the petition.

When the clergy presented King Fahd with the memorandum of advice, they profoundly changed political discourse in Saudi Arabia. It was an innovative collective action conducted in such a way that it had to be taken seriously. The muzakharat al nasiha gave people permission to talk about politics and religion in Saudi Arabia, a right they had long been denied. Without this permission, no change would ever occur, and permission had to come in an Islamic vocabulary and with Islamic authority. Only an Islamically based permission could overpower a state law and a social norm of self-censorship. The nasiha gave ordinary Saudis "cognitive liberation" (McAdam 1982); that is, it gave people permission to talk. It freed them from the shackles of the past, the fear of retribution for talking.

Agency, or empowerment to effect change, is stunted among Saudis by very real fears of retaliation. However, with the bold act of submitting the nasiha to the king, the popular clergy assumed the risk of political activity for Saudis who were hesitant to speak out themselves. The popular clergy used their voices to give people a sense of empowerment. The nasiha gave Saudis what we may call "agency by proxy."

The critical attribute for agency by proxy to work is trust. Trust is crucial in the articulation, transmission, and resonance of ideas that challenge a status quo. While Saudis may have doubted their own ability to alter the system, they did have confidence in the power of Islam. The popular clerics were able to amplify the latent sense of agency that people carried around dormant (Gamson 1995). Islamists opened the floodgates of criticism in the kingdom by invoking the Islamically grounded right to advise the ruler (hence, the memorandum of advice). Once opened, it could not be closed.

The status quo dogma made the kinds of contention traditionally recognized in social movement theory unthinkable because unseemly behavior in public reflects upon the entire family unit in Saudi Arabia. Media debates and public outbursts were considered unacceptable, but advising the king is an age-old legitimate form of criticism. Some argued that it was also a civic obligation. Written petitions to the king were arguably compatible with the national organizational form and the status quo dogma in Saudi Arabia. The dogma had to be stretched a bit because it traditionally placed two conditions on advising the king: advice to the king could be given only in private and only by the ulama. (The nasiha had been circulated in society before it reached the king. Also, while the dogma may imply that only the official ulama reserve the right to advise the king, popular-level clergy are not explicitly barred from it.) Demanding reform through the right to advise "fit" within the legitimate cultural repertoire (Williams and Kubal 1999).

Furthermore, the cognitive liberation that was critical to the sustenance of the movement was directed less toward collective action (as would be anticipated by McAdam) and more toward the construction of a common identity. At this time, there was not a sense of collective identity in the country (indeed, it is only emerging now). Collective action was thus not the end; the construction of meaning as a nation was the end. The resulting mobilization was less action-oriented and more about the identification, justification, and legitimation of counterhegemonic narratives. Only Islam could do that successfully.

Why Islamism? Free-Riding the Effective Frame

Several other frames had been attempted to effect reform in Saudi Arabia, but none were able to cut across multiple social cleavages in the country. At the time of the Gulf war, the first petition to be presented to the king was signed by the "liberals," that is, reformists who were not self-consciously Islamist in their political efforts. They decried corruption and authoritarianism in the kingdom, but their petition did not resonate among the population. People called it "fawning" and "obsequious" in its pledge of loyalty to the ruling family.

When women kicked their foreign drivers out and drove cars through Riyadh, this gendered frame appealed to only a part of the population—and support could not be shown publicly for fear of dishonoring the family unit. Williams and Kubal (1999) argue that successful collective action frames must have a center of gravity within the repertoire; otherwise, they will be disadvantaged in the political struggle for public symbolic meaning. In Saudi Arabia at the time, it was disconcerting for many to see women driving—the action was incompatible with the legitimate cultural repertoire.

Historically, still other frames have attempted to distill and propel dissent into action. Private businessmen have been vocal and well organized in their criticism of mismanagement in the country. But observers charge them with being co-opted by the very regime they criticize (dependent upon it for the receipt of state contracts). Nationalists (*al watanyun*) attempted to promote sweeping reform, but any sense of national identity was crosscut by more salient identities such as family, region, and Islam. One frame that has been quite resonant is regional identity; but for obvious reasons, regional identity does not carry a country.

While Islamists do not work in a vacuum (they are intimately tied to this fabric of communal, regional, and economic networks), they clearly are the most articulate and powerful of the various social forces in Saudi Arabia. They are better organized and more cohesive than other social forces, and although the Islamist movement may threaten the al-Saud, the ruling family cannot easily quash or oppose Islamist arguments, since they stake their right to rule largely on Islamic grounds. Given the authoritarian content of the regime, all organization, assembly, and expression are strictly controlled. Islamism is the only voice that has proven difficult to legally prohibit. In effect, then, Islamists express the grievances of many people. The ideational and material grievances articulated by the Islamist social movement are held in common by other social forces in Saudi Arabia (whether Sunni or Shiᶜa of diverse orientations, women, business groups, regions, urban social networks, or nationalists). Even though people may disagree on strategy and the ultimate end of opposition movements, they do concur on grievances. And on the overarching political questions of predictability, regularity, and the rule of law, there is a consensus.

Because of the convergence on grievances, other social forces were, in a sense, content to "free-ride" on the back of the Islamist social movement. It is the Islamists who took the risks and pushed the edges. They offered a cogent material and symbolic critique of the regime; they contested the dominant historical narrative on the founding of the kingdom; and they worked within the embedded social structure in Saudi Arabia, meaning, the horizontal networks of family and tribe. It is Islamists who engaged in sit-ins and protests. They were jailed, exiled, and tortured. It is the Islamists who posed the greatest threat to the regime through their loose organization into study groups throughout the country. Islamists were responsible for the bombings in Riyadh and Dhahran. It is Islamists who called international attention to internal problems through the fax, the Internet, and the press. Indeed, Islam is one movement idiom that can effectively cross gender, regions, class, and social status. Other social forces will benefit from this, as they share concern for the separation of public and private and the call for predictability and regularity. But Islamists in Saudi Arabia did the really messy work of confronting the regime on difficult issues such as corruption, mismanagement, behavior, and historic memory.[13]

Conclusion

Only three years ago, it was fashionable to dismiss Islamism in Saudi Arabia as a failed movement or as a mere postwar hiccup on the domestic front. Observers argued that Islamism had been quashed or co-opted by the al-Saud regime because shaykhs and dissidents were less vocal than before. This was a mistake. Those who made this error were using an inappropriate yardstick, looking only for "regime overthrow" as a measure of success. In fact, Islamist pressures have initiated significant steps toward reform, in both policy and in discourse. For example, it is unlikely that King Fahd would have created the consultative council in 1992 without the pressure of Islamists (it had been promised regularly since 1975) or that he would have created provincial councils or later expanded the membership of the council from 60 to 90. Most significantly, Crown Prince Abdullah would have had a harder time asserting his position in the succession struggles against Sultan and his brothers that followed Fahd's stroke in 1995 had it not been for the power of the Islamist voice in Saudi Arabia. After consolidating his position in the struggles in late 1998, Abdullah allowed a popular clergy to voice opinions, and he reined in the more ostentatious behavior of princes. He instituted limits on the extent to which princes and princesses can freely use the telephone services, water, airline, and electricity, and he paid off government debts to farmers and contractors. He limited the extent to which members of the ruling family can be involved in oil-related endeavors. This is significant because people wanted Fahd to do this for years. The Islamists now had the leverage to force the issue.

Abdullah must deal with the voices of contending ulama. It appears that he will respond to Islamists in a way that grants concessions to the opposition and protects the position of the ruling family. In summer 1999, he released the popular-level shaykhs who had been jailed. He allowed the press a bit more leeway than before and publicly criticized U.S. policy toward Israel and Palestine. Still, one month after September 11, Abdullah summoned many religious authorities to his side. He warned them to be cautious in their rhetoric and to "not be emotional or provoked by others." He exhorted them to avoid inflammatory comments and "to weigh each word before saying it." The role of Islamism in the post–Abdullah succession struggle will tell us much about the coherence, sustainability, and power of this social movement in rewriting history and reformulating the pact in Saudi Arabia.

Even more important than policy changes, what Islamists have done is capture the discourse in Saudi Arabia. Above all, in my view, the struggles of the Islamist movement have made conversation permissible in Saudi Arabia. This is an enormous feat in the authoritarian circumstances of the country. Ideas that were oppositional have become normalized. Islamists have initiated a renegotiation of the social contract in Saudi Arabia and an alternative telling(s) of history. The al-Saud occupy all positions of authority, but they now must make some compromises in accordance with the historical, material, and ideological critique eloquently articulated by Islamists. This is a measure of success, not the sign of an exhausted Islamist social movement.

If you measure the success of a movement by regime change, then Islamists have failed in Saudi Arabia. But if you measure success by discourse and meaning, then clearly Islamists have succeeded. They have provided people with common scripts and symbols to utilize when confronting the overwhelming power of state institutions. The success of a movement can be judged by the "transformations wrought in culture and consciousness, in collective self-definitions, and in the meanings that shape everyday life" (Polletta 1997, 432). Resonance, for Williams and Kubal (1999), is a measure of success—it is the reception of symbolic challenges at a wider cultural level. The goal of the Islamist social movement in Saudi Arabia was not simply mobilization and collective action; rather, it was to engender support for the collective action that had already occurred.

Now that conversation has become more permissible, the larger debates in Saudi Arabia today are about the construction of meaning as a nation. People are talking about the terms and content of their belonging together and about the right to talk about such sensitive topics. The contemporary debate is about what it means to "be Saudi," that is, the meaning of citizenship. It was the Islamists who began this national conversation about what it means to belong and about the relationship of ruling family, state, citizen, and religion. This is no small accomplishment in Saudi Arabia, where only a decade ago the most controversial criticism that could be published in the papers was parental complaints about school lunches.

The Islamist frame was absolutely critical to prompting this long overdue national debate. Without the Islamist frame, the floodgates of criticism would have remained closed. Once opened, the torrent of criticism poured forth. In many ways, the Islamist social movement focuses on ends that may not be specifically Islamic. In my conversations with activists, once familiar with their grievances, I pushed them to give substance to their ends. When I asked, "What do you hope to achieve? What is your ideal state?" I was provided with a laundry list of reforms that included elections, shariᶜa, representation, open media, contending clergy, rights, a written constitution, public ownership of resources, parties, and, most important, an independent judiciary. I then asked, "But what would you settle for? What would you accept in the end?" The answer was automatic: "Police off the phone and the right to organize."

Many Islamists in Saudi Arabia, then, advocate freedom of expression and freedom of assembly. These are certainly compatible with Islam but are not peculiar to the Islamist frame. The language, reference points, and organization were Islamist; the ends were common to many alternative frames. Given this convergence, the reformist movement may be transformed from a specifically Islamist movement to a nationalist movement that is grounded thoroughly in Islam. In Saudi Arabia, perhaps the mantle of leadership of the reformist movement will pass to another social force that is better situated to achieve the normative ends that are shared in common with the Islamists (transparency, regularity, law, rights). The next master frame will likely be about national identity and citizenship, about meaning and memory.

Notes

I thank the participants on the MESA 1998 panel on Culture, Ideology, and Mobilization in Social Movements and the APSA 1999 panel on Social Movements and Democratization in Theory and Practice, Kiren Aziz Chaudhry, Dale Eickelman, Suzanne Maloney, Rich Martin, David Medicoff, Mary Ann Tetreault, and Carrie Rosefsky Wickham. For his invaluable criticism and support, I thank Patrick Conge.
The analysis in this chapter is based largely on structured, open-ended interviews conducted in 1997 and 1999 with Sunni Islamists in London who represent three social movement organizations: Saᵓad al Faqih from the Movement for Islamic Reform in Arabia (*al harakah al islamiyya lil islah*); Muhammad al Massᵓari from the Committee for Defense of Legitimate Rights (*lajnah al difa an huqooq al shariah*); and Khaled al Fawwaz from the Advice and Reformation Committee (*lajnah al nasiha wa islah*), and multiple interviews with representatives of the Shiᶜa Reform Movement (*al harakah al shiat lil islah*) in the United States. All quotations are taken from these interviews. Parts of this argument appeared in "Networks of Dissent: Islamism and Reform in Saudi Arabia," *Current History* (January 2002): 22–28.

1. Likewise, functional theorists who emphasize structural strain, psychological alienation, aggression, and deprivation might be hard-pressed to find such attributes in a meaningful way in the family-centered rentier welfare state context of Saudi Arabia. Political process theorists would find that internal rather than external factors are central to the political struggles.

2. I use "Islamist social movement" to refer to those societal forces which seek to effect meaningful political change through reference to vocabulary, symbols, and historical developments that are firmly grounded in Islamic tradition. The social movement incorporates many groups, formal and informal, Sunni and Shiᶜa.

3. This chapter is not directly about September 11 or al-Qaeda. The political debates today, post–September 11, are the issues discussed in the conclusion to this chapter. Discourse now changes rapidly in Saudi Arabia.

4. This historic choice between confrontation and co-option of the religious Right seems instructive today. Crown Prince Abdullah, too, is faced with the rise of the radical Right. He may respond differently than Fahd because he has stronger religious credentials and greater legitimacy among broad segments of the population.

5. In an interview with the author, Al Faqih relays that Fahd considered a crackdown against these groups in 1987 to dismantle their leadership. The king was unable to mount such action, however, because of the recent massacre of 400–450 Iranian pilgrims in Mecca. Iran questioned the credentials of the al-Saud to serve as "keepers of the holy cities," and there were mutual calls for the downfall of the Khomeini and al-Saud regimes. The king needed the support of the Saudi Sunni Islamists to counter the power of Iranian Shiʿa Islamists, even though he was discomfitted by their swelling numbers.

6. These terms have always been used variously by dissenters (who disagree among themselves about meaning), ordinary Saudis, and scholars. Believers would never refer to themselves as Wahhabi, as that implies worshiping someone other than God. Some people use the term *neo-Wahhabi*, but most adherents tend to refer to themselves as Salafis. Terminology has been complicated further by September 11. The term *Wahhabi* seems to have taken on a hegemonic meaning in the international press that does not accurately reflect its usage in Saudi Arabia before September 11. I use *Wahhabi* to refer to the private reassertion of strict religious practices that adhere to the literalist understanding of the Qurʾan and Sunna, and I use the term *Salafi* when referring to individuals or actions that transform these practices into political activism. Others, however, may use the terms differently, indicating a need to carefully construct definitions. This may be a difficult undertaking, since Islamists themselves disagree over the terminology.

7. Internal grievances about maldistribution of oil revenues, inequity, and authoritarianism were supplemented by external grievances, primarily U.S. hegemony in the region, including U.S. support for Israel, sanctions against Iraq, and support for repressive regimes. The U.S. troops in Saudi Arabia are both an internal and external issue.

8. Some scholars argue that the Gulf war, the use of female soldiers, and the presence of the foreign press were the crucial components of the political opportunity structure that provided an opening for the social movement. I disagree. If this framework is utilized, the relevant opportunities are the stationing of U.S. troops (the objective condition) and the alliance between the official clerics and the ruling family (the subjective condition).

9. Others use the terms *corrupt, subservient,* or *evil* versus *genuine, authentic,* or *good.*

10. One drew a fascinating parallel between the Ikhwan of the 1920s and 1930s and the Taliban of contemporary Afghanistan. "The Ikhwan would go from town to town, ridding them of corrupt and evil elements. Then they would move on to the next village. The problem was that they never replaced the corrupt leaders with their reformers. Abdulaziz caught on and sent his men from Riyadh to assume the vacant positions. He put in his own men after the Ikwhan did the work. History repeats itself now in Afghanistan. People beg the Taliban to clean their village of corruption. The

Taliban do so, but then move on to the next town without placing their own reformers in positions."

11. Al Rasheed has thoughtfully analyzed the Shiᶜa construction of their cultural history. She documents their transformation from a focus on military confrontation to a search for cultural authenticity. Shiᶜa intellectuals and opposition leaders deconstruct official narratives, which dismiss them as a nonindigenous community, and provide alternative narratives that anchor their community in Saudi history and society (1998). The Sunni Islamists are self-consciously recording the history of their movement even as it unfolds in a text entitled "The History of Dissent in Arabia." They document internal debates within the social movement and with the regime. Chapters cover, among other topics, the Gulf Crisis, the Women's Demonstration, the American-Saudi Propaganda Machine, the Full Story behind the Letter of Demands, the Memorandum of Advice, and the Establishment of the CDLR.

12. One activist repeatedly emphasized the importance of the relationship between society and the desert, as a part of training and the mobilization of opposition. He explained, "People know the desert well. They are able to survive in it because families regularly spend three months of the year in desert camps as a part of holiday. The smallest camp cannot have less than 50 people. Americans need mineral water to survive in the desert. A Saudi Arabian can drink mud and survive."

13. Now, however, especially in the wake of September 11, alternative voices and frames are once again being heard as distinct from the Islamists.

Works Cited

Benford, Robert, and David Snow. 2000. "Framing Processes and Social Movements: An Overview and Assessment." *Annual Review of Sociology* 26: 611–39.

Brysk, Allison. 1995. "Hearts and Minds: Bringing Symbolic Politics Back In." *Polity* 27, 4 (Summer): 559–85.

Dekmejian, R. Hrair. 1994. "The Rise of Political Islamism in Saudi Arabia." *Middle East Journal* 48, 4 (Autumn): 627–43.

Fantasia, Rick, and Eric Hirsch. 1995. "Culture in Rebellion: The Appropriation and Transformation of the Veil in the Algerian Revolution." Pp. 144–59 in *Social Movements and Culture,* ed. Hank Johnston and Bert Klandermans. Minneapolis: University of Minnesota Press.

Gamson, William. 1995. "Constructing Social Protest." Pp. 85–106 in *Social Movements and Culture,* ed. Hank Johnston and Bert Klandermans. Minneapolis: University of Minnesota Press.

Al Hawali, Safar Ibn Abd al Rahman. "An Open Letter to President Bush." Posted on IANA Radionet, November 2001.

Jenkins, Craig. 1983. "Resource Mobilization Theory and the Study of Social Movements." *Annual Review of Sociology* 9: 527–53.

Johnston, Hank, and Bert Klandermans, eds. 1995. *Social Movements and Culture.* Minneapolis: University of Minnesota Press.

Kechichian, Joseph. 1986. "The Role of the Ulama in the Politics of an Islamic State: The Case of Saudi Arabia." *International Journal of Middle East Studies* 18: 53–71.

Krimly, Riyad. 1992. "The Political Economy of Rentier States." Ph.D. dissertation, George Washington University.

McAdam, Doug. 1982. *Political Process and the Development of Black Insurgency, 1930–1970.* Chicago: University of Chicago Press.

McAdam, Doug, John McCarthy, and Mayer Zald, eds. 1996. *Comparative Perspectives on Social Movements: Political Opportunities, Mobilizing Structures, and Cultural Framings.* Cambridge: Cambridge University Press.

McCarthy, John D., and Mayer N. Zald. 1977. "Resource Mobilization and Social Movements: A Partial Theory." *American Journal of Sociology* 82, 6 (May): 1212–41.

Melucci, Alberto. 1985. "The Symbolic Challenge of Contemporary Movements." *Social Research* 42, 4 (Winter): 789–815.

Oberschall, Anthony. 1973. *Social Conflict and Social Movements.* Englewood Cliffs, N.J.: Prentice-Hall.

Piscatori, James. 1983. "Ideological Politics in Saudi Arabia." Pp. 56–72 in *Islam in the Political Process,* ed. James Piscatori. Cambridge: Cambridge University Press.

Polletta, Francesca. 1997. "Culture and Its Discontents: Recent Theorizing on the Cultural Dimensions of Protest." *Sociological Inquiry* 67, 4: 431–50.

Al Rasheed, Madawi. 1998. "The Shiʿa of Saudi Arabia: A Minority in Search of Cultural Authenticity." *British Journal of Middle Eastern Studies* 25, 1: 121–38.

——. 1999. "Political Legitimacy and the Production of History: The Case of Saudi Arabia." In *New Frontiers in Middle East Security,* ed. L. Martin. New York: St. Martin's.

Swidler, Ann. 1995. "Cultural Power and Social Movements." Pp. 25–40 in *Social Movements and Culture,* ed. Hank Johnston and Bert Klandermans. Minneapolis: University of Minnesota Press.

Williams, Rhys, and Timothy Kubal. 1999. "Movement Frames and the Cultural Environment: Resonance, Failure, and the Boundaries of the Legitimate." Pp. 225–48 in *Research in Social Movements, Conflicts, and Change,* ed. Michael N. Dobkowski and Isidor Wallimann. Stamford, Conn.: JAI Press.

Eleven

Opportunity Spaces, Identity, and Islamic Meaning in Turkey

M. Hakan Yavuz

[handwritten annotations:]
— talks about the opening of opportunity spaces — what about the closing of opp. spaces in W. democ. context?
— differentiated movements & opp. spaces — intra movement diff. enhanced by type of opp. (?)

In Turkey, Turgut Özal's (1980–1993) program of economic liberalization created an assortment of new "opportunity spaces"—social sites and vehicles for activism and the dissemination of meaning, identity, and cultural codes. These opportunity spaces included independent newspapers, TV stations, magazines, financial institutions, and private educational facilities, all of which provided autonomous networks of association for the production and dissemination of religious values and ways of life. For Islamic groups, these new avenues for collective engagement produced emancipation from the strictures of the Kemalist secularization project by offering alternative, market-oriented venues for Islamic ideas and practices.

Although new opportunity spaces suggest mechanisms of empowerment, the impact on movement communities is typically uneven. Shifts in the structure of opportunities do not inexorably empower or disempower entire movements; rather, they selectively produce differentiated effects that likely help some groups while hurting others, thus reshaping the internal dynamics and distribution of power within the movement. In Turkey, the economic reforms were welcomed and embraced by society-centered Islamic movements that appropriated Islamic symbols for the marketplace to encourage the production of religious interpretations, values, and meaning through businesses and patterns of consumption. These society-centered groups did not seek to capture state institutions and impose Islamic mores from above; rather, they represented everyday life–based movements determined to challenge Kemalist cultural codes and produce new meaning according to an Islamic identity. Constituted, in part, by socioeconomic groupings that stood to gain from the liberalization of the economy, these Islamic groups effectively mobilized into

270

capitalist venues to propagate religious values and empower the Muslim community.

State-centered Islamic groups, however, did not fare as well. Supporters of such groups often derive from socioeconomically marginalized communities with little access to the instruments of capitalist growth. These communities *same as* instead sought to affect state policy to produce socioeconomic justice from *w. Erk?* above, and economic liberalization reforms, which weakened state welfare policies, undermined this goal. These groups were thus unable to take advantage of the new opportunity spaces in the same way as society-oriented Islamic groups, thereby fragmenting Islamic positions vis-à-vis the new capitalism of Turkey.

This chapter explores the differential impact of the new opportunity spaces of economic reform. It argues that the impact of new opportunities on social movements can only be understood if movements are disaggregated into their constituent elements. To this end, the chapter offers a typology of Islamic activism that distinguishes groups according to goals and strategies. Such distinctions help us better comprehend the relationship of specific groups to Kemalism, the state, and economic liberalization reform. Once a movement is deconstructed into smaller elements, the heterogeneous consequences of shifts in the structure of opportunities become clear. Changes viewed as openings for some groups may be seen as obstacles or setbacks by other groups in the movement. A comparison of state-centered and society-centered Islamic groups in Turkey highlights this point.

state v society - centered groups

"Opportunity Spaces" and Contestation

To a large extent, Islamic activism is best explained within the context of new social movement theory, which focuses on identity, beliefs, symbols, and values in the restructuring of everyday life (Melucci 1980, 1996; Calhoun 1995). New social movements involve personal and intimate contacts with others in an effort to create "networks of shared meaning" predicated upon alternative cultural codes and ways of living. The creation of these networks produces new shared identities and communities of agents connected through common understandings about norms of everyday life (in this volume, see Clark, chapter 6, and Wickham, chapter 9). Much of the work of new social movements is centered on meaning construction and emancipation from dominant cultural codes to sanction new ways of living (Okruhlik in this volume, chapter 10). Islamic movements, which do not uniformly seek an Islamic state, are agents of meaning production and offer an alternative set of norms to guide social interactions and individual behavior. Because Islamic movements consist of diverse, complex, and multisided Muslim agents with different goals and means by which they interact with, shape, and guide political and social action, this meaning production is an inherently contentious project.[Islamic groups challenge the hegemony of state-sponsored Islam, but they also experience intramovement differences over visions, goals, and tactics.]

New "opportunity spaces" can enhance such projects of transformation by providing previously inaccessible or limited social arenas for the transmission of values. Opportunity spaces are not merely new resources; they are fora of social interaction that create new possibilities for augmenting networks of shared meaning and associational life. Such arenas include political fora, electronic media and cyberspace, and the market. Opportunity spaces are also not simply mobilizing structures, since they adhere through social interactions and expressive space rather than formal or informal organizational structures. Within these spaces, new social movements can form shared identities, resist state hegemony, or change the meaning of everyday life, since these spaces free diverse voices and transform stocks of knowledge into a *project* and shared rules of cooperation and competition (Featherstone 1998). Moreover, because social movements "are 'acted out' in individual actions," opportunity spaces are central to an understanding of the transformation of everyday life (Johnston 1995, 7). In these spaces, not only is the distinction between the individual and collective action blurred, but the boundary between the public and private is constantly redrawn as well. Islamic social movements represent the "coming out" of private Muslim identity in the public spaces. It is not only a struggle for recognition of identity but also "going public" through private identities. In these opportunity spaces, identities and lifestyles are performed, contested, and implemented.

In Turkey (as elsewhere), economic growth fueled by an export-driven market has led to the dynamism and proliferation of opportunity spaces as seen in the explosion of market-oriented vehicles for the dissemination of meaning, including "print-capital" magazines, newspapers, television channels, the Internet, and a private education system. These new opportunity spaces opened up new possibilities to Muslim actors in terms of having their own distinct voice and institutional networks in public discussions. They tied Islamic groups into broader cultural and political processes of social change and helped them form a new sociopolitical consciousness.

In Turkey, the privatization and pluralization of fashion, journalism, new tastes, architecture, and music through new market mechanisms have all allowed multiple Islamic voices to become public, thereby empowering economically and culturally excluded groups vis-à-vis the state. But because the Islamic movement comprises variegated groups with alternative interpretations of Islamic mores and self-interest, the effect of the economic reforms in terms of empowerment and goals is heterogeneous. Before detailing the differential impact of new opportunity spaces, it is necessary to first sketch a typology of Islamic groups.

A Typology of Islamic Social Movements

Kemalism is the top-down state-imposed political and cultural reform of Mustafa Kemal (1881–1938) to create a secular society and state (Gellner 1994). It was a crude imitation of the European experience and an attempt to institutionalize nationalism as a substitute for Islam (Göle 1996). The ruling Kemalist elite who worked within the framework of orientalism constructed Islam as irrational, traditional, precapitalist, and stagnant as compared with a civilized, rational, and modern Europe. As a result, since the 1920s, the Republican elite has aimed at Westernizing every aspect of social, cultural, and political life to create a secular and national Republican space with a Westernized identity (see Rustow 1957; Berkes 1998). In spite of the state-led secularization policy, Islam, for this segmented society, has still offered a set of rules for regulating and constituting everyday life. Given the ongoing struggle between a militantly antireligious state elite and ideology and the majority of society, which never has broken fully from its Ottoman Islamic heritage, Islam continues to serve as a repertoire, a source of counterstatist discourse, and an organizational framework for social mobilization to deal with the stresses of development.

The centralization and interference of the state has politicized religion in a manner that is unprecedented and that has led many people to perceive Islam increasingly in the language of opposition. Thus, the large Sunni periphery embraced Islam as a way of challenging the policies of the center. This "oppositional Muslimness" of the periphery tried to develop a new language to counter Kemalist positivism and scienticism while concurrently opening a war against folk Islam by stressing the textual basis of Islam (the Qur'an and *hadith*, or recorded sayings of the prophet Muhammad). The concept of secular no longer denotes just the separation of state and religion. It has become almost a devotional creed and designation for the ruling elite. Thus the debate between Islamic activism and a secularist state is a debate about the boundary of state and society, top-down vs. bottom-up modernity, and the public and private. It is also a debate over the codes of everyday life.

The reforms of Mustafa Kemal aimed to create state-monitored public spaces to secularize and nationalize the society. The resulting opportunity spaces were limited and the repertoires of action have varied from rebellion to full withdrawal (intended to create inner spaces against the penetration of state power). This differentiation is based on each group's access to opportunity spaces, their goals, and group strategies to further expand these spaces to produce social change.

The goals of these social movements range from state-oriented to society-oriented changes, with strategies that may include legitimate (legal) and ille-

✳ ✳ Table 11.1. A Typology of Islamic Social Movements

		Repertoire of Action (Strategies and Means)	
		Legitimate	Illegitimate
G O A L S	**Vertical** Leninist state-centric elite-based vanguard movement from above	**Reformist** Participation in the hope of controlling the state or shaping policies through forming their own Islamic party or in alliance with other parties **Target:** Education, legal system, social welfare **Outcome:** Accommodation	**Revolutionary** Rejects the system and uses violence and intimidation **Target:** State **Outcome:** Confrontation
	Horizontal Society-centric associational identity-oriented from below	**Societal (Everyday Life-Based Movements)** Groups using the media and communications networks to develop discursive spaces for the construction of Islamic identity; seek to use the market to create heaven on earth; view Islam as cultural capital; use associational networks to empower community **Target:** Media, economy, (private) education **Outcome:** Integration	**Spiritual/Inward** Withdraws from political life to promote self-purification and self-consciousness **Target:** Religious consciousness **Outcome:** Withdrawal

gitimate (illegal) components. Although some social movements can be placed along a continuum, the classification suggested here offers four generic categories of Islamic movements. At one end is a state-oriented and elite-based vanguard movement from above that is more ideological and statist, and at the other end lies a society-centric, gradual, and reformative pragmatic movement. This classification is diagrammed in table 11.1.

These four generic categories help us disaggregate Islamic movements at the national and global level. While society-oriented movements seek to further expand opportunity spaces and integrate political society into civil society, state-oriented movements conversely seek to integrate and subordinate civil society into political society. The latter movements aspire to negate particular interests and identities within Islam to achieve an idealized unity.

Categories improve our understanding of how different movement groups or tendencies are affected by the emergence of new opportunity spaces and the possible consequences for the movement as a whole.

State-Oriented Islamic Movements

State-oriented vertical Islamic movements tend to be authoritarian and elitist in terms of decision-making. Such movements believe that the ills of society can be cured by the control of the state and its enforcement of a uniform and homogenizing religious ideology. These movements are more likely to form either when the state is too oppressive or when it is in the process of opening new opportunity spaces (Hafez, chapter 1 in this volume).

Those who seek state-imposed change from above stand on the vertical level of our model of socioreligious movements. Such movements consist of people who dogmatically follow Islamist precepts and perceive both religion and nationalism as belonging within the framework of the state. They seek total transformation of society by means of the state, and the degree of change sought is cataclysmic. The goal of replacing the state or, at the very least, providing a substitute for it, means that this becomes the locus for the production of popular identity. The goal of forging a standardized modern religious identity requires a leader to determine the definitive set of dogma and practices. Thus dialogue (*muhabbet*) or deliberation are problematic for state-oriented Islamic movements and may cause corrosion within the movements.

As intimated, another defining feature of a state-oriented, vertical Islamic movement is that in seeking to accommodate itself to a hostile environment it has attempted to assimilate the external world into its own religious dogma. The resulting identity is characterized by textual uniformity and a desire for homogeneity. The movement perceives diversity and differences generated by market forces, emerging discursive spaces, and technology as a threat to its faith in unity.

We can divide state-oriented Islamic movements into two subsections based upon their strategies and means of accessing power and shaping society. (1) *Revolutionary* Islamic movements reject the legitimacy of the prevailing political system and use violence as their means of accessing power, usually because all other avenues are blocked by the establishment (Rapoport 1993). Some Islamic groups treat violence as a means to create opportunity spaces, while others seek a complete overthrow of the current sociopolitical system. The purpose of violence is to establish the Islamic state and apply Islamic law. (2) *Reformist* Islamic movements participate in the political processes (as political opportunity space) currently available to them in the hope of gaining control of the state or shaping state policy; such movements take the form of Islamic political parties or alliances with other parties. In keeping with their ideological and social priorities, their main focus is on matters within the spheres of education, law, and the welfare program.

Society-Oriented Islamic Movements

Society-oriented Islamic movements seek to transform society from within by utilizing new societal opportunity spaces in the market, education, and media to change individual habits and social relations. In terms of strategies and means, there are two distinct subhorizontal movements. (1) *Everyday life-based* movements are concerned with influencing society and individuals and use both modern and traditional communications networks to develop new arguments for the construction of newly imagined identities and worldviews. Since societal movements target the media, the economy, and the information industry, they favor active participation in all facets of life. (2) *Inward-oriented contemplative* movements seek to withdraw within their own private realm in order to disengage, or exit, from what are viewed as illegitimate sociopolitical systems. These movements focus on individuals as the object of change through cultivating the inner self as the inner space in order to construct a reinvigorated Islamic consciousness along very traditional lines. Passive resistance is the major characteristic of the inward-oriented Islamic movement. Muslim activists seek to raise social consciousness by deeply involving religious rituals of praying, fasting, reading the Qur'an, and giving alms to the poor and needy. Through the repertoire of pious activism, believers achieve personal transformation and construct a shared moral discourse to critique power relations. For instance, the Nur faith movement and Sufi orders believe that if individuals are redeemed, a larger societal transformation will become possible (Mardin 1989). Thus, personal redemption is seen as the key to societal change. This inner and micro-level mobilization attracted those who are looking for enriching and satisfying emotional experiences, some of which are produced during the collective rituals and meetings. One needs to see these social movements as moral protests against the introduction of a new identity and code of conduct. Emotions such as anger, shame, and outrage play an important role in inner mobilization. In the case of Turkey, the Naksibendi Sufi order has been the major institution for this inner mobilization (Özdalga 1999).

The Impact of Neo-Liberal Economic Policies on Opportunity Spaces

The "modernizing" Republic had full official control over education and telecommunication until the early 1990s. This enabled the state to organize and monitor the public sphere to ensure it was adhering to the official national (i.e., Turkish) and secular (i.e., European) identity. Moreover, the state used high tariffs to create a pro-statist secular, not necessarily national, bourgeoisie by implementing exclusivist policies against Armenian, Greek, and Jewish merchants who hitherto, with the aid of Western imperial powers, had dominated the trade of the Ottoman state. Although the formation of a culturally diverse bourgeoisie began in the late 1960s, the economic policies following the 1980 military coup, which were implemented by Turgut Özal, helped the crystallization and expansion of a countercultural bourgeoisie class with Anatolian roots (for more, see Sezal and Dağı 2001).

In the 1980s and 1990s, Özal's free market policies were supported by small-scale provincial businessmen and the petite bourgeoisie of the cities. This sector, which includes peddlers, dealers, builders, restaurant owners, small and mid-size industrialists, and food processors, receives no public funding and thus opposes state intervention in the economy in favor of economic liberalization. Muslim entrepreneurs, who were not dependent on state subsidies and who were concentrated in foreign exchange–earning export industries like food processing and textiles, were particularly well placed to prosper in this period. This economic elite funded many prominent new publications including the newspapers *Turkiye, Zaman,* and *Yeni Safak* and many national and regional TV stations. Ironically, the policy of economic liberalization in Turkey encouraged by the International Monetary Fund did not favor those sections of society that were well disposed toward Kemalism because of their long dependence on the privileges of the Republic's statist economic policies.

Özal's privatization policies provided an independent resource for the development of associational life, separate from the state, which enriched collective life and even stabilized governance by serving as a buffer between the state and the individual. Reforms expanded the boundaries not only of political society but also of civil society in order to reshape the identity and parameters of the Turkish state. The neo-liberal economic policies of Özal have created and enlarged the space in which people can establish new contractual ties and have incorporated a large segment of the population into economic and political spaces. Therefore, neo-liberalism, by creating gaps between the rich and poor and spaces between religious and secular groups, has led to a more pluralist society marked by differences rather than unity.

Özal replaced the statist and corporatist Kemalist developmental strategy with a new vision of free-market policies that supported his neo-populist coalition. The "losers" within the Islamic movement have suffered the dislocations of modernity and development without the attendant economic benefits and have maintained an authoritarian and socially rigid view of Islam, which favors a strong welfare state. The claims for social justice are made through the politics of identity. They are very suspicious of the relativism and mobility fostered by the market and modernity. The "winners" within the Islamic movement are Islamic groups tied to new businesses that used the marketplace to transmit a societal-centered understanding of transformation. Through the reproduction and commodification of Islamic symbols, these groups have effectively exploited the new opportunity spaces created by economic reform. Case studies based on detailed fieldwork in two neighborhoods in Istanbul exemplify the divergent effects of economic liberalization on groups within the Islamic movement in Turkey.

The Erzurumlular Neighborhood: Society-Centric Islamic Movement

The predominant Islamic social movement in Erzurumlular is market-based, associational, and print-oriented, and it stresses "difference" more than commonality. The movement seeks to expand autonomous spaces and integrate political society into civil society; it is mediatic and print-based and has undergone what I call "a process of pluralist-fragmentation." The fulcrum of Islamic social movement action shifted from a concern for large-scale societal change to narrower, more self-oriented goals of claiming and realizing individual and group identities.

The residents of the Erzurumlular neighborhood include Islamist merchants, industrialists, financiers, and academics. This quarter is dominated by the Nakşibendis and the Nurcu community of Fethullah Gülen, which is in banking (al-Baraka Türk and Asya Finance), media (AK-TV, Moral FM), textiles (Huzur Giyim, Aydinli, and Topbaş), and ceramic production. Korkut Özal, the brother of the late president Turgut Özal, is the head of the association of the private mosque Zahidiyye Cami. A number of leading textile producers with several businesses in the Central Asian republics live in this quarter. Some families are also active in the diamond and gold businesses. This well-integrated Muslim bourgeoisie community finds that it has little in common with the worldview of the impoverished Muslim neighborhood of Sultanbeyli (the other case study in this chapter).

One of the main reasons for the success of what I characterize as a society-centric Islamic movement, as illustrated by the Erzurumlular neighborhood, is the expansion of the economic opportunity spaces that resulted from Turkey's export-led trade policies. In the late 1980s and early 1990s, Özal's free market (liberal economic) policies were supported by small-scale merchants, small industrialists, and the new emerging textile industry in Anatolia. This sector of the economy was critical for the distribution lines of major companies, and it opposes state intervention in the economy because the state has always been on the side of the pro-Kemalist large industrialists who formed the TÜSİAD (the Association of Turkish Industrialists and Businessmen) in 1974. This new emerging sector finds Islamic ethics and networks to be the best means of generating public opinion against both the state and the big corporations that benefit from the high tariff measures.

[This new bourgeoisie used Nurcu reading circles and Sufi networks as social capital to overcome the problem of information, trust, reciprocity, and connection in the market environment.] In Turkey, Nakşibendi and Nurcu groups also function as business "clubs." The more personally valuable the services provided by "religious clubs," the greater the demand for religious affiliation and the more cogent the feeling of Islamic identity (Congleton 1995, 72).

This sector benefited from Islamic networking to consolidate its economic position and formed the MÜSİAD (Association of Independent Industrialists and Businessmen) in 1990 (Özel 1996; Buğra 1999). This marks a turning point in the history of Islamic movements and the economy in Turkey. The task of the MÜSİAD has been the construction of "Islamic ethics in the Spirit of Capitalism." They identified the market as the realm of "jihad" and have been seeking to dominate this competitive zone. MÜSİAD supports Turkey's full economic integration into the globalized economy, advocates free trade zones and less state intervention, and argues that the prophet Muhammad (himself a merchant renowned for his ethical virtues prior to undertaking his religious mission) built a market-based society in Medina (Tabakoğlu 1997). MÜSİAD has organized several international conferences to codify Islamic market ethics and publish books, including *Homo Islamicus*. In the MÜSİAD vision, *Homo Islamicus* is a replica of homo economicus (MÜSİAD 1994; Mert 2001). In other words, the Islamization of the economy, rather than Islamic economics, is, for the MÜSİAD, a way of translating cultural capital into economic capital. The economic sector within Islamic movements seeks to carve a space for itself to prepare for a major leap to economic hegemony within Turkey. In fact, MÜSİAD already has deep ties with the informal sector of the economy, which constitutes more than 30 percent of the Turkish economy.

As the market forces generated a material base, new modes of distinction emerged in the new opportunity spaces in art, literature, fashion, and food. Literature and music have been the main arena in which the competition takes place. The dwellers of the Erzurumlular quarter all have Sufi music in their homes, although Nakşibendi families tend to listen to Sufi music more than do Nurcu families. Moreover, Nakşibendi families tend to have more Ottoman-style furniture and artworks in their homes than do Nurcus. The people of this quarter criticize Arabesk music as being corrupt and un-Islamic, and the dominant culture of the neighborhood is a mix of Ottoman and Republican culture and symbols. The evolution of this quarter supports the theses of Ernest Gellner (1983) that modernity creates its own high culture, and that there is no high culture in Turkey outside an Islamic ethos. This emerging hierarchy of taste classifies Islamic groups and their respective positions in society.

With the formation of the new Anatolian bourgeoisie, consumption habits of religious groups transformed into bourgeoisie consumption patterns. New forces that seek to enter and control the center establish coalitions with forces of the periphery so that they can redefine power relations. The integration of religious groups into the consumer culture has several implications: religious identity is objectified through mass production of goods that signify Islamic images; modern spaces of media, education, market, and fashion are "Islamicized" through consumer patterns; and religious needs and obligations are transformed into modern commodities through restylization. For instance, one of the opportunity spaces is the Caprice Hotel, as a site where modernity intermingles with Islam and molds the conduct and expectation of Muslims in accordance with the consumer economy (Göle 2000). Although the hotel was opened in 1996, with 2,000 rooms, Fadil Akgündüz, the owner of the JetPa Corporation, bought it in 1997. Akgündüz is a culturally conservative, politically liberal, and economically free market–oriented person. Akgündüz, who is from a traditional Nurcu family, did not support the Islamic political party (Welfare Party of Necmettin Erbakan) but rather voted for the True Path Party of Tansu Çiller. The example of the Caprice Hotel represents the ability of new bourgeoisie to commodify Islamic values to carve a larger market space for their goods. The Hotel represents the internal secularization of Islam; that is, Islam has been commodified as a good in the market competition. This is not an act of "Islamic radicalism" but rather reconstitution of Islam in the spirit of modern leisure time. In order to create a clientele for himself, Akgündüz "Islamicized" the hotel by prohibiting alcohol and creating gender-segregated pools. According to the owner of the Caprice, "The name of alternative holiday is Caprice" (*Yeni Safak*, July 3, 1996). This very example illustrates that Islam has become a strategic tool for Turkey's rational business groups to translate Islam into a commodity. Some Islamists, who defend the welfare state system, sharply criticized the presentation of the Caprice Hotel as an "Islamic vacation site." Ali Bulaç, for instance, treated this case as the total dominance of neo-liberalism over Islamic values and a dangerous process (Bulaç 1996; Tasgetiren 1996).

New economic spaces lead not only to the Islamization of leisure but also to changes in fashion (Barbarosoğlu 1995). The owners of the textile chains Tekbir and Tesettür[1]—the latter means Islamic dress code—live in the Erzurumlular quarter and produce Islamic fashions as a consumer item for the religiously conservative segment of the Turkish population.[2] They meet the religious needs of this segment of Turkish society by redefining *tesettür* as a modern commodity that facilitates Muslim women's participation in modern spaces. When *tesettür* turned into a consumer item and was articulated through fashion shows to legitimize it as a modern and desirable form of dress, women's femininity was not negated but rather negotiated through yearly changes in varieties, colors, and models exhibited in heterogeneous forms. Moreover, *tesettür* fashions in the Erzurumlular quarter have become status symbols. The content of *tesettür* is thus modernized and consumed as a commodity. This, in turn, objectifies religious needs through commodification. In conversations with college students in this quarter, they all argued that modern *tesettür* enhances their participation and roles in public space without negating their religious identity.[3] In other words, new opportunity spaces like the market and fashion empowered religiously oriented women to negotiate their identity by uplifting "backward" identity through commodification. Consumerism and stylized modest-women fashion shows offer new avenues for Muslim women to express their earned status in modern life. The owners of the Tekbir and Tesettür companies informed me that there are two religious scholars who visit the production factory and inspect the various fashions on women to determine whether they are in accordance with the Islamic dress code.[4] The Nakşibendi owner of the chain argues that "religious scholars should help us to set the boundaries of Islam for new modern fashions."[5] The religious decree, *fatwa*, is issued by these scholars to validate modern styles of consumerism in accordance with their somewhat subtle understanding of Islamic teachings and way of life.[6]

Residents in the neighborhood see the state as a problem and societal initiative and the market as a cure to social ills. Islam, for them, is a network for social mobility and a way of solving the transaction costs of information and enforcement in the market. For example, Aydınlı textiles has one of the largest distribution networks in the country, and almost all of them are controlled by members of the Nakşibendi order. They are extremely critical of state intervention in the economy and education. They run their own well-equipped elementary and high schools and emphasize bilingual education in Turkish and English with a focus on science and computer training. The consistently high academic performance of graduates of these schools has led even many well-to-do "secular" parents to enroll their children in them. Their *jihad* focuses not on the state and politics but rather on civil society and the market. Like English Puritans of the seventeenth century, they view worldly success and hard work as a manifestation of divine grace. Esad Coşan (1938–2001), former shaykh of the Nakşibendi order, argues, "A good society is a just society which is based on a powerful economy where people have businesses and work to meet their needs. This powerful economy only could be based on a work and business ethic, and this ethics/morality only could be derived from Islam."[7] The core group of Nakşibendis is very much involved in the leading Turkish export industries of textiles and ceramics. They also naturally support Turkey's economic and political integration into the European Union.

The expanding influence of societally centered Islamic groups through new opportunity spaces did not go unnoticed by the regime. On February 28, 1997, the Turkish National Security Council, the country's most powerful decision-making body in which generals sit ex officio, openly moved into politics by ordering the government of Necmettin Erbakan to implement the 18-

measure plan. Measure number 14 calls on the government to monitor "finance organizations and companies under the control of religious groups" so that they are "prevented from becoming economic forces."[8] The Turkish Armed Forces declared Islamic movements to be "enemy number one" of the state and quickly forced the removal of the democratically elected Welfare Party–led coalition government. The army targeted 100 major companies whose only apparent sin was to be run by conservative Muslims. The army included the prominent Ülker biscuit company, İhlas corporation, and the Kombassan Conglomerate on its blacklist (Yavuz 2000). Despite economic openings and concomitant opportunity spaces, the state has still been trying to exclude the Muslim "presence" in the political, economic, and cultural spheres.

Sultanbeyli and the Islamic Political Parties: State-Centric Islamic Movement

The Islamic movement in the quarter of Sultanbeyli, founded in 1978, is state oriented, oral, populist, and party based, and it highlights particular village and sectarian identities as a social safety net at the expense of more cosmopolitan Muslim ones (Işik and Pinarcioğlu 2001). This movement seeks populist outcomes and struggles to integrate civil society into political society. Although self-declared Islamists preach that Muslims must negate particular interests and identities within a uniform "Islamic" framework, the more particularistic identities are used as instruments to further defend their interests. Sultanbeyli is also referred to by the establishment as "the Qum of Turkey." There are 87 mosques and only four (impoverished) high schools.[9] By referring to it as "Qum," state officials and journalists seek to indicate that it is politicized Islamism and radicalism.

The people of Sultanbeyli often are known as *pazarci*, or street vendors. If land occupation has been the main solution to the housing problem, street vending is the way to solve the employment question. These vendors constitute an illegal segment of Turkish society through their informal commerce and occupation of state land. However, a high degree of competition among these vendors in the Sultanbeyli market politicizes village or regional-based identities for the purpose of protecting turf. Moreover, the street vendors of Sultanbeyli use primordial loyalties to escape the control and regulation of the state. Since the streets are under the authority of the municipality, the people seek to cultivate their ties with the mayor's office. Regional and other forms of identity-based loyalties prevent any dominant institution from controlling or co-opting the people of Sultanbeyli. As a result, everyday interactions of exchanges and marriages are still dominated by regional village identities rather than Islamic ones.

Sultanbeyli is one of the fastest-growing shantytowns in Istanbul. It has limited sewage and plumbing, and its water and health-care facilities are very poor. There are ten state mosques and more informal small mosques (known as *mesjid*).

There are also 27 coffeehouses where there are always pictures of Orhan Gencebay and Mahsun Kirmizigül, prominent populist musicians. This popular music, which is referred to as "Arabesk" by state officials, is a hybrid genre. Because it is officially disapproved of by the state, it is used by subalterns to express feelings and resistance to the establishment (Tanrikorur 1998). The first-generation Arabesk music includes Turkish, Arabic, and European lyrics and rhythms (Stokes 1992; Tanrikorur 1998).[10] This music does not lead people to desperation and fatalism but rather resonates with the deepened self of the fragmented personality in an urban environment in flux. It constitutes emotional vocabulary to express the feelings and views of this urban subaltern community. Arabesk has become a vehicle for stirring social themes of corruption, displacement, and deprivation, functioning in much the same way as the blues and the music of the Grateful Dead in American society. Music has penetrated social institutions and minds in a way that was not possible by other means. Popular notions of justice and alienation are the main themes of Arabesk music, which was banned on state-owned TV and radio stations. It was only with Özal in 1986 that the state-owned television opened its channels for Arabesk music. Turgut Özal, in fact, was the first president to attend Arabesk concerts. This music challenged the Kemalist cultural establishment through a fusion of popular tradition and new market values. With the privatization of the media in 1988, Arabesk had access to a larger segment of the population.

Although most apartments lack a finished roof (people build as they accumulate income to complete the next floor), the images and consciousness of people in the neighborhood are more articulate and contemporary than their living conditions. They derive these images from global images transmitted to them through 45 national, 2 local, and many international television stations. American television and American-made movies or the lifestyle in rich neighborhoods of Istanbul shape their dreams. The people in Sultanbeyli are not fax or e-mail users, but they usually have a phone and one or two televisions, and they listen to the radio. They are a part of Turkey's expanding working class, fresh from the countryside and hungry for social change.

They collectively construct their homes without permits from municipal authorities, and the local Islamist party (Saadet Partisi) leadership dominates the construction networks. This network of home building on state land has created cohesive ties among the members, and there are several overlapping informal associations that regulate relations in this neighborhood.

At the intracommunal level, all residents seek to utilize their common "language" of Islam for communication and interaction and to build trust. They utilize Islamic idioms and institutions to develop survival strategies on a group basis and demand an exclusive social space where their sense of traditional morality is supposed to reign. Such moral economies claim to derive from utopian solutions of the Medina Charter as the basis of a just state–Islamic polity (Bulaç 1998).

People identify state policies as the source of their problem and are extremely skeptical about the equity of the market. They constantly refer to a common *hadith*, or saying of the Prophet: "Money is the trial (*fitna*) of my community." They have little confidence in the market system. They all stress that the prophet Muhammad was a just ruler and that the Islamic state was the just state which incorporated a high degree of social welfare for the less fortunate of society. In the case of Sultanbeyli, "Economic polarization and social marginalization, which seem to result from liberal restructuring in the periphery, give rise to concomitant separation and secession from the national ideal" (Keyder 1993, 12). Thus Islamic fundamentalism is a community-building movement seeking to prevent the negative ramifications of the market, which is identified with secularist immorality and callous Darwinian capitalist market ethics.

The people of Sultanbeyli, due to their class background, use Islam as a "resource" to challenge the state and empower themselves against the forces of the market economy. Their version of the Islamic state promises prosperity. They believe that the "Islamic state will distribute wealth whereas the Kemalist state is distributing poverty."[11] For the residents of Sultanbeyli, an Islamic state is a "just state" in which the basic needs of the poor are met by the state while providing opportunities for the social advancement of their children in the future.[12] They want the state to offer health care, proper education, and unemployment insurance and even to protect their family against pornography, which is rampant on Turkish channels and is viewed approvingly by some opposed to Islamic tradition as a symbol of modernity.

Islam, in Sultanbeyli, is thus a resource to mobilize the have-nots and to extract resources for their needs. The residents of Sultanbeyli have constructed Islam not just as a religion but more importantly as an oppositional identity. It articulates a language of social justice and identity. It is for these reasons that the residents are loyal supporters of the Islamic parties (FP of Reaci Kutan and the JDP of Tayyip Erdoğan) and find protection within the Felicity-dominated municipal government.[13] This neighborhood supported the Welfare/Virtue parties because they promised a double transformation: a political revolution to redefine national identity and an economic revolution to end exploitation and distributive injustice. The most critical factor in the strength of the JDP of Erdoğan, incarnated after the closure of the Virtue Party by the Constitutional Court in response to the wishes of the National

Security Council, are to be found in its discourse of identity and justice. The JDP seeks the creation of a strong state capable of providing welfare and socioeconomic justice. This is in sharp contrast to Erzurumlular, where inhabitants do not support any Islamic party. Residents of Erzurumlular overwhelmingly voted for Özal in the 1983 and 1987 general elections, and in the 1995 elections the center-right of Çiller and Yilmaz received over 70 percent of the vote in the neighborhood.

Conclusion

The possibility of new opportunity spaces does not inexorably produce movement empowerment and a unified surge of contention. In fact, these new opportunities may serve as a force of intramovement pluralization by creating alternative venues for the expression of self and identity, especially among new social movements. Greater access to new spaces creates the possibility for the entrance and enhancement of new movement voices, perspectives, and projects. Such a process, in turn, may actually lead to even greater movement differentiation, rather than the consolidation of a unified movement.

In Turkey, the new opportunity spaces offered by economic liberalization have created greater opportunities for the construction of a new Muslim identity independent of state control over religion, which tended to privatize it in Kemalist fashion. They have created an arena for making Muslim identity "public" through market mechanisms, new media, and other venues for meaning dissemination. But instead of using such an opportunity to unify and push for a single Islamist project, the expression of Muslim identity has led to the proliferation of competing Islamic projects and the decentralization, in market fashion, of understandings about Muslim cultural codes.

In addition, by disaggregating the Islamic movement in Turkey, this chapter has attempted to show how the new opportunity spaces of economic liberalization divergently affected Islamic groups. Economic reform tended to empower society-centered Islamic movements, rather than state-centered groups, and produced myriad vehicles for the transmission of values, identities, and meaning in everyday life. Rather than giving rise to an emancipated Islamic movement capable of undermining the regime through a coordinated counterhegemonic project, the new opportunity spaces actually accentuated intramovement differentiation, leading to a certain degree of fragmentation.

While social movement theory has long recognized that movements are constituted by a number of oftentimes conflicting groups, the relationships among various social movement groups and movement processes remain undertheorized. There is broad recognition that movements compete over resources (Zald and McCarthy 1987, 161) and engage in "framing contests" (Benford 1993), but more work needs to be done to discern how intramovement differences relate to shifting opportunity structures, micromobilization contexts, recruitment processes, movement success, and other relevant movement issues. By examining the ways in which new opportunity spaces impacted different groups within the Islamic movement in Turkey, this chapter has attempted to encourage a step in this direction.

Notes

This essay emerged out of my research while I was a visiting Rockefeller Fellow at the Kroc Institute of the University of Notre Dame. I thank the Institute for its support and Charles Kuzman, Quintan Wiktorowicz, Paul Lubeck, and Reşat Kasaba for their comments.

1. Mustafa Karaduman owns the largest Islamic-style clothing chain, Tekbir Giyim (which means Allah is Great apparel). Karaduman's chain includes 600 stores throughout Turkey and in Sarajevo, Berlin, and Sydney. See Zaman (1999).

2. "Pijama değil, tesettür mayosu," *Milliyet*, May 9, 2001. This news item examines the new swimming bikini fashion show in Istanbul.

3. Interview with a group of female students on April 23, 1995, and May 10–12, 1996, in Istanbul.

4. Interview with the owners of these magazines on May 10, 1996, in Istanbul. I also visited the textile production shop in Kurtköy, Istanbul.

5. Interview on May 10, 1996, in Istanbul.

6. Some Islamic groups sharply criticized this consumerization of *tesettür*. See Özcan (1994), Sever (1994), Saraçgil (1998), and Alpay (1994).

7. Interview with Esad Coşan, April 24, 1996, in Istanbul.

8. For the recommendations of the National Security Council, see *Turkish Daily News*, March 3, 1997.

9. "İstanbul'da İslam Cumhuriyeti," *Milliyet*, May 29, 2001. Qum is a city in Iran where many religious seminaries are located.

10. When Ferdi Tayfur sings "Re-create Me, My Lord" (*Tanrim beni baştan yarat*) and "Let the World Sink Down" (*Batsin bu dünya*), music constitutes a new communication among listeners, telling them they belong to a larger identity of "strangers." In the 1960s and 1970s, the best-sellers were "Comfort Me" (*Bir teselli ver*), "This Is What I Am" (*Ben buyum*), "Let Them Say" (*Desinler bee*), and "You Are in Love, My Friend!" (*Sen aşiksin arkadaş*). The beats of these songs genuinely attempted to reflect the pain and hardship of modernization, as experienced by the vast and yet marginalized sectors of Turkey's nascent capitalist economy. These songs articulated the feeling newcomers had that they were "strangers" within their own country. When Orhan Gencebay, the star of Arabesk music, sings "You Are a Stranger" (*Yabancisin sen*), he not only expresses this alienation but also offers avenues for escape from it.

11. Interview on December 12, 1996, in Sultanbeyli, Istanbul.

12. Interviews on May 23, 1996, and October 12, 2000, in Sultanbeyli, Istanbul.

13. Although political Islam is spread out from the center-right parties, the dominant force representing political Islam is the National Outlook Movement of Necmettin Erbakan (NOM: *Milli Görüş Hareketi*), which after being closed down formed,

in succession, the National Order, National Salvation, the Welfare, and the Virtue. The movement spilled into the Felicity Party and Justice and Development Party of Tayyip Erdoğan in 2001.

Works Cited

Alpay, Kenan. 1994. "Islami Mesajli Tüketim Kültürü mü? Veya Islamci Beymen Status 'Elif Kadin.'" *Hak Söz* 39 (June): 55–56.

Barbarosoğlu, Fatma Karabiyik. 1995. *Modernleşme Sürecinde Moda ve Zihniyet*. Istanbul: İz Yayıncılık.

Benford, Robert D. 1993. "Frame Disputes within the Disarmament Movement." *Social Forces* 71: 677–701.

Berkes, Niyazi. 1998. *The Development of Secularism in Turkey*. 2d ed. New York: Routledge.

Buğra, Ayşe. 1999. *Islam in Economic Organizations*. Istanbul: TESEV.

Bulaç, Ali. 1996. "Dinlenmek ve tatil kültürünü tüketmek." *Yeni Safak*, July 3.

———. 1998. "The Medina Document." Translated by Duygu Koksal and Betigul Ercan. Pp. 169–78 in *Liberal Islam: A Sourcebook*, ed. Charles Kurzman. New York: Oxford University Press.

Calhoun, Craig. 1995. "'New Social Movements' of the Early Nineteenth Century." Pp. 173–215 in *Repertoires and Cycles of Collective Action*, ed. Mark Traugott. Durham, N.C.: Duke University Press.

Congleton, Roger D. 1995. "Ethnic Clubs, Ethnic Conflict, and the Rise of Ethnic Nationalism." Pp. 71–97 in *Nationalism and Rationalism*, ed. A. Breton et al. New York: Cambridge University Press.

Featherstone, Mike. 1998. *Undoing Culture: Globalization, Postmodernism, and Identity*. London: Sage.

Gellner, Ernest. 1983. *Muslim Society*. Cambridge: Cambridge University Press.

———. 1994. "Kemalism." Pp. 81–91 in *Encounters with Nationalism*. Oxford: Blackwell.

Göle, Nilüfer. 1996. *The Forbidden Modern: Civilization and Veiling*. Ann Arbor: University of Michigan Press.

———. 2000. "Snapshots of Islamic Modernities." *Daedalus* 129: 91–118.

Işik, Oğuz, and M. Melih Pinarcioğlu. 2001. *Nöbetleşe Yoksulluk: Sultanbeyli Örneği*. Istanbul: Iletişim.

Johnston, Hank, Enrique Laraña, and Joseph R. Gusfield. 1995. "Identities, Grievances, and New Social Movements." Pp. 3–35 in *New Social Movements: From Ideology to Identity*, ed. Enrique Laraña, Hank Johnston, and Joseph R. Gusfield. Philadelphia: Temple University Press.

Keyder, Cağlar. 1993. "The Rise and Decline of National Economies on the Periphery." *Review of Middle East Studies* 6: 6–23.

Mardin, Şerif. 1989. *Religion and Social Change in Modern Turkey: The Case of Bediüzzaman Said Nursi*. Albany: SUNY Press.

Melucci, Alberto. 1980. "The New Social Movements: A Theoretical Approach." *Social Science Information* 19: 99–226.

———. 1996. *Challenging Codes: Collective Action in the Information Age.* Cambridge: Cambridge University Press.

Mert, Nuray. 2001. "MÜSİAD Müslümanliği." *Radikal,* October 20.

MÜSİAD. 1994. *İş Hayatinda Islam Insani (Homo Islamicus).* Istanbul: MÜSİAD.

Özcan, I. Faruk. 1994. "Tesettür Modasi ve Ulema." *Hak Söz* 39 (June): 56–57.

Özdalga, Elisabeth. 1999. *The Naqshbandis in Western and Central Asia.* London: Curzon Press.

Özel, Mustafa. 1996. "Changing Economic Perspectives in Contemporary Turkey." *Islamic World Report* 3: 87–93.

Rapoport, David C. 1993. "Comparing Militant Fundamentalist Movements and Groups." Pp. 429–61 in *Fundamentalisms and the State,* ed. Martin E. Marty and R. Scott Appleby. Chicago: University of Chicago Press.

Rustow, Dankwart A. 1957. "Politics and Islam in Turkey, 1920–55." Pp. 69–107 in *Islam and the West,* ed. Richard Frye. The Hague: Mouton.

Saraçgil, B. 1998. "Islami Giyimde Moda ve Tüketim." *Yeni Zemin* 8.

Sever, Martin. 1994. "Elhamdüllilah Tüketiyorlar." *Nokta* 12 (May 1–7): 34–38.

Sezal, Ihsan, and Ihsan Daği. 2001. *Kim bu Özal?: siyaset, iktisat ve zihniyet.* Istanbul: Boyut.

Stokes, Martin. 1992. *The Arabesk Debate: Music and Musicians in Modern Turkey.* Oxford: Oxford University Press.

Tabakoğlu, Ahmet. 1997. "Islam Iktisadinda Işçi-Işveren Münasebetleri." *Cevre* 5, 20 (October): 74–85.

Tanrikorur, Cinucen. 1998. *Musiki Kimliğimiz.* Istanbul: Ötüken Yayinlari.

Tasgetiren, Ahmet. 1996. "Kapris'ten Çeçenistan görünüyor mu?" *Yeni Safak,* August 16.

Yavuz, M. Hakan. 2000. "Cleansing Islam from the Public Sphere and the February 28 Process." *Journal of International Affairs* (Columbia University Press) 54, 1 (Fall): 21–42.

Zald, Mayer N., and John D. McCarthy. 1987. "Social Movement Industries: Competition and Conflict among SMOs." Pp. 161–84 in *Social Movements in an Organizational Society,* ed. Mayer N. Zald and John D. McCarthy. New Brunswick, N.J.: Transaction Books.

Zaman, Amberin. 1999. "Spreading Faith through Fashion: Turkish Chain Promotes Islamic Clothing." *Washington Post,* December 2.

Conclusion
Social Movement Theory
and Islamic Studies

Charles Kurzman

Over the past generation, the fields of social movement theory and Islamic studies have followed parallel trajectories, with few glances across the chasm that has separated them. This volume helps to bridge that chasm, offering insights from Islamic movements to contribute to social movement theory, and insights from social movement theory to assist the study of Islamic movements.

Parallels

In the 1970s, social movement theory and Islamic studies underwent parallel paradigmatic revolutions: social movement theory shunted aside collective behavior, and Islamic studies turned against Orientalism. The previously dominant perspectives, largely unchallenged for generations, shared a variety of features in common. Both had their origins in the entry of the masses into the political calculations of Western elites. In the case of collective behavior, the era of mass democracy spurred Gustave Le Bon, Robert E. Park, and other founders of the field to examine the mysteries of the new political actors. In the case of Orientalism, the era of imperialism spurred William Jones, Ernest Renan, and other major figures to explore the religion, culture, and history of the newly colonized peoples. Both fields adopted similar approaches to their subjects, emphasizing the grip that social forces had over them, although these forces were inverted in the two fields: the weight of tradition was said to bear down on Muslims, and the lack of tradition was said to make crowds susceptible to contagion. The subjects in both fields were often treated as irrational and in need of salvation through the gaze of the (presumably rational) scholar.[1]

Self-doubt appeared in collective behavior and Orientalism about the same time in the 1960s. Already in the 1950s, Ralph Turner and Lewis Killian, authors of the authoritative textbook on collective behavior, criticized the field's "often biased descriptions" and "the tendency to single out for study only those collective phenomena of which the observer disapproves" (1957, 12, 16)—but their goal in making these criticisms was to improve the field by making it more "scientific" and "objective." Similarly, Carl Couch (1968) urged the field to distance itself from derogatory stereotypes that littered earlier works. In Islamic studies, Anouar Abdel-Malek charged that the end of the colonial era had set Orientalism "in crisis." The field's institutionalization "dates essentially from the period of colonial establishment," with academic societies founded in Batavia in 1781, Paris in 1822, London in 1834, and the United States in 1842 (Abdel-Malek 1963, 104). Orientalist scholarship was "profoundly permeated" by the state's need "to gather intelligence information in the area to be occupied, to penetrate the consciousness of the people in order to better assure its enslavement to the European powers," with the result that "the scientific value of arduous work" was often "compromise[d]" (106). Now that the colonized regions had won their independence, Abdel-Malek concluded, Orientalism "had to be thought anew" (112; see also Hourani 1967; Issawi 1981). Similarly, A. L. Tibawi argued, "Gone are the days when Orientalists used to write largely for the benefit of other Orientalists." They have a large and growing readership in the Muslim world, and in "their present mood, after repeated polemic and missionary onslaughts against their faith, and prolonged Western political and cultural domination of their lands, the Muslims are more prone to take offense than ever before" (Tibawi 1963, 191–92). These critiques were offered from within the fold, explicitly cast as attempts to improve collective behavior and Orientalism, not to dismiss them.

By the 1970s, though, the fields of Orientalism and collective behavior were having difficulty reproducing themselves. The second edition of Turner and Killian's collective behavior textbook, published in 1972, vehemently rejected the pejorative biases in the field. At the same time, a series of works—Oberschall (1973), Gamson (1975), Tilly, Tilly, and Tilly (1975), McCarthy and Zald (1977), and Tilly (1978) being among the most influential—launched a direct assault on the premises of collective behavior. In Islamic studies, the 29th International Congress of Orientalists, held in Paris on the 100th anniversary of the first such meeting, voted to remove Orientalism from its name, replacing it with "Human Sciences in Asia and North Africa" (*Le XXIXe Congrès* 1975, 67). A series of works—Laroui (1973), Coury (1975), Naraghi (1977), el-Zein (1977), Djaït (1985), Turner (1978), Tibawi (1979), and most famously Said (1978)—rejected Orientalist premises. In the United States, Orientalism was displaced almost completely by Middle East "area studies," whose flagship organization (the Middle East Studies Association of North

America, founded in 1966) was later replicated throughout Western Europe (for ideologically polar, yet strikingly similar reviews of this transition, see Hajjar and Niva 1997; Kramer 2001). The field of Middle East studies viewed Orientalism as a noble relic: "The orientalists have achieved immense works of scholarship, and their attainments stand like the monuments of the ancients which induce awe in us even though our technology far exceeds theirs. . . . We are nearly all agreed now that we wish to study Islamic civilization as related to the living societies of the Middle East today. This goal leads us beyond the possibilities of Orientalism" (Binder 1976, 9–10).

Both paradigmatic revolutions were the work, in large part, of the subjects of study who had entered Western academia. In the United States, the long march of youthful activists through the universities (Jacoby 1987) was linked with a sea change in the study of social protest (Lofland 1993, 53), most concretely by Morris and Herring (1987, 182–84), who interviewed theorists about their experience with the movements of the 1960s. "When you are participating, you inevitably look at it from the standpoint of participants," said one social movement theorist. The collective behavior school struck him as "slightly insulting" and as "denigrating the motives of participants." "Since many social scientists sided with the activists and were debating issues of strategy and tactics, the irrationalist assumptions of the collective behavior approach seemed outmoded," wrote another social movement theorist who participated in the paradigm shift (Zald 1992, 331). Orientalism, too, was most vehemently attacked by "Orientals" whose training and careers had brought them to Western universities, where they found the dominant approach to be mismatched with their own experiences and values. In the words of one defender of Orientalism: "The accuser in this trial, needless to say, is now the East itself, which from a passive object of history and study has revived as a subject, which seeks with profound travail its own soul and does not recognize it in its past or present in the mirror of European orientalistic investigation" (Gabrieli 1965, 130).[2]

The shift from object to subject was central to the substance of both paradigmatic changes. In both collective behavior and Orientalism, the people being studied were deemed largely unaware of the forces governing their lives. In collective behavior this view expressed itself through analogies with herds of animals—most famously in Herbert Blumer (1939)—or natural processes like wildfires and avalanches—most famously in Elias Canetti (1963). In Orientalism this view took the form of blanket statements about Muslims' lack of interest in Islamic studies, such as Ernest Renan's comment in 1862 that "Islam is the complete negation of Europe; . . . Islam is the disdain of science, the suppression of civil society; it is the appalling simplicity of the Semitic spirit, restricting the human mind, closing it to all delicate ideas, to all refined sentiment, to all rational research, in order to keep it facing an eternal tautology: God is God" (quoted in Kurzman 1998, 3). Renan's successor at the Collège de France, Jacques Berques, suggested in 1957 that "in this period the Arabs neglect their own past, and stammer their noble language. Contemporary orientalism was born from this vacancy. The exploration, the resurrection of such moral treasures was the chance of the erudite Christian, who as well as the Christian of the Bank concurrently revived the wasted space and filled the warehouses" (quoted in Abdel-Malek 1963, 131). This supposed "vacancy" was the product of what Tavakoli-Targhi (1996) has called "Orientalism's genesis amnesia": the willful forgetting of Orientalists' dependence, especially in the early years, on the historical and philological work of their Muslim teachers.

The new perspectives, by contrast, emphasized the subjects' knowledge. For social movement theory, this expressed itself in rational-actor models, with protesters treated as cost-benefit calculators and utility maximizers with the same level of sophistication as anybody else. The application of resources to collective ends, the response of protesters to the opening of political opportunities, and the development of persuasive ideological frames—major themes in the new approach—all expressed this view of the subject as knowledgeably strategic. Islamic studies did not elaborate a new consensus as self-consciously as social movement theory did. Yet post-Orientalist work shared social movement theory's respect for the perspective of the subject. It treated Islamic interpretation as an act of piety, meaning-making, and strategic advancement.

In both fields, the new perspectives treated their subjects as fundamentally similar to the observers. In answer to Ralph Coury's sarcastic query—mocking Orientalists for allegedly wondering, "Why can't they be more like us?" (Coury 1975)—both fields began emphasizing similarities and downplaying differences. The subjects did not always reciprocate. Some social movement activists were displeased to be cast as cost-benefit calculators, preferring instead the activist identity of self-sacrificing hero or martyr (e.g., Jasper 1997, chapter 8). In the same vein, some Muslims preferred the Orientalist image of Islam to the post-Orientalist image, viewing their religion as monolithic and unchanging, austere and authoritarian—not socially constructed and potentially liberal (Tibi 1990).

The collective behavior school more or less politely incorporated the new approach. The third edition of Turner and Killian's textbook on collective behavior couched crowd processes within a structural analysis of political opportunities and resource mobilization. The final chapter of the book, which in previous editions had examined the effects of collective behavior on social structures, reversed this formulation in the third edition to examine "the conditions of social structure that are most conducive to collective behavior" (Turner and Killian 1987, 388). Similarly, Neil Smelser, author of a major work on collective behavior (Smelser 1962) that is rarely cited in social movement theory—even the portions that discussed political opportunities (under

the rubric of "social control"), a topic of central interest to the new approach
—simply combined collective behavior and social movement theories in his
introductory sociology textbooks, with the implication that they are complements, not competitors (Smelser 1991, 365–86). In later work, Smelser allowed himself to express regret at the dismissal of the collective behavior
school by social movement scholar-partisans who failed to appreciate the reforms he had tried to achieve in the field, and who attributed bias—"real or
imagined"—to scholars such as himself who had tried to "maintain a posture
of neutrality and dispassion" (Smelser 1997, 41–44).

Orientalism died a harder death. Bernard Lewis, the dean of American
Orientalism, fulminated angrily against the new turn in Islamic studies.
Said's famous book *Orientalism* was so wrongheaded that it struck him as "one
of those alternative universes beloved of science fiction writers." In the paradigm shift that followed, "the term 'Orientalism' has been emptied of its previous content and given an entirely new one—that of unsympathetic or hostile
treatment of Oriental peoples. For that matter, even the terms 'unsympathetic' and 'hostile' have been redefined to mean not supportive of currently
fashionable creeds or causes" (Lewis 1993, 109, 100). Among the fashionable
creeds that Lewis objected to was the "taboo" against "generalizations about
ethnic, racial or religious groups": "We live in an age when ethnic generalizations of any kind are tantamount to blasphemy—or rather have supplanted
blasphemy as the ultimate unspeakable offense, in the most literal sense of
that word" (Lewis 2000, 3–4; see also Lewis 2002). Other Orientalists, while
less irate, were also troubled by the attack on Orientalism, which involved "a
certain danger," "was a bit Stalinist," and "had some unfortunate consequences," according to scholars of the earlier generation interviewed in a recent collection of life stories (Gallagher 1994, 41, 124, 144; see also the auto-
biographies in Naff 1993).

If Orientalists refused to go quietly into the dark night, anti-Orientalists
began to turn on one another. Not long after the publication of *Orientalism*,
supporters of Said's approach began to use it against Said himself, beginning perhaps with Al-ᶜAzm's (1981) charge that Said essentialized the West
much in the same way that Orientalism essentialized the Orient. The post-
Orientalist field has no name aside from the geographically delimited area
studies moniker "Middle East Studies," while the older term "Orientalist" is
now wielded as an epithet. I have sat in academic meetings where competing
scholars have insulted one another's perspectives as "Orientalist," just as leftists often call one another "reactionaries."

The Chasm

The two traditions exchanged few glances as the parallel trajectories of social
movement theory and Islamic studies unfurled on two sides of a chasm.[3] This

chasm is strange for at least two reasons. First, a number of major social scientists of this period had academic roots in the Islamic world, conducting formative empirical work on Muslim societies and later speaking to Western social theory in its broadest reaches, including Pierre Bourdieu (France), who studied Algeria; Ernest Gellner (Britain), who studied North Africa; and Clifford Geertz (United States), who studied Indonesia and Morocco. Yet the influence of these scholars in Western social science seems to have been dissociated from their fieldwork in Islamic lands. Second, just at the moment when the new paradigms were consolidating their positions, the Iranian Revolution brought Islamic social movements to international prominence, spawning a large academic literature and Western policy interest. Yet neither Bourdieu et al. nor the Iranian Revolution prompted a commingling of social movement studies and Islamic studies.

Leading figures in social movement studies have acknowledged in recent years that a "core democracy bias" may have limited the scope conditions of the theory, since so few studies were conducted on movements outside of North America and Western Europe (McAdam, McCarthy, and Zald 1996, xiii; McAdam, Tarrow, and Tilly 1997, 143). A further bias may be implicated in the tendency of social movement scholars to study movements with which they sympathize, a pattern that would seem to be linked with the field's biographical roots in the social movements of the 1960s. There are a handful of exceptions, including studies of the religious right in North America. Yet social movement theory has largely been generated in conversation with movements that scholars support. It may be harder to apply contemporary social movement approaches—the rationality of protesters, for example—to protesters who appear to be, and claim to be, so different from the secular, Western, liberal-left norms that social movement theorists generally espouse. The absence of Islamic movements was particularly egregious in one book on world-system theory and the study of anti-systemic movements, which managed to overlook Islamic movements almost entirely—though these were arguably the most active anti-systemic movements in the world, then and now (Arrighi, Hopkins, and Wallerstein 1989).[4]

Yet on the few occasions when social movement theorists did glance across the chasm at Islamic movements, they did so to emphasize difference, focusing on Islamic ideas and critiquing social movement theory for ignoring ideology (e.g., Snow and Marshall 1984). The most famous instance involved sociologist Theda Skocpol, whose book on *States and Social Revolutions* (1979) dismissed the importance of revolutionaries in favor of structural explanations, particularly state collapse. In a reversal several years later, Skocpol (1982) argued that her theory did not apply to the Iranian Revolution, where ideology and purposive action played a larger role than in the revolutions she had studied (France, Russia, and China). It was only in the 1990s that the Iranian Revolution was incorporated into the broader field of social movement studies (see essays in Foran 1997; Goldstone, Gurr, and Moshiri 1991; Smith 1996).

From the other direction, too, Iran specialists were slow to join contemporary social movement discourse. They turned instead to older approaches, if they looked across the chasm at all. Some adopted "relative deprivation" approaches (protest ensues when rising expectations are dashed) (among others, Saikal 1980, 187; Keddie 1983, 589–91; Benard and Khalilzad 1984, 53–58). Others went ever further back to the "natural history" approach to revolution, citing Crane Brinton's (1965) schematic outline of the stages of revolution, which was first published in the 1930s (among others, Fischer 1980, 189; Bill 1982, 30; Sick 1985, 187). Said Arjomand (1988, 110) preferred "old-fashioned [Emile] Durkheim" and his theory of normative disorientation from the turn of the twentieth century.

A new generation of Iran specialists, entering graduate school after the revolution, effected a rapprochement. In the decade after 1979, three dozen doctoral dissertations were produced in North America on the Iranian Revolution, many of them drawing on the most recent approaches in social movement theory. This second wave of studies on the Iranian Revolution began to draw on and contribute to social movement studies (among others, Moshiri 1985; Milani 1988; Moaddel 1992, 1993; Kurzman 1994, 1996).

It took another decade for this rapprochement to diffuse beyond Iran. Saad Eddin Ibrahim's foundational article on the Islamist movement in Egypt made no mention of contemporary social movement theory, though it drew parallel conclusions, critiquing earlier social-psychological explanations for presuming that protesters "must be alienated, marginal, anomic, or must possess some other abnormal characteristic" (Ibrahim 1980, 440). Later studies paralleled the social movement focus on the institutional bases of protest (Eickelman 1987) and framing (Burke 1986, 1988, citing the "moral economy" literature), while ignoring social movement studies. Only at the turn of the millennium did scholars studying Islamic movements outside Iran begin to look across the chasm at contemporary social movement theory. Four colloquia were held on this theme in 1999–2000—one each at the University of California at Santa Cruz, New York University, the University of Lausanne, and the Middle East Studies Association meeting in Orlando, Florida—and a number of publications emerged (among others, Vergès 1997; Lubeck 2000; Wiktorowicz 2001, 2003; Wickham 2002; Bennani-Chraïbi and Fillieule 2002; Clark 2003; and the chapters in this volume).

Contributions

In this section, I wish to propose several contributions that the study of Islamic movements may offer social movement studies, with a focus on the relationship of the observer and the observed. First, post-Orientalist discourse involves a level of reflexivity that other social movement scholars can generally avoid, a "rigorous self-examination that would do a puritan proud, or a strictly observant Sufi" (Krämer 2000, 6). The critique of Orientalism means a critique of Western treatment of Muslims, both politically (colonialism, imperialism, neo-imperialism) and cognitively (derogatory, essentializing, stereotyping). At the same time, studies of Islamic movements are themselves written from a Western standpoint, even when the authors are Muslims—that is, they only "count" as "studies of Islamic movements" if they have the trappings of Western academic discourse, which includes a commitment to the Western project of understanding social movements. This double position, Western and anti-Western, generates anxieties that are frequently near the surface. As Edmund Burke notes, it is "perilous to advance an explication of the so-called Islamic revival without reproducing the concerns of the ambient political culture of our own society, with its deeply grounded fears and phantasms about Islam. The discourse on the Other, especially the Muslim Other, is politically saturated" (Burke 1988, 18). Many scholars worry that their contribution to the understanding of Islamic movements will be misunderstood —or worse, understood—by a hostile audience that includes policymakers who see all Islamic movements as an undifferentiated threat that needs to be undermined. Specialists on Islamic movements seem to be more routinely consulted by U.S. and other governmental officials than specialists on other sorts of social movements. (I have no data on this, but such stories are prevalent at Middle East Studies Association conferences and only occasionally mentioned at American Sociological Association meetings.) If studies of Islamic movements are not intended to contribute to the project of "knowing thine enemy," then what is their purpose? Whatever each scholar's answer to this question may be, the question itself generates more reflexivity than in other studies of social movements.

Second, these studies frequently acknowledge the difficult combination of likeness and difference that complicates the relationship of the observer and the observed. Value congruence cannot be assumed, since the observers of Islamic movements rarely share the full set of goals that the movements aspire to achieve, such as the adoption of certain behaviors as markers of piety (as they interpret it) or the implementation of an Islamic state (as they envision it). The field holds itself in tension, unable to deny the obvious cultural differences between Islamic activists and Western scholars, yet unwilling to claim irreducible difference for fear of falling into Orientalist patterns. Between these poles, emphases could vary, with some observers, such as Paul Rabinow (1977, 162), emphasizing difference: "Different webs of significance separated us [his subjects and himself], but these webs were now at least partially intertwined. But a dialogue was only possible when we recognized our differences, when we remained critically loyal to the symbols which our traditions had given us." Others, such as Gregory Starrett (1998, 246–47), emphasized similarity: "If we treat Islamism as a pathology, the result of the faulty operation of modern institutions rather than of the potentials and contradictions inherent within them, we can continue to believe that our own personal, religious and political convictions are, by contrast, consistent, coherent, and grounded in truth and reason, rather than desperate practical refuges always on the verge of crisis and change." A series of post-Orientalist works have looked beyond Islamic exceptionalism to examine common patterns in Islam and other faith traditions, such as Talal Asad's (1993) study of the emergence of modern religion in Islam and Christianity; Roxanne Euben's (1999) juxtaposition of Islamic and Christian critiques of modernity; and several projects that place Islamic fundamentalist movements in the context of other fundamentalist movements (Marty and Appleby 1991–1995; Juergensmeyer 1993; Lawrence 1995). In this volume, many of the chapters emphasize the similarities between Islamic and other social movements. Whatever the emphasis, the issue is never neatly resolved.

Third, studies of Islamic movements cannot presume that the people they study will respond to macro structures in the same way that Western researchers would. The problematic value congruence between researcher and researched means that political opportunities, mobilization structures, and other factors common to social movement studies cannot be translated automatically from one context to another. A response that seems commonsensical to the observer—say, reducing one's exposure to risk as repression increases—may not seem commonsensical to the activist. This is not to suggest that the usual tools of social movement studies are useless, or that Islamic activists are all irrational or seeking martyrdom. The upshot, rather, is that such matters are open for empirical research. Value congruence can hide this from view by making the subjects' preference structures seem transparent. Researchers who identify with their subjects can look straight through their eyes to focus on shifts in macro structures. In Islamic studies, the eyes of the subjects and the researchers don't line up, so the subject's perspective must be addressed.

The subject's perspective is thus frequently a topic of analysis in this volume. Some essays ask to what extent Islamist activists respond to cues such as shifts in the political economy (Fred Lawson, Benjamin Smith); some examine Islamists' understandings of political opportunities and their moves to make the most of the spaces available to them (Mohammad Hafez, Hakan Yavuz); some study the calculations that shape the decision to engage in violence (Mohammad Hafez and Quintan Wiktorowicz, Glenn Robinson), construct networks and alliances (Jillian Schwedler, Diane Singerman), or engage cultural contexts for movement purposes (Gwenn Okruhlik, Carrie Wickham). Most of these studies offer a punch line of universalism. Islamic

activists, in these accounts, are not wild-eyed fanatics with preference structures that are completely different from those of Western activists, but rather
rational actors who respond to stimuli and create social movements much in
the same way as others around the world. Still, these studies cannot, and do
not, assume universalism. The extent to which Islamic activists conform to
the theoretical expectations of social movement studies is an empirical matter.

Such empiricism is often difficult to come by. Islamic activists have been
driven underground in many Muslim societies by authoritarian states, supported by the governments of the United States and Western Europe. These
activists are frequently hostile to Western analysts, sometimes for their generally secular worldview, more often because they are suspected of serving the
interests of their governments. The contributors to this volume are among the
few academics who have actually interviewed Islamic activists and observed
their meetings. This sort of research takes considerable fieldwork skills, which
may be why it is not performed more frequently. Yet the payoff is irreplace-
able. By interacting with Islamic activists, we begin to become familiar with
their perspectives. By learning their perspectives, we may understand how
they engage and restructure the institutions around them. Through this understanding, we may bridge the chasm that has separated Islamic studies and
social movement theory.

Notes

1. The origins of the collective behavior school have been studied in detail by
historians (Barrows 1981; McClelland 1989; Nye 1975). Orientalism, by contrast, has
not yet been subjected to the same sort of scrutiny; its historians have tended to be
its polemical critics.

2. The top leaders in this revolt were not so much subjects as supporters who
identified with the subjects: young professors (such as Gamson, Oberschall, and
Tilly) rather than student activists, Arab Christians (such as Abdel-Malek and Said)
rather than Muslims. This situation might be considered "curious" (Lewis 1993,
106), but—if we liken paradigmatic revolutions to the political uprisings studied in
social movement theory—the mobilization of allies within the "polity" (in this case,
academia) may be considered a crucial aspect of the revolt's success.

3. A similar chasm exists between the fields of history and Islamic studies (Tucker
1990, 210; Gelvin 2001).

4. Other world-systems approaches, I should note, took somewhat greater notice
of Islamic movements. Boswell (1989), for example, included three chapters on the
Iranian Revolution, and a 1999 collection of world-systems approaches to *The Future
of Global Conflict* noted that "a revitalized Islamic fundamentalist model could, on
ideological grounds, be a basis for a potential future counter-core. But this is not
likely to be a serious challenger to capitalist neo-liberalism for global hegemony"
(Bornschier and Chase-Dunn 1999, 7).

Works Cited

Abdel-Malek, Anouar. 1963. "Orientalism in Crisis." *Diogenes* 44: 103–40.

Arjomand, Said Amir. 1988. *The Turban for the Crown: The Islamic Revolution in Iran.* New York: Oxford University Press.

Arrighi, Giovanni, Terence K. Hopkins, and Immanuel Wallerstein. 1989. *Antisystemic Movements.* London: Verso.

Asad, Talal. 1993. *Genealogies of Religion: Discipline and Reasons of Power in Christianity and Islam.* Baltimore: Johns Hopkins University Press.

Al-ᶜAzm, Sadik Jalal. 1981. "Orientalism and Orientalism in Reverse." *Khamsin* 8: 5–26.

Barrows, Susanna. 1981. *Distorting Mirrors: Visions of the Crowd in Late Nineteenth-Century France.* New Haven: Yale University Press.

Benard, Cheryl, and Zalmay Khalilzad. 1984. *"The Government of God": Iran's Islamic Republic.* New York: Columbia University Press.

Bennani-Chraïbi, Mounia, and Olivier Fillieule, eds. 2002. *Les mouvements sociaux dans le monde musulman.* Paris: Karthala.

Bill, James A. 1982. "Power and Religion in Revolutionary Iran." *Middle East Journal* 36: 22–47.

Binder, Leonard. 1976. "Area Studies: A Critical Reassessment." Pp. 1–28 in *The Study of the Middle East: Research and Scholarship in the Humanities and the Social Sciences,* ed. Leonard Bonder. New York: Wiley.

Blumer, Herbert. 1939. "Collective Behavior." Pp. 221–80 in *An Outline of the Principles of Sociology,* ed. Robert E. Park. New York: Barnes and Noble.

Bornschier, Volker, and Christopher Chase-Dunn, eds. 1999. *The Future of Global Conflict.* London: Sage.

Boswell, Terry, ed. 1989. *Revolution in the World-System.* New York: Greenwood.

Brinton, Crane. [1938] 1965. *The Anatomy of Revolution.* Rev. cd. New York: Vintage.

Burke, Edmund, III. 1986. "Understanding Arab Social Movements." *Arab Studies Quarterly* 8: 333–45.

———. 1988. "Islam and Social Movements: Methodological Reflections." Pp. 17–35 in *Islam, Politics, and Social Movements,* ed. Edmund Burke III and Ira M. Lapidus. Berkeley: University of California Press.

Canetti, Elias. 1963. *Crowds and Power.* Translated by Carol Stewart. New York: Viking.

Clark, Janine. 2003. *Faith, Networks, and Charity: Islamic Social Welfare Activism and the Middle Class in Egypt, Yemen, and Jordan.* Bloomington: Indiana University Press.

Couch, Carl L. 1968. "Collective Behavior: An Examination of Some Stereotypes." *Social Problems* 15, 3: 310–22.

Coury, Ralph. 1975. "Why Can't They Be Like Us?" *Review of Middle East Studies* 1: 113–33.

Djaït, Hichem. 1985. *Europe and Islam.* Translated by Peter Heinegg. Berkeley: University of California Press.

Eickelman, Dale. 1987. "Changing Interpretation of Islamic Movements." Pp. 13–30 in *Islam and the Political Economy of Meaning,* ed. William R. Roff. London: Croom Helm.

Euben, Roxanne L. 1999. *Enemy in the Mirror: Islamic Fundamentalism and the Limits of Modern Rationalism—A Work of Comparative Political Theory.* Princeton, N.J.: Princeton University Press.

Fischer, Michael M. J. 1980. *Iran: From Religious Dispute to Revolution.* Cambridge: Harvard University Press.

Foran, John, ed. 1997. *Theorizing Revolutions.* London: Routledge.

Gabrieli, Francesco. 1965. "Apology for Orientalism." *Diogenes* 50: 128–36.

Gallagher, Nancy Elizabeth, ed. 1994. *Approaches to the History of the Middle East: Interviews with Leading Middle East Historians.* Reading, U.K.: Ithaca.

Gamson, William A. 1975. *The Strategy of Social Protest.* Homewood, Ill.: Dorsey.

Gelvin, James L. 2001. "The Power of Religion: Why We Don't Have a Clue, and Some Suggestions to Clue Us In." <http://www.humnet.ucla.edu/humnet/religion/gelvin.html>, last modified December 17, 2001. Accessed March 28, 2003.

Goldstone, Jack A., Ted Robert Gurr, and Farrokh Moshiri, eds. 1991. *Revolutions of the Late Twentieth Century.* Boulder: Westview.

Hajjar, Lisa, and Steve Niva. 1997. "(Re)Made in the USA: Middle East Studies in the Global Era." *Middle East Report,* no. 205: 2–9.

Hourani, Albert. 1967. "Islam and the Philosophers of History." *Middle Eastern Studies* 3: 206–68.

Ibrahim, Saad Eddin. 1980. "Anatomy of Egypt's Militant Islamic Groups: Methodological Note and Preliminary Findings." *International Journal of Middle East Studies* 12: 423–53.

Issawi, Charles. [1964] 1981. "Reflections on the Study of Oriental Civilizations." Pp. 147–57 in *The Arab World's Legacy.* Princeton, N.J.: Darwin.

Jacoby, Russell. 1987. *The Last Intellectuals: American Culture in the Age of Academe.* New York: Basic Books.

Jasper, James M. 1997. *The Art of Moral Protest.* Chicago: University of Chicago Press.

Juergensmeyer, Mark. 1993. *The New Cold War? Religious Nationalism Confronts the Secular State.* Berkeley: University of California Press.

Keddie, Nikki R. 1983. "Iranian Revolutions in Comparative Perspective." *American Historical Review* 88: 579–98.

Krämer, Gudrun. 2000. "On Difference and Understanding: The Use and Abuse of the Study of Islam." *ISIM Newsletter,* no. 5: 6–7.

Kramer, Martin S. 2001. *Ivory Towers on Sand: The Failure of Middle Eastern Studies in America.* Washington, D.C.: Washington Institute for Near Eastern Policy.

Kurzman, Charles. 1994. "A Dynamic View of Resources: Evidence from the Iranian Revolution." *Research in Social Movements, Conflicts, and Change* 17: 53–84.

———. 1996. "Structural Opportunities and Perceived Opportunities in Social Movement Theory: Evidence from the Iranian Revolution of 1979." *American Sociological Review* 61: 153–70.

———. 1998. "Liberal Islam and Its Islamic Context." Pp. 3–26 in *Liberal Islam: A Source-Book,* ed. Charles Kurzman. New York: Oxford University Press.

Laroui, Abdallah. 1973. "For a Methodology of Islamic Studies." *Diogenes* 83: 12–39.

Lawrence, Bruce B. 1995. *Defenders of God: The Fundamentalist Revolt against the Modern Age.* Columbia: University of South Carolina Press.

Le XXIXe Congrès International des Orientalistes, Paris—Juillet 1973. 1975. Paris: L'Asiathèque.

Lewis, Bernard. 1993. "The Question of Orientalism." Pp. 99–118 in *Islam and the West.* New York: Oxford University Press.

———. 2000. *A Middle East Mosaic: Fragments of Life, Letters, and History.* New York: Random House.

———. 2002. *What Went Wrong? Approaches to the Modern History of the Middle East.* New York: Oxford University Press.

Lofland, John. 1993. "Theory-Bashing and Answer-Improving in the Study of Social Movements." *American Sociologist* 24: 37–58.

Lubeck, Paul. 2000. "Antimonies of Islamic Movements under Globalization." Pp. 146–64 in *Global Social Movements,* ed. Robin Cohen and Shirin M. Rai. London: Athlone.

Marty, Martin E., and R. Scott Appleby. 1991–1995. *The Fundamentalism Project.* 5 vols. Chicago: University of Chicago Press.

McAdam, Doug, John D. McCarthy, and Mayer N. Zald. 1996. "Introduction: Opportunities, Mobilizing Structures, and Framing Processes—Toward a Synthetic, Comparative Perspective on Social Movements." Pp. 1–20 in *Comparative Perspectives on Social Movements: Political Opportunities, Mobilizing Structures, and Cultural Framings,* ed. Doug McAdam, John D. McCarthy, and Mayer N. Zald. Cambridge: Cambridge University Press.

McAdam, Doug, Sidney Tarrow, and Charles Tilly. 1997. "Toward an Integrative Perspective on Social Movements and Revolution." In *Comparative Politics: Rationality, Culture, and Structure,* ed. Mark Irving Lichbach and Alan S. Zuckerman. Cambridge: Cambridge University Press.

McCarthy, John D., and Mayer N. Zald. 1977. "Resource Mobilization and Social Movements: A Partial Theory." *American Journal of Sociology* 82: 1212–41.

McClelland, J. S. 1989. *The Crowd and the Mob: From Plato to Canetti.* London: Unwin Hyman.

Milani, Mohsen. 1988. *The Making of Iran's Islamic Revolution: From Monarchy to Islamic Republic.* Boulder: Westview.

Moaddel, Mansour. 1992. "Ideology as Episodic Discourse: The Case of the Iranian Revolution." *American Sociological Review* 57: 353–79.

———. 1993. *Class, Politics, and Ideology in the Iranian Revolution.* New York: Columbia University Press.

Morris, Aldon D., and Cedric Herring. 1987. "Theory and Research in Social Movements: A Critical Review." *Annual Review of Political Science* 2: 137–98.

Moshiri, Farrokh. 1985. *The State and Social Revolution in Iran: A Theoretical Perspective.* New York: Peter Lang.

Naff, Thomas, ed. 1993. *Paths to the Middle East: Ten Scholars Look Back.* Albany: SUNY Press.

Naraghi, Ehsan. 1977. *L'Orient et la crise de l'occident.* Translated by Brigitte Simon. Paris: Entente.

Nye, Robert A. 1975. *The Origins of Crowd Psychology.* London: Sage.

Oberschall, Anthony. 1973. *Social Conflict and Social Movements.* Englewood Cliffs, N.J.: Prentice-Hall.

Rabinow, Paul. 1977. *Reflections on Fieldwork in Morocco.* Berkeley: University of California Press.

Said, Edward W. 1978. *Orientalism.* New York: Pantheon.

Saikal, Amin. 1980. *The Rise and Fall of the Shah.* Princeton, N.J.: Princeton University Press.

Sick, Gary. 1985. *All Fall Down: America's Tragic Encounter with Iran.* New York: Random House.

Skocpol, Theda. 1979. *States and Social Revolutions.* Cambridge: Cambridge University Press.

——. 1982. "Rentier State and Shiʿa Islam in the Iranian Revolution." *Theory and Society* 11: 265–83.

Smelser, Neil J. 1962. *Theory of Collective Behavior.* New York: Free Press.

——. 1991. *Sociology.* 4th ed. Englewood Cliffs, N.J.: Prentice-Hall.

——. 1997. *Problematics of Sociology.* Berkeley: University of California Press.

Smith, Christian, ed. 1996. *Disruptive Religion: The Force of Faith in Social Movement Activism.* New York: Routledge.

Snow, David A., and Susan E. Marshall. 1984. "Cultural Imperialism, Social Movements, and the Islamic Revival." *Research in Social Movements, Conflicts, and Change* 7: 131–52.

Starrett, Gregory. 1998. *Putting Islam to Work: Education, Politics, and Religious Transformation in Egypt.* Berkeley: University of California Press.

Tavakoli-Targhi, Mohamad. 1996. "Orientalism's Genesis Amnesia." *Comparative Studies of South Asia, Africa, and the Middle East* 16: 1–14.

Tibawi, A. L. 1963. "English-Speaking Orientalists: A Critique of Their Approach to Islam and Arab Nationalism." *Muslim World* 53: 185–204, 298–313.

——. 1979. "Second Critique of the English-Speaking Orientalists." *Islamic Quarterly* 23: 3–54.

Tibi, Bassam. 1990. *Islam and the Cultural Accommodation of Social Change.* Boulder: Westview.

Tilly, Charles. 1978. *From Mobilization to Revolution.* Reading, Mass.: Addison-Wesley.

Tilly, Charles, Louise Tilly, and Richard Tilly. 1975. *The Rebellious Century, 1830–1930.* Cambridge: Harvard University Press.

Tucker, Judith E. 1990. "Taming the West: Trends in the Writing of Modern Arab Social History in Anglophone Academia." Pp. 198–227 in *Theory, Politics, and the Arab World,* ed. Hisham Sharabi. New York: Routledge.

Turner, Bryan S. 1978. *Marx and the End of Orientalism.* London: George Allen and Unwin.

Turner, Ralph H., and Lewis M. Killian. 1957. *Collective Behavior.* Englewood Cliffs, N.J.: Prentice-Hall.

——. 1972. *Collective Behavior.* 2d ed. Englewood Cliffs, N.J.: Prentice-Hall.

——. 1987. *Collective Behavior.* 3d ed. Englewood Cliffs, N.J.: Prentice-Hall.

Vergès, Meriem. 1997. "Genesis of a Mobilization: The Young Activists of Algeria's

Islamic Salvation Front." Pp. 292–305 in *Political Islam*, ed. Joel Beinin and Joe Stork. Berkeley: University of California Press.

Wickham, Carrie. 2002. *Mobilizing Islam: Religion, Activism, and Political Change in Egypt*. New York: Columbia University Press.

Wiktorowicz, Quintan. 2001. *The Management of Islamic Activism: Salafis, the Muslim Brotherhood, and State Power in Jordan*. Albany: SUNY Press.

———. 2003. "Islamic Activism and Social Movement Theory: A New Direction for Research." In *Shaping the Current Islamic Reformation*, ed. B. A. Roberson. Portland, Ore.: Frank Cass.

Zald, Mayer N. 1992. "Looking Backward to Look Forward: Reflections on the Past and Future of the Resource Mobilization Research Program." Pp. 326–48 in *Frontiers in Social Movement Theory*, ed. Aldon D. Morris and Carol McClurg Mueller. New Haven, Conn.: Yale University Press.

El-Zein, Abdul Hamid M. 1977. "Beyond Ideology and Theology: The Search for the Anthropology of Islam." *Annual Review of Anthropology* 6: 227–54.

Contributors

Janine A. Clark is Associate Professor in the Department of Political Science at the University of Guelph, Canada. She is coeditor of *Economic Liberalization, Democratization, and Civil Society in the Developing World* and author of *Islam, Social Welfare, and the Middle Class: Networks, Activism, and Charity in Egypt, Yemen, and Jordan.*

Mohammed M. Hafez is a visiting assistant professor in the Department of Political Science at the University of Missouri–Kansas City. He is author of *Why Muslims Rebel: Repression and Resistance in the Islamic World.*

Charles Kurzman is Assistant Professor of Sociology at the University of North Carolina, Chapel Hill. He is the editor of the anthologies *Liberal Islam: A Source-Book* and *Modernist Islam, 1840–1940: A Source-Book* and author of *The Unthinkable Revolution in Iran, 1977–1979.*

Fred H. Lawson is Professor of Government and Chair of the Department of Government at Mills College. He is author of *Why Syria Goes to War* and *Bahrain: The Modernization of Autocracy.*

Gwenn Okruhlik is a political scientist and Fulbright scholar to Saudi Arabia (2002–2003), where she is conducting research on meaning and memory. Her publications cover a range of topics, including identity, citizenship, and Islamism in Saudi Arabia; alternative historic narratives; tourism; gender and civic mythology; and migrant labor in the Arabian Peninsula.

Glenn E. Robinson is Associate Professor of Political Science at the Naval

305

Postgraduate School. He has written on democratization, the peace process, and state-building in Palestine, Jordan, and Syria, including *Building a Palestinian State: The Incomplete Revolution.*

Jillian Schwedler is Assistant Professor of Government and Politics at the University of Maryland. She has edited several books on civil society and Islamist movements and has written a number of articles on issues related to democratization. She is a member of the editorial committee of *Middle East Report* and a member of the Steering Committee for the Palestinian-American Research Center in Ramallah.

Diane Singerman is Associate Professor of Government at American University. She is author of *Avenues of Participation* and coeditor of *Development, Change, and Gender in Cairo.*

Benjamin Smith is a postdoctoral fellow at the Harvard Academy for International and Area Studies. He will be Assistant Professor of Political Science and Asian Studies at the University of Florida, starting in 2004. His research focuses on state-building and the politics of resource wealth and economic development. He is currently working on a book focused on the politics of state-building and development in oil-rich countries.

Carrie Rosefsky Wickham is Associate Professor of Political Science at Emory University and author of *Mobilizing Islam: Religion, Activism, and Political Change in Egypt.*

Quintan Wiktorowicz is Assistant Professor of International Studies at Rhodes College in Memphis, Tennessee. He is author of *The Management of Islamic Activism* and *Global Jihad: Understanding September 11.* He is currently conducting research on radical Islamic groups in London.

M. Hakan Yavuz is Associate Professor of Political Science at the University of Utah and author of *Islamic Political Identity in Turkey.* His current projects focus on transnational Islamic networks in Central Asia and Turkey; the role of Islam in state-building and nationalism; and ethno-religious conflict management.

Index

Index